The One Year® Unlocking the Bible Devotional

THE ONE YEAR®

UNLOCKING THE BIBLE

DEVOTIONAL

COLIN S. SMITH
with TIM AUGUSTYN

Tyndale House Publishers, Inc.
Carol Stream, Illinois

Visit Tyndale online at www.tyndale.com.

TYNDALE, Tyndale's quill logo, *One Year*, and *The One Year* are registered trademarks of Tyndale House Publishers, Inc. The One Year logo is a trademark of Tyndale House Publishers, Inc.

The One Year Unlocking the Bible Devotional

Copyright © 2012 by Colin S. Smith. All rights reserved.

Cover photograph of doors copyright © Barbara Chase/Corbis. All rights reserved.

Author photo taken by LifeTouch photography, copyright © 2011. All rights reserved.

Designed by Mark Anthony Lane II

Edited by Jonathan Schindler

Published in association with the literary agency of Wolgemuth & Associates, Inc.

Portions of *The One Year Unlocking the Bible Devotional* are adapted from *Unlocking the Bible Story* by Colin S. Smith, volumes 1 through 4. Used by special permission of Moody Publishers.

Unless otherwise indicated, all Scripture quotations are taken from the *Holy Bible*, New Living Translation, copyright © 1996, 2004, 2007 by Tyndale House Foundation. Used by permission of Tyndale House Publishers, Inc., Carol Stream, Illinois 60188. All rights reserved.

Scripture quotations marked ESV are taken from *The Holy Bible*, English Standard Version® (ESV®), copyright © 2001 by Crossway, a publishing ministry of Good News Publishers. Used by permission. All rights reserved.

Scripture quotations marked KJV are taken from the *Holy Bible*, King James Version.

Scripture quotations marked NASB are taken from the New American Standard Bible,® copyright © 1960, 1962, 1963, 1968, 1971, 1972, 1973, 1975, 1977, 1995 by The Lockman Foundation. Used by permission.

Scripture quotations marked NIV are taken from the Holy Bible, *New International Version,*® *NIV.*® Copyright © 1973, 1978, 1984, 2011 by Biblica, Inc.™ Used by permission of Zondervan. All rights reserved worldwide. www.zondervan.com.

ISBN 978-1-4143-6935-8

Printed in the United States of America

18   17   16   15   14   13   12

7   6   5   4   3   2   1

A NOTE FROM THE AUTHOR

Many people know some stories from the Bible but do not know the Bible's story.

Whether you've been reading the Bible for years or are just starting out, one of the great dangers you face is the real possibility of missing the forest for the trees. But once you begin to see the Bible as one story that begins with two people in a garden, ends with a vast crowd of people in a city, and all along the way points to Jesus Christ, God's Word will be wonderfully unlocked for you.

For years I've been encouraging people to read through the Bible in order to grasp the big picture of the Bible's story line. I first gave a series of eighty messages through the Old and New Testaments at The Orchard Evangelical Free Church, which were later adapted by Moody Publishers into four volumes called *Unlocking the Bible Story*. In this devotional, I've collected and arranged that material—and added some fresh insights—so that it can most profitably be read over the course of one year.

As you get started, you'll notice that you can travel either by date (January 1, January 2, etc.) or by day (Day 1, Day 2, etc.). I encourage you, whatever the date today, to start at the beginning with Day 1. As with any good story, the Author has left clues at the beginning that will help you to understand what is happening (and why it's happening) later on. Starting with Day 1 will help you better understand and more fully appreciate each part of the story so that you can see how it all fits together.

Welcome to the journey!

INTRODUCTION: GOD'S BIOGRAPHY

In the beginning God . . . GENESIS 1:1

THE BIBLE IS one marvelous story that people sometimes shelve in the *fiction* section of their mind, alongside myths, legends, and fables. But it belongs in the *biography* section. In this book God reveals himself. He tells us about who he is. He also tells us who we are, why we are here, what we were made for, and where we are going.

The Bible is one story that begins with two people in a garden and ends with a crowd, too many to number, in a city. In the Bible, God tells us the story of how we got from this beginning to where we are today, and how we will get from where we are today to the ending he has revealed.

Many people today know a number of stories *from* the Bible, but they do not know the story *of* the Bible. That is like holding a bunch of pearls in your hand but having no string to hang them on.

What we want to do this year is string the pearls together to make a necklace. If you stay on this one-year journey, you will be able to do that, and you will have a good grasp of the story of the Bible.

The Bible was written over a period of fifteen hundred years, beginning with Moses and ending with the apostle John, fifty to sixty years after the death and resurrection of Jesus. But the whole Bible has one main subject or focus, and that is Jesus Christ himself.

After his resurrection, Jesus began with Moses and the prophets and taught the Old Testament to two disciples on the road to Emmaus. As far as he was concerned, the whole of the Old Testament is about him. It shines a light on who he is, why he came, what he has done, and what he can do in our lives today.

As we move through the Bible's themes, it will be like taking a diamond and turning it in the sun. Each facet reflects another brilliant shaft of light. Each of these themes will help us to understand something of the glory of our Lord Jesus Christ.

FOR FURTHER READING, SEE LUKE 24

PROLOGUE: RAISING THE CURTAIN

In the beginning . . . GENESIS 1:1

SUPPOSE YOU AND a friend have tickets to a major play called *The Bible Story*, but because of traffic, you arrive late to the theater. You walk into the lobby and discover that it's already intermission! You figure you might as well stay. Besides, you've heard that the New Testament is the best part.

You hear the buzz of conversation about act 1, then the lights fade. It's time to get a seat. You sit down just in time for the beginning of act 2. But you have entirely missed act 1, so you know nothing about what came first, the Old Testament.

The curtain rises, and a manger and a newborn child are at center stage. As the scene unfolds, you learn that this is no ordinary child. Unlike any other character in human history, he has no human father. He is born of a virgin, and an angel announces that this child is the Son of God, "God . . . with us" (Matthew 1:23), and that "he will save his people from their sins" (1:21).

You overhear a wife say to her husband, "This is it! He will be the one who was promised. You wait and see; it will all center around him. He'll be the answer to the problem."

But you've just arrived, and you don't know what the problem is.

You hear that he is the Son of God, but you don't know who God is. You hear that he will save his people, but you don't know who his people are or what they need saving from! Having missed act 1, you struggle to grasp what this story is about.

That is the position many people are in today. They hear the story of Jesus, but they do not understand it because they don't know the Bible story. If you don't know who God is, humanity's problem, or the promise God has made, the coming of Christ will seem like nothing more than a sentimental story. This is why we need to unlock the Bible story. Act 2 won't make sense until we have grasped act 1.

FOR FURTHER READING, SEE ACTS 17

THE AUTHOR TAKES THE STAGE

In the beginning God created the heavens and the earth. GENESIS 1:1

IMAGINE YOURSELF AT a theater for the performance of a new play. The curtain goes up and the stage is empty. Then the author walks out and introduces himself. He tells you who he is, why he wrote the play, and what it is about. Without apology or argument, the author simply begins to speak about himself and his work.

The Bible begins with God walking onto the stage and introducing himself. This is his story, and so right at the beginning, God introduces himself to us. As we follow the Bible story, we will discover more about who he is and what he has done, but the first thing God wants us to know is that he is here.

God wants us to know that what we are about to see is entirely his work. This is of great importance because the creator has the rights of an owner. If I say, "Have it your way," you will probably think of Burger King, or if I say, "Just do it," you will think of Nike—because a slogan belongs to its creator.

A creator always has the rights of ownership, and God owns all that he has made. If your life were an accident arising from millennia of human history, then you would be a free agent, accountable to no one but yourself. But if you were created, then your Creator has the full rights of ownership over your life.

Either you are an accident of history and completely free to do whatever you please with your life—to indulge it or trash it or end it—and if that is the case, your life is ultimately meaningless; or you are a created being, and your Creator has absolute rights of ownership over your life.

God introduces himself as our Creator and therefore our owner. You are not your own. Your life is a trust given to you from God. You are not worthless or aimless; God chose to bring you into being. He did it on purpose, and you will discover that purpose as you get to know him.

FOR FURTHER READING, SEE GENESIS 1

January 4 | DAY 4

THE IMAGE OF GOD

Then God said, "Let us make human beings in our image." GENESIS 1:26

AFTER FIVE DAYS of creation, the crowning moment has come: "Let *us* make human beings . . ." It is almost as if God has a conversation with himself: "Let's do it! Let's make them in our image, in our likeness." An image is a reflection, so God is telling us that he made us, male and female (see Genesis 1:27), to reflect something of his own nature and glory.

This image of God is what distinguishes people from animals. The animals were made *by* God, but they were not made to be *like* God. That is why no man or woman should ever be treated like an animal or behave like an animal.

At the center of the Bible story, we find God taking on the form of a human. Why did he take the form of a man and not an animal? Because man was made in the image of God. People who believe that they are simply developed animals have missed the most fundamental thing God says about them.

God made the first man from the dust of the ground, so we should not be surprised that animals have a biological makeup similar to ours. But there is more to man than biology: "The LORD God formed the man from the dust of the ground. He breathed the breath of life into the man's nostrils, and the man became a living person" (Genesis 2:7).

God formed a corpse, complete with a skeletal frame, and breathed his own breath into it. It became a living being. God is always doing what he did that day, giving "everyone life and breath" (Acts 17:25, NIV). He sustains you one breath at a time. You are absolutely dependent upon God.

If you can grasp that you are made in God's image and that you are dependent on him, you will discover great dignity, and at the same time, profound humility.

FOR FURTHER READING, SEE COLOSSIANS 1

TAKING A WALK WITH GOD

When the cool evening breezes were blowing, the man and his wife heard the LORD God walking about in the garden. GENESIS 3:8

GOD IS INVISIBLE. He is Spirit. Yet right from the beginning of the Bible story, he has been reaching out to make himself known. That's why the Lord God made himself visible, "walking" with Adam in the Garden.

God revealed himself first in a beautiful garden called Eden. We call each appearance of God in visible form a "theophany." The Old Testament has many examples of this, and in the New Testament the Son of God became a man, so it should not seem strange that he should appear in a visible form here. These appearances show us God's intense desire to establish fellowship with humans.

It is almost as if the Son of God could not wait to come. He burst out of heaven, entering human time and space, and he came to earth so that he could walk with the first man and woman in the Garden. Adam and Eve heard the crackling of twigs and the rustling of leaves. They walked with the Son of God in Eden as surely as Peter, James, and John walked with the Son of God in Galilee.

As Adam and Eve walked with God, they asked questions and enjoyed conversation. Can you imagine what this must have been like? God was interested in what Adam had done during the day, and he listened to whatever was on Eve's mind. God also spoke to them. The man and the woman were literally walking in fellowship with God.

When God appeared *visibly* to Adam and Eve, he did for them what he does *invisibly* for all his people. We cannot see God, but Jesus Christ gives us access to the Father when we come in faith. This is God's way of creating a relationship with you. His presence is as real as it was when he appeared in visible form to Adam. Think about that when you pray.

FOR FURTHER READING, SEE 1 JOHN 1

A PLACE CALLED HOME

The LORD God planted a garden in Eden in the east,
and there he placed the man he had made. GENESIS 2:8

IT IS DIFFICULT to be precise about the location of Eden, but it is important to grasp that it was a real place. The book of Genesis is part of the revelation God gave to Moses at Mount Sinai, so when it says Eden was "in the east," we are talking about a location somewhere east of Sinai.

We are also told about four rivers (see Genesis 2:10-14)—the Pishon and the Gihon, which are not known to us, and the Tigris and the Euphrates, which run through modern-day Iraq. These landmarks do not give us an exact location, but we can have confidence that the Lord planted a garden somewhere in this area of the Middle East. What a garden it must have been!

The significant thing is that the Lord put the man there. God created a particular place where Adam would know and enjoy his blessing. It is quite possible that God created Adam outside the Garden and then brought him to Eden, saying, "This is the place I have prepared for you!"

I find it helpful to remember that God does the same thing for us. He has determined the exact places for us to live (see Acts 17:26). Try to imagine God walking with you into your home, saying, "This is where I want you to be," or walking with you into your church, saying, "This is the place I have prepared for you to grow."

The place where God puts you will not be perfect—even Eden was exposed to the possibility of evil. But there is no better place to be than where God has set you down. You are not where you are by accident, but by the plan and purpose of God. This is one of God's greatest blessings to us. When we know, as Adam did, that God has placed us where we are, we will find strength in the most difficult of times.

FOR FURTHER READING, SEE PSALM 16

THERE'S WORK TO BE DONE

> *[God] brought them to the man to see what he would call them,*
> *and the man chose a name for each one.* GENESIS 2:19

ONE OF THE contributions of science is naming things. Scientists observe, reflect on what they see, and then describe it. You may remember that it was God who named the day and the night (see Genesis 1:5), but now he invites Adam, the world's first scientist, to participate in his work, giving him the responsibility of naming each creature.

Right from the beginning, Adam was occupied with the work of naming the animals and caring for the Garden: "The LORD God placed the man in the Garden of Eden to tend and watch over it" (Genesis 2:15). This should not surprise us, because the Bible begins with God working. Work is a good gift from God, a reflection of his own character and activity.

It is important to note that Adam was never overwhelmed by his work *while he was in the Garden*. Work existed *before* sin entered the world, and work will continue *after* sin has been taken away. Adam never knew what it was like to be frustrated with his work until after he was outside the Garden.

Unfortunately, frustration with work did not end with Adam. It is something we all need to be saved from, and God's saving purpose includes restoring us to the position from which Adam fell—that means being master *over* our work instead of being mastered *by* our work.

Notice that God brought the animals to Adam. God took a personal interest in Adam's daily work. That's worth thinking about as you work at your desk, on the shop floor, in school, or by the kitchen sink.

It may be hard for you to imagine that God would enjoy the documents you prepare, the tests you take, the components you assemble, or the home you create, but he does. When you know this, you'll begin to find a new joy in your work.

FOR FURTHER READING, SEE ROMANS 6

A MARRIAGE MADE IN HEAVEN

Then the LORD God made a woman from the rib,
and he brought her to the man. GENESIS 2:22

ONCE AGAIN THE Lord appeared to Adam, and he said, "Adam, I have someone I want you to meet." I have no doubt that Adam's jaw dropped wide open: "At last! . . . This one is bone from my bone, and flesh from my flesh!" (Genesis 2:23).

The Lord himself brought the two together. The first wedding service was conducted by almighty God. Try to picture it in your mind: the Lord God takes her hand, puts it into Adam's hand, and says, "Here is the partner I have made for you!"

This marriage had more than its fair share of troubles. When Eve was tempted, Adam became a passive observer. He did nothing to help his wife. And then when God confronted them, they both tried to avoid their responsibilities by passing the blame. Whatever problems they had, both of them knew that the reason they were together was that they had been joined together by God.

There will be times in every marriage when a husband and wife need to come back to this. Marriage is the joining of one man and one woman by God. As the Scripture says, "This explains why a man leaves his father and mother and is joined to his wife, and the two are united into one" (Genesis 2:24).

Marriage is a wonderful gift from God. When two people marry, God does invisibly what he did for Adam and Eve visibly. Try to picture God taking your hand and the hand of your spouse and joining them together. As he does that, God says, "Go through life together. Be partners. Love each other and forgive each other." If you are married, this is what God has done. When you know God has joined you together, it will help you weather the most difficult times.

And if you are looking for a marriage partner, remember that it was God who brought the woman to Adam. I'm not suggesting that you should be passive, but there is no need to panic. You can trust the Lord with every area of your life.

FOR FURTHER READING, SEE EPHESIANS 5

RECRUITING FOR THE REBELLION

Now the serpent . . . said to the woman . . . GENESIS 3:1, NIV

IMAGINE LIFE IN Eden: Adam's work is fulfilling and fascinating. He enjoys the companionship of his wife and the company of God. When he is hungry, he reaches up and picks his food from the trees. His whole life is one of blessing and joy. This is the picture at the end of Genesis 2.

By the end of Genesis 3, everything has changed, and the man and woman find themselves struggling to make a life in a very different world. They are now outside the place where God blessed them. They live out in the wilderness, where all kinds of wild animals threaten and where they must work to get their food. They experience pain and fear and guilt, and when evening comes, they no longer see God. Something has gone terribly wrong.

The Bible never fully explains the origin of evil, but it does tell us where it started. Alongside the visible world that we know, God created an invisible realm in heaven and filled it with angels. One of those angels, known as the devil or Satan, became inflated with pride and tried to usurp the position of God (see Isaiah 14:12-14).

Satan's rebellion was unsuccessful and led to his being excluded from the presence of God and cast down to the earth. So right from the beginning of human history, there was an enemy bent on destroying the work of God. This enemy came to the woman in an attempt to recruit the human race into his rebellion.

As we will see, Satan successfully recruited Adam and Eve into his rebel cause, introducing a virus known as "sin" into the entire human race. Like sick people in need of a doctor, we need an accurate diagnosis and an appropriate prescription. But until we understand that sin is the source of our sickness, we won't be ready to receive the cure God has provided for us in Jesus Christ.

FOR FURTHER READING, SEE ISAIAH 14

READING YOUR OPPONENT'S PLAYS

The serpent was the shrewdest of all the wild animals
the LORD God had made. GENESIS 3:1

A GOOD FOOTBALL team will spend hours studying their opponents' plays so that they can defend against them. When Satan came into the Garden of Eden to do battle with Adam and Eve, he used the most deceptive plays in his playbook.

Satan's first play was to pose a question to Eve: "Did God really say you must not eat the fruit from any of the trees in the garden?" (Genesis 3:1). God had given one simple instruction, and Satan's first action was to question it. If Satan could undermine the clarity of God's Word and generate enough confusion about it, it would be easier to disregard.

God made it clear that sin would result in death (see Genesis 2:17), but Satan suggested in his second play that the consequences of sin have been exaggerated: "You won't die!" (3:4). It's as if he said, "Eve, come on. You can't seriously believe you will die from eating one piece of fruit! God loves you. He won't allow anything bad to happen to you."

Adam and Eve were made in the *image* of God, but Satan suggested in his third play that the man and the woman could actually *be* God: "God knows that your eyes will be opened as soon as you eat it, and you will be like God, knowing both good and evil" (Genesis 3:5). Again, it's as if Satan was saying, "Why is God telling you what to do? You can decide what's good and evil for yourself!" Satan knows how much we like that suggestion. Humans are made in the image of God, but we are not content with that. We want to *be* God.

Now that you know Satan's primary tactics, it is not difficult to organize a defense. Start by taking the Word of God seriously and refusing to twist its meaning. Next, settle in your heart that sin always brings consequences. When God speaks about judgment, he is not making idle threats. Finally, let God be God. What he has declared "good" is good, and what he has declared "evil" is evil. These are the basic building blocks of any successful defense against the enemy.

FOR FURTHER READING, SEE GENESIS 3

THE KNOWLEDGE OF EVIL

*The LORD God warned [Adam], "You may freely eat the
fruit of every tree in the garden—except the tree of the
knowledge of good and evil."* GENESIS 2:16-17

GOD'S FIRST LAW was a wonderful expression of love. God made everything good, so good was the only thing Adam knew. But it was not the
only thing in the universe.

When God told Adam he must not eat from the tree of the knowledge of good and evil, it was as if he had said, "Adam, you need to
understand. There is a terrible reality in the universe, and I want to
protect you from it. It's called evil. You don't know anything about it,
but it already exists. I don't want you ever to experience it. So whatever
you do, don't eat from this tree!"

But later Adam and Eve felt they would like to have this knowledge
of evil. Perhaps they felt they were lacking something. Perhaps curiosity
drew them to this forbidden knowledge. Satan worked with this grain of
curiosity, and it wasn't long before both Adam and Eve were convinced
that this was what they wanted.

The first couple disobeyed God's one command and got what they
wanted—the knowledge of evil. But there was a terrible hook behind
this bait. Adam found that once he had this knowledge, he could not get
rid of it. The knowledge of evil changed him. Evil gained a grip on his
life—in Eve's, too—and it would be the same with all of their children.
Today it has a grip on us, as well.

Yet God has not abandoned us. He sent his Son into this fallen
world and into our ongoing battle with evil. He was tempted in every
way, just as we are, but with a different outcome (see Hebrews 4:15).
Jesus Christ stood his ground against the enemy and triumphed where
Adam failed. The reign of sin and death has been broken. All who
belong to Christ have been set free.

FOR FURTHER READING, SEE HEBREWS 4

THERE'S NO WAY BACK

*The LORD God banished them from the Garden of Eden, and he sent Adam
out to cultivate the ground from which he had been made.* GENESIS 3:23

OVER TIME, ADAM and Eve would begin to notice lines and wrinkles
on their skin. They would experience pain, and they would begin to
realize that the death God had spoken about was a terrible reality they
could not avoid.

Adam and Eve were outside the place of God's blessing. They no
longer enjoyed fellowship with him. Their lives had become a terrible
struggle in a hostile place. They were exposed to all kinds of danger
from the wild animals, there were thorns and thistles they had never
seen before, and even their perfect marriage had become strained. They
were alienated from God and alone in the world. Paradise was lost.

After God drove the man and woman out of the Garden, he placed
cherubim and a flaming sword to guard the way to the tree of life (see
Genesis 3:24). We are told that the flaming sword was flashing back
and forth, so getting around it would have been impossible. The sword
would cut you down.

Try to imagine yourself standing with Adam and Eve outside Eden.
As you look back at the angels and the flashing sword of God's judgment,
you see that there's no way back into the presence of God.

Then someone comes out from the presence of God and stands
beside you. He advances toward the flaming sword flashing back and
forth. You see what will happen to him when he gets there, but he just
keeps walking forward. The sword strikes him and kills him, breaking
his body. But the sword itself lies shattered on the ground, and the way
back into the presence and blessing of God is opened.

That's a picture of what happened when Jesus Christ died on the
cross. The judgment that kept us out of God's presence struck him. It
was spent and exhausted on him, and the way back into God's blessing
was opened for all who will come through Jesus.

FOR FURTHER READING, SEE EPHESIANS 2

FALLING TO THE GROUND

The LORD God said to the serpent, . . . "You are cursed." GENESIS 3:14

HOPE BEGAN ON the very day that the man and woman sinned. And it began with a curse! When a person or thing is "cursed," it is set apart for destruction. So when God cursed the serpent, he was announcing that evil would not stand. Satan would not have the last word. Adam and Eve must have been overjoyed at hearing this news.

If God had not promised an end to evil, who else could? Without the Curse, we would be stuck with the knowledge of evil forever. Our newspapers continue to report another massacre, another atrocity, another dictator—we can't get free from it. But God said, "You are cursed," and from that moment on, our enemy was under a sentence of destruction.

Then God pronounced a second curse. He turned to the man and began to speak. Adam must have held his breath. God was looking straight at Adam as he spoke that dreadful word, but Adam was in for a surprise. Instead of saying to Adam, "You are cursed," God said, "The ground is cursed because of you" (Genesis 3:17).

God announced he would destroy evil, and he deflected the Curse away from Adam so that it fell on the ground instead. God is just, so the Curse must go somewhere, but he directed it away from the man and the woman. At the right time, God would direct the Curse to fall on his Son. That is what the cross is about: "Christ has rescued us from the curse pronounced by the law. When he was hung on the cross, he took upon himself the curse for our wrongdoing. For it is written in the Scriptures, 'Cursed is everyone who is hung on a tree'" (Galatians 3:13).

Whenever the man and the woman experienced the pain and disappointment of life in this fallen world, they were reminded of the Curse that fell on the ground, not on them. On the very day that they sinned, they discovered the grace and mercy of God.

FOR FURTHER READING, SEE GALATIANS 3

ONGOING BATTLE, DECISIVE VICTORY

*The LORD God said to the serpent, . . . "I will put enmity between you
and the woman, and between your offspring and hers; he will crush
your head, and you will strike his heel."* GENESIS 3:14-15, NIV

GOD CALLS THE relentless human battle against evil "enmity." Man is
always trying to get rid of evil, but evil is constantly spilling over into our
communities, our families, and even our own lives. Man simply cannot
get free from the knowledge of evil.

But God promises someone who will come to us through the woman's
offspring. This person is not described as the man's offspring, but as the
woman's, and when he comes, he will engage in a great struggle against
the evil one.

This deliverer will inflict a fatal blow to the head of the enemy. And
in the process, the enemy will bite the heel that crushed him. Imagine
standing on the head of a venomous snake. In the same moment, he
bites you and inflicts a wound, but then that wounded foot bears down
on him and brings his destruction.

All this points to the coming of Jesus Christ, the Deliverer, who was
born of a virgin—without a human father. He would not come *from* us;
he would come *to* us. And he would not face the enemy in a beautiful
garden filled with fruit, but in a barren wilderness, weak and hungry
after forty days of fasting.

Satan tried all the same strategies in a vain attempt to bring Jesus
under the control of evil, but Christ stood his ground against the enemy
and triumphed where Adam failed. When all his efforts failed, the devil
withdrew in defeat to wait for another opportunity.

Three years later, through his death on a cross, Jesus inflicted a
mortal wound on the enemy. When the sword of God's judgment struck
Jesus—instead of us—it broke, clearing a new and living way into the
presence of God. Jesus has opened the way to all who will come to God
through him.

FOR FURTHER READING, SEE MATTHEW 4

SAME START, DIFFERENT DIRECTIONS

The LORD accepted Abel and his gift, but he did not accept Cain and his gift. This made Cain very angry, and he looked dejected. GENESIS 4:4-5

RIGHT FROM THE beginning, the human family has been divided in its response to God. Adam and Eve had two children, and the world's first brothers set the rudders of their boats in two totally different directions. Abel sought God; Cain struggled against God.

The reason people choose different lifestyles is that they operate with very different convictions about who God is and about who they are. People either place *themselves* at the center—believing that they are accidents of history who must write their own rules, that they are accountable to nobody but themselves, and that their greatest need is to be at peace with themselves; or they place *God* at the center—believing that he is their Creator, that he writes the rules and people are accountable to him, and that their greatest need is to find peace with him.

These convictions are like a rudder on a boat, determining the course you take in life. Convictions formed deep in your heart today determine where you will be tomorrow. Cain's convictions led him to develop a fierce hatred for Abel, and he eventually killed him.

God had warned Cain earlier that "sin is crouching at the door, eager to control you" (Genesis 4:7). But Cain ignored God's warning, and his life drifted further into sin. Even though God showed Cain mercy by protecting him and by allowing him and his descendants to build a new city and to make contributions to music, art, and culture, Cain's hostility brought severe consequences: isolation from his family and from God (4:10-16).

Similarly, men and women who do not know what they believe about God or about themselves are like people sitting in a boat with no hand on the rudder. Their boat will go wherever the prevailing winds and currents are going. If your boat is heading for the rocks, the first thing to do is to thank God for his mercy, and then grab hold of the rudder.

FOR FURTHER READING, SEE GENESIS 4

AMAZING GRACE

Noah found favor with the LORD. GENESIS 6:8

EVEN AS HUMANITY'S wickedness increased, God did not abandon people or lose interest in them. All throughout the Bible story we find God reaching out to save people by grace, through faith. This pattern is established right at the beginning in the story of Noah.

Noah found "favor" with God. This is the first word we find in the Bible that means "grace." God looked with kindness and compassion on Noah, and the first way he expressed this grace was by warning Noah about the coming judgment: "I have decided to destroy all living creatures, for they have filled the earth with violence" (Genesis 6:13).

It is possible that Noah actually heard an audible voice, or maybe he had a dream. Either way, God spoke to Noah and made it clear to him that judgment was coming. Noah didn't keep this message to himself. The New Testament tells us that he was "a preacher of righteousness" (2 Peter 2:5, NIV). Noah was the first preacher in the Bible. God spoke *to* him and *through* him so that a whole community would hear the Word of God.

The Bible records a number of occasions when God brought judgment on particular communities—including the Flood, the destruction of Sodom and Gomorrah, and the fall of Jerusalem in 586 BC. These examples of God's judgment in history point forward to the final calamity when God will judge the whole world in righteousness.

Notice that God demonstrated his grace to Noah in a second way, by telling him clearly and specifically what he should do in order to be kept safe from the judgment: "Build a large boat from cypress wood" (Genesis 6:14). Knowing about a coming judgment would not be of much help to Noah unless there was some way he could be saved from it.

The message of judgment is not merely the angry outburst of a fierce God; it is the gracious call of a loving God, who says, "I must destroy evil, and I will destroy it. But I do not want to destroy you, so here is the way you can escape."

FOR FURTHER READING, SEE GENESIS 6

THE OPEN DOOR

In those days before the flood, the people were enjoying banquets and parties
and weddings right up to the time Noah entered his boat. People didn't realize
what was going to happen until the flood came and swept them all away.
That is the way it will be when the Son of Man comes. MATTHEW 24:38-39

THERE IS NOTHING wrong with banquets, parties, or weddings. Noah was married, and so were his three sons. They all ate every day. But Noah's great priority was to be ready for the day God had told him about. The only way to be ready was to believe what God had said and to do what he had commanded.

True faith always shows itself in action. Noah built the boat; he believed what God told him, and he acted on it. Then God told Noah to get into the boat seven days before the rain began (see Genesis 7:1-10), when there wasn't a cloud in the sky! This too was an act of faith. There was no reason for getting in there except God's Word.

Then the rain came. The ship that was built in the desert slowly rose, and Noah and his family were lifted up and taken into a new world. All those who were outside the boat were destroyed, and all those who were in it were saved.

The Flood is a judgment that will never be repeated (see Genesis 9:8-16), but Jesus warns us about another more terrible judgment to come. On that day, many people will be in the same position as those who heard Noah and did not believe.

Just as God provided the boat for Noah, he has provided a way for you to be saved from the final judgment. When Jesus Christ died on the cross, the judgment of God for our sins fell on him. If you will come to Christ by faith, then you will be safe from the judgment of God. Are you "in Christ"? Why would you stand outside, when the door is open for you to come in?

FOR FURTHER READING, SEE GENESIS 7

CONFUSION ON THE TWENTIETH FLOOR

*Come, let's build a great city for ourselves with a tower that
reaches into the sky. This will make us famous and keep us
from being scattered all over the world.* GENESIS 11:4

IN THE TIME of Noah, evil multiplied, so God cut it back with the Flood.
But sin kept growing, so it was not long before a community of people
at Babel found a new way to express their defiance toward God.

The people developed a new technology called "bricks," and with
this marvelous discovery a whole new world of possibilities was opened
up. The people said, "Now we will be able to build higher than ever
before. Let's see how far we can go. Let's build a tower right up to the
heavens!"

The problem with this building was not its height, but its purpose—
to proclaim man's greatness. God allowed the work to proceed to a
certain point, and then he cut it back: "Let's go down and confuse the
people with different languages" (Genesis 11:7).

Imagine you've been working with the same man on the twentieth
floor, and one morning you ask him about last night's game. He
responds with a confusing grunt. You ask if he needs an aspirin, and
you cannot make heads or tails of his answer. What's wrong with him?
Then you realize that you cannot understand a word that any of your
coworkers are saying. Is this some kind of joke?

Eventually, to your great relief, you find someone else on the building site who speaks just like you. The two of you find a few others, and
you agree to pack up your tools and create a new community where
everyone speaks the same language.

God allows nations and individuals to pursue their own greatness
to a certain point, but then he acts. Do you have a secret sin you have
cherished? God will allow you to get to a certain point, and then he will
cut you back. He must do that, because he disciplines those he loves (see
Hebrews 12:6). But when you respond to God's discipline, it creates
more room for his grace.

FOR FURTHER READING, SEE GENESIS 11

LOOKING FOR A CITY

I will bless those who bless you and curse those who treat you with contempt.
All the families on earth will be blessed through you. GENESIS 12:3

GOD'S JUDGMENT IS never his final word. When God cuts sin back, it is always to create room for his grace. Adam and Eve were excluded from the Garden, but there was the promise of a Deliverer. Cain murdered Abel, but when Seth was born, there was a new line of hope. The Flood destroyed all life, but Noah and his family were saved. So when we read about God judging Babel, we wonder what shape grace will take.

God scattered the people at Babel, but then he took the initiative with a man named Abraham, who was worshiping other gods with his family in Ur (see Joshua 24:2). God appeared to him and promised to bless him, pledging that through his line, every nation on earth would be blessed (see Genesis 12:1-3). So Abraham left Ur looking for "a city designed and built by God" (Hebrews 11:10).

The rest of the Old Testament follows Abraham's family—Isaac, Jacob, Judah, and David. Then the New Testament begins with the birth of a baby from Abraham's line named Jesus, who would "save his people from their sins" (Matthew 1:21). Jesus taught God's words and did God's work, and then he was crucified. But on the third day, he rose from the dead, appeared to many, and then ascended back to heaven.

A few days after Jesus' ascension, God reversed the events that had happened at Babel. Men from every nation were in Jerusalem for Pentecost, and God caused the apostles to speak in different languages, so that each one heard the gospel in his own tongue (see Acts 2:5-6). Do you see the grace of God here?

At Babel, humankind was exalted, and God confused their language—they were divided and scattered. At Pentecost, Christ was exalted, and God spoke to people from every nation in their own languages—they were united and gathered. The book of Acts tells how the good news of God's promised blessing to all nations—through the line of Abraham—has come to us in Jesus Christ.

FOR FURTHER READING, SEE GENESIS 12

LIFT UP YOUR EYES

The LORD said to Abram . . . , "Lift up your eyes and look from
the place where you are, northward and southward and eastward
and westward, for all the land that you see I will give to you
and to your offspring forever." GENESIS 13:14-15, ESV

HAVE YOU EVER been promised something and it never came? God
promised to bless Abraham with a family and a home. Abraham's faith
was stretched to the limit as he trusted God for both of these promises.
Years passed without any sign of Sarah's conceiving a child.

In their old age, when all human hope of conceiving a child was
completely gone, God intervened, and Isaac was born. God had fulfilled the first promise. Isaac had two sons, Jacob and Esau, and Jacob
had twelve sons, who became the fathers of the twelve tribes of Israel.

Abraham obeyed God's call, leaving the comforts of his home in Ur
to go to the place God would show him. But when he came to Canaan,
he found that the land was already occupied. It would be some time
before God's promise to give the land to his descendants would be
fulfilled.

In Jacob's later years there was a famine, and it looked like the family
would not survive. But God brought Jacob's son, Joseph, to a promi-
nent position in Egypt, and through him provided for the family when
all hope seemed lost. Abraham's descendants remained in Egypt for the
next four hundred years and during that time grew from an extended
family of seventy people into a nation of around two million. God fulfilled his promise, even though it seemed impossible.

Maybe you have been waiting on God for something. You've even
prayed about it, but your prayers have become little more than "worry
on your knees." You say "Dear God" at the beginning and "Amen" at
the end, but in the middle all you do is rehearse your problems. When
you come to pray, look away from your problems and up into the face
of God. God will do everything that he has promised, and his timing
is perfect.

FOR FURTHER READING, SEE GENESIS 13

WHAT HAVE YOU FOUND?

It was by faith that Moses, when he grew up, refused to be called the
son of Pharaoh's daughter. He chose to share the oppression of God's
people instead of enjoying the fleeting pleasures of sin. He thought it was
better to suffer for the sake of Christ than to own the treasures of Egypt,
for he was looking ahead to his great reward. HEBREWS 11:24-26

AFTER JACOB MOVED his family to Egypt, Jacob's descendants remained there and grew into a nation of over two million people. They began to face persecution from the Egyptians.

This is the Bible's first recorded outbreak of violent racism, and especially of anti-Semitism, one of the great evils of history. The Egyptians subjected the Hebrews to forced labor, and eventually Pharaoh decreed that all of the male Hebrew babies were to be thrown into the Nile River.

When Moses was born, his mother defied Pharaoh's decree and placed him in a basket on the river. Pharaoh's daughter found him floating in the reeds and took pity on him, bringing him into the palace to care for him. In God's wonderful providence, Moses' mother was appointed to nurse him.

When he became an adult, Moses was outraged over the way the Egyptians treated his people. Eventually, he took matters into his own hands and killed an abusive Egyptian. When word of this got out, he ran for his life—all the way to Midian, where he married Zipporah and settled down to make a living as a shepherd.

On one occasion, Moses was tending his sheep in the area of Mount Horeb (also called Mount Sinai). It was here that God appeared to him in the burning bush and told him to go back to Egypt and confront Pharaoh. And he did.

The world sees little of value in Christ. But to us who believe, Christ is the treasure in the field, the pearl of great price. What Moses found in him made him glad to give up the comforts of a palace in Egypt and suffer with the people of God. The joyous response of finding Christ often results in worship and sacrifice. What have you found in Christ?

FOR FURTHER READING, SEE EXODUS 3

THE GOD WHO DELIVERS

*I have certainly seen the oppression of my people in Egypt. I have
heard their cries of distress because of their harsh slave drivers.
Yes, I am aware of their suffering. So I have come down to rescue
them from the power of the Egyptians.* EXODUS 3:7-8

FACED WITH AN oppressive Egyptian regime, the defenseless Hebrews cried out to God. What else could they do? They were completely powerless.

The great question raised in the book of Exodus is whether the living God can do anything to rescue his suffering people. And if he is capable of doing something, does he care enough to act? We still ask the same questions of God when we see suffering around us today: Can he do something? Does he care enough to act? God gives us the answer in the judgment that he brings on Egypt.

The people could be saved from oppression only if Pharaoh repented of his evil or if the evil was destroyed. God spoke to Pharaoh through Moses, telling him to let the people go, but the Egyptian leader refused. Then God spoke through a plague, but Pharaoh still refused. More plagues followed. Every time Pharaoh defied God, the cost of his defiance grew—for himself and for the people he led.

The reason God brings judgment is that he will not allow evil to stand. God made that plain on the day sin entered the world. If you do not understand that God will destroy all evil, you will fail to understand the Bible's message. The modern world does not feel the need for a Savior because it does not believe in a God who will bring judgment.

When God wanted to deliver his people from the tyranny of the Egyptians, he sent a man named Moses with a litany of plagues. When he wanted to deliver his people from the tyranny of sin, he sent his Son to take on human flesh. If you ever doubt God's determination to destroy evil, look to the cross, where the Son of God experienced all the plagues of hell so that you never would.

FOR FURTHER READING, SEE ROMANS 5

GOD BREAKS HIS SILENCE

God replied to Moses, "I AM WHO I AM." EXODUS 3:14

IT HAD BEEN four hundred years since Jacob and the family moved to Egypt, and in all of that time, God had been silent. No doubt Moses' mother would have taught him about the God of Abraham, Isaac, and Jacob. But by Moses' time, these stories must have seemed like ancient history.

Moses received a secular education in Pharaoh's palace, learning about the gods of Egypt—Osiris, Heqet, Apis, and Ra. Like students in secular universities today, he would have heard his teachers talk about the God of the Bible as only one god among many, a reflection of the culture in which a person is raised.

But Moses would no longer have to wonder who God is after he saw a fire resting on a bush—without actually burning the bush! All other fires go out when they exhaust their fuel; a candle burns only until the wax is gone, and then the flame goes out. This fire was unlike any other. It sustained its own life.

Moses had never seen anything like it, and as he came closer, God spoke to him from the fire: "I am the same God who called Abraham, appeared to Isaac, and wrestled with Jacob, and now I am speaking to you." Then he presented to Moses the name by which he wanted to be known: "I AM WHO I AM." Like fire on the burning bush, God is dependent on no one, and he cannot be confined to any time or place in history.

When people say they don't believe in a God who will judge or in a God who would save people only through Jesus, what they are really saying is that they don't like the God of the Bible, so they have decided to shape God into a more pleasing image. But this is idolatry, the casting of a false god. The God of the Bible is not whoever you want him to be. He is who he is!

FOR FURTHER READING, SEE ISAIAH 44

THE POINT OF THE PLAGUES

I will execute judgment against all the gods of Egypt,
for I am the LORD! EXODUS 12:12

IT IS ALL very well for the God of the Bible to say, "I AM," but how do we know that he is and that the other gods are not? That is the point of the plagues. Pharaoh refused to obey God's command to let his people go because he did not recognize the authority of God.

As long as Pharaoh believed he could worship his own gods, he would never submit to the authority of the one true God. So God gave proof of who he is by bringing down the powers behind Egypt's gods— Osiris, the god of the Nile; Heqet, the goddess of fertility; and Ra, the sun god.

Much more was at stake in the plagues than a conflict between Moses and Pharaoh or between Israel and Egypt. The living God was bringing down the demonic powers masquerading behind Egypt's false gods. Those powers were real. That is why the magicians were able to produce frogs—though they could not get rid of them! (See Exodus 8:7.)

In effect, God was saying, "You claim that the Nile sustains you, but I can turn the Nile into a lifeless swamp. You bow down to Heqet, the image of a frog, but I will give birth to so many frogs, you will wish you had never known her. You claim the power of the sun, but I will turn the sun to darkness. What you have put in my place will become a plague to you!"

God will not tolerate our putting anything in his place. He wants nothing to detract from the one true image of the invisible God. God took human flesh and entered the world, making himself known in Jesus Christ, "the exact imprint of his nature" (Hebrews 1:3, ESV). That is why Jesus could say, "Anyone who has seen me has seen the Father" (John 14:9). You won't find your way to the God of the Bible through any other so-called "gods," but God has drawn near to you in Jesus Christ.

FOR FURTHER READING, SEE 1 JOHN 5

ARE YOU COVERED?

When I see the blood, I will pass over you. EXODUS 12:13

GOD GAVE MOSES very careful instructions for the people. When the greatest and the last of God's ten judgments came on Egypt, God made a way in which all who believed and obeyed could be kept safe. Every family was to choose a lamb. They were to keep it for four days, and then they were to kill it. The lamb's blood was then to be painted onto the doorframes of their houses.

Can you imagine the pressure on Moses to communicate this message? He had been in the presence of the living God at the burning bush. He had seen the fire and heard God's voice. He had seen the plagues, and he knew that God would strike Egypt with judgment. He knew that God had provided one way in which families could be kept safe through this night of terror. The way of deliverance was by blood. Only blood would save them from death.

I can imagine Moses going around to each house asking, "Are you covered by the blood of the lamb? Have you shed that blood yet? Is it over your door? The day of judgment is coming. God said, 'When I see the blood, I will pass over you.' Now, get it on your house! Why haven't you done it yet?"

When night came, I have no doubt that some of the people were shaking with fear as they ate the Passover meal. They must have looked up at their doors and wondered if the blood would make any difference when God's judgment broke. All they had to go on was the Word of God. About two million people believed and obeyed, and every one of them was kept safe through God's judgment.

God never said, "If you offer a certain number of prayers, I will pass over you." He did not say, "If you are sincere, I will pass over you." He said only, "When I see the blood, I will pass over you" (Exodus 12:13). Likewise, our salvation does not depend on the quantity of our prayers or on our sincerity; it depends on whether we are covered by the blood of Jesus Christ through faith.

FOR FURTHER READING, SEE EXODUS 12

THE SUBSTITUTE TEACHER

Go, . . . slaughter the Passover animal. . . . Take a bundle of hyssop branches and dip it into the blood. Brush the hyssop across the top and sides of the doorframes of your houses. EXODUS 12:21-22

WHEN ADAM AND Eve sinned in the Garden, "God made clothing from animal skins" for them (Genesis 3:21). That means God killed an animal on the very day the first sin was committed. God warned Adam that disobedience would lead to death, and there was a death in the Garden that day. Adam's life was spared, and an animal died instead.

We find the same pattern in the story of Abraham and Isaac. God told Abraham to take his son up the mountain, and God provided an animal that was killed in Isaac's place. The animal's blood was shed, and Isaac's life was spared.

Now a lamb would be killed for every Hebrew family in Egypt. God was teaching the same lesson to a new generation: "The way you will be saved from judgment is through the death of another. It will involve the shedding of blood, like it did for Adam and for Abraham."

Jesus Christ is "the Lamb of God who takes away the sin of the world" (John 1:29). Like the sacrificed animals, he died in the place of Adam and Isaac and in the place of God's people in Egypt. He died in your place too. He bore the judgment of God so that it would not fall on you. As Paul says, "Christ, our Passover Lamb, has been sacrificed for us" (1 Corinthians 5:7).

Just as there had to be an act of faith and obedience in which the blood was applied to the doorframes of the Israelites' homes in Egypt, so there must be an act of faith in which Christ's blood is applied to your life. The blood must not only be shed; it must also be applied.

Since the blood of Christ has been shed, why would you not, in an act of faith, ask that his blood cover you? Then you can rest on God's promise, and God will bring you safely through the day of judgment.

FOR FURTHER READING, SEE ROMANS 4

THE LAW WAS NEVER A LADDER

Then God gave the people all these instructions:
"I am the LORD your God, who rescued you from the land
of Egypt, the place of your slavery." EXODUS 20:1-2

MOSES RETURNED TO the place where God had spoken to him out of the burning bush, surrounded not by a flock of sheep, but by two million people. God had been faithful, and the seemingly impossible had happened. In one of the greatest miracles in the Old Testament, God parted the waters of the Red Sea. Now, a couple of months later, the people of God arrived at Mount Sinai, where they set up camp.

The God who came down to speak with Adam, Abraham, Isaac, and Jacob was coming down to give his law to the people, but his law was never intended as a ladder for unsaved people to climb up to heaven. It was always a pattern of life for God's people who had been saved from judgment by the blood of the lamb.

God was not saying, "I'm giving you these commands, and by keeping them you may become my people." He was saying, "I'm giving you these commands because you are my people." The law tells us how people who belong to God ought to live.

This is important, because some people have the idea that in the Old Testament God tried to save people by getting them to keep the law, but since they couldn't, he came up with a better way of saving people— through his Son, Jesus Christ. If this were true, we would naturally conclude that the Old Testament is a book of law and the New Testament is a book of grace, so the Old Testament has nothing to do with us, because we're not under law; we're under grace.

That is a complete misunderstanding of the Bible. The whole Bible is a book of grace. God promised a Redeemer on the very day that sin entered the world. There is one God and one story. The law is given specifically to people who have experienced the grace of God and have become his people, and for this reason, it continues to speak to us today.

FOR FURTHER READING, SEE EXODUS 20

LAYING TRACK FOR THE TRAIN

I will give you a new heart, and I will put a new spirit in you. I will take out your stony, stubborn heart and give you a tender, responsive heart. And I will put my Spirit in you so that you will follow my decrees and be careful to obey my regulations. EZEKIEL 36:26-27

GOD'S ULTIMATE PURPOSE is to restore in us a true reflection of his glory. Since God's glory is expressed in his law, that means the purpose of the gospel is to bring us to the position where we live according to the law of God.

The whole of the Christian life is a process in which we are changed from one degree of glory to another, until the day when we see God, and then we shall be like him. This transformation is the work of the Holy Spirit, and it is spoken of in both the Old and New Testaments.

In the new covenant, God not only tells us what to do, he also gives us the power to move in that direction. The law of God is like the rails for a train. The rails give direction, but the train will not go anywhere unless there is power in the engine. It is the special work of the Holy Spirit to give God's people the power to move in the direction laid out in God's law.

The Christian life is not a matter of believing in Jesus and then trying your best to live according to God's law. God's promise is that when you believe in the Lord Jesus Christ, the Holy Spirit will come and reside in your life, and when the Spirit comes into your life, you will receive power (see Acts 1:8).

That power will make the difference between a battle in which you are destined for defeat and a battle in which there will be ultimate victory. When the Holy Spirit lives within you, the law is no longer a list of impossible demands, but a description of new possibilities. What are the greatest battles of your life? Can you hear God's promise of victory?

FOR FURTHER READING, SEE EZEKIEL 36

PUT TO THE TEST

*Moses . . . remained on the mountain forty days
and forty nights.* EXODUS 24:18

WHEN GOD GAVE the Ten Commandments, he spoke with an audible voice that all the people heard: "The LORD said to Moses, 'I will come to you in a thick cloud, Moses, so the people themselves can hear me when I speak with you. Then they will always trust you'" (Exodus 19:9).

Moses came down the mountain and told the people what was going to happen, and then God spoke to them (see Exodus 20:1). Imagine hearing the audible voice of God! "When the people heard the thunder and the loud blast of the ram's horn, and when they saw the flashes of lightning and the smoke billowing from the mountain, they stood at a distance, trembling with fear. And they said to Moses, 'You speak to us, and we will listen. But don't let God speak directly to us, or we will die!'" (20:18-19).

So Moses went back up the mountain and remained there forty days and nights (see Exodus 24:18), almost six weeks, and by the end of that time, the people were tired of waiting. They gathered around Aaron and said, "Come on, make us some gods who can lead us. We don't know what happened to this fellow Moses" (32:1).

Only six weeks had passed since the people heard God himself telling them not to make any idols. Now, within a matter of days, they made a choice that directly contradicted one of God's simplest instructions. The effects of their remarkable experience of God had faded quickly. Here is the mystery of sin and the weakness of human nature.

Six weeks of silence from God and the absence of their spiritual leader, Moses, was all it took to put their faith to the test. Does it seem like God has been hiding himself from you? What is putting your faith to the test? Don't give in to despair. Watch and pray (see Matthew 26:41), and you will see the faithfulness of God.

FOR FURTHER READING, SEE HEBREWS 3

BREAKING UP THE PARTY

The people got up early the next morning to sacrifice burnt offerings
and peace offerings. After this, they celebrated with feasting and
drinking, and they indulged in pagan revelry. EXODUS 32:6

MOSES WAS AT the top of the mountain in the presence of God when he
received the bad news: "Quick! Go down the mountain! Your people
whom you brought from the land of Egypt have corrupted themselves"
(Exodus 32:7).

Moses faced the uncomfortable task of breaking up the party. His
first step was to confront Aaron. "What did these people do to you to
make you bring such terrible sin upon them?" (Exodus 32:21). Had
the people subjected Aaron to some horrible torture? All it took to persuade him to disobey God's law was public demand. Aaron was unable
to resist the pressure of their felt needs.

Notice Aaron's attempt to deflect responsibility. We are told that
Aaron actively shaped the gold into the form of an idol, but when Moses
challenged him, Aaron gave a sanitized version of the story: "When they
brought [their gold] to me, I simply threw it into the fire—and out came
this calf!" (Exodus 32:24). In Aaron's telling, it just happened!

After confronting his brother, Moses called the people to a point of
decision: "All of you who are on the LORD's side, come here and join
me" (Exodus 32:26). Everyone was given opportunity to repent. They
were invited to declare their allegiance to the Lord. There were nearly
two million people in the camp, and for the three thousand people who
refused the invitation, this was the last day of their lives (see 32:28).

This devastating judgment was not so much the result of their sin
as of their refusal to give it up. They had seen the glory of God, heard
his voice, and refused to come to him. The commandments of God are
not a list of suggestions. They are real laws with real penalties for those
who break them. Ultimate rejection of God's invitation to repent always
leads to devastating consequences.

FOR FURTHER READING, SEE EXODUS 32

WHAT MORE DO YOU WANT?

You have committed a terrible sin. EXODUS 32:30

THREE THOUSAND PEOPLE were already dead, and the 1,997,000 people remaining had made some indication of repentance toward God. So why does Moses get up the next day and say, "You have committed a terrible sin"? These people already know they've done wrong. Talk about preaching to the choir!

What happened to forgiveness? Why doesn't Moses draw a line under it? Isn't it his duty to tell them that they are forgiven? These people are sorry. What more does Moses want from them? Notice there is no forgiveness offered by God here. Why? Isn't it God's duty to forgive them?

No, something must happen before forgiveness can be granted. Moses announces, "I will go up to the LORD; perhaps I can make atonement for your sin" (Exodus 32:30, NIV). It is at this point in the Bible story that we discover a new word, *atonement*. What is an atonement? Atonement is what it costs to take something that is wrong and put it right.

The English word *atonement* can be split into three parts: "at-one-ment." If two people are divided by a dispute, an atonement is what it will take to restore their relationship so they are "at one." Wherever there is an offense, we face the question of atonement. What will it cost to take what is wrong and put it right?

Are you feeling that God is far removed from you? Have you wondered what it would take to restore a right relationship with God? Maybe you are sorry for your sins. Maybe you have even tried to make things right with God. There is nothing wrong with these things, but by themselves they cannot make you right with God.

If you and God are going to be at peace with each other, you need an atonement. This atonement for sin was offered by Jesus Christ through his death on the cross. Put your trust in that sacrifice, and you will be "at one" with God.

FOR FURTHER READING, SEE HEBREWS 2

A GREAT LEADER

Leave me alone so my fierce anger can blaze against them, and I will destroy
them. Then I will make you, Moses, into a great nation. EXODUS 32:10

THIS WAS QUITE an offer! Put yourself in Moses' shoes: God offers you
a fresh start and the prospect of leading a whole new group of people.
What would you do?

But when Moses thought about the people God had given him,
he could not give them up. No doubt Moses had thought about the
Passover and the death of the lamb. Perhaps *he* could be the substitute!
He was ready to lay down his life if it meant that these people could be
spared.

The next day Moses said to the people, "Perhaps I can make atonement for your sin" (Exodus 32:30, NIV). Then Moses went back to the
Lord: "These people . . . have made gods of gold for themselves. But
now, if you will only forgive their sin—but if not, erase my name from
the record you have written!" (32:31-32).

We have a volunteer—the greatest spiritual leader in the Old Testament—ready to lay down his life for the people. But God does not accept
his offer. "No deal, Moses," he seems to say. "This is out of your league."
Moses had a murder on his record, and a man with his own sins is in no
position to atone for the sins of others.

What Adam and Eve had discovered, the nation of Israel now discovers—that sin causes God to hide and withdraw his presence. Without
an atonement, God "will not travel" with them to the Promised Land
(Exodus 33:3). The immediate presence of God is dangerous for them,
because it is a fearful thing to be in the presence of an angry God.

When the people hear they will have to face the future without God's
presence, they begin to mourn (see Exodus 33:4). They are now facing
the most fundamental question in the most personal way: What will it
take to bring back the presence of God?

FOR FURTHER READING, SEE EXODUS 33

PAINSTAKING OBEDIENCE

The Israelites had done everything just as the LORD
had commanded Moses. EXODUS 39:32

GOD HAD ALREADY given precise instructions for building the Tabernacle (see Exodus 25–30). Then as we read the details of the actual workmanship—the making of the Ark, the table, the lampstand, the altar, the courtyard, and the priestly garments—it is exactly the same (see 35–39). We are told both the detailed instructions and the details of all their work to make a single point: the people did *exactly* what God told them to do, down to the tiniest detail.

Many people have the idea that a serious commitment to obeying God's commands will make up for their sins. Some of the people of Israel may have thought, *If we are sincere in our obedience, God's blessing will return.* Imagine a woman sewing embroidery on the curtains for the Tabernacle, and as she follows God's exact instructions, she thinks, *I've got to be obedient to God. Perhaps this will bring back his presence.* Picture a man working with bronze, thinking, *If my hands can do what God has commanded, his blessing might return to us.*

For seven months, the people gave themselves to a daily, detailed obedience of the law of God, but at the end of it all, there was still no sign of God's presence. By this point they must have been wondering, *How is it possible to bring back the presence of God? How can we take what is wrong and put it right?*

This is a key issue to grasp if we are to understand the story of the Bible. Many people feel that if they are sorry enough, things will become right with God. There are others who think that if they shape up to a more detailed obedience to God's laws by attending church, saying prayers, or reading the Bible, this will make things right with God. But right here, God is teaching us that although these things are good, they are not enough. What we need is an atonement.

FOR FURTHER READING, SEE ROMANS 3

A WORTHY SACRIFICE

*This is what the LORD has commanded you to do so that the
glory of the LORD may appear to you.* LEVITICUS 9:6

AFTER SEVEN MONTHS of longing for the presence of God to return,
Moses told the people how it could happen. There must have been a
stunned silence as the people listened to the instructions he gave Aaron:
"Come to the altar and sacrifice your sin offering and your burnt offering
and make atonement for yourself and the people; sacrifice the offering
that is for the people and make atonement for them" (Leviticus 9:7, NIV).

The priests took an animal and slaughtered it so that the blood of the
animal was poured out. The blood was then taken to the altar. "Moses
and Aaron went into the Tabernacle, and when they came back out,
they blessed the people again, and the glory of the LORD appeared to
the whole community" (Leviticus 9:23).

God was back! That could only mean that what had been wrong had
finally been put right. Then the Lord gave evidence of his presence:
"Fire blazed forth from the LORD's presence and consumed the burnt
offering and the fat on the altar. When the people saw this, they shouted
with joy and fell face down on the ground" (Leviticus 9:24).

Can you imagine the impact of this? A woman sits in her tent, talking about the day: "I've never seen anything quite like that! Who would
have imagined that shedding the blood of an animal would bring back
the presence of God?" Her husband agrees: "We've learned something
today. Where there is sin, we need a sacrifice. It's the sacrifice and the
shedding of blood that makes atonement with God."

The Old Testament sacrificial system always pointed forward so
that we would be able to understand why the Son of God had to come
into the world. The sacrifices help us to see that in his death on that
cross, Jesus Christ did in reality what the sacrifice of animals did only
in symbol. Christ made atonement for our sins, and he brings back the
presence of God for all who trust in his sacrifice.

FOR FURTHER READING, SEE LEVITICUS 9

WHY YOU NEED A PRIEST

The LORD said to Moses, . . . "I myself am present in the cloud above the atonement cover." LEVITICUS 16:2

IF YOU EVER find yourself in a court of law, you will probably want an attorney to present your case. Law courts are intimidating places, and they operate under some fairly complex rules, so you need the help of an attorney to speak on your behalf before the judge.

Old Testament priests did something similar for the people of God. A priest would represent the people to God and speak to him on their behalf, operating in a mobile worship center called the Tabernacle. The Tabernacle was separated into different areas by a series of curtains and contained various pieces of symbolic furniture.

At the center of the Tabernacle was the Most Holy Place, which was screened off from view by a heavy curtain. If you could have gone into the Most Holy Place—nobody but the high priest was allowed to, and he only once a year—you would have seen the Ark of the Covenant, a wooden chest with an ornate lid.

Rising from the lid were two golden statues. These were angelic figures called cherubim, whose work was associated with the judgment of God. The cherubim were placed at the entrance to the Garden of Eden with swords flashing back and forth to prevent sinful men and women from entering the presence of God. So also these golden statues on top of the Ark of the Covenant were a visual reminder that you can't come near God without coming close to judgment.

Between the cherubim was a flat area called the atonement cover (or mercy seat). God told Moses, "I will meet with you there . . . above the atonement cover between the gold cherubim that hover over the Ark of the Covenant" (Exodus 25:22).

Once a year, on the Day of Atonement, the high priest would go behind the curtain into the Most Holy Place. God would come down, just as he had done on Mount Sinai. But he did not make himself visible; he appeared in the cloud. God met with the high priest at a place that speaks of both his mercy and his judgment.

FOR FURTHER READING, SEE LEVITICUS 16

ACT 1: THE PRIEST APPEARS

[Aaron] must put on his linen tunic and the linen undergarments
worn next to his body. He must tie the linen sash around his
waist and put the linen turban on his head. LEVITICUS 16:4

THE DAY OF Atonement was like a great drama in five acts. Even today
it remains the most visual presentation of the gospel in the Old Testament. The whole day was filled with symbolism that points us forward
to Jesus Christ and helps us to understand the significance of his death
on the cross.

You would have understood that the high priest was one of the most
important people in the nation just by looking at his clothes. Rich in
symbolism, his breastplate contained twelve precious stones, representing the twelve tribes of Israel. Under his breastplate he wore an ephod,
a sleeveless tunic of fine linen, decorated with gold, blue, purple, and
scarlet trim. His clothing displayed the dignity of his office.

But on the Day of Atonement, the high priest did not wear his magnificent clothes. He appeared in the streets wearing a simple white
cloth, the sort of clothing that the lowest servant would wear.

Imagine the man who holds the most dignified office in the land
dressed as a common slave, onlookers lining the route where he walks.
He makes his way toward the Tabernacle like a boxer entering the ring,
a vast crowd pressing round in anticipation of what is about to happen.

In the New Testament another high priest appears. Every high priest
descended from Aaron, but this high priest is not one of Aaron's sons.
This priest is the Son of God! His glory, the glory that he shared with
the Father before the world began, is much greater than the splendid
clothes worn by the high priest.

However, just as the high priest discarded his magnificent clothing on the Day of Atonement, Christ laid aside his glory. He took on
himself the form of a servant (see Philippians 2:6-7). He was wrapped
in strips of cloth and laid in a manger. When Christ was born, the real
drama of atonement was about to begin.

FOR FURTHER READING, SEE PHILIPPIANS 2

ACT 2: THE PRIEST PREPARES

When Aaron enters the sanctuary area, he must follow these instructions fully. He must bring a young bull for a sin offering. LEVITICUS 16:3

AARON, THE FIRST high priest, had led God's people into the worship of the golden calf. No doubt he tried to honor God and live by the commandments, but before he could enter the presence of God to deal with the people's sins, his first priority was to deal with his own.

A bull was brought forward and slaughtered in public view. Then Aaron took some of the blood behind the curtain into the Most Holy Place, where God had said he would come. There, Aaron sprinkled the bull's blood as a sacrifice for his own sins.

This must have made a powerful impression. The high priest was saying, "Before we get to offering a sacrifice for the people, I want to recognize publicly that I stand in need of a sacrifice myself." He was saying, like every other priest, pastor, or religious leader of any denomination would always have to say, "I have sins of my own, and therefore I am in no position to deal with yours."

As we read through the Gospels, we find that Jesus Christ lived a life that was different from any other life that has ever been lived. He did the will of the Father and fulfilled all the work that the Father had given him to do.

When Jesus asked his enemies if they could find even one sin in him, they responded by calling him names, but not by naming any sins (see John 8:46-48). This high priest was unlike any other. He did not need to offer a sacrifice for his own sin, because he had committed no sin (see 2 Corinthians 5:21; I Peter 2:22).

Jesus was what every other priest wished he could be. He lived the life that no other high priest was able to live, and his perfect life qualified him to achieve the atonement that all the other high priests could only illustrate.

FOR FURTHER READING, SEE HEBREWS 5

ACT 3: ATONEMENT IS MADE

*Then Aaron must slaughter the first goat as a sin offering for the people
and carry its blood behind the inner curtain. There he will sprinkle
the goat's blood over the atonement cover.* LEVITICUS 16:15

AFTER THE HIGH priest had dealt with his own sins, he would come back
out of the Tabernacle, and all the people would see him again. Then
a goat was brought forward and slaughtered, and the high priest took
the blood behind the curtain and sprinkled it on the atonement cover.

Remember, the atonement cover was the flat surface on the Ark of
the Covenant between the huge golden figures of the cherubim. God's
agents of judgment looked down at the atonement cover where the
blood would be sprinkled. When Aaron sprinkled the goat's blood on
the atonement cover (also called the mercy seat), it was as if judgment
and mercy were meeting together.

Judgment, which demands death as the penalty for sin, was satisfied;
mercy, which demands forgiveness for the sinner, was sustained. Mercy
was released in the place of judgment as the blood of the sacrifice was
sprinkled.

Back in the Garden of Eden, God made it clear that the consequence
of sin is death (see Genesis 2:17). That is why blood had to be sprinkled
on the atonement cover. The blood demonstrated that a death had taken
place. This death would satisfy the justice of God in relation to sin.

After three years of public ministry, Jesus was arrested and sentenced
to be crucified. As he was nailed to the cross, his blood was shed and his
life poured out. Darkness covered the face of the earth, and he cried out,
"My God, my God, why have you abandoned me?" (Mark 15:34). The
judgment of God represented by the cherubim fell on him.

When Christ cried out in a loud voice, "It is finished" (John 19:30),
the inner curtain in the Temple that surrounded the Most Holy Place
was ripped in two from top to bottom (see Mark 15:37-38). Atonement
was made by our great High Priest, and a new and living way was opened
up into the presence of God!

FOR FURTHER READING, SEE HEBREWS 9

ACT 4: SIN IS CONFESSED

> *[Aaron] will lay both of his hands on the goat's head and confess over it*
> *all the wickedness, rebellion, and sins of the people of Israel. In this way,*
> *he will transfer the people's sins to the head of the goat.* LEVITICUS 16:21

THE PEOPLE SAW the goat being slaughtered, and then all they could do was wait as the high priest went into the Most Holy Place to sprinkle the blood on the atonement cover. Now, a second goat was brought to him.

The high priest was charged with confessing all the sins of Israel while laying both hands on the head of this live goat. That would have been a long prayer! While he was unable to confess the details of every individual sin, the high priest prayed in such a way that the people recognized there were specific sins that needed to be dealt with. If you had been standing in the crowd listening, eventually you would have thought, *That sin is one of mine.*

When the high priest confessed the sins of the people, his hands on the head of the goat, a transfer took place. God moved the guilt of these sins onto the goat. He regarded these sins as placed on the goat's head and carried by the goat.

Now God says to us, "That is what I want you to do. I want you, in an act of faith, to lay hold of the Lord Jesus Christ. I want you to confess your sins, and when you do, this is what will happen: your guilt will be transferred to Christ. It will be laid on him and included in the sin for which he died."

Have you done that? Christ, the perfect High Priest, has appeared. Atonement has been accomplished in his death. The question is whether that atonement has been applied to your sins. That happens when you lay hold of Jesus Christ in faith and confess your sin to him. When faith has laid its hand on Christ and confession has been made, then guilt is transferred and you can look back to the cross and know that your guilt and your sin were dealt with there.

FOR FURTHER READING, SEE 1 JOHN 1

ACT 5: GUILT IS REMOVED

*As the goat goes into the wilderness, it will carry all the people's
sins upon itself into a desolate land.* LEVITICUS 16:22

WHAT HAPPENED NEXT on the Day of Atonement is a marvelous picture
of how God deals with our sins when they have been confessed and
atonement has been made.

Picture yourself in the crowd. The high priest has finished confessing your sins. Your guilt has been transferred to the goat, and now
someone leads the goat away.

You watch him weave in and out between the tents and then outside
the camp and into the desert. You watch until the man and the goat are
only a dot on the horizon, and then you can no longer see them at all.

Apply this picture to your own life. When atonement has been made
for your sin and your sin has been confessed, then your guilt will be
removed. It will be taken out of sight.

Can you see your sins laid on Jesus, as you lay hold of him by faith
and confess your sins to him? Can you picture your sins being taken
away into the distance and out of sight? Can you believe that through
the finished work of Christ your guilt is removed, that "he has removed
our sins as far from us as the east is from the west" (Psalm 103:12)?

The Day of Atonement was a series of visual aids in which God was
teaching us: 1) We need a priest who will lay aside his dignity and come
as a servant to make atonement for us. 2) A man with his own sins cannot atone for the sins of others. 3) Atonement can be made only by the
shedding of blood, satisfying the justice of God and releasing mercy. 4)
When sin is confessed, its guilt is transferred. 5) When atonement is
made and sin is confessed, then guilt is removed.

This five-act drama was like a dress rehearsal for the real performance that took place when Jesus Christ came into the world. It told us
what to look for and what to expect when he came.

Fast-forward fifteen hundred years, and you move from the dress
rehearsal to the opening night, from the preview to the main event,
featuring Jesus Christ in the role of the High Priest.

FOR FURTHER READING, SEE HEBREWS 10

GOD'S UNCONDITIONAL LOVE

The LORD did not set his heart on you and choose you because
you were more numerous than other nations, for you were
the smallest of all nations! DEUTERONOMY 7:7

ON THIS OCCASION, God seemed almost to tease his people with the prospect of an explanation of why he loved them. Have you ever wondered why God loves you? Our appetite for an answer is piqued. "Lord, tell us why you love us."

God gave his people an answer: "It was simply that the LORD loves you" (Deuteronomy 7:8). That is the reason God loves you, and you will never get a deeper answer! The explanation of the love of God for you lies in God alone—in the source and not in the object.

This is quite beyond the range of our experience. It is easy for me to explain why I love my wife. The reasons are not hard to find. Her charming character, striking appearance, unusual gifts, and warm personality evoke a response from me. It was like that when we met, and it is still like that today.

But God's love is different. The reason God loves you is not that he was smitten with your appearance, bowled over by your personality, knocked out by your good works, or swept away by the sheer genius of your talent. The explanation of God's love for you does not lie in anything within you; it lies in God alone.

Only God is able to love the unlovely, the unskilled, the wounded, the inhibited, and even the rebel. Only God still loves you in your worst moments. So when you wonder, *How can God love me?* the problem is that it focuses all of the attention on you, and when you're depressed or struggling with a personal failure, thinking about yourself is not very encouraging.

Thankfully, the reason God loves you has nothing to do with you at all. The explanation lies in God. If you can get your attention away from yourself and focus your thoughts on God, it will not be long before you are rejoicing in his love.

FOR FURTHER READING, SEE DEUTERONOMY 7

WHY OBEDIENCE MATTERS

Those who hear the warnings of this curse should not congratulate themselves, thinking, "I am safe, even though I am following the desires of my own stubborn heart." DEUTERONOMY 29:19

TOWARD THE END of his life, Moses was concerned that some people who knew God's unfailing love—the love expressed in, "The LORD . . . is the faithful God who keeps his covenant for a thousand generations and lavishes his unfailing love on those who love him and obey his commands" (Deuteronomy 7:9)—might already have been turning away from him.

Can you see how one of God's people might reach this point? "We're God's people. God has given us the sacrifices to cover our sins and a high priest who goes into the Holy Place for us. Since God loves us unconditionally, all we need to do is perform this ritual, and then for the rest of the week, we can do what we want. Why does obedience matter? No matter what I do, God will keep blessing me."

Moses saw that some people were beginning to think like that. But God had addressed the issue (see Leviticus 26). He gave a long list of promises that were all conditional—promises predicated on the little word *if*: "If you follow my decrees and are careful to obey my commands, I will . . ." (26:3-4). And God listed the blessings that would follow: a strong economy (abundant harvests) and national security (victory over enemies), and the greatest blessing that follows from obedience: "I will live among you" (26:11).

Then God spoke about disobedience and its results: "If you do not listen to me or obey all these commands, and if you break my covenant by rejecting my decrees, treating my regulations with contempt, and refusing to obey my commands, I will punish you" (Leviticus 26:14-16). The consequences of disobedience were terrible, some of which would make your hair stand on end—ill health, bad harvests, and military defeat.

Once you begin thinking, *It doesn't matter what I do; God will still bless me*, you are walking away from the presence of God and into his loving discipline.

FOR FURTHER READING, SEE HEBREWS 12

AGREEING WITH GOD'S CURSES

When you cross the Jordan River . . . the tribes of Reuben,
Gad, Asher, Zebulun, Dan, and Naphtali must stand on
Mount Ebal to proclaim a curse. DEUTERONOMY 27:12-13

SHORTLY BEFORE GOD'S people came into the land of Canaan, God brought them to a place where there were two hills, Mount Ebal and Mount Gerizim. When the people came to the pass between the mountains, Moses sent representatives from each tribe to the tops of these two hills.

The Levites were to shout out curses from God's law as the people passed through the valley below. Imagine you are one of a vast crowd of people walking along a path, and high on a rock above, you hear a group of men shouting, "Cursed is anyone who carves or casts an idol and secretly sets it up" (Deuteronomy 27:15). When you hear this, you have to join with all the other people by saying, "Amen!"

You walk another few yards, and you hear somebody else shouting, "Cursed is anyone who dishonors father or mother" (Deuteronomy 27:16), and again you say, "Amen." The word *amen* means "so be it," and so when you say this, you are saying, "That's what I am asking God to do."

When the people said "amen" to the curses, they were saying to God, "Lord, if I am stupid enough to choose a path of disobedience, I want you to intercept me and bring that plan to nothing (that's what the word *curse* means, something is set apart for destruction). If I use deception, expose me. If I sin in secret, bring it into the open. If I start living for myself and for my pleasure, take pleasure from me until I find pleasure in you."

How do you feel about making that kind of commitment to God? Suppose you want to keep your options open. If you had been at Mount Ebal, you might have mumbled your response and tried to mask that you never said "amen" at all. There is only one way into God's blessing, and it goes past Mount Ebal, where you renounce sin and call on God to keep you from it.

FOR FURTHER READING, SEE DEUTERONOMY 27

CHOOSING YOUR PATH

When you cross the Jordan River, the tribes of Simeon, Levi, Judah,
Issachar, Joseph, and Benjamin must stand on Mount Gerizim to
proclaim a blessing over the people. DEUTERONOMY 27:12

BEYOND MOUNT EBAL lies Mount Gerizim, the mountain of God's blessing. Having passed Ebal, where they renounced sin, God's people now
walked under Mount Gerizim, where the Levites shouted out the blessings of God: "Wherever you go and whatever you do, you will be blessed"
(Deuteronomy 28:6).

God was saying, "I will be with you to bless you. My hand will be
upon you. Though enemies come against you, I will protect you. You
will know my presence and my peace."

Whenever the people looked up to the hills, these two mountains
would have reminded them that there are two ways to live and that they
lead to two entirely different experiences of the love of God. The path
of disobedience leads to an experience of God's discipline, in which he
loves us by doing whatever it takes to bring us back to himself. The path
of obedience leads to an experience of God's blessing, in which he loves
us by showering good gifts upon his people.

Jesus Christ came into the world, "that [we] may have life, and have
it to the full" (John 10:10, NIV). He made it clear that the paths of obedience and disobedience lead not only to different experiences in this
life, but to two different destinations (see Matthew 7:13-14). Christ
bore the Curse for us so that it would be possible for us to get off the
road that leads to destruction and onto the road that leads to life.

Look back on the last ten years of your life. Is there a pattern of
pushing outside the boundaries of God's commands? Is there a pattern
of resisting God and then God confronting the problem to bring you
back? Have you been wearing yourself out by resisting his will and his
truth? What will the next ten years look like? Choose life! Choose the
path of God's blessing.

FOR FURTHER READING, SEE DEUTERONOMY 28

PREPARING FOR BATTLE

*From the whole community of Israel, record the names of all
the warriors by their clans and families. List all the men . . .
who are able to go to war.* NUMBERS 1:2-3

GOD WAS LEADING the people into warfare, preparing them for a military campaign in which they would enter the land he had promised them. Costly battles and ultimate victory lay ahead.

But in the early days after the Exodus, God shielded his people from the full cost of their calling: "When Pharaoh finally let the people go, God did not lead them along the main road that runs through Philistine territory, even though that was the shortest route to the Promised Land. God said, 'If the people are faced with a battle, they might change their minds and return to Egypt'" (Exodus 13:17).

Jesus declares, "If any of you wants to be my follower, you must turn from your selfish ways, take up your cross, and follow me" (Mark 8:34). He does not tell us what that cross will be, only that we must be ready to take it up.

It took Moses' traveling caravan two months to get from the Red Sea to Sinai, and by the time the Tabernacle was set up, a year had passed. God used that time to turn a confused crowd into a disciplined nation. The people had an ordered way of worship, a functioning legal system, and a government.

Genesis tells us God chooses his people; Exodus tells us he redeems his people; Leviticus tells us God is among his people; Deuteronomy tells us God loves his people; and Numbers tells us God commissions his people. God's chosen, redeemed, holy, and dearly loved people were now being sent to war.

Our calling is to a life of unconditional obedience to all that God has told us to do. God's revealed will for Israel was to enter the land of Canaan. The revealed will of God for his people today includes the great commandment, "You must love the LORD your God with all your heart . . . [and] love your neighbor as yourself" (Mark 12:30-31), and the great commission, "Go and make disciples of all the nations" (Matthew 28:19).

FOR FURTHER READING, SEE EPHESIANS 6

AVOIDING THE DETOUR

The LORD now said to Moses, "Send out men to explore the land of Canaan, the land I am giving to the Israelites." NUMBERS 13:1-2

MOSES SENT THEM off, and the spies traveled through the Promised Land for forty days gathering information. But when they got back, things began to go horribly wrong. The majority of the spies took the view that the land couldn't be conquered.

Their pessimism spread, and the people lost heart. They were unwilling to press forward in obedience to God's command. At the very point where great things lay ahead, a negative spirit emerged: "The people began to complain about their hardship, and the LORD heard everything they said" (Numbers 11:1). This group of people who had been uniquely blessed by God became deeply dissatisfied with what God had given them.

It is difficult to make good decisions when you have a bad attitude. If in your heart you feel deeply dissatisfied with what God has given to you, be careful! That's where God's people were when they made the mistake of a lifetime. God determined that this generation of grumblers and complainers would not enter the land he promised them. So they spent the next thirty-eight years in the desert, until that whole generation had died and their children were old enough to take their place.

Numbers is a book that need never have been written. It is the story of an unnecessary detour by a group of God's people who held back when they should have pressed forward. God recorded this sad experience of his people to warn us about the long-term consequences of cowardly choices.

Even though we belong to God, there is still the danger that we may miss our calling and become a group of wandering, aimless people who merely mark time for a generation. The prospect is frightening, and that is why the book of Numbers is so valuable to us. If we can understand where these people went wrong, it will help us to avoid repeating their mistakes.

FOR FURTHER READING, SEE 1 CORINTHIANS 10

THE CANAAN REPORT

> *But the other men who had explored the land with*
> *[Caleb] disagreed. "We can't go up against them!*
> *They are stronger than we are!"* NUMBERS 13:31

WHEN THE TWELVE spies were sent out, there was one representative sent from each of the tribes, "all . . . leaders of Israel" (Numbers 13:3). They were sent out to gather information that would help Moses form a plan to accomplish the will of God.

After a forty-day trip behind enemy lines, they returned, and the majority of these leaders told Moses that, in effect, what God had commanded them to do was not practical. They said, "We can't do it! The land is good, but it is already occupied by powerful forces. This whole project is beyond us."

Notice that they made no reference to God in their report (see Numbers 13:27-33). They announced the view that "on the basis of the available data, we are unable to progress further with the purposes of God at this time."

These leaders had stopped asking, "What does God want us to do?" and had begun asking, "What seems manageable?" Whenever leadership makes that shift, it will be costly for the people of God. We must focus our attention on what God is calling us to do. If we lose this focus, we will operate at a purely pragmatic level. That often is the beginning of years of aimless wandering in ineffective ministry.

The Canaan report was a catalog of disasters. The research team was commissioned by Moses, but they made their report to all the people. They were asked to bring back information, but they went beyond that and made a recommendation. The question to be decided was not *if* they should go into Canaan, but *how* they should go into Canaan.

Only two members of the team took a different view: Joshua and Caleb. Their minority report focused on the fact that God was with them, and so the land was theirs for the taking. But by the time they were given opportunity to speak, the people had already made up their minds.

FOR FURTHER READING, SEE NUMBERS 13

CASTING YOUR VOTE

"If only we had died in Egypt, or even here in the wilderness!"
they complained. "Why is the LORD taking us to this country
only to have us die in battle?" NUMBERS 14:2-3

"LET US DIE in this desert rather than deal with these fierce enemies!" That's what the people said, and that's exactly what God allowed them to do. It is easy for us to sit in comfortable surroundings and imagine that if we had been asked to vote on entering Canaan, we would have shouted, "Yes!" I wonder if we would have.

True, God had done many things for the people. He had led them out of Egypt, forgiven their sins, and provided them with food every day in the desert. But they recognized that now the Lord was asking them to do something that would be very costly—enter a pagan land, Canaan, and take ground that had become a stronghold of Satan. That would mean war, and people would die in the fighting.

Put yourself in their shoes. If you were one of the women, would you vote for entering Canaan when you knew your husband could be one of those whose lives would be taken? If you were one of the men, would you vote for a military campaign that could involve up to seven years of active military service?

I can understand why, when crunch time came, many people were happy to stay in the desert, offering their sacrifices and enjoying God's presence. They could have all their evenings at home, raise their children in peace, and continue to enjoy the blessing of God that they had known since they left Egypt. Yet it was God who was calling them forward.

This seemed to have carried little weight with these people. Many of them seemed to have lost their first love for the Lord. Maybe you can relate. Maybe you still remember the joy of having new faith in Christ, but now you wonder if the personal cost of obedience to the will of God is too high.

Don't lose heart. Begin by asking God for crystal clarity about your calling. Then ask him to make you ready to pay any cost, and finally, ask him to help you keep your eyes focused on the crown that lies beyond the cross.

FOR FURTHER READING, SEE LUKE 14

HOLDING OUT YOUR HANDS

The LORD said to Moses, "How long will these people treat
me with contempt? . . . They will never even see the land
I swore to give their ancestors." NUMBERS 14:11, 23

IT IS IMPORTANT to understand the point of what God says here. God was faithful to the people, even in the desert. They were still God's people, and God provided food for them every day. He never left them. The point is not that they were saved and then somehow lost. The point is that this generation of people who had experienced the abundant grace of God contributed nothing to advancing the purpose of God.

If your commitment to the will of God is conditional on your personal comfort, then you are treating God with contempt. That is, you are glad to receive his good gifts but care little for him personally. God saw his people holding out their hands every day for fresh blessings, but they were not willing to serve him if that involved going outside their comfort zones. God found that to be personally insulting.

The apostle Paul applied this story to a local church where some people had become complacent. He reminded the believers that "God was not pleased with most of [the generation that had left Egypt], and their bodies were scattered in the wilderness" (1 Corinthians 10:5). In effect, Paul said, "Be careful that you don't become unprofitable like the generation that rebelled in the desert." He told them this was why he exercised self-discipline in his own life. Having preached to other people, he did not want to become unprofitable, someone who is of little use in advancing the purposes of God (see 9:26-27).

It would be very easy for us to live as redeemed children of God within our own comfort zones, holding worship services, rejoicing in the love of Christ, and doing nothing significant to advance the purposes of God. Similarly, it's easy for churches that have been greatly blessed to grieve the Spirit and become unprofitable in the purposes of God. Once we see the danger, the great question is, how are we going to avoid being like that?

FOR FURTHER READING, SEE EPHESIANS 4

MOSES' LAST WORDS

*Beware that in your plenty you do not forget the LORD your God
and disobey his commands, regulations, and decrees. . . . For when
you have become full and prosperous . . . do not become proud at that
time and forget the LORD your God.* DEUTERONOMY 8:11-14

THE ATMOSPHERE WAS electric as the old man began to speak for the last time. He had been their leader for forty years, and it was hard to imagine life without him.

Moses spoke with passion, like a father speaking to his children. His beard had turned white decades ago, but his memory was still sharp as he recounted the years of their journey together; his vision was still clear as he spoke of critical choices that would shape their future.

Deuteronomy records the last words God spoke through Moses. The people were about to enter the land God gave to their forefathers, but Moses would not go with them. He would die before they entered the land, the mantle of leadership placed onto Joshua's broad shoulders.

Forty years had passed since the people left Egypt (see Deuteronomy 1:3), and Moses reminded them where they had come from. God brought their parents to the edge of the Promised Land, but they had lacked the courage to press forward. Now God was giving the same opportunity to the next generation, and they were ready for the challenge.

As the new generation stood on the verge of entering their inheritance, the great question was how they would handle the intoxicating effects of sudden prosperity. Financial security has a way of sucking the spiritual life out of you. Success brings its own subtle tests; it can dull your spiritual passion.

The more God gives you, the more you will want to keep. Money is powerful, and it can gain a grip on your heart. But God calls his people in every generation to develop a culture of kindness by practicing proportional giving and by exercising restraint. By the grace of God, these regular practices will help break the power that money can so easily hold over us.

FOR FURTHER READING, SEE DEUTERONOMY 8

NO MORE MANNA

You must set aside a tithe of your crops—one-tenth of all the crops you harvest each year. DEUTERONOMY 14:22

MOSES WAS SPEAKING in the desert to a group of people who didn't own an acre of land. The land was still in the hands of their enemies. Moses was saying, "What God has done for the last forty years with manna from heaven, he will now do through the crops of the land. But remember, it is still God who gives you everything you have. So every year, work out your income, divide it by ten, and give that portion to God."

In addition, every person in Israel had to attend three festivals: the Passover (the Feast of Unleavened Bread), the Feast of Weeks, and the Feast of Booths. These festivals were to be marked by joyful giving: "All must give as they are able, according to the blessings given to them by the LORD your God" (Deuteronomy 16:17).

God's principles of giving have not changed. The New Testament emphasis is on the spirit in which we give—"God loves a person who gives cheerfully" (2 Corinthians 9:7)—but the act of giving is still important. When you write a check supporting your local church, let it be an act of worship! Let it be an expression of your joy in what God has given you. The more the Lord prospers you, the larger your tenth will be, and the greater your joy in giving will be.

God was teaching his people how to maintain their spiritual health in a materialistic culture. When they entered the land of Canaan, the greatest danger was that their spiritual life would be swamped by the pursuit of wealth and that the blessing of God would stifle their spiritual life. So God called them—as he calls us—to develop a habit and a culture of giving.

How is your giving to God? Jesus says, "Wherever your treasure is, there the desires of your heart will also be" (Matthew 6:21). If you keep all your treasure, then God will never have your heart.

FOR FURTHER READING, SEE MATTHEW 6

THE BOTTOM LINE

When you have entered the land I am giving you, the land itself must observe a Sabbath rest before the LORD every seventh year. For six years you may plant your fields . . . but during the seventh year the land must have a Sabbath year of complete rest. LEVITICUS 25:2-4

THE SABBATH DAY was to be "dedicated to the LORD your God" (Exodus 20:10). It was a day for worship, a day to be renewed in body, soul, and spirit. People will make different choices about what is appropriate on this day, but whatever we do, we must not make it another day of work. And if you think that the principle of the Sabbath day is challenging, you ain't heard nothing yet!

Not only did God say that the people were to rest from their work one day out of seven, but he also said that the land was to lie inactive one out of every seven years.

God gave a special promise in connection with the Sabbath year: he would send a bumper crop in the sixth year so that there would be enough food to sustain the people in the seventh year and in the planting of the eighth year (see Leviticus 25:20-22).

How would you have reacted to the Sabbath year? Perhaps you would look at your fields and say to yourself, "What a waste! This Sabbath law is costing me a whole year of income. Think of the money I could make if I worked my fields!"

The Sabbath law placed a restraint on greed. God's people were to learn how to say no to something good in order to say yes to something better. So one year in every seven, they passed up a year's wages in order to learn again that there is more to life than work and money.

In a world of greed, practice restraint. Maybe you're the kind of person who wants to say yes to every opportunity. Without the Sabbath principle of restraint, your life would have no margins. You need to take a day off, and you need to take a vacation. These are not luxuries; they are God's principles for maintaining spiritual health.

FOR FURTHER READING, SEE HEBREWS 4

WRITING OFF DEBT

*At the end of every seventh year you must cancel the debts of
everyone who owes you money.* DEUTERONOMY 15:1

LENDING WAS ENCOURAGED in Israel: "If there are any poor Israelites
in your towns when you arrive in the land the LORD your God is giving
you, do not be hard-hearted or tightfisted toward them. Instead, be
generous and lend them whatever they need" (Deuteronomy 15:7-8).

You could charge reasonable interest to a foreigner, but not to your
neighbor. If you received a loan from a neighbor, you were obligated to
repay it as quickly as possible. Christians are still under an obligation to
repay their debts. Paul says, "Owe nothing to anyone" (Romans 13:8).
We honor God as we plan to repay our loans. If we have benefited from
someone else's generosity through a loan without interest, we should
not take advantage of that kindness by failing to repay.

Suppose you lived in ancient Israel, and after seven years, your
neighbor was unable to repay you. There were circumstances of misfor-
tune in which this could easily happen. What were you to do? According
to the law, you were to write off the debt: "Everyone must cancel the
loans they have made to their fellow Israelites. They must not demand
payment from their neighbors or relatives, for the LORD's time of
release has arrived" (Deuteronomy 15:2).

This law was wide open to abuse. Suppose you were given a $10,000
interest-free loan. Now, in the sixth year of the loan, you have $7,000
in the bank. You open your checkbook, and as you are about to write a
check, your hand freezes. *I could give him $5,000, but it's only a few months until
the year of canceling debts*, you think. *I'll wait. He doesn't really need the money.*

God's law hangs on two foundational principles: 1) We must love
God with our whole hearts, and 2) we must love our neighbors as ourselves. These principles of love extend to our handling of money. Love
means that when I receive a loan through the kindness of my brother,
I am under an obligation of love to repay him in full as soon as possible.

FOR FURTHER READING, SEE DEUTERONOMY 15

INDEPENDENCE DAY

*If a fellow Hebrew sells himself or herself to be your servant
and serves you for six years, in the seventh year you must
set that servant free.* DEUTERONOMY 15:12

IF GOD'S PEOPLE were unable to pay back their loans, one way they could fulfill their responsibility was by working for the lender. The problem was that those who were forced to sell themselves to others could set their families up for generational poverty, in which the children of one family could end up serving the children of another. So God gave additional laws to protect the poor.

As a result, the lender was not to become a slave master: "If one of your fellow Israelites falls into poverty and is forced to sell himself to you, do not treat him as a slave. Treat him instead as a hired worker or as a temporary resident who lives with you" (Leviticus 25:39-40).

The obligation of the employer went beyond kind treatment of the worker. The law protected freedom by requiring that a servant be released after seven years. If a man was working to repay a debt, he could always look forward to the day when his freedom and independence would be restored.

This law was great for the debtor but costly for the creditor. Of course, this reminds us of our debt to God: the cost to God of canceling all our sin was incalculable. It cost the death of his Son, Jesus Christ. And the benefit to us is also incalculable.

The only way to write off a debt is to incur the loss of the debt amount personally. And if God is to write off all our debts to him, it means that he has to incur the total cost of that debt himself. That is why Christ went to the cross. He bore the loss and in this way canceled our debts.

This is good news for the spiritually poor. You can look forward to the day when Christ returns and your freedom will be completely restored.

FOR FURTHER READING, SEE LUKE 7

PERMANENT DEEDS

Set this year apart as holy, a time to proclaim freedom throughout the land
for all who live there. It will be a jubilee year for you, when each of you
may return to the land that belonged to your ancestors. LEVITICUS 25:10

EVERY FIFTY YEARS, the trumpet was to sound, and the land was to be returned to its original owners. Ownership of the land could never be permanently transferred because the land really belonged to the Lord (see Leviticus 25:23).

Imagine the impact this would have on a community. Once in a lifetime, the poor would be given a fresh start with the land the Lord had given that family at the beginning, and the rich would not be able to rely on massive inheritances of land.

Land sold in the fortieth year of the cycle would sell low because the buyer could use the land for only ten years. Land bought in the tenth year of the cycle would be sold high because the buyer could use the land for forty years. All that could be bought or sold was the use of the land for a limited time.

Would you have liked to live under these laws? Your answer to that question would probably have depended on whether you were a lender or a borrower. Borrowers were probably grateful for these laws, but lenders probably viewed them differently.

The Sabbath rest for the land was systematically ignored. God's people failed to let the land rest seventy different years, but God kept track, and when the Babylonians took God's people into exile, the land enjoyed its rest in one long Sabbath that lasted seventy years in a row (see 2 Chronicles 36:21)!

Do you know how often the Jubilee happened? Never! Not once. The people who had the power to call the Jubilee never had the will to do so, because for them it would have been very costly. Jesus proclaimed, "The Spirit of the LORD is upon me, for he has anointed me . . . to proclaim . . . that the time of the LORD's favor has come" (Luke 4:18-19). Jesus was saying, "The Jubilee is here! God will cancel all debts; God will restore lost inheritances." Indeed, in Jesus Christ, that is exactly what he has done.

FOR FURTHER READING, SEE LUKE 4

WHAT MOST PEOPLE FIND ACCEPTABLE

When you enter the land the LORD your God is giving you,
be very careful not to imitate the detestable customs of
the nations living there. DEUTERONOMY 18:9

AS THE PEOPLE of God gathered at the edge of the Promised Land, Moses had one last opportunity to prepare them. What would the community do when one of their number broke God's law? Would God's people confront the problem, or would they ignore it? A culture can be defined as "what most people think is acceptable." The way in which the community responded to different kinds of evil would determine which ones would multiply and which ones would diminish.

Moses challenged the people of God to create a culture conducive to holiness—to regard every sin as God does. This is a burning issue for the church today. What most people consider acceptable in a church will multiply, and what is unacceptable in that church will diminish. If a member of Christ's body refuses to give up a pattern of sin, the most powerful statement that can be made this side of God's final judgment is the disapproval of the whole community.

In ancient Israel, it would not be long before you got the message: "Around here we live by God's law. If you honor his law, you will be blessed; if you fail to live up to God's law, you will be forgiven; if you flout God's law, you will be in trouble."

A healthy church is a community of people who care enough to encourage one another in the pursuit of a consistent, holy life. It is also a community of people who care enough to confront one another over issues of sin.

Our choices are heavily influenced by our nature and our environment, and when we come to Christ, God changes both. He changes our nature through the new birth, and he brings us into a new environment called the church. We need the encouragement of the church because we are often weak, and we need the restraint of God's people because we are often willful.

FOR FURTHER READING, SEE 1 CORINTHIANS 5

PROTECTING THE VULNERABLE

*You must set apart three cities of refuge in the land the LORD your
God is giving you. . . . Then anyone who has killed someone can flee
to one of the cities of refuge for safety.* DEUTERONOMY 19:2-3

MOSES GAVE AN example of the kind of situation when cities of refuge
would be used: Two men are out in the forest cutting trees, and there
is a terrible accident. The head of one man's ax flies off the handle, and
it hits his colleague and kills him. When the dead man's family hears
about it, they do not believe that it was an accident. They're convinced
it was criminal negligence, and they set out after the hapless woodcutter,
intent on vengeance (see Deuteronomy 19:5-6).

The cities of refuge provided a place of protection for vulnerable
people until there could be a proper inquiry into what happened. The
incident with the ax may have been criminal negligence, or it may have
been a terrible accident, but among God's people there was to be a
proper, legal process for determining the truth. The community was to
make sure that vulnerable people were protected from those who would
take the law into their own hands.

A while back our church hosted some people from a remote part
of Venezuela. They had not heard the gospel until some missionaries
from our denomination brought the message of Christ's love to them.
Many of the tribal people received Christ, and it transformed their
whole culture.

One of the tribal leaders explained, through double translation—
first to Spanish and then to English—the difference that the gospel had
made. "Before the gospel came to our culture," he told our congregation, "disputes were always resolved with the sword. Now we have a
council to resolve disputes." That is a wonderful reflection of how God
calls a community to function.

There are only two places where we can hope to find a culture in
which the vulnerable are protected—in the home and in the church.
So when your Christian brothers and sisters are vulnerable, you must
protect them. Stand with them in the storm and don't back off. They
need you.

FOR FURTHER READING, SEE 1 THESSALONIANS 5

AN EYE FOR AN EYE

You must show no pity for the guilty! Your rule should be life for life, eye for eye, tooth for tooth, hand for hand, foot for foot. DEUTERONOMY 19:21

SOME PEOPLE ARE surprised that this statement is in the Bible. But God never intended that if you knock my tooth out, you should stand against a wall while I line up my punch to knock yours out! "Eye for eye" is not an invitation to retaliatory violence. God's command simply established the principle of fair compensation.

Suppose a slave owner struck his slave and blinded him. The law demanded that the slave should be compensated in some way, "an eye for an eye, a tooth for a tooth" (Exodus 21:24). God was not telling the blinded slave to put out his owner's eye! But there should be some compensation, and in this case, God says the slave should be given his freedom (see 21:26).

"An eye for an eye" also teaches us that compensation should be in proportion to the damage done. It is an eye for an eye—not two eyes, an arm, and a leg! God's law places restraints on the injured person who says, "You have made me suffer, so I will make you suffer ten times over!"

God's law gives guidance to judges by telling them that they are not to make huge and disproportionate awards, but are to keep a due sense of proportion: "Eye for eye, tooth for tooth." Properly understood, this is a principle that we desperately need today, in a society where a simple injury is sometimes seen as an opportunity to make a fortune.

When a culture is given over to selfishness and greed, the courts become about winning, not about what is true and right. It's about who can present the most compelling story. When truth is lost, we find ourselves in a world of "spin," where it is hard to know what is true and what is right, and the value of life itself is lost. We must work to protect truth and offer just compensation to those to whom it is due.

FOR FURTHER READING, SEE MATTHEW 5

RESTRAINING THE WICKED

Purge from Israel the guilt of murdering innocent people;
then all will go well with you. DEUTERONOMY 19:13

SUPPOSE SOMEONE "IS hostile toward a neighbor and deliberately ambushes and murders him" (Deuteronomy 19:11). Here is an example of deliberate, premeditated, cold-blooded murder. If the murderer runs to one of the cities of refuge, he is not to be protected from the consequences of his actions. The elders of the town are to bring him back, and his life is to be taken (see 19:12).

This theme of purging evil is repeated like a refrain in Deuteronomy. In the case of perjury, where someone has deliberately lied in order to harm another person, God said, "You must impose on the accuser the sentence he intended for the other person. In this way, you will purge such evil from among you" (Deuteronomy 19:19). Or in the case of adultery, "If a man is discovered committing adultery, both he and the woman must die. In this way, you will purge Israel of such evil" (22:22).

In the case of kidnapping, "If anyone kidnaps a fellow Israelite and treats him as a slave or sells him, the kidnapper must die. In this way, you will purge the evil from among you" (Deuteronomy 24:7). False prophets who call the people to follow other gods "must be put to death. . . . In this way you will purge the evil from among you" (13:5).

This might give the impression that God's people were in constant danger of capital punishment, but the number of offenses that called for the death penalty was remarkably few, and they related to three primary values: the worship of God ("you must not have any other god but me," Deuteronomy 5:7), the sanctity of life ("you must not murder," 5:17), and the sanctity of marriage ("you must not commit adultery," 5:18). These are the central pillars of society, and God called the whole community to uphold them.

One way we can do this is through our parenting. God has given parents the responsibility of communicating the message that sin leads to painful consequences. Christian parents need to make it clear that the way of the sinner is hard. If we fail to do this, we will raise children who are unable to make the connection between sin and its consequences.

FOR FURTHER READING, SEE DEUTERONOMY 19

SERVING THE LORD

Fear the LORD and serve him wholeheartedly. JOSHUA 24:14

IT IS IMPORTANT to remember that when God made a covenant with his people, he gave them his laws, but he also gave them the system of sacrifices.

God established the death sentence for idolatry, but he also gave his people a way to make atonement for their sinful rebellion. After the Israelites made the golden calf in the desert, God provided a sacrifice as a way of deliverance. Forgiveness and restoration were always in the mind and heart of God. The sacrifices provided a way out of the full penalties of the law and a way back into covenantal relationship.

In the ancient world, it was common for the terms of a covenant to be written out. Two copies would be made. This is probably the significance of the two tablets of stone on which the commandments were written. These were the terms of the covenant between God and his people, and just as with any legal contract today, there was a copy for both parties—one for God and one for the people.

A covenant is a binding promise. The book of Joshua tells us how God gave his people remarkable success in driving out their enemies. Then the people gathered, full of joy from their victories, and Joshua challenged them to renew their commitment to the Lord. For the first time in their lives, God's people were facing the test of prosperity. Joshua was concerned that as they settled into their comfortable homes, they might lose their passion for serving the Lord.

When Joshua spoke about serving the Lord, he wasn't talking about volunteering to get involved in some program or ministry. Serving the Lord meant then—as it does now—making sure that the first commitment of your life is to do what God wants done.

This is never easy. We can talk about God being first in our lives, but there is a daily battle to work this out in practice. Joshua gives us three strategies to help us reignite our spiritual passion: 1) remember God's faithfulness, 2) make a decisive commitment, and 3) throw out our idols.

FOR FURTHER READING, SEE 1 TIMOTHY 6

REMEMBERING GOD'S FAITHFULNESS

Joshua summoned all the tribes of Israel to Shechem. JOSHUA 24:1

SHECHEM WAS A place of great significance. It was a small town in the valley between Mount Ebal and Mount Gerizim, where the Levites had shouted out God's blessings and curses. When Abraham camped there by the oak tree more than five hundred years earlier, "the LORD appeared to [him] and said, 'I will give this land to your descendants'" (Genesis 12:6-7).

Now two million descendants of Abraham were gathered at that same town. Imagine the emotion and excitement as these people came over the brow of the hill and looked down into the valley. Moms and dads would be saying to their children, "You see those trees down there? That's where God appeared to our father Abraham more than five hundred years ago. God promised him that his descendants would live in this land, and here we are! God is as good as his word."

The value of a promise depends on the character of the person who makes it. What you do with your promises is a defining point of your character. God's character is reflected in his faithfulness to his promises.

Joshua gathered all the people together and recalled the faithful acts of God: that God had led Abraham, who was serving other gods, safely to the land of Canaan; that he gave Abraham many offspring—Isaac, Jacob, and Esau—and gave each of them land; that God sent Moses and Aaron to Egypt, along with the plagues, and afterward brought the people out (see Joshua 24:2-5). God summarized all that he had done in bringing the people to the Promised Land in this statement: "I gave you land you had not worked on, and I gave you towns you did not build" (24:13).

If you want to restore your commitment to the Lord, come back to the trees—not the trees at Shechem where the Lord appeared to Abraham, but the tree outside Jerusalem where Christ died for you. Take some time to think about God's love and faithfulness to you. Our commitment is always a response to God's grace. Spiritual passion begins with a mind that is gripped by God's faithfulness.

FOR FURTHER READING, SEE JOSHUA 24

MAKING A DECISIVE COMMITMENT

*If you refuse to serve the LORD, then choose today whom
you will serve. Would you prefer the gods your ancestors served
beyond the Euphrates? Or will it be the gods of the Amorites
in whose land you now live?* JOSHUA 24:15

JOSHUA CHALLENGED THE people who were struggling to make a wholehearted commitment to the Lord. If they didn't want to serve the Lord, they needed to be clear about whom they would serve.

You see, the real issue is not whether you will serve the Lord; it is, which god are you serving? If you are not serving the Lord, you have put something or someone else in the place that belongs to him. It is of the greatest importance that you be clear and honest about who or what that is.

Just in case the people were struggling to think of alternative gods, Joshua gave them some suggestions: "You could, for example, return to the gods your forefather Abraham worshiped." Before Abraham knew the living God, his life did not count for much. Then God promised to bless him and make him a blessing to the nations. "Perhaps you would like to go back to the gods who did nothing at all for Abraham!"

Then Joshua had another suggestion: "Why not consider the gods of the Amorites?" That was laying it on a bit thick, because Israel had just driven the Amorites out of the land! It was clear the gods of the Amorites were unable to save their people.

No one is likely to follow the gods of the Amorites today, but Joshua's question is important for us. If we are not serving the Lord, what have we put in his place? When you are finding it difficult to serve the Lord, try to identify what has taken his place. Then take an honest look at where that substitute will lead you.

Joshua confronted the people with a radical choice, and then he led the way in saying, "As for me and my family, we will serve the LORD" (Joshua 24:15). When you have considered the alternatives, it won't be long before you say the same.

FOR FURTHER READING, SEE ROMANS 6

THROWING OUT YOUR IDOLS

We would never abandon the LORD and serve other gods.
For the LORD our God is the one who rescued us and our ancestors
from slavery in the land of Egypt. . . . So we, too, will serve
the LORD, for he alone is our God. JOSHUA 24:16-18

THE PEOPLE GOT the point! Then Joshua made an extraordinary statement: "You are not able to serve the LORD" (Joshua 24:19). The people had responded to the challenge, and then Joshua told them that they couldn't do it! They were offended by this and insisted that they could (see 24:21).

Then Joshua said, "All right then, . . . destroy the idols among you, and turn your hearts to the LORD" (Joshua 24:23). Evidently, God's people had held on to some idols the Canaanites had left behind. These were offensive to God.

Suppose Jesus Christ came into your house or your office. Is there anything you would not want him to find?

Here, Joshua spoke like a prophet: "You say you want to serve the Lord, but you can't until you deal with this stuff. Get rid of it!" As long as the idols remained, the people's commitment to serve the Lord was only words.

In the past, God had blessed them despite these things. He is incredibly gracious and sometimes overlooks inconsistencies in our lives. But when God puts his finger on a particular issue, you have to deal with it.

When Joshua said, "[God] will not forgive your rebellion and your sins" (Joshua 24:19), he was not telling the people they had committed an unforgivable sin. He was making it clear that God would not forgive a sin they were not willing to forsake. Repentance precedes forgiveness. You cannot ask God to forgive you for a sin you have no intention of abandoning.

Joshua would not allow the people to renew the covenant in words only. Commitment to the covenant involves a clear and decisive rejection of all that displeases God. What are you holding on to that keeps you from serving the Lord?

FOR FURTHER READING, SEE JAMES 1

A LOST GENERATION

The Israelites served the LORD throughout the lifetime of Joshua
and the leaders who outlived him—those who had seen all the
great things the LORD had done for Israel. JUDGES 2:7

THE ISRAELITES FOLLOWED through on their promise. That generation had grown up in the desert and had directly and personally experienced God's saving action. Some would have been small children at
the time of the Exodus and in their late forties or early fifties when they
arrived in Canaan. By the time the land was conquered, they would have
been retirement age.

But those born in the desert were now in their twenties and thirties.
These folks would have seen what the Lord did for Israel on the day the
walls of Jericho fell down and the remarkable day when the sun stood
still. When they recalled what God had done for them, they made a
commitment to serve him. But eventually, "that whole generation had
been gathered to their ancestors" (Judges 2:10, NIV); they died.

The next generation was different: "Another generation grew up
who did not acknowledge the LORD or remember the mighty things he
had done for Israel" (Judges 2:10). This is one of the saddest verses in
the Bible, and it sets the scene for the rest of the book of Judges.

If you had asked the folks out in the desert, "Who is God?" they
would have said, "He is the God of Abraham, Isaac, and Jacob. He is the
God who appeared to Moses and said, 'I AM WHO I AM.' He is the God
who came down on Mount Sinai and gave the Ten Commandments.
He is the Creator of all things, and he is our Savior and Judge. He is
holy, righteous, loving, gracious, and good. He is to be worshiped and
feared and loved. He is the living God."

This new generation was in an entirely different situation. Their
problem was not that they failed to believe in God; it was that they did
not know God. It took only one generation for that knowledge to be
lost. But it's also true that what can be lost in one generation can also
be restored in one generation.

FOR FURTHER READING, SEE JUDGES 2

GOING AROUND IN CIRCLES

> *Whenever the LORD raised up a judge over Israel, he was*
> *with that judge and rescued the people from their enemies*
> *throughout the judge's lifetime.* JUDGES 2:18

THE BOOK OF Judges records a cycle of events that occurred many times over a period of several hundred years. It began when people forsook the Lord and turned to idols: "The Israelites did evil in the LORD's sight and served the images of Baal. They abandoned the LORD . . . [and] went after other gods, worshiping the gods of the people around them" (Judges 2:11-12).

Then God became angry and gave his people into the hands of their enemies: "This made the LORD burn with anger against Israel, so he handed them over to raiders who stole their possessions" (Judges 2:14).

In response, the people cried out for God's help, and God raised up a leader, or a judge, to deliver them. These "judges" were not like the ones you would normally find at a courthouse; they were more like military leaders who led the people into battle against their enemies.

The people of Israel followed the Lord while the judge was alive, but when the judge died, the people returned to their previous ways, and the cycle started all over again. "When the judge died, the people returned to their corrupt ways, behaving worse than those who had lived before them. They went after other gods, serving and worshiping them. And they refused to give up their evil practices and stubborn ways" (Judges 2:19). The people were going around in circles—idolatry, judgment, crying out to God, deliverance, and then idolatry again.

God will create a crisis in order to bring his people back to himself. He will withdraw his protection and allow us to live with the consequences of our own choices. This is the way in which God most often deals with persistent sin.

If you recognize this cycle in your own life, it means you're facing a choice between the gods of your imagination and the living God of the Bible. You may feel you're in control of your gods, but they're powerless to help you and deeply offensive to God. Only the living God can deliver you, and he sent his Son to save you from sin, death, and hell.

FOR FURTHER READING, SEE PSALM 106

IDENTIFYING THE IDOLS

So the people of Israel lived among the Canaanites,
Hittites, Amorites, Perizzites, Hivites, and Jebusites, and
. . . the Israelites served their gods. JUDGES 3:5-6

AS YOU READ through the Old Testament, you will keep coming across this business of idolatry. Every few pages, there seems to be something about one of the idols: the Baals, the Asherahs, Molech, or Dagon.

It all seems remote to us, but it comes up so often that it is obviously important. I found a solid definition of idolatry in a recent *Wall Street Journal* article: "Across the country, the faithful are redefining God. . . . [They] are embracing quirky, individualistic conceptions of God to suit their own spiritual needs."

You will never get a clearer definition of idolatry than that. The *Journal* could have entitled their article "Idolatry in America." Of course, we do not hear about Baal, the Asherahs, Dagon, or Molech; we have replaced them with "a force field of positive energy," or "pure intense feelings of love," or "seeing the fog lift up at sunrise." Redefining God is pure idolatry.

Idolatry is powerfully attractive because it puts us in a position of control. Instead of worshiping the living God who says, "I AM WHO I AM," we prefer to create a god that suits our own perceived spiritual needs.

Idolatry is attractive, but it is also deeply offensive. Suppose some folks in the church that I serve said, "We like the idea of having a sort of 'Colin figure' around here, but we don't like who you are and we don't like what you do." That is exactly what idolatry does in relation to God. Idolatry says to God, "We like the idea of some kind of god, but we don't like you. We don't like what you say, and we don't like what you do! So we'll redefine you."

God responds by saying, "I AM WHO I AM. You cannot redefine me. But I hear you clearly, and I will withdraw. I will take away my hand of protection, and I will deliver you into the hands of your enemies." But remember, God is gracious to all who call upon him. If you turn to him in faith and repentance, he will deliver you.

FOR FURTHER READING, SEE ROMANS 1

CHANGE THAT LASTS

Then Gideon said to God, "Please don't be angry with me, but let me make one more request. Let me use the fleece for one more test. This time let the fleece remain dry while the ground around it is wet with dew." JUDGES 6:39

AS YOU READ through Judges, it is clear that while these military leaders achieved remarkable things, they also had significant limitations. Most of them were seriously lacking in character, making it difficult to admire them.

Gideon was so lacking in faith that he needed multiple confirmations of what God was telling him to do. Samson's failures are legendary (see Judges 14–16) and qualify him as the weakest strong man who ever lived!

The judges brought a change in the people's circumstances, but they were never able to bring a change in the people's hearts. As soon as a judge died, the people returned to their idols, and the whole cycle started over. God's people needed a better deliverer than these judges—someone who could bring lasting change.

Fourteen hundred years later the people of God were under another oppressor—the Romans. They were hoping God would raise up a deliverer. Some wanted God to raise up another Samson—a strong, aggressive, one-man army. Others, like Simeon and Anna, were praying for a deliverer who could touch the issues of the heart. And as they cried out, God sent his Son into the world.

When Judas Iscariot saw what Jesus could do, he knew Jesus could deliver the people from the power of Rome. But Christ refused to follow that agenda. God could change the external circumstances of our lives a thousand times, but if he does not change our hearts, our lives will go round in circles like the story of Judges.

When Jesus was nailed to a cross, all hopes of deliverance seemed shattered. But on the third day, Jesus rose from the dead. Here, for the first time in human history, was a Deliverer who would never die. Today he continues to deliver us from our greatest enemies—sin, death, and hell.

FOR FURTHER READING, SEE HEBREWS 7

CIRCUMSTANCES BEYOND OUR CONTROL

In the days when the judges ruled in Israel,
a severe famine came upon the land. RUTH 1:1

THE BIBLE RECORDS what life was like in Israel when there was no king: "All the people did whatever seemed right in their own eyes" (Judges 17:6). Law and order had broken down, and Israel was no longer a safe place to raise children.

What would you do if you lived in a crime-infested neighborhood and you had a wife and two young children to support, but your income wouldn't buy the food you needed? Elimelech watched his family suffer and finally felt he had waited on God long enough. So he packed up his family and his belongings and headed to Moab.

Moab wasn't the kind of place any self-respecting Jew would live. The Moabites were known for worshiping idols, and they were the enemies of Israel. So Moab was not the first choice for an Israelite planning a vacation. But desperate times call for desperate measures, and Elimelech decided Moab was his best option.

He left the people of God and the land God had chosen to bless in order to make a new beginning. The whole family moved to Moab, and soon after they arrived there, Elimelech died. His widow, Naomi, and her two sons—probably in their teenage years—were trying to make a life for themselves in a foreign land.

The boys eventually married two local girls—Orpah and Ruth. Another ten years passed, and Naomi's two sons died. Now she was alone in a foreign land. She had come to Moab because of her husband, stayed in Moab because of her sons, and now she was left in Moab with two daughters-in-law.

Maybe because of unforeseen circumstances, you find yourself living a life that is only a shadow of the one you were hoping for. Put your hope in the Lord, for "with him is plentiful redemption" (Psalm 130:7, ESV). Redemption is what God will bring out of your painful circumstances. What God redeems will not be just enough to make it worthwhile; it will be plentiful!

FOR FURTHER READING, SEE PSALM 130

LOVE CHOOSES TO PAY A PRICE

Wherever you go, I will go; wherever you live, I will live.
Your people will be my people, and your God will be my God.
Wherever you die, I will die, and there I will be buried. RUTH 1:16-17

NEWS SPREAD THAT the famine in Israel was over. There was food in Bethlehem! An aging single woman like Naomi could no longer run the farm, but it was home, so she decided to return. Maybe she could generate some income by selling the land.

Naomi knew that if her daughters-in-law came back with her to Israel, they would face the same problems she had endured in Moab. Without husband or father, two foreign women in Israel would be vulnerable. It was better that they should stay in Moab where there was still hope of remarrying.

But Naomi was struggling with a deeper problem. She was convinced that God was against her. She believed in God, like a good Jewish woman should, but as she grew older, the experiences of life led her to believe that God was her enemy instead of her friend.

When Naomi arrived back in Bethlehem, the women asked, "Is it really Naomi?" (Ruth 1:19). This remark can only be an indication of how bad she looked. She had left Bethlehem as a bright-faced mother; she returned a haggard-looking widow.

Naomi (whose name means "pleasant") asked her friends to call her "Miss Bitter" (*Mara*) and told the townspeople, "The Almighty has made life very bitter for me" (Ruth 1:20). If God was against her, it would do her daughters-in-law no good to stay: "Leave me alone with my grief. Go and make a new life for yourselves." So Orpah left, but Ruth wouldn't go, and that was when she said some of the most beautiful words of commitment ever spoken.

Here was a young lady making a costly commitment of love and loyalty to a rather difficult, bitter older woman. At the same time, she was making a costly commitment to the God of Israel, who had allowed great pain and disappointment in her own life. Love proves its commitment when it chooses to pay a price.

FOR FURTHER READING, SEE RUTH 1

LIFE ON THE BREADLINE

May the LORD, the God of Israel, under whose wings you have come to take refuge, reward you fully for what you have done. RUTH 2:12

IT COULD NOT have been easy for Naomi and Ruth when they arrived back at the farm. The fields had not been cultivated for at least ten years, and the whole area would have been overgrown. It would be weeks before they cleared the fields for planting and months before they could raise a harvest. So the women had no source of income. They were poor.

The poor were permitted to pick the leftovers from the edge of any field; they would follow the harvesters to pick up any grain that remained on the ground. It was like sorting through the trash, and it was not the kind of thing most people wanted to do. Sometimes the "gleaners" were viewed as pests, and landowners could be abusive.

Yet Ruth went out, willing to glean in the fields behind "anyone who is kind enough to let me do it" (Ruth 2:2). If anyone would allow her to gather the leftover grain, that was what she would do to meet her and Naomi's needs.

The field she chose belonged to a man named Boaz, providentially a distant relative of Elimelech. Boaz had a considerable estate and ran a large farming operation. He was supervising the harvest when he noticed a foreign woman picking up the grain behind the harvesters. He asked, "Who is that young woman over there?" (Ruth 2:5).

The harvesters replied, "She is the young woman from Moab who came back with Naomi" (Ruth 2:6).

Boaz heard about Ruth's kindness to Naomi, and he told her to stay in his fields. He also made sure that the harvesters were kind to her. Ruth was surprised that a complete stranger would treat a foreigner so well.

Boaz's kindness is a powerful challenge for the church. Jesus Christ has broken down the dividing walls so that people from every background can find a place in God's family (see Ephesians 2). Whoever wants to take refuge under God's wings may do so, and all who come are to be received by the people of God with kindness.

FOR FURTHER READING, SEE RUTH 2

AN INITIATIVE OF FAITH

*I am your servant Ruth. . . . Spread the corner of your covering
over me, for you are my family redeemer.* RUTH 3:9

NOW WE COME to the best part of Ruth's story, but first a legal briefing, so you can understand what's about to happen. The law of levirate marriage said that if a man died without children, his brother should take responsibility to support the widow, including marrying her and raising children with her (see Deuteronomy 25:5-10). The closer the relationship, the greater the obligation.

Boaz was not Elimelech's nearest relative, and it had not occurred to him that he would have any greater role in the lives of these women than the kindness he had already shown. Naomi came up with the plan, but it was Ruth who took the risky initiative of faith.

Boaz was working around the clock on the harvest. During the day, he was harvesting, and in the evening, he would go to the threshing floor, where he would lie down and sleep by the grain.

Ruth went over to the threshing floor and lay down by his feet. During the night, Boaz stirred, and as he wakened, he realized that somebody else was there. "Who are you?" he asked.

Ruth answered, "Spread your wings over your servant" (Ruth 3:9, ESV). If you want that in plain English, she said, "Marry me." Boaz had prayed that God would bless Ruth as she had taken refuge under his wings (see 2:12). Ruth was saying, "Boaz, you prayed that *God's* wings would be spread over me. But I think that the way this should happen is for you to spread *your* wings over me too. Marry me!"

This was one gutsy lady! She placed her trust in God, but she was not afraid to take action in faith. She was willing to take a risk in order to see the fulfillment of God's purpose for her life. Faith trusts, but it also acts.

If you have never done so, I invite you to follow the example of Ruth and take a risky initiative of faith. You can come to Christ today and say, "Spread your wings over me." If you come to him, he will not turn you away.

FOR FURTHER READING, SEE RUTH 3

AT THE CITY GATE

Praise the LORD, who has now provided
a redeemer for your family! RUTH 4:14

BOAZ WAS READY to marry Ruth, but there was one problem. Another relative was closer to the family than Boaz. Now this relative appeared on the scene, and it seemed that he might ruin Boaz's plans.

So Boaz went to the city gate, where legal contracts were struck. He sat there until this unnamed relative came by. Boaz persuaded him to sit down, and he gathered some town elders together as legal witnesses. Their conversation went like this:

"Naomi is selling Elimelech's farm, and you have the first right to buy it."

"I'll buy it! It's a good farm at a nice price. It'll cover my costs in a few years."

"There are two laws to consider: one gives you the right to buy the land; the other gives you the responsibility of supporting the widows. You can't claim the privilege of the one and deny the responsibility of the other!"

The price was going to be higher than the relative thought. It would not be a one-time payment, but a lifelong commitment! The close relative didn't like that idea: "I can't redeem it. I might endanger my own estate! You redeem it."

"I am ready to pay the price for the farm and to support the women," Boaz answered.

The nearer relative breathed a sigh of relief and handed Boaz his sandal—the sign of agreeing to a legal deal. Then he disappeared, never to be heard from again.

Boaz acted as a redeemer, a blood relative of a person in need, able and willing to pay a price. To become our Redeemer, Christ took upon himself our flesh and blood. In his birth, he entered the human family and became our close relative.

Christ bought us out of spiritual poverty and alienation from God with his own blood: "You know that it was not with perishable things such as silver or gold that you were redeemed from the empty way of life handed down to you from your ancestors, but with the precious blood of Christ" (1 Peter 1:18-19, NIV). God has not left you without a Redeemer!

FOR FURTHER READING, SEE RUTH 4

A TWIST IN THE TALE

Boaz was the father of Obed. Obed was the father of Jesse.
Jesse was the father of David. RUTH 4:21-22

LIKE ALL THE best stories, this one has a fascinating twist at the end. Indeed, that twist is probably the reason God has preserved Ruth's story for us in the Bible.

Following her marriage, Ruth gave birth to a son, whom she and Boaz named Obed (see Ruth 4:17). The story concludes by saying that Obed was the grandfather of David.

This David was Israel's second king, and if you follow the line of David for another thousand years, you will find that it was into this line that Jesus Christ was born. Matthew gives special mention to Ruth in the human ancestry of Christ (see Matthew 1:5).

God was at work through all of this family's tears of disappointment. Through this foreign widow who trusted in God and in her mother-in-law, King David was eventually born—and the Messiah would appear in his line.

You may sometimes feel that God's plans for the world turn on governments, businesses, kings, and armies. But the book of Ruth reminds us that at one point, God's plan of salvation flowed through one woman who decided to trust God and love a rather bitter old woman.

The extraordinary thing is that Naomi, Ruth, and Boaz all died without having any idea what God would do as a result of their faithfulness. Naomi died an old lady with an empty family nest. As a younger woman, Ruth probably thought she would never have children. But unwittingly, the lives they lived were caught up in God's redemptive plan for the world.

Never underestimate the significance of what God has given you to do. It may be a hidden, costly commitment to a rather difficult person or a simple act of kindness to a foreigner you've never seen before. It may be an initiative of faith to get the will of God done. But the story of Ruth reveals that the most ordinary acts of faith and obedience can lead to extraordinary results.

FOR FURTHER READING, SEE MATTHEW 1

FRUSTRATIONS OF LIVING BY FAITH

The LORD replied [to Samuel], . . . "It is me they are rejecting, not you. They don't want me to be their king any longer." 1 SAMUEL 8:7

FOR FOUR HUNDRED years, from the time of the Exodus to the end of the time of the judges, God led his people Israel. The whole story is the story of God's miraculous deliverances.

Israel's victories were not by might or by power, but by the intervention of the Spirit of God. At times when they were likely to win, God cut their numbers back so it would be absolutely clear that God had given them the victory. But the people of God were becoming dissatisfied with this.

When there was a crisis, the people waited on God to raise up a judge, but the other nations had kings and standing armies. When a king died, his successor was crowned immediately. "The king is dead; long live the king!"

The people wondered why Israel could not have this kind of stability and continuity. Eventually the elders of the community came to Samuel, who was a judge and a prophet, and asked him to appoint a king (see 1 Samuel 8:5).

Why didn't Israel have a king? Because God was their king. God led them into battle and into blessing. He did everything a king would do for his people, and much more. But the people weren't satisfied. They didn't want to go into battle depending on God alone, and they didn't want to wait on God to raise up their leaders. They wanted a system of succession, a flesh-and-blood person to lead them.

It is quite clear from the Lord's words to Samuel that this was not pleasing to God. When the people asked for a king, they were turning away from a life of faith in which they were directly dependent on the Lord.

But God let them have their way: "Do as they say, and give them a king" (1 Samuel 8:22). God's people made a decision that was displeasing to him, but he allowed their decision to stand, even though it wasn't in their best interest (see 8:10-18). Your choices matter, and they have long-term consequences.

FOR FURTHER READING, SEE 1 SAMUEL 8

THE JURY HAS REACHED A VERDICT

You will beg for relief from this king you are demanding. 1 SAMUEL 8:18

THE FIRST BOOK of Samuel tells the story of how God's people made a poor choice. They knew their desire for a king was displeasing to God. Samuel even warned them of the consequences of this choice: "If you have a king, there will be taxes and military service. Your sons and daughters will wish you had never made this choice." But the people were not listening. Their minds were made up, so God gave them what they asked for.

Poor choices always lead to painful consequences. Experience is a great teacher, but her school fees are high. God is sovereign, and that means that no choice, however poor, can put us beyond the grace of God. But the Bible also teaches us personal responsibility. That means each choice has consequences.

As we follow the rest of the Old Testament story, we ask, "How did Israel's kings do?" Saul, Israel's first king, looked promising at first, but eventually his self-willed disobedience led God to reject him as king (see 1 Samuel 15:23). Solomon, Israel's third king, wrote Scripture, built the Temple, and made some wise choices, but eventually his seven hundred wives turned his heart toward other gods (see 1 Kings 11:3).

David was Israel's most promising king, but even he had committed sins with terrible consequences. Still, he had a genuine desire in his heart to follow the Lord. Some kings were better, some kings were worse, but none were able to completely fulfill God's mandate.

Because of this, God himself took on human flesh in Jesus Christ and became the King his people had asked for. Christ is the King who leads his people into victory and blessing.

Where you are today is the result of the grace of God, but it is also related to a series of choices that you have made. Where you are tomorrow will be by the grace of God too, but it will also be affected by your choices today.

FOR FURTHER READING, SEE PROVERBS 1

A BLUEPRINT FOR HONORING GOD

Go ahead and do whatever you have in mind,
for the LORD is with you. 2 SAMUEL 7:3

DAVID WAS AN unknown shepherd boy until he defeated Goliath; then everybody knew who he was. But when the ancient equivalent of cheerleaders started singing, "Saul has killed his thousands, and David his ten thousands" (1 Samuel 18:7), David had to run for his life. Eventually a bitter, disillusioned King Saul died, and David was crowned king.

Under David's leadership, Israel captured Jerusalem, and David established his palace there. During Saul's reign, the Ark of the Covenant had been in storage and forgotten (see 1 Samuel 7:1-2). But now King David wanted the presence of God at the center of national life; so he brought the Ark to Jerusalem.

Then this godly man, with a good heart and a great idea, called his adviser Nathan. "It's not right that I get to live in this lavish palace, while the ark of God is in a tent," David said. "The palace is a statement of the king's greatness, but I want to put up a building that will be a statement of God's greatness."

Nathan told David to go for it, but later that night he had an uncomfortable time with God. Nathan was a prophet, and that meant God revealed things directly to him. "Nathan," God was saying, "you gave David bad advice. I will establish David's dynasty, but he will not build my home. I will give that privilege to his son" (see 2 Samuel 7:9-13). God was essentially saying, "David, if the Temple is for my glory, it should not matter to you who builds it!"

Have you ever wanted to do something good and then God closed the door? Maybe a friend encouraged you to pursue some initiative you thought would be for the glory of God, but it didn't work out. Or you had a great idea, but then God gave somebody else the opportunity to develop it! This is the ultimate test of humility. David was humbled, but in accepting this position, he would be honored.

FOR FURTHER READING, SEE 2 SAMUEL 7

DISAPPOINTMENT AND THE DOOR OF PROMISE

The LORD declares that he will make a house for you. 2 SAMUEL 7:11

IT WOULD NOT have been surprising if David had lost all interest in the Temple project after God told him he would not be able to complete it. But David's humility is shown by the fact that he gathered the necessary materials and then handed the privilege of building the Temple over to his son.

None of us is naturally humble. Yet it is the mark of true greatness in God's Kingdom. Jesus said, "Whoever wants to be a leader among you must be your servant, and whoever wants to be first among you must be the slave of everyone else. For even the Son of Man came not to be served but to serve others" (Mark 10:43-45).

When David faced the disappointment of a closed door, God gave him a wonderful promise: "Your idea was to build a house for me, David, and that isn't going to happen. But I have a better idea: I am going to build a house for you."

God was not talking about brick and mortar. He was making a promise about one of David's descendants: "When you die and are buried with your ancestors, I will raise up one of your descendants, your own offspring, and I will make his kingdom strong" (2 Samuel 7:12). This was similar to the promise given to Eve, when God said one of her offspring would crush the head of the serpent (see Genesis 3:15).

God gave three promises: "David, here is what I am going to do: 1) Your son will build a house for my name, 2) I will establish his throne forever, and 3) I will be his father, and he will be my son. Your son will be my son!" (see 2 Samuel 7:13-14).

David was so overwhelmed by the weight of these promises that he had to sit down (see 2 Samuel 7:18). He was struggling to take it all in. How could a son of David possibly be the Son of God? How could any king's reign last forever? These were incredible promises. The question was, which son of David would fulfill them?

FOR FURTHER READING, SEE HEBREWS 1

WHICH SON OF DAVID?

Will God really live on earth? Why, even the highest heavens cannot contain you. How much less this Temple I have built! 1 KINGS 8:27

SOLOMON FULFILLED DAVID'S dream of putting up a magnificent building. And when the Temple was dedicated, the cloud of God's glory came down and filled it. God filled the Temple with his presence.

The people must have thought, *This is what God promised to David. Solomon has built the Lord's house. His kingdom will last forever*. But a few years later, Solomon died, the kingdom was divided in two, and after only a few hundred years, Solomon's Temple was destroyed.

Fast-forward a thousand years, to the opening of the New Testament: "This is the genealogy of Jesus the Messiah the son of David" (Matthew 1:1, NIV). The first thing we learn is that Jesus is the son of David. But the angel Gabriel also announced, "You will name him Jesus. He . . . will be called the Son of the Most High" (Luke 1:31-32). That is, the Son of God.

In the Temple courts one day, Jesus announced, "Destroy this temple, and in three days I will raise it up" (John 2:19). Those who heard him thought he was inviting them to bulldoze the building so he could rebuild it. They responded, "It has taken forty-six years to build this Temple, and you can rebuild it in three days?" (2:20).

Jesus was not talking about the building; he was talking about his body. It was as if Christ was saying, "From now on, my body is the Temple." The presence of God is found in Jesus Christ, "for in Christ lives all the fullness of God in a human body" (Colossians 2:9).

When Jesus was crucified, his body was torn down, and when he rose three days later, it was built again! In AD 70, the Temple building in Jerusalem was destroyed, and it has never been rebuilt. This is significant. The place where men and women can meet with God is not a building in Jerusalem, or anywhere else. The place where you meet with God is through Jesus Christ.

FOR FURTHER READING, SEE JOHN 2

THE BIBLE'S GREATEST MIRACLE

The Holy Spirit will come upon you, and the power of the
Most High will overshadow you. So the baby to be born will be
holy, and he will be called the Son of God. LUKE 1:35

WHEN JESUS WAS born, he came into the line of David through his mother, Mary. Joseph was a descendant of David too (see Matthew 1:1-16), but Jesus was not conceived through him, but by a creative miracle of God.

We normally think of a son as someone who is born twenty or thirty years after his father. But there was never a time when the Son Jesus was not with the Father God. When the Bible says, "Jesus is the Son of God," it is telling us that he shares the Father's nature. Like the Father, the Son has no beginning: "In the beginning the Word already existed. The Word was with God, and the Word was God" (John 1:1).

Once this truth is grasped, it makes sense of everything else. The eternal Son, who had always been beside the Father, became a son of David and in his own nature brought God and man together.

When you came to faith in the one and only Son of God—Jesus Christ—God received you as an adopted child into his family: "To all who believed [Jesus] and accepted him, he gave the right to become children of God" (John 1:12).

Let the truth of who Christ is and what he does for us sink in. Christ is reigning on the throne of the universe, and he is the Son of God. Faith joined you to Christ so that in him you have become God's temple, a place where God's presence will come. You are a citizen of God's Kingdom, living under the benefits of his rule. You are a son or a daughter of the living God, and your destiny is to enjoy him forever.

Take that into your most ordinary day or your darkest hour. Let it lift you to see the honor God has given to you and lead you to praise and glorify his name.

FOR FURTHER READING, SEE LUKE 1

THE ULTIMATE COVER-UP

The LORD was displeased with what David had done. 2 SAMUEL 11:27

PEOPLE WHO ARE given positions of great power often begin to feel they are beyond the rules that apply to others. That's how it was for David. One day, the king saw a married woman named Bathsheba. He ignored God's law and took the woman.

David loved the Lord, but even a heart that loves God can harbor some strange affections. David's feelings for Bathsheba were utterly offensive to God, but they were also very powerful. No Christian is ever beyond the power of temptation, and the moment we think we are is probably our time of greatest danger.

When Bathsheba told the king she was carrying his child, he became involved in a cover-up. The woman's husband, Uriah, was on the battlefield, and David ordered that he be sent home. David hoped the man would spend a few nights with his wife so that he could be identified as the child's father.

But Uriah was a good soldier, and he did not feel he should be at home with his wife while the other men were risking their lives on the battlefield. So David ordered that Uriah be put into the front lines of battle, making his death almost inevitable. The field commander obeyed, and Uriah died in fierce fighting (see 2 Samuel 11:5-17).

Then David took Bathsheba as his wife. The whole thing happened without anyone getting wind of it. David's marriage to Saul's daughter, Michal, had been a disappointment, and the outcome probably pleased Bathsheba, too. There is little doubt she made a play to attract the king's attention. She must have known, when she went out to sunbathe on her roof, that she was in sight of the palace.

End of story . . . except for one thing: God saw what had been done. The Lord could have remained silent, but David's sin would have remained hidden, and he would have lived as a believing man at a distance from God. Or God could bring the sin out into the open, so forgiveness and restoration would be possible. Guess which God chose?

FOR FURTHER READING, SEE 2 SAMUEL 11

THE TERRORS OF GOD'S VOICE

The LORD sent Nathan to David. 2 SAMUEL 12:1, NIV

WHEN GOD SPOKE to Moses at Mount Sinai, there was thunder and lightning and the sound of trumpets announcing the glory of God's presence. The people saw the mountain surrounded in smoke, and then they heard an audible voice. God spoke!

Imagine yourself in an earthquake or a hurricane to get a sense of what this must have been like. Even Moses was trembling with fear, and when the people heard the voice of God, they begged that no further Word would be spoken directly to them because they could not bear it (see Hebrews 12:18-21). They must have felt something of what it will be like for sinners to stand before almighty God on the last day: "God's voice thunders, and the earth melts" (Psalm 46:6).

When God was present at Mount Sinai, the people said to Moses, "You speak to us, and we will listen. But don't let God speak directly to us, or we will die!" (Exodus 20:19). So Moses went up the mountain, and God spoke to him, and then Moses came down from the presence of God and repeated the words of God to the people. This was the beginning of what we call prophecy.

God sent prophets to bring his Word so that the people would be saved from the terrors of hearing God speak to them directly. When God sent a prophet, it was always a sign of his grace. Sometimes the prophets said pretty fierce things, but nothing that any of the prophets said could ever come close to what it would have been like for the people to hear God's voice directly.

That was how David would hear God's rebuke—through the strong, direct words of a prophet sent by God. People sometimes say, "I don't want to go to church to hear the preacher talk about my sins." Well, it would be better for the Holy Spirit to convict you through a preacher than to have your sins remain hidden until the last day and have God speak to you about them himself.

God graciously chooses to speak to us about our sins so that we may turn from them and be forgiven. If you hear him speaking to you today, open your heart to him.

FOR FURTHER READING, SEE 2 SAMUEL 12

IN THE KING'S COURT

Nathan said to David, "You are that man!" 2 SAMUEL 12:7

DAVID WAS CONVINCED that his cover-up had been a success. But God knew what had happened, and he told the prophet Nathan to speak to David about it. God told Nathan some things he didn't want to know. He was being carried along by the Spirit, and he knew that when God spoke, he could not be silent.

With fear and trembling, and in the power of the Spirit, Nathan went to the palace to speak the Word of God to his friend David. Using a clever parable, Nathan told David about a rich man who stole a poor man's lamb. As David listened, he was filled with anger. He wanted to know who the man was so he could bring him to justice. But Nathan looked at David and said, "You are that man!" (2 Samuel 12:7).

David thought he had sidestepped a potential scandal. He moved into the darkness and lost fellowship with God, so God sent a prophet to expose what was hidden and to bring David back. This was God's grace in action.

The prophets were like God's prosecuting attorneys. They were also like wise counselors who helped God's people face the truth about themselves so they could return to God and find grace and forgiveness.

Down through the centuries, God sent his prophets to his people, but they were despised, brutalized, and sometimes murdered. Then God sent his Son. The Word of God was *given to* man in the prophets, but in Jesus Christ the Word of God *became* a man: "The Word became human and made his home among us" (John 1:14).

Christ did not *hear* the Word of God. He *is* the Word of God. Everything God has to say to you is expressed in him. This is why we don't need other prophets today. God spoke in the past by the prophets, but they were pointing to Christ, who is the Word of God. There can be no further Word beyond the one who is the Word made human.

FOR FURTHER READING, SEE JOHN 1

RESPONDING TO GOD'S WORD

I have sinned against the LORD. 2 SAMUEL 12:13

WHEN GOD SPOKE to David about his sin, he could have responded, "Nathan, she threw herself at me!" and there may have been some truth to that. He might have said, "Nathan, my marriage has been dead for years." This may also have been true. Instead David said, "I have sinned against the LORD."

Would you have said that? How you respond to the Word of God when it hurts you is one of the most revealing statements about you. It will determine whether you remain on a spiritual casualty list or you are restored to living fellowship with God. David's honest confession led to forgiveness. His conscience was released, and the joy of his salvation was restored.

A thousand years later, another king sat on the throne in Jerusalem. God spoke to him through the prophet John. King Herod was interested in spiritual things, and he liked listening to John the Baptist's preaching. One day God gave John some words to speak to Herod about his relationship with his brother's wife. The king didn't want to hear it, and eventually he ordered John's execution.

Herod's sin did not dull his interest in spiritual matters. He wanted to see Jesus, and eventually he had the opportunity. Herod "asked Jesus question after question, but Jesus refused to answer" (Luke 23:9). Herod had refused God's Word to him through John; now the Savior had nothing more to say to him.

As far as we know, the next time God spoke to Herod it was without a prophet or a Savior. If you will not hear the Word of God today, there will come a day when he will speak to you directly. That is why the Bible says, "What makes us think we can escape if we ignore this great salvation that was first announced by the Lord Jesus himself and then delivered to us by those who heard him speak?" (Hebrews 2:3).

God promises, "If we confess our sins to him, he is faithful and just to forgive us our sins and to cleanse us from all wickedness" (1 John 1:9). That is what happened to David, and it can happen for you as well.

FOR FURTHER READING, SEE MARK 6

THE RIGHT TOOLS FOR THE JOB

There was no sound of hammer, ax, or any other
iron tool at the building site. 1 KINGS 6:7

GOD HAD GIVEN his people wise and stable leadership and had entrusted them with significant resources. And right from the start, Solomon knew what God wanted him to do with this moment of opportunity. God had told Solomon's father, David, "Your son will build a house for me."

Solomon knew from the prophecy given to his father that God had a building project for him to do. He had the stones cut, shaped, and dressed at the quarry, and then delivered to the building site. Then, when all of the materials were assembled, a command was given to build. The whole building went up in silence.

This picture is taken up in the New Testament, where God's people are described as "living stones" who are being built into a temple that will be for the glory of God (see 1 Peter 2:5). Every stone has to be shaped for its place in the building.

Who are God's stonecutters in your life? The pain that God may allow in your life or the hardships that you struggle with are like the hammer and chisel in the quarry. But God will use that pain in his great purpose of shaping you into the likeness of Christ so you can take your place in his living temple.

I don't know who or what God is using in your life to cut you into shape. It may be a challenging problem such as a health, job, or financial issue. No matter the cutting instrument—a person or a situation—the process can be painful.

But when Christ returns, the stones will all be sized and dressed and he will give the command to build, and all the people of God will be brought together. On that day the church will be all that Christ died for it to become, and you will be a part of the place where God's glory is known and enjoyed forevermore.

FOR FURTHER READING, SEE 1 PETER 2

NO BUILDING CAN CONTAIN HIM

*May you watch over this Temple night and day, this place where
you have said, "My name will be there."* 1 KINGS 8:29

WHEN THE TEMPLE building was complete, the people gathered for
a service of dedication. This was one of the greatest occasions in the
nation's history. Solomon summoned the elders of Israel, the heads
of the tribes, and the chiefs of the families to bring up the Ark of the
Covenant (see 1 Kings 8:1).

The priests brought the Ark of the Covenant into the inner sanctuary, and a cloud so filled the Temple that they could not perform their
service (see 1 Kings 8:10-11). The last time God's glory had shown
itself like this was four hundred years before. The same God whose
glory rested on the Ark of the Covenant in the desert had come into
the Temple!

Solomon's first response was to worship: "Praise the LORD, the
God of Israel, who has kept the promise he made to my father, David"
(1 Kings 8:15). Then Solomon turned to God and expressed the longing of his heart, that God would hear as the people of Israel directed
their prayers toward the Temple (see 8:30).

Solomon was a wise man, and he knew that no building could ever
contain God and that the cloud could leave as quickly as it had come.
Solomon longed for much more than a once-in-a-lifetime experience
of God's presence. He wanted the Temple to be a place where God's
presence could always be found. People who were living many miles
from Jerusalem would also want to seek the face of God.

Solomon asked that God would listen to every prayer directed toward
the Temple. Jesus Christ is the place where the presence of God can
always be found. In fact, Christ promises that God will hear every prayer
offered in his name: "I tell you the truth, you will ask the Father directly,
and he will grant your request because you use my name" (John 16:23).
We can approach God confidently, knowing that through Jesus Christ,
our prayers will be heard.

FOR FURTHER READING, SEE 1 KINGS 8

A VERY SHORT DISTANCE

In Solomon's old age, [his foreign wives] turned his heart to worship other gods instead of being completely faithful to the LORD his God. 1 KINGS 11:4

WHEN SOLOMON CAME to the throne, the people of God had everything going for them, and they accomplished remarkable things. Solomon assembled a two-hundred-thousand-person workforce, and after seven years of construction, the Temple of God was completed. When the building was dedicated, God's glory filled the Temple. It was one of the greatest moments in the history of Israel.

God's people became the envy of the nations. The queen of Sheba came to visit Solomon to learn from his wisdom and to marvel at what he had accomplished. But there is a very short distance between triumph and disaster. As time passed, we find that Solomon's success began to breed complacency, and the seeds of future disaster were planted in the later years of his reign.

While people in the South were prospering, the people in the North were struggling. Solomon had focused his forced labor program in the North. The result was a significant group of people who were feeling marginalized among the people of God. Solomon lost touch with these hurting people. Perhaps he thought they were unimportant. But whatever the reason, that shortsighted leadership decision had long-term consequences.

Solomon could do virtually anything he wanted—he had almost unlimited power and great wealth. In his early days, he was a man on a mission. He knew God had called him to build the Temple, and he threw his time, energy, and money into accomplishing something for the glory of God. But later in his life, he used his position to support his own indulgence. Solomon had seven hundred wives and three hundred concubines (see 1 Kings 11:3). That's indulgence, and it was the root of his own downfall.

Solomon, who was so wise in his early years, became very foolish in his later years. The relationships he had chosen became a burden and a snare to him. The constant influence of ungodly people eroded his faith. Be very careful about your choice of significant relationships, friendships, and partnerships because they will greatly impact the course of your life.

FOR FURTHER READING, SEE 2 CORINTHIANS 6

HOW TO START AN AVALANCHE

> *On the Mount of Olives, east of Jerusalem, he even built a pagan*
> *shrine for Chemosh, the detestable god of Moab, and another for*
> *Molech, the detestable god of the Ammonites.* 1 KINGS 11:7

IT'S NOT HARD to imagine the circumstances that led Solomon to do this. One of his favored wives said to him one day, "Solomon, I have a favor to ask. It's for a number of us Moabites. Each one of us left our home and our family to be your wife, and we would like to have a little taste of home here in Israel. I know you wouldn't want us going back to Moab, so what about us having a little bit of Moab here? Just a little shrine to Chemosh would be wonderful!"

Solomon built a pagan shrine to Chemosh for his Moabite wives. You know what happened next. One of Solomon's other wives came to him, this one from Ammon, asking for similar treatment. So Solomon set up a shrine for Molech.

Then the rest of Solomon's wives came forward with their petitions. Maybe he finally said, "To make it fair, the rule is that all of the women may have a shrine of their own choosing." The record reads, " Solomon built such shrines for all his foreign wives to use for burning incense and sacrificing to their gods" (1 Kings 11:8).

When the queen of Sheba came to Jerusalem, she saw a Temple that spoke of the unique glory of God. Now the Temple of the living God was surrounded by a smorgasbord of shrines to other gods, so that any visitor to Jerusalem would draw the conclusion that the God of Israel was one among many. This was the beginning of a radical transformation that infected God's people.

Solomon's choices were the beginning of the erosion of true worship in Israel. Our personal worship may also be stifled by poor choices. The apostle Peter, for example, warns husbands to be careful about the way they treat their wives, "so your prayers will not be hindered" (1 Peter 3:7). If we intentionally hide sin in our hearts, then the Lord will not hear us.

FOR FURTHER READING, SEE 1 PETER 3

THE STORY IN THE NORTH

It is too much trouble for you to worship in Jerusalem. Look, Israel,
these are the gods who brought you out of Egypt! 1 KINGS 12:28

SOLOMON HANDED HIS son Rehoboam a troubled kingdom. Rehoboam immediately faced rumbling discontent among the people in the North, and eventually the northern tribes rallied around Jeroboam and crowned him as their king.

The ten tribes in the North were separating from the line of David that God had promised to bless. The kingdom was now divided and at war—the North (called Israel) against the South (called Judah).

But Jeroboam realized the cohesive power of religion. He saw that if people from the North kept going down to the Temple in Jerusalem, it would remind them of the unity they shared. So Jeroboam established his own worship centers for the North—using golden calves! This was politically shrewd but entirely wrong, and deeply offensive to God. He was using religion to strengthen the corporate identity of the people he was leading, and when that is the aim, any religion will do.

After Jeroboam, for the next fifty years a succession of kings in Israel followed the same policies—Nadab, Baasha, Elah, Zimri, Omri, and finally Ahab, who did "what was evil in the LORD's sight, even more than any of the kings before him" (1 Kings 16:30). He married Jezebel and served Baal. Jezebel initiated a persecution, hunting down and killing the prophets of God.

The nation of Israel had changed beyond recognition. At the beginning of Solomon's reign, the king said, "There is one God," and the kingdom was in one piece. By the time of Jeroboam, the kingdom was divided, and the official position in the North was, "There are many gods." By the time of Ahab, anyone who served God was subject to violent persecution.

A few years before, God's presence had filled Solomon's Temple; now the knowledge of God was all but lost, even among God's own people. What happened in Israel eight centuries before the birth of Christ can certainly happen in America twenty-one centuries after his birth.

True worship will be fostered where God's truth is proclaimed, where Jesus Christ is exalted, and where God's people give freedom to the work of the Holy Spirit in their lives. Everything else is secondary.

FOR FURTHER READING, SEE 1 TIMOTHY 4

BEFORE YOU CAN WORSHIP

*How much longer will you waver, hobbling between
two opinions? If the LORD is God, follow him!
But if Baal is God, then follow him!* 1 KINGS 18:21

THE PROPHET ELIJAH was on Mount Carmel, facing 450 prophets of
Baal and 400 prophets of Asherah. Elijah said to them, in effect, "If
Baal is God, then follow him. But if he's not, then return to God!" That
is like saying today, "If Allah is God, then leave the church and go to the
mosque! If Vishnu is God, then adopt Hinduism!"

Elijah did not appeal to tradition. He was not interested in perpetu-
ating a system of vested interests that are used to dominate the culture.
He appealed to the truth: the single reason for worshiping the Lord is
that he is God.

Nobody has the right to say you should be a Christian because your
parents are Christians or because Christianity is the dominant religion
in your country. These are not good enough reasons. Christianity rises
or falls on the claim that it is true. Authentic worship is a response to
revealed truth: "If the LORD is God, follow him."

The people found it very difficult to respond to Elijah's challenge;
"the people were completely silent" (1 Kings 18:21). Elijah's question
assumed categories of truth and error, and the people found it difficult
to think in these terms. They had been brought up believing probably
what many of us have been brought up to believe, that the God you
worship is a personal choice. Faith is a private matter, and every person
must find a way to worship that fits their personality.

Elijah's first task was to confront the people with the claims of truth.
Before you can truly worship, you need to know who God is. So if
worship is to be restored, truth must be proclaimed. We should sing
the truth, read the truth, pray the truth, and preach the truth in our
worship services.

If you want to know a greater depth of worship in your life, get your
Bible open and engage with the truth. Soak your mind in it. The Holy
Spirit will use the truth to stimulate a response within your heart, and
this will help your prayers.

FOR FURTHER READING, SEE 1 KINGS 18

THE TRAGEDY OF FALSE RELIGION

*O LORD, answer me! Answer me so these people will
know that you, O LORD, are God and that you have
brought them back to yourself.* 1 KINGS 18:37

ELIJAH INVITED THE prophets of Baal to call on their god to show himself by sending fire. The prophets took up the challenge. They cried out and danced around the altar, working themselves into a frenzy. This went on for hours.

You have to give these prophets top marks for sincerity and effort. Their worship was probably meaningful and made them feel good, but after all the activity, "still there was no sound, no reply, no response" (1 Kings 18:29). That is the tragedy of false religion. Even though they had done everything with sincerity and at great personal cost, there was no one there.

At some point in history, people made up mythical stories about Baal and wrote them down. Then other people made images of Baal and carved them out of wood. But there was nothing in the worship of Baal beyond what human minds had dreamed up and what human hands had made. It had no authority and no power. Elijah wanted to save the people from that.

Many people have concluded that Christianity started in the same way. They assume the Bible is a book of ancient myths, and that it has no authority. If they are right in their assumptions, then they are right in their conclusion. A religion created by one culture should not be imposed on another.

Elijah longed for the knowledge of the living God to be restored in the land. So he prayed about the most fundamental truth in the Bible—before the world began; before cultures developed; before religious writing; before animal, vegetable, or mineral; "in the beginning" there was God. The world and all that is in it are his handiwork. This living God revealed himself to Abraham, Isaac, and Jacob, but that knowledge was being drowned out by a thousand substitutes.

You will struggle to worship whenever you lose a sense of the weight and glory of the Lord. But Elijah knew that where God's glory was known, worship would follow. So he stepped forward and prayed that God would make himself known.

FOR FURTHER READING, SEE EPHESIANS 3

FIRE FELL FROM THE SKY

The LORD—he is God! Yes, the LORD is God! 1 KINGS 18:39

ELIJAH DELIBERATELY USED twelve stones, representing the twelve tribes of Jacob, to build the altar. This was politically incorrect: his audience from the northern tribes would have preferred he take ten stones. But Elijah took twelve, because he was about to offer a sacrifice to the God of *all* Israel.

Elijah prepared his sacrifice, and then, in order to make the revelation of God's power compelling even to skeptics, he poured water on the altar, drenching the sacrifice. Then "the fire of the LORD fell and consumed the burnt offering" (1 Kings 18:38, ESV).

Imagine yourself in the crowd. You have bought into the prevailing belief that all religions are a human creation. As you are sitting at the top of Mount Carmel, the sky is filled with fire. Suddenly, your mind is lucid; everything falls into place: "Elijah is telling the truth! The Lord *is* God, and the fire of his judgment is falling!"

But when God's fire came, it did not fall on the thousands of people who were there. God's fire was diverted away from them and onto the altar, where the sacrifice had been prepared.

On a different day on a different hill, another sacrifice was offered. Jesus Christ died, and the judgment of God fell. But it did not fall on the people; it fell on the sacrifice. It struck him, and in this way, God created room for men and women from every culture and in every generation to be reconciled to himself.

When the people saw the fire, they fell down in worship. Witnessing the Lord's grace and power, a group of people made a new and decisive commitment as they confessed their faith in the living God.

Maybe you've seen something of the glory of God and his grace to you in Jesus Christ. Don't stay at a distance. Take your stand with Christ by confessing your faith in him today. God's Word promises, "If you confess with your mouth that Jesus is Lord and believe in your heart that God raised him from the dead, you will be saved" (Romans 10:9).

FOR FURTHER READING, SEE ROMANS 10

TURNING AWAY FROM GOD

> *This disaster came upon the people of Israel because they worshiped other gods. They sinned against the LORD their God. . . . They worshiped idols, despite the LORD's specific and repeated warnings.* 2 KINGS 17:7, 12

GOD'S PEOPLE BECAME divided after the death of Solomon, and the northern tribes declared their independence from the southern tribes. The tragedy of the northern tribes was that they separated themselves from the blessing of God.

God promised to bless the line of David's descendants who ruled in the South. There the royal line of David continued, with each king transferring power to his son. But in the North, most kings came to power by murdering their predecessor.

Nineteen kings ruled over the northern kingdom's two hundred years, and every one "did what was evil in the LORD's sight" (see, for example, 1 Kings 15:26). Eventually, God allowed their enemies to overrun them, and the people were deported. The whole area became a wasteland.

When Jeroboam, the first northern king, set up two golden calves, it was the beginning of two hundred years of turning away from the Lord. Amos described the northern kingdom in its later years: the rich lived in opulence, showing a total disregard for the poor, and the streets were filled with violence. Some parents even allowed their unwanted children to be burned in the fire.

This society had become sick, but the first charge God brought against his people was not violence, murder, greed, or cruelty. His first complaint was that they had worshiped other gods (see 2 Kings 17:7). Why?

The first four commands are God's fundamental requirements: "You must not have any other god but me. You must not make for yourself an idol of any kind. . . . You must not misuse the name of the LORD your God. . . . Remember to observe the Sabbath day by keeping it holy" (Exodus 20:3-8). Our first calling is to give God his place.

When Jesus was asked which is the greatest commandment, he answered, "You must love the LORD your God with all your heart, all your soul, and all your mind" (Matthew 22:36-37). This is godliness.

FOR FURTHER READING, SEE EXODUS 20

LIFE WITHOUT GOD

They worshiped worthless idols, so they became worthless themselves....
They rejected all the commands of the LORD their God. 2 KINGS 17:15-16

GOD CALLS US to a life of godliness, and then he speaks about our attitudes and actions toward others: "Honor your father and mother. . . .
You must not murder. You must not commit adultery. You must not
steal. You must not [lie]. You must not covet" (Exodus 20:12-17). This
is God's second calling for his people.

The Bible calls this kind of self-restraint "righteousness." Righteous
living is faithfully reflecting God's attitudes and actions in our relationships with other people. Christ confirmed this when he said that the
second greatest commandment is to "love your neighbor as yourself"
(Matthew 22:39).

True godliness will result in increasing evidence of righteousness
because righteousness is built on the foundation of godliness. So when
people reject godliness, they find that righteousness is beyond their
grasp. You cannot reflect the attitudes and actions of God until you
have a God-centered life!

The story of the northern kingdom teaches us that when a nation
turns away from the living God, the result is moral confusion and the
unleashing of sin and evil. It began with the people rejecting God, and
it ended with them putting their children into the fire. The reason they
lost the morality of the Bible is that they rejected the God of the Bible.
You cannot have righteousness without godliness.

It is a great mistake to think our hearts are naturally filled with love for
God: "The sinful nature is always hostile to God" (Romans 8:7). Unless
God changes our hearts, it is natural for us to resent him because his
power seems to threaten our freedom, his holiness offends our pride,
and his complete knowledge feels like an invasion of privacy. There will
never be a time when God steps down from power or becomes more
tolerant of our sins.

Unless God changes our hearts, our sinful minds are hostile to him,
and that is the root of our sin. Sin originates with our rejection of God.

FOR FURTHER READING, SEE ROMANS 8

ONE OF THE BIBLE'S MOST MISUNDERSTOOD TRUTHS

They . . . sold themselves to evil, arousing the LORD's anger. 2 KINGS 17:17

THE ANGER OF God is one of the most misunderstood truths of the Bible. Anger is not part of the nature of God. God is always holy, he is always love, and he is always true, but he is not always angry.

The pagan gods were always smoldering. Offerings were given to pacify them, but their anger never went away; it was only contained. Anger is not a part of God's nature. "The LORD is . . . slow to get angry" (Psalm 103:8), but he can be provoked.

God is immensely patient. For two hundred years, he restrained judgment and sent the prophets to call the people back to godliness and righteousness, but "the Israelites would not listen" (2 Kings 17:14). Eventually, God was provoked: "Because the LORD was very angry with Israel, he swept them away from his presence" (17:18). We are told how this happened: "Israel was exiled from their land to Assyria" (17:23).

In the Garden, when Adam decided that he did not want to live under God's rule, he broke God's commandment and was driven from God's presence. At the end of the Bible story, we find that every person who has ever lived will stand before God, and the ungodly and unrighteous will be driven from God's presence. That is hell—eternity outside the blessing of God. If a person refuses to bow before God, saying, "Your will be done," a time will come when God will say to that person, "Your will be done; depart from me forever."

The message to an unbelieving world is not, "Following Jesus is the best way to a more satisfying life," but, "God shows his anger from heaven against all sinful, wicked people who suppress the truth by their wickedness" (Romans 1:18). That's why the gospel is so urgent. That's why we must be passionate about the gospel and why we must use all possible means to communicate its message today.

FOR FURTHER READING, SEE 1 KINGS 17

DISCOVERING THE MERCY OF GOD

The king of Assyria transported groups of people from Babylon,
Cuthah, Avva, Hamath, and Sepharvaim and resettled them in the
towns of Samaria, replacing the people of Israel. 2 KINGS 17:24

WHEN GOD WAS provoked, he drove the people out of his presence, and the land that he had promised to bless lay uninhabited. But it wasn't long before the king of Assyria repopulated the area with people from all over his empire.

Apparently, while the Promised Land was empty, the number of wild animals increased, so when these immigrants arrived, they were attacked by lions. These people were brought up to believe that the lions were a plague from whichever god was in charge of the area.

Word got back to the king of Assyria, who thought the best way to deal with the problem was to find a priest from among God's people who used to live there. He assumed a local priest would know what to do to placate whatever god was causing this problem, so he gave orders to find a priest and send him back to Israel.

In God's mercy, "one of the priests who had been exiled from Samaria returned to Bethel and taught the new residents how to worship the LORD" (2 Kings 17:28). God brought people from the north, south, east, and west into the place he had promised to bless, and while they were there, God sent one of his own people to them so they could discover him too. God's promise was not to bless just Israel, but God promised that through Israel, all the nations of the earth would be blessed (see Genesis 22:18).

This multiethnic population eventually combined the worship of God with the worship of its own gods (see 2 Kings 17:29). Although they became confused, there was a witness to the truth among them for the first time. The Samaritans, as these people came to be known, built their own temple on Mount Gerizim, where God spoke of his blessings to his people when they first came into the Promised Land. And God sent another witness to them later in the person of his Son (see John 4). Has God sent a witness to the truth to you? Praise him for his wonderful mercy today!

FOR FURTHER READING, SEE JOHN 4

HOW A SUPERPOWER GOT CARRIED AWAY

In the ninth year of King Hoshea's reign, Samaria fell,
and the people of Israel were exiled to Assyria. 2 KINGS 17:6

HOW WOULD YOU feel if forty-two of the fifty American states left the union? What if each of the forty-two had a completely independent government and armed forces and refused to pay taxes? Then, what if several years later, those forty-two independent states collapsed and were overrun by enemies?

As a citizen in one of the eight remaining states, you would no longer be part of a world superpower. Instead, you would be a citizen of a rather small and vulnerable country. Enemies who were once thousands of miles away could now move military installations very close to your border. What once seemed strong and secure would now seem weak and helpless.

That must have been how it was for the people of God in the two tribes that made up the southern kingdom of Judah. In the time of David, Israel had been a dominant power, with the twelve tribes united and the kings—Saul, David, and Solomon—ruling from the south. During Solomon's reign, admiring heads of state came to Jerusalem to see the achievements of the world's leading country.

After ten of the twelve tribes declared their independence, things changed radically for the South. The nation was diminished militarily and economically, and within two hundred years, the whole of the northern area was overrun by enemies.

If you were in the South at that point, you were among the remaining few of a once magnificent kingdom. You were part of a vulnerable group of the descendants of Judah and Benjamin. All that remained were two tribes.

God's promise to bless Abraham and then to bring blessing to all the nations of the world through him must have looked very doubtful. But God's promise had never been revoked, and although the people of the southern kingdom went through some harrowing times, God was faithful to his promise. Don't let doubtful circumstances undermine your confidence in God's faithfulness today.

FOR FURTHER READING, SEE ROMANS 11

BEGIN SEEKING GOD TODAY

*[Josiah] did what was pleasing in the LORD's sight and
followed the example of his ancestor David. He did not turn
away from doing what was right.* 2 KINGS 22:2

THE PEOPLE OF Judah had the benefit of better leadership than their brothers and sisters in the North. Every one of the nineteen northern kings "did what was evil in the LORD's sight" or "refused to turn from the sins that [the previous king] had led Israel to commit" (see, for example, 2 Kings 3:2; 10:31), but in the South, a number of kings "did what was pleasing in the LORD's sight" (see, for example, 2 Kings 15:3).

Things took a turn for the worse in Judah when Manasseh came to the throne. He reigned for fifty-five years (see 2 Kings 21:1) and brought more trouble to God's people than anyone else. "Manasseh led them to do even more evil than the pagan nations that the LORD had destroyed when the people of Israel entered the land" (21:9).

Manasseh promoted the worship of Molech and the evil practice of sacrificing children in a fire (see 2 Kings 21:6). After half a century of this, God's anger was provoked. God's people were called to be a light in the dark, but they were living in the same darkness as the people around them!

At the end of Manasseh's reign, his son Amon reigned for two years before he was murdered. Then Amon's son Josiah became king when he was only eight years old. He began to seek the Lord in the eighth year of his reign (see 2 Chronicles 34:3). As a teenager, he developed a heart for God, and with this foundation, he became a man of great character. It is never too early to seek God.

Here we have a godly young leader who wanted to get Judah back on track. What was he to do? He had no Bible training to draw on. His father and grandfather had not given him any kind of model to follow. Josiah grew up in a spiritually confused and biblically illiterate culture, and yet deep within his heart, there was a longing to know God.

Regardless of your age, your spiritual background, or your lack of Bible knowledge, you can begin seeking God. Don't put it off another day.

FOR FURTHER READING, SEE 2 KINGS 22

CHICKEN SOUP AND YOUR SOUL

*Hilkiah the high priest said to Shaphan the court secretary,
"I have found the Book of the Law in the LORD's Temple!"* 2 KINGS 22:8

KING JOSIAH BEGAN his attempt to turn things around in Judah by refurbishing the Temple of God. He raised money through taxes collected at the Temple. Then, at age twenty-six, the king began renovation (see 2 Kings 22:3-6). Josiah sent his secretary, Shaphan, to Hilkiah the high priest to get the money and pay the builders.

Hilkiah entered the Temple, and while he was there, he discovered a dusty old book. This "Book of the Law" was almost certainly a copy of Deuteronomy. One wonders how it could have become lost in the Temple!

God's law condemned most of the things the previous kings Amon and Manasseh had done, and everybody knew that Jezebel had put the prophets who spoke the Word of God in the North to death. So it's not difficult to imagine why the priests ignored the Scriptures. If they had preached from the Word of God, "There is one living God, and the worship of all other gods is an offense to his glory," that would have led to trouble, just as it would lead to trouble today.

So the priests continued their work in the Temple without ever using the Scriptures! What were they doing all day? They must have become experts in administration, counseling, and organizing social events, but apparently the priests never opened the Scriptures. The high priest likely placed the Bible in a Temple vault and offered, in its place, short encouraging talks. Within fifty years, a new generation of God's people knew nothing of God's law.

Indeed, many people today seek pastors who tell stories and jokes and offer the people "chicken soup for the soul." You don't need the Bible to do that. But if the church chooses this path, then within a generation we may well have young people like Josiah growing up, who long to know God but do not know where to find him. They go to church, but they do not find him there. If you're longing to know God today, it's important to ask yourself, *Am I attending a church that faithfully teaches the Word of God?*

FOR FURTHER READING, SEE 2 TIMOTHY 4

GRIPPED BY A RADICAL NEW VISION

When the king heard what was written in the Book of the Law,
he tore his clothes in despair. 2 KINGS 22:11

THE "BOOK OF the Law" contains the Ten Commandments and all the regulations about how God's people were to live when they entered the land. The book of Deuteronomy describes the blessings and curses that would follow obedience or disobedience, and it ends with a record of how the people of God renewed their covenant with him and committed themselves to live according to his law.

When Josiah heard this, he tore his robes. He took the Bible seriously. When the commands were read, he said, "We're not doing this. How could we have strayed so far from God's requirements?" Without God's Word, the people had no criteria for telling right from wrong, so they operated on consensus. By the time of Manasseh, the consensus said, "It's sometimes right to sacrifice your children in the fire."

The Bible has a very simple definition of righteousness. What God calls "right" is right, and what God calls "evil" is evil. And if righteousness is to be restored to our nation, then the Bible must be restored in the churches, and those who love God must get serious about putting the Bible into practice.

Josiah gives us a wonderful model of this. He heard the Word of God, took it seriously, and then he said, "This is how I am going to live." Josiah did more than read the Bible; he wanted to put it into practice, and he began with his own life.

Then Josiah called for a rally at the Temple. Imagine the sea of faces as a great crowd gathered in the Temple area. Josiah read the whole book of Deuteronomy to the people and made a personal commitment to obey the Lord (see 2 Kings 23:2-3). Then he had all the rest of the people make the same commitment (see 2 Chronicles 34:32).

As Josiah listened to the Scriptures, he was gripped by a radical new vision of obedience to the Word of God: *What would life be like if it was lived fully according to the Law of God?*

FOR FURTHER READING, SEE 1 THESSALONIANS 1

WHERE CHANGE BEGINS

> *Never before had there been a king like Josiah, who turned to the LORD*
> *with all his heart and soul and strength, obeying all the laws of Moses.*
> *And there has never been a king like him since.* 2 KINGS 23:25

WHEREVER JOSIAH FOUND altars, Asherah poles, or other evidences of idolatry in the land, he completely destroyed them. It was the greatest onslaught against pagan practices in the history of Israel. Josiah went right through Judah and even extended his activity into the North.

Josiah destroyed the altars Solomon had authorized for the sake of his foreign wives (see 2 Kings 23:13). These altars had stood for three hundred years. Other kings had promoted the worship of God, but no other kings in the North or the South had the courage and political will to destroy the pagan altars in the land.

Later, a prophetess named Huldah sent Josiah this message: "This is what the LORD, the God of Israel, says concerning the message you have just heard: You were sorry and humbled yourself before the LORD when you heard what I said against this city and its people—that this land would be cursed and become desolate. . . . I have indeed heard you, says the LORD. So I will not send the promised disaster until after you have died and been buried in peace. You will not see the disaster I am going to bring on this city" (2 Kings 22:18-20).

God honored Josiah's leadership and held back judgment on the nation during his lifetime. King Josiah died in peace, but there were limitations to his achievement: "Even so, the LORD was very angry with Judah because of all the wicked things Manasseh had done to provoke him" (2 Kings 23:26).

God is not satisfied with outward conformity to the law. He is looking for an inward desire for righteousness. This is the work of the Holy Spirit. It involves changing our hearts to give us a new capacity to pursue a life that is pleasing to God.

FOR FURTHER READING, SEE EPHESIANS 2

WHAT NO STATE, CHURCH, OR PARENT COULD EVER DO

Judah has never sincerely returned to me. She has only pretended to be sorry. I, the LORD, have spoken! JEREMIAH 3:10

JOSIAH PERSONALLY OVERSAW the reforms. It was not a popular uprising of the people; it was a state program. Josiah did away with the pagan priests, the Asherah poles, and the pagan shrines (see 2 Kings 23:5-8). So it is not surprising that "throughout the rest of his lifetime, [the people of Judah] did not turn away from the LORD" (2 Chronicles 34:33).

But as soon as Josiah died, things went back to the way they were. With the right leader you can change the laws of the land, but unless the hearts of the people are changed too, revival will be short-lived.

If you are just conforming to the expectations of others, then when you are with a different crowd, you will adapt your behavior to fit the new social pressures. Righteousness flows from the heart!

It must have been hard for the prophet Jeremiah to watch the people slide back into their old, idolatrous ways after King Josiah's death, but then God gave one of the most wonderful promises in all the Old Testament: "The day is coming . . . when . . . I will put my instructions deep within them, and I will write them on their hearts" (Jeremiah 31:31, 33).

God was promising to do what no state, church, or parent could ever do: get his law into the minds and hearts of the people. Jeremiah must have wondered how God would do this.

More than six hundred years later, another King came, not to impose new laws but to bring new life. The risen Lord Jesus Christ invites us to come as we are, with our confused minds and our stubborn hearts.

And when we come to him, his Spirit enters our soul, and he puts the desire for righteousness within us. That is why a Christian loves God and longs for righteousness. That is why a Christian prays, and why, when a Christian sins, it is not long before he or she feels the need to come to Christ and be forgiven.

FOR FURTHER READING, SEE MARK 7

STUNNED SILENCE

Ezra was a scribe who was well versed in the Law of Moses. . . .
The gracious hand of the LORD his God was on him. EZRA 7:6

JOSIAH'S ATTEMPT TO call people back to the God's Word quickly faded, and then God allowed enemies to reduce his own city to a pile of rubble. The Babylonian army laid siege to Jerusalem, and those who survived fled for their lives or were taken prisoner and marched off to resettlement camps in Babylon.

The city of God became a smoldering ruin, and silence reigned where a community of believers once lifted their voices in worship. The Temple that was once filled with the cloud of God's presence was completely destroyed.

But God had not forgotten his promise. After seventy years in captivity, the exiled people watched the Babylonian empire fall. Then the new king, Cyrus, decreed that Jewish exiles who wished to return to Jerusalem and rebuild the Temple could do so. Fifty thousand people caught a vision for rebuilding the city of God and responded to the challenge.

The land had been uninhabited for years, so the first challenge was to build homes. When they were complete, Zerubbabel called the people together to build an altar (see Ezra 3:1-2). When it was finished, the people offered the sacrifices God had commanded Moses, and they began to rebuild the Temple.

Soon Ezra arrived in Jerusalem. When he discovered the spiritual condition of the people, he sat down in stunned silence until evening (see Ezra 9:2-4). He could hardly believe that the people of God in the city of God knew so little about the Word of God.

Ezra was faced with the challenge of teaching the Bible to people who thought they knew the Lord, but who knew very little of the Bible. Surrounded by the language and literature of the Babylonians, many had become assimilated into their culture. The returned exiles knew they were the people of God, but they knew very little about the God whose people they were. This is true of many people today. How well do you know the God of the Bible? As you spend more time in his Word, you will come to know God better.

FOR FURTHER READING, SEE EZRA 9

A REMARKABLE CHANT

They asked Ezra the scribe to bring out the Book of the Law of Moses,
which the LORD had given for Israel to obey. NEHEMIAH 8:1

A FEW YEARS later, God raised up Nehemiah, a brilliant planner and organizer. He came to Jerusalem and saw that although the Temple had been completed, nothing had been done about the walls. The great city of God had no defenses and precious little infrastructure. God put it into Nehemiah's heart to do something about this.

More than five hundred years had passed since the cloud of God's glory had filled Solomon's Temple. By the time of Nehemiah, these events were ancient history! So how could the people be molded into a worshiping community who loved the Lord and were committed to obeying his law? The answer was the Word of God!

On one remarkable occasion, fifty thousand people gathered in a public square to worship God, and they requested that God's Law be brought out. Now, how do fifty thousand people make a request? They chant! This crowd, gathered in high spirits and with a great hunger for the Word of God, grew impatient for events to get underway. So they began to shout, "We want the Bible! Bring out the Bible!" or something similar.

It must have been a great joy for Ezra to bring out the Scriptures and to teach the Word of God to this vast crowd. These people had been starved for Bible teaching for most of their lives, and now they were committing themselves to a new life of faith and obedience to God, and they were hungry for his Word.

Ezra brought the Word of God to those assembled, "men and women and all the children old enough to understand" (Nehemiah 8:2). It is a powerful thing to bring children into an environment where they see adults worshiping and taking the Word of God seriously. I am grateful for programs that are geared specifically to our children and young people, but there is something special about allowing the next generation to witness Mom and Dad's commitment to the Word of God. If you have children, let them see your love for and commitment to the Word of God.

FOR FURTHER READING, SEE NEHEMIAH 8

UNDERSTANDING YOUR BIBLE

Ezra praised the LORD, the great God, and all the people chanted,
"Amen! Amen!" as they lifted their hands. Then they bowed down and
worshiped the LORD with their faces to the ground. NEHEMIAH 8:6

GOD HAD SPOKEN these words to Moses a thousand years earlier, but when Ezra read and explained them, the people believed that God was speaking directly to them. They recognized that when they heard this book read and explained, they were not listening to the words of a man, but to the Word of God, so they gave it their full attention.

They did not ask Ezra to visit Mount Sinai to see if there was a new word from the Lord. They asked him to open the Book of the Law, which was a thousand years old, because they believed what God had said then was still his Word to them now.

Ezra and the Levites who assisted him "read from the Book of the Law of God and clearly explained the meaning of what was being read, helping the people understand each passage" (Nehemiah 8:8). Ezra did not decide on a message and then come to the Bible to find some verses to support it; he came to the Scripture and allowed the Scripture to determine the message.

The Levites were interspersed in the crowd. Ezra would read part of the law and explain the meaning, and then he would stop. The Levites would then ask the smaller family groups gathered around them if there were any questions. People had some break-out time to work through the application of the preaching, and when everyone in the group was clear, Ezra would continue (see Nehemiah 8:7-8).

If we lose confidence in the power of the Word, we will soon be trying just about anything to hold on to our young people, attract our neighbors, or make our services more interesting. God still speaks through his Word, so if we want to disciple a community of people, then reading and explaining the Bible must be central to all that we do.

FOR FURTHER READING, SEE 1 THESSALONIANS 2

A DIFFERENT KIND OF MINISTRY

"Don't mourn or weep on such a day as this! For today is a sacred
day before the LORD your God." For the people had all been weeping
as they listened to the words of the Law. NEHEMIAH 8:9

AS EZRA READ the law of God, the people realized how far they were
from what God was calling them to be. One of the first effects of receiving the Word of God is that it humbles us. We start to see things in our
lives that we didn't see before. We become sensitive to attitudes and
actions that grieve the heart of God.

It is often the purpose of God to humble us, but it is never his
purpose to leave us feeling defeated. You may have experienced legal-
istic preaching that made you feel small. You came out saying, "What
a miserable person I am; I must do better," but eventually you lost the
strength to keep trying.

Ezra and Nehemiah's ministry was different. Their ministry reduced
people to tears, but it did not leave them there. Nehemiah said, "Go
and celebrate with a feast of rich foods and sweet drinks, and share gifts
of food with people who have nothing prepared. This is a sacred day
before our Lord. Don't be dejected and sad, for the joy of the LORD is
your strength!" (Nehemiah 8:10).

Conviction of sin is always a means to an end—to bring sinners to
Christ. When Nehemiah spoke about the joy of the Lord, he wasn't
telling the people to cheer up. He was reminding them that the grace
of God could wipe away all their tears.

The Christian life is not an endless attempt to fulfill God's law.
When you feel your failure and your weakness, look up into the face of
God. You will find that he is gracious and merciful and that his hand is
extended to you in Christ.

When people left the great service of worship in Jerusalem, they were
not going home preoccupied with themselves and their failures. They
went home with a fresh glimpse of the grace and mercy of God. This
gave them new hope, new joy, and new strength to face the challenge
of another week.

FOR FURTHER READING, SEE 2 CORINTHIANS 7

SEARCHING FOR JOY

> As they studied the Law, they discovered that the LORD had
> commanded through Moses that the Israelites should live in shelters
> during the festival to be held that month. NEHEMIAH 8:14

THE RATHER UNUSUAL festival that the Israelites rediscovered involved each family making a temporary shelter from branches and then living in it for seven days. The festival reminded the people how God had protected their forefathers in the desert and that everything in this world is temporary. Like Abraham, they were to look for a heavenly city.

I love the spontaneity of this festival. These men read the teaching in the Word of God, and then they went and did it: "The people went out and cut branches and used them to build shelters on the roofs of their houses, in their courtyards, in the courtyards of God's Temple, or in the squares" (Nehemiah 8:16). Their obedience was visible in the home, among their neighbors, in their place of worship, and in the workplace. It was a marvelous example of the power of a group of people who are committed to doing whatever the Word of God says.

Their obedience to the Word of God was infectious: "Everyone who had returned from captivity lived in these shelters during the festival, and they were all filled with great joy! The Israelites had not celebrated like this since the days of Joshua son of Nun" (Nehemiah 8:17). Eight centuries had passed since the days of Joshua! The people were never happier than when they were fully obedient.

God had spoken to his people through his Word. It had humbled them in their sins, but it had also lifted them up to see the grace and mercy of God, and then had directed them into a new life of obedience.

In all our desperate searching for ways to find joy, God is telling us that we will never find joy like the joy of knowing God, being humbled in our sins, experiencing his grace, and walking in a life of obedience.

FOR FURTHER READING, SEE PHILIPPIANS 2

THE GREATEST MAN IN THE EAST

There once was a man named Job who lived in the land of Uz.
He was blameless—a man of complete integrity. JOB 1:1

THIS VERSE DOES not mean Job was perfect, but that if people were looking for anything to stick on him, they wouldn't find it. Job "feared God" and "stayed away from evil" (Job 1:1). That means he experienced the same temptations the rest of us do, but he had learned to push them off. He avoided evil, and the reason he was able to do this was because he feared God.

Job lived a highly successful life under God's blessing. In those days, wealth was measured in livestock. We are told that he had seven thousand sheep, three thousand camels, five hundred teams of oxen, and five hundred donkeys (see Job 1:3). His net worth was very impressive.

Job also had seven sons and three daughters (see Job 1:2), and it seems they were the one shadow on his horizon. Their lives were an endless round of parties, and his sons used to take turns holding feasts in their homes (see 1:4).

Their lifestyle seems to have been built around the pursuit of pleasure. If you had asked them what they were living for, they would have said, "We live for the weekend." Job did not like this. After the parties were over, he used to offer a sacrifice for each of his children. "Perhaps my children have sinned and have cursed God in their hearts," he said (Job 1:5).

Most people probably would have thought that Job's sons and daughters were fine, upright people, but Job was worried that when the wine had loosened some of their inhibitions, they had cursed God. Job was wonderfully blessed, but his one nagging fear was that what was going on in his family was not pleasing to God.

Parents who fear God and are well acquainted with their own souls will be grateful for their children's successes yet aware of the battle going on for their hearts and minds. Are you engaged in the battle against sin in your own life? If you are a parent, do you recognize the battle going on in the lives of your children?

FOR FURTHER READING, SEE JOB 1

THE DAY EVERYTHING CHANGED

Your oxen were plowing, with the donkeys feeding beside them, when
the Sabeans raided us. They stole all the animals and killed all the
farmhands. I am the only one who escaped to tell you. JOB 1:14-15

ONE DAY EVERYTHING in Job's life changed. The day was like any other—
until a terrified servant broke through the door of the house with desperate news.

Job did not even have time to take this in, because while the servant
was still speaking, another messenger came with the news that the sheep
and other servants had been killed in what was probably something like
a lightning storm: "The fire of God has fallen from heaven and burned
up your sheep and all the shepherds. I am the only one who escaped to
tell you" (Job 1:16).

While he was still speaking, a third messenger came with news that
the Chaldeans had swept down from the hills and taken off with the
camels. Then a fourth messenger arrived with the worst news of all—
Job's sons and daughters had been eating and drinking at one of their
parties, when suddenly the house was hit by a mighty wind. The house
collapsed on them, and they were all dead (see Job 1:17-19).

In one day, Job lost every familiar landmark of his life. His business
was destroyed, his wealth was plundered, and his entire family was tragi-
cally killed. It all happened in one day. By any standards, this is a catalog
of unspeakable suffering.

When God chose to speak to us about suffering, he did not merely
give us a book of philosophy. When we are in deep personal pain, we
don't have a great deal of interest in theory or arguments. God speaks
to us through the real-life experience of a man who suffered, and he
records for us his thoughts and his struggles. As you enter Job's struggles, God will speak into your pain. Wherever you look in human history, pain is still pain, and God is still God.

FOR FURTHER READING, SEE MARK 15

GOD'S PEOPLE WILL SUFFER

[Job] was the greatest man among all the people of the East. JOB 1:3, NIV

BAD THINGS HAPPEN to good people. Sometimes terrible things happen to wonderful people, and God allows it to be so. The story of Job clearly teaches us that the pursuit of a godly life will not put us beyond suffering.

Many Christians instinctively feel that if they pursue a life of worship and service, God will keep them from significant suffering in their lives. But there is no such deal on the table. The book of Job makes that clear. Christian faith does not inoculate us against suffering in a fallen world. That is why it is an absolute travesty of the gospel to suggest that if people come to Jesus, all their problems will be solved.

At the heart of the Bible story, we learn that the greatest and most godly person who ever lived suffered more than any other. Jesus Christ was rejected by his family. He wept at the graveside of one of his dearest friends. He was betrayed and suffered injustice, and then he was crucified. When he calls us to walk in his footsteps, that includes following him into the mystery of the suffering that God allows in the life of a godly person.

When you suffer, you will probably ask why. Jesus did. But as fallen human beings, we often frame the question wrongly, reflecting a mind-set that while it may be appropriate that other people should suffer, suffering should not happen to us. *We are churchgoers,* we might think. *We tithe. We give to others. We are, generally speaking, good people.* But our faith in Christ does not and will not grant us immunity from suffering in this life.

The apostle Peter writes, "Don't be surprised at the fiery trials you are going through, as if something strange were happening to you" (1 Peter 4:12). The important question to ask is not "Why does suffering happen?" but "How can I stand when all the navigating points of my life disappear?"

FOR FURTHER READING, SEE 1 PETER 4

GOD'S PEOPLE WILL FEEL PAIN

What I always feared has happened to me. What I dreaded has come true.
I have no peace, no quietness. I have no rest; only trouble comes. JOB 3:25-26

THE BOOK OF Job exposes the lie that if we "take it to the Lord in prayer," then that will somehow remove the pain. Job discovered that prayer doesn't act as a painkiller.

God reveals himself in Scripture and in Christ in order that we may know him, love him, and trust him, but he also hides himself (see Job 34:29; Isaiah 45:15). There will be times when we ask why but get no answer.

Job's friends said many things—some misguided and some true—but Job was not able to hear them. In the past, Job might have enjoyed their theological discussions, but now he was overwhelmed by pain. The comfort of God eventually broke through, but it was a long time coming, and Job never pretended he was experiencing comfort when he was not. There is a relentless honesty about this man.

God's people are not always so honest. Perhaps the reason is that we are afraid of "not having the answers." Job's testimony releases us from the pressure of feeling we have to say that things are going well when they are not. There are times of pain and turmoil, when peace seems to be beyond our grasp. And we must not be afraid of this; this was the experience of the greatest man in the East.

If the Christian life is portrayed as a life of victory, where the triumphs are always greater than the pain and the certainties are always greater than the questions, then Christians will not be able to make sense of their experience when the pain seems greater than the victory and the questions greater than the answers.

I thank God for a book of the Bible that tells us how the greatest man of his time struggled in the dark with unresolved questions and battled a level of pain even his closest friends could not begin to understand. Yet in all this, he did not turn away from God.

FOR FURTHER READING, SEE JOB 3

THE STORY BEHIND THE STORY

Satan [said] to the LORD, . . . "You have always put a wall of protection
around him and his home and his property. You have made him
prosper in everything he does. Look how rich he is! JOB 1:9-10

GOD PULLS BACK the curtain so we can get a glimpse of another story that is going on behind the pain Job experienced. God wants us to know that there is more at stake in this story than Job ever knew.

One day God summoned the angels to present themselves to him, and we are told that Satan, an outcast of heaven, came with them. God asked him, "Have you noticed my servant Job? He is the finest man in all the earth. He is blameless—a man of complete integrity. He fears God and stays away from evil" (Job 1:8).

Satan used the occasion to slander God's name: "Does Job fear God for nothing?" (Job 1:9, NIV). In effect, Satan told God, "You think he loves you freely, but that's impossible! Job is a man, and men love themselves! He will profess to love you as long as you give him everything he wants. But take away his wealth, his work, his family, and his health, and he will curse you to your face!"

Satan, who himself had rejected God's law and authority, in essence told God, "Nobody could love you for who you are! Men may love your gifts, but men will never come to love you for who you are." Satan was convinced that sin is an incurable disease and that restoration is impossible. So God said, "Let's see."

As far as Job was concerned, his story was one man struggling to understand a series of unexplained tragedies. But something much more important was happening. The story behind the story was about vindicating the name of God.

Even though Satan was a direct factor in Job's suffering, his activity was within strict limits determined by God. When suffering comes into your life, whatever its shape or cause, you have the opportunity to vindicate the name of God.

FOR FURTHER READING, SEE EPHESIANS 6

WHAT'S AT STAKE IN YOUR SUFFERING

*Job stood up and tore his robe in grief. Then he shaved his
head and fell to the ground to worship.* JOB 1:20

WHEN TRAGEDY CAME to Job and his family, it produced two entirely
different responses. Job's wife said to him, "Are you still trying to maintain your integrity? Curse God and die" (Job 2:9). That was exactly
what the devil had figured she would say. Suffering did to Job's wife
exactly what Job feared wine might do to his children: it lowered her
inhibitions and exposed what she thought.

But when Job worshiped, Satan was confounded. The worship of
one man in the middle of his suffering vindicates the name of God. I
like to think about Satan shrinking back in silence, dumbfounded by
the power of God's grace in this ordinary man's life.

Your response to God in times of trouble will be one of the most
revealing things about you. For Job's wife, integrity was a means to an
end. It was God's responsibility to fill her life with good things, keep
the family healthy, and keep the business prospering. As long as that
continued, she "loved" God.

But when suffering came to this couple, their different responses
were telling: Job loved God for who he is; his wife loved God for what
he gave. One loved God as a means to an end; the other loved God as
an end in himself. One proved that the devil is sometimes right; the
other gave evidence that the devil is ultimately wrong. It is possible for a
person to love God, not simply as a means to an end, but for who he is.

Job never knew what was at stake in his suffering. After he died and
went into the presence of God, the angels may well have said to him,
"When we heard Satan slander the name of God, we trembled, and we
held our breath as we watched to see what you would do. God placed
his name and reputation on the line, and when you worshiped, Job, we
can't tell you the shouts of joy and triumph that went up as we watched
the enemy shrink away in defeat and humiliation!"

FOR FURTHER READING, SEE 1 PETER 1

AFTER THE CRISIS

I wish [God] would crush me. . . . At least I can take comfort in this:
Despite the pain, I have not denied the words of the Holy One. JOB 6:9-10

THE UNANSWERED QUESTIONS don't go away after the funeral. (Remember, Job had lost seven sons and three daughters.) Faith may have triumphed yesterday, but there is still today, and then there will be tomorrow.

Those who have walked the path of suffering know that after the moment of crisis there is an ongoing process of living with a new and unwelcome situation. Job made a magnificent confession of faith, but he still had to find a way to get through another day with his mind in turmoil and his body in pain.

Job began to wonder how much longer he could keep this up. Sometimes he felt it would be best if his own life ended immediately; at least he could say, "I have fought the good fight and kept the faith" (see 2 Timothy 4:7). But God kept calling him to face another day, and Job didn't know how much more he could take!

There are three stages to seasickness. First you think you are going to die, then you are sure you are going to die, and then you are afraid that you might not die. Job may not have been seasick, but he was heartsick, and he had reached stage 3: he was more afraid of the pain of living and denying God than he was of dying.

Job might have looked forward to grandchildren, but his children were gone. He might have looked forward to a comfortable retirement, but his wealth was plundered. What was left for him to look forward to?

In anger, Job cried out to God, "I don't have the strength to endure. I have nothing to live for. Do I have the strength of a stone? Is my body made of bronze?" (Job 6:11-12).

It's easy to get the idea that when you're angry or in pain God must be distant. But you can find God in the middle of your anger and pain. He reaches out to you there. Job did precisely the right thing when he poured out his anger in the presence of God. That's where the journey from pain to peace begins.

FOR FURTHER READING, SEE JOB 6

WHEN NOBODY UNDERSTANDS

I know that my Redeemer lives. JOB 19:25

JOB LOOKED TO three friends—Eliphaz, Zophar, and Bildad—for support. You have to give them credit for being there, but these friends were quite certain that all suffering is a punishment for sin and that Job must have had some skeleton in his closet. Job told them he wasn't hiding anything, but they didn't believe him.

For all their sincerity, Job's friends were of no help to him whatsoever. Eventually Job said, "How long will you torture me? How long will you try to crush me with your words? You have already insulted me ten times. You should be ashamed of treating me so badly. Even if I have sinned, that is my concern, not yours" (Job 19:2-4). That's a nice way of saying, "Why don't you go away and mind your own business?"

Job's wife was ready to throw in the towel—on her faith and apparently on Job, too, for Job said, "My breath is repulsive to my wife" (Job 19:17). Sounds like she didn't want him anywhere near her, and the same was true for the other members of Job's extended family (see 19:13). Job's wife came back at the end of the story, and so did his relatives, but in the middle of his suffering, he was utterly alone.

It is difficult to imagine a more desperate situation. This man lost everything. His friends were no help to him, his wife didn't want to know him, and his health was deteriorating ("I have been reduced to skin and bones"—Job 19:20).

When there are a thousand things you don't know, affirm what you do know. Never doubt in the darkness what God has taught you in the light. In the darkness of your suffering, hold on to what you know is true.

Everything around Job was collapsing, and the only way to avoid being sucked down was to grab hold of something solid. That's what Job did when he confessed the fundamental conviction on which he would stake his life. This was Job's secret to survival: he knew there was a living Redeemer, ready and able to deliver him.

FOR FURTHER READING, SEE JOB 19

THIS IS NOT THE END

I know that my Redeemer lives, and he will stand
upon the earth at last. JOB 19:25

JOB TURNED TO his friends: "You have seen the tough situation I'm in, but I'm absolutely sure of two things: I have a Redeemer, and I know that my Redeemer lives."

If they had asked him who this Redeemer was, he wouldn't have been able to answer. All he knew was that God had somebody somewhere who would have the will and the means to do whatever was necessary to deliver Job from this mess.

Job's physical condition was getting so bad he was beginning to feel he might well die before this Redeemer appeared on the scene. But that would make no difference. He was convinced that this Redeemer would come, and even if he did not come until long after Job had died, he would still be able to deliver Job from ultimate loss.

Can you imagine the Son of God listening to this? There were at least another two thousand years before Jesus Christ came into the world. But here was a man already looking for him, staking his life on it.

After Adam and Eve sinned, God promised that someone would come to get men and women out of the mess they were in, and Job held on to that promise. He believed that the pain, suffering, and loss of life in this fallen world would not be the end.

God looked at this sinful world and said, "I can't leave them there like this. I must go down and rescue them." That took God giving up his Son. The cross tells us that when the Redeemer came, he did something more difficult than anything else God had done in all the history of the world.

The Redeemer has come and paid the price. "God paid a ransom to save you. . . . And the ransom he paid was not mere gold or silver. It was the precious blood of Christ" (1 Peter 1:18-19). And on the third day, he rose again. So even through your tears, you can say with absolute confidence, "I know that my Redeemer lives."

FOR FURTHER READING, SEE HEBREWS 7

EVEN IF I DIE . . .

After my body has decayed, yet in my body I will see God! JOB 19:26

JOB SAID TO his friends, "If I die before the Redeemer comes, some of you might be tempted to think my faith was in vain. But even though worms destroy my body, I will see God. Death will not put me beyond the range of the Redeemer's power."

Right here, at least two thousand years before Christ, it is as if God gave Job a candle in a dark room. In its short flame, this man had enough light to see that God had more in store *after* his funeral service. God "broke the power of death and illuminated the way to life and immortality through the Good News" (2 Timothy 1:10)—Good News already recorded in what is perhaps the oldest book of the Bible. Christ came into a dark room and switched on a brilliant light.

Job's wife had a very different philosophy: "What you don't get now, you won't get ever!" There are a lot of people today who would agree with her. Whatever lies on the other side of death cannot be half as attractive as life here and now!

But when Jesus Christ came into the world, he declared, "I am the resurrection and the life. Anyone who believes in me will live, even after dying" (John 11:25). In his resurrection, Christ became the prototype of a new humanity.

That means the day is coming when you will be done with sin forever. You will be responsive only to what is good and pure and true. You will be filled with all the fullness of God. Temptation will be gone, confusion past, and pain forgotten. The heaven God has planned will make the joys Adam and Eve knew in the Garden fade into insignificance.

The joys of body and soul in that life are so great that they're difficult to imagine, but God says what he has prepared is beyond anything that has ever entered our minds (see 1 Corinthians 2:9). Job discovered he was not in the land of the living on his way to the land of the dying. He was in the land of the dying, yet on his way to the land of the living.

FOR FURTHER READING, SEE 1 CORINTHIANS 2

UNANSWERED QUESTIONS

Then the LORD answered Job from the whirlwind. JOB 38:1

JOB ENDURED A period of great suffering, struggling with many unanswered questions, but then almighty God spoke to him. Later Job would say, "I had only heard about you before, but now I have seen you with my own eyes" (Job 42:5).

God gave Job not an explanation, but a revelation. This will disappoint people who are looking for an explanation for suffering. God's revelation did not answer all of Job's questions, nor does it answer all of our questions. But it does tell us who God is. When Job saw the glory of God, he was satisfied.

God asked Job nearly seventy questions that Job couldn't answer. It was as if the Lord was saying, "Job, you want to enter into God's counsel. Let's see if you are qualified." So God conducted an interview. You may have endured an interview in which high-powered people asked you hard questions, but this was the most devastating interview of all time.

Let's listen in on the interview: "Job, I understand that you want to know all things. You want to be God of the universe? That is a pretty exclusive position, so let me ask you, 'Where were you when I laid the foundations of the earth, . . . as the morning stars sang together and all the angels shouted for joy? Who kept the sea inside its boundaries?' [Job 38:4, 7-8]. Have you ever tried talking to the waves or telling the sun to rise? [see 38:11-12]. If you wish to know all things, you need to learn how to do this."

Job wanted to lay his case before God, but now, in God's presence, he was silent. He thought he needed to understand why things were happening, but now he knew this knowledge was out of his league. "I am nothing—how could I ever find the answers? I will cover my mouth with my hand" (Job 40:4).

Perhaps you have imagined that when you see God, you will ask him some pretty tough questions. But when Job was in the presence of God, it was altogether different from what he expected. He was not the one asking the questions; in God's presence, his questions melted away.

FOR FURTHER READING, SEE JOB 38

THE OUTCOME OF THE INTERVIEW

I had only heard about you before, but now I have seen you with
my own eyes. . . . I sit in dust and ashes to show my repentance. JOB 42:5-6

WHEN THE INTERVIEW finally ended, Job must have been exhausted. But when God relented, Job had an entirely new perspective on his life and his suffering: "I know that you can do anything, and no one can stop you. . . . I was talking about things I knew nothing about, things far too wonderful for me" (Job 42:2-3).

The book of Job is dominated by the opinions of his friends—Eliphaz, Bildad, and Zophar, with another man, Elihu, throwing in his long-winded contribution. When Job's friends had finished all their counsel, Job was in absolute misery. But then God took center stage. You might think God's words to this broken man seem crushing, but God's speech had exactly the opposite effect. After his encounter with God, Job was filled with a vision of the glory of the God who is sovereign over all things.

The friends had focused Job's attention inward; God focused Job's attention upward. That's what the Word of God does. It takes you outside of yourself, and it brings you to God. When Job saw the glory of God, it changed the way he was thinking and the way he was feeling. His encounter with God did not end with his saying, "Now I understand," but, "Now I repent."

Job was a man of faith. When tragedy struck, Job tore his robes and worshiped! But in the course of his suffering, and under the influence of his friends, he became increasingly consumed with himself and his unanswered questions.

Some people sin by thinking too highly of themselves, others sin by thinking too lowly of themselves, but all of us sin by thinking too *much* about ourselves. That's where Job was until the revelation of God broke through. In a fresh encounter with the living God, this man of faith once again became a worshiper.

FOR FURTHER READING, SEE JOB 42

WHAT YOU THINK ABOUT GOD

These are the visions that Isaiah son of Amoz saw . . . during the years when
Uzziah, Jotham, Ahaz, and Hezekiah were kings of Judah. ISAIAH 1:1

ISAIAH HAD A long ministry, spanning somewhere between four and six decades. But it was a vision from God given in the year King Uzziah died that would shape Isaiah's whole life and ministry.

King Uzziah ruled in Jerusalem for fifty-two years. During these years, there was a huge increase in construction, a remarkable growth in farming, and a significant strengthening of Judah's defenses. This generated a feeling of confidence among the people, and as that confidence grew, they became increasingly casual toward God.

The people offered sacrifices and observed the feasts and festivals, yet God called it "parad[ing] through my courts" (Isaiah 1:12). Their religion seemed to have little impact in their lives; God rebuked them for "bringing me your meaningless gifts" (1:13). The Temple that was once filled with God's glory was now something of a national treasure, a symbol of traditional values. There seems to have been little difference between these people and the pagan nations around them.

Their situation speaks powerfully to the church today. America is also a prospering nation where many people acknowledge God but behave in a way that is hardly different from the surrounding culture. Like the nation of Israel in the time of Isaiah, we have people who participate in worship services and lie to their parents, claim false expense reimbursements from their employers, abort their babies, cheat on their spouses, and throw themselves into materialism. The important thing to grasp is that this is not new. It always happens when people lose their vision of God.

What you think about God is the clearest indicator of where your spiritual future will be. If a man thinks of God only as loving and forgiving, we should not expect him to be too diligent in the pursuit of a moral life. If a woman thinks of God primarily as someone who affirms everyone, then it should not surprise us if she feels affirmed even while she is still in her sins. The great issue in Isaiah's time, and in ours, is that many people have lost sight of the awesome holiness of God.

FOR FURTHER READING, SEE 2 TIMOTHY 3

LOSING SIGHT OF THE GLORY OF GOD

It was in the year King Uzziah died that I saw the Lord. ISAIAH 6:1

WHEN GOD'S PEOPLE lost sight of his glory, he revealed himself to one man and commissioned him to tell the people who God is. Isaiah was given that incredible privilege and awesome responsibility.

When Isaiah says he "saw the Lord," one wonders what he actually saw. What does God look like? Isaiah writes, "He was sitting on a lofty throne, and the train of his robe filled the Temple" (Isaiah 6:1). We wait for more, but that is all that Isaiah can say.

When Moses saw the God of Israel, he said, "Under his feet there seemed to be a surface of brilliant blue lapis lazuli, as clear as the sky itself" (Exodus 24:10). Moses could not look directly at God's glory; he could only describe the brightness beneath God's feet.

When John saw the glory of the risen Christ, he said, "His face was like the sun in all its brilliance" (Revelation 1:16). You can't look directly at the sun. John is telling us, "I couldn't look into the face of Christ; his glory was too bright."

Let's go back to this curious detail in Isaiah's vision: "The train of his robe filled the Temple." The Temple was an enormous building that had taken years to build. But the whole place could scarcely contain the end of God's robe!

Then Isaiah tells us what he heard—seraphs, or angelic creatures, calling out to one another, "Holy, holy, holy is the LORD of Heaven's Armies!" (Isaiah 6:3). If we want to emphasize something, we can underline it or put it in italics. There is only one truth in the whole of the Bible that is *triple underlined*, and that is the holiness of God.

There is never a time when the Bible says that God is "wrath, wrath, wrath" or "love, love, love." The holiness of God is so foundational to who God is that if we do not grasp his holiness, we do not know him as he is.

FOR FURTHER READING, SEE ISAIAH 6

WHEN GOD CAME DOWN

*Attending [the Lord] were mighty seraphim, each having six
wings. With two wings they covered their faces, with two they
covered their feet, and with two they flew.* ISAIAH 6:2

THE BEST WAY to understand fire is by observing its effect. What happens
when fire touches something will give you some sense of the awesome
thing that it is. Similarly, the best way to understand the holiness of God
is by watching its effect.

The seraphim were calling to each other, announcing the presence
of God. You would think that angels, who inhabit heaven, would be
comfortable in the immediate presence of God, but they were covering
their faces. Why would they do that?

These angels had nothing to be ashamed of—their lives were spent
in obedience to God. The angels covered their faces because they are
creatures, awed in the presence of their Creator. If you were to live a
perfect life and then enter the presence of God, you would still tremble
in awe before the glory of your Creator.

When God came down, the foundations of the Temple shook, and
it was filled with smoke (see Isaiah 6:4). This must have been absolutely
terrifying; the earth shook like an earthquake when God came near.
How could the people who worship this God possibly be satisfied to
remain "a sinful nation . . . loaded down with a burden of guilt" (1:4)?

In Isaiah's day thousands of people crowded into the Temple, enjoying
their favorite music and hearing positive messages, but never experiencing God's presence. It would never have occurred to them that if God
came near, the very foundations of the building would shake. If you think
God is boring, then you have never encountered the God of the Bible.

The great irony about the worshipers in Isaiah's day is that they were
the people of God, but they did not know God. They had no experience
of the God they claimed to be worshiping. So God revealed himself to
one man in order that he could bring God's truth to his generation.
As you rediscover the awesome holiness of God, you, like Isaiah, will
appreciate the wonder of what God has done for you in Jesus Christ,
and your greatest privilege in life will be to serve this awesome, glorious, holy God.

FOR FURTHER READING, SEE HEBREWS 12

COMING APART AT THE SEAMS

Woe is me! For I am lost. ISAIAH 6:5, ESV

THE MOST SIGNIFICANT effect of God's holiness was not on the angels or on the foundations of the Temple, but on Isaiah the prophet. The word translated *lost* literally means "coming apart at the seams." If someone is competent or successful, we sometimes say, "He's got it all together." But when Isaiah saw God, he said, "It all fell apart."

Isaiah had already been engaged for some time in a prophetic ministry of speaking the Word of God, and he was one of the most respected people of his day. Up until this point in his ministry, he had been saying "woe" to all kinds of people, but now in the presence of God, he can only say "woe" to himself! The holiness of God makes even the best people feel their own sinfulness.

Isaiah felt that sin had infected the area of his greatest gift: "I have filthy lips" (Isaiah 6:5). As a preacher and a prophet, Isaiah used his lips as the tools of his ministry. But in the presence of God, he felt that even his greatest gift had to be cleansed lest it be subverted for another purpose. Similarly, our best efforts need God's cleansing lest they be subverted by sin—"Our righteous deeds . . . are nothing but filthy rags" (64:6). Sometimes even our greatest strength will become the point at which we are most vulnerable to the sin of pride.

Then Isaiah said, "I live among a people with filthy lips" (Isaiah 6:5). Things he had become used to now seemed dirty to him. He had a new sensitivity to just how far the whole community was from the purity of God.

Some people spend their whole lives avoiding the woe that Isaiah experienced in the presence of God. But a God who loves and forgives is compelling only to those who have stood in his presence and have felt their need for forgiveness. Your need for Jesus Christ will not become evident to you until you have seen the holiness of God.

FOR FURTHER READING, SEE LUKE 5

THE FOUNDATION FOR MINISTRY

He touched my lips with [a burning coal] and said,
"See, this coal has touched your lips. Now your guilt is
removed, and your sins are forgiven." ISAIAH 6:7

THE KNOWLEDGE OF the Holy One leads people to feel that they have come apart at the seams, that their whole lives have been unraveled—but God will never leave them there.

After Isaiah had seen the glory of God and the seraphim had announced the imminent presence of the holiness of God, smoke filled the Temple. So after a momentary glimpse of the glory of God, Isaiah was surrounded by darkness. He was conscious of the presence of God, but God was hidden from his view. Then the foundations of the Temple shook. It must have been absolutely terrifying!

As Isaiah peered into the smoke, one of the angels came toward him with a burning coal he had taken from the altar with a pair of tongs. He pressed the hot coal to Isaiah's lips. It seared the prophet's flesh. Then the angel said, "See, this coal has touched your lips. Now your guilt is removed, and your sins are forgiven" (Isaiah 6:7).

The altar was the place where the sacrifice of atonement was made. Now the effect of that atonement was applied to Isaiah's particular need. Isaiah had made his confession, "I have filthy lips," and now the angel of God said, "Your guilt is removed" (Isaiah 6:7).

God's grace had touched Isaiah's life at the point of his deepest need, and this was the foundation for a life of ministry. Having discovered the grace of God in this personal way, Isaiah wanted to serve: "I heard the Lord asking, 'Whom should I send as a messenger to this people? Who will go for us?' I said, 'Here I am. Send me'" (Isaiah 6:8).

And God sent Isaiah, almost as if saying, "You go, Isaiah, because you've understood who I am, you know what sin is, and you have grasped what grace is." Isaiah went out into a culture that had lost touch with the reality of God, to make him known, just as you are called to do if you have received God's grace.

FOR FURTHER READING, SEE 1 TIMOTHY 1

A FATAL MISTAKE

Hezekiah . . . showed [the Babylonian envoys] everything in
his treasure-houses—the silver, the gold, the spices, and the
aromatic oils. . . . There was nothing in his palace or kingdom
that Hezekiah did not show them. ISAIAH 39:2

WHEN HEZEKIAH BECAME king of Judah, the world superpower Assyria had already invaded the northern kingdom of Israel. Assyria then scattered the ten tribes, and its empire extended right up to the borders of Judah.

Soon afterward, Sennacherib, the king of Assyria, was camped outside Jerusalem, but Hezekiah managed to buy him off with silver and gold. Hezekiah had the gold plating removed from the doors and the doorposts of the Temple. Payments for peace are rarely successful, and it was not long before Sennacherib was back at the gates of Jerusalem, intimidating Hezekiah's army. Then God intervened, and a plague hit Sennacherib's army. They withdrew. God had delivered!

Sometime later, God spared Hezekiah from a terminal illness (see 2 Kings 20:1-6). When the king of Babylon heard about Hezekiah's health, he sent messengers bearing gifts. But by the time they arrived, Hezekiah had already recovered. He welcomed these messengers and showed them all the riches of his kingdom. That was a fatal mistake. Isaiah told him that Assyria's power would decline and that Babylon's power would rise. Hezekiah had just shown all his treasures to his future enemy.

Isaiah prophesied, "The time is coming when everything in your palace . . . will be carried off to Babylon" (2 Kings 20:17). And that's exactly what happened. Babylon became a world superpower, and one hundred years after Hezekiah's death, under the leadership of Nebuchadnezzar, the Babylonian army reduced Jerusalem to a heap of rubble and deported the most able people.

God was in control when Sennacherib's armies came to the gate of Jerusalem and when they suddenly withdrew in retreat. God was in control when Assyria's power weakened and when Babylon's power rose. God was as much in control when Jerusalem was destroyed and the exiles were taken off to Babylon as he was when Nehemiah led the exiles back and Jerusalem was rebuilt. Keep that in mind today: no matter what you are facing, God is in control.

FOR FURTHER READING, SEE ISAIAH 39

WHEN YOU CAN'T FIX IT

God sits above the circle of the earth. The people below seem like
grasshoppers to him! . . . He judges the great people of the world
and brings them all to nothing. They hardly get started, barely taking
root, when he blows on them and they wither. ISAIAH 40:22-24

GOD'S PEOPLE HAD all kinds of hopes and dreams, but Isaiah's prophecy about the rise of Babylon made it clear that the future would bring hardship and suffering.

We thrive on solutions, but what about the things we cannot fix—serious illness, crippling disability, or irreplaceable loss? People may pray for a miracle, but what if God has called you to live with a burden that will not be lifted? There's a hollow sound when people say, "I hope things will be better soon," because deep in your heart you feel that they may well get worse.

How do we find strength when the future does not hold hope for something better, but dread of something worse? This is God's Word to people who have just received devastating news: "'Comfort, comfort my people,' says your God. 'Speak tenderly to Jerusalem'" (Isaiah 40:1-2).

When God tells Isaiah to comfort his people, Isaiah's response is predictable: "What should I [say]?" (Isaiah 40:6). Isaiah is told to remind the people that God is in control, reigning over all the events of history. This is God's Word to people who face circumstances in which there is no reasonable prospect of change.

God is in control in our disasters and in our triumphs. On the darkest day in human history, when God's own Son was nailed to a cross, God was in control. And on the greatest day in human history, when Christ rose from the dead, God was in control.

God is in control through the darkest day of your life. The sovereignty of God does not make God the author of evil, but it does mean that no evil, however great, can finally overturn the purpose of God. Feed your faith on God's sovereignty.

FOR FURTHER READING, SEE ISAIAH 40

EVEN WORLD-CLASS ATHLETES

He gives power to the weak and strength to the powerless. Even youths
will become weak and tired, and young men will fall in exhaustion.
But those who trust in the LORD will find new strength. ISAIAH 40:29-31

ISAIAH REMINDS THE people that God will sustain them. God knows
that unrelenting pressures can wear us down. Even at our strongest, we
do not have unlimited resources—"even youths will become weak and
tired." The word Isaiah uses for "young men" is related to a word that
means "chosen men." So Isaiah is talking about men who are the pick
of the bunch, like athletes who would catch a recruiter's eye.

Even Olympic athletes at the very peak of conditioning have limited
resources and strength. And when that strength is drained, they will
stumble and fall, but those who hope in God will renew their strength.
Those who know that God is in control and believe that he will fulfill
his purposes will be given the ability to persevere.

When Jesus Christ came into the world, his disciples had great
hopes and dreams about what the future might hold. And then the
unthinkable happened: Christ was crucified. It must have seemed to
the disciples that God's purposes had been thwarted. And yet God was
in control even when evil was unleashed in its most horrendous and
violent form—the death of God's Son. There is a deep mystery in this,
but God's greatest purpose was fulfilled in the world's darkest hour.

Think about this when it seems that your life has been thrown into
chaos or confusion. What has taken you by surprise and brought you
deep disappointment was always known to God, and it has its place in
his purpose.

God leads his people through some pretty dark valleys, where it will
not be possible for us to see what he is doing, but he promises to sustain
us while we walk through them: "If you are walking in darkness without
a ray of light, trust in the LORD and rely on your God" (Isaiah 50:10).
This is the foundation of your faith.

FOR FURTHER READING, SEE JOHN 16

WHAT WOULD IT TAKE?

Look at my servant . . . ISAIAH 42:1

GOD CALLED HIS people to be a model community in the world. They were to live by his laws and bear his name. But they became divided and then turned to other gods. Now they were coming under God's discipline. Isaiah prophesied that Jerusalem, the place where God had put his name, would become a smoldering ruin. So what hope would there be of God's blessing coming to the nations?

God told Isaiah to comfort his people. He told them that he was in control, that he would sustain his people through the dark times, and that his purposes would be fulfilled. God's people must have wondered how this could possibly happen. What would it take to get the will of God done?

At this point in the story, we are introduced to someone who is simply called the "servant." A servant is a person who gets his master's will done. If you are a servant, your job description is very simple—whatever your master tells you to do, do it! The servant waits on his or her master, doing what the master wants.

God introduces the servant, essentially saying, "Let me tell you about the person who will get my will done in the world." God is telling us how his ancient promise to Abraham to bless his people and to bless the nations will be fulfilled. As we read through the book of Isaiah, it becomes increasingly obvious that this servant is of great importance. He is the executor of the will of God, and he delivers the promises of God.

When we come to the New Testament, the servant is clearly identified with our Lord Jesus Christ. But before we see how Jesus fulfills the role of the servant, it is important to remember that Isaiah was speaking to the people of God seven hundred years before Christ came into the world. God was telling his people, long before Jesus was born, that he would accomplish his will through a coming servant.

FOR FURTHER READING, SEE JOHN 13

MAKING MAXIMUM IMPACT

Look at my servant, whom I strengthen. He is my chosen one,
who pleases me. I have put my Spirit upon him. He will
bring justice to the nations. ISAIAH 42:1

GOD'S SERVANT HAS some remarkable privileges! This servant will be chosen, loved, anointed, and sustained in his ministry. The servant's calling is to bring justice to the nations. This is more than getting right decisions in a court of law. The servant's task is to put things in order and make them as they ought to be.

By any standards, that is an extraordinary ministry, and when God tells us about the magnificent results of the servant's ministry—"he will not falter or lose heart until justice prevails throughout the earth" (Isaiah 42:4)—we are bound to ask how this kind of transformation could possibly be achieved.

How would a servant of God go about changing the world? If you were casting a vision for a ministry that would restore right order in the world, where would you begin? Perhaps you would call a national press conference, initiate an education program, or go on the road in a white suit to lead religious revival meetings. The servant Isaiah was describing would do none of these things: "He will not shout or raise his voice in public" (Isaiah 42:2).

God was saying, "The person I am going to use to get my will done is not going to have anything of the showman about him. He will not promote himself. He will not be the kind of person who tries to dominate everybody else. He will not shout. In fact, the outstanding thing about him will be the quietness of his ministry. He will get on with doing my will without drawing attention to himself."

God's words about the servant give us a pattern for the kind of ministry that will get his will done in dark places and the kind of person God will use to bring his blessing to the nations. How does this mesh with your ideas about effective ministry and the kind of person that God uses?

FOR FURTHER READING, SEE ISAIAH 42

THE POWER OF COMPASSION

*He will not crush the weakest reed or put out
a flickering candle.* ISAIAH 42:3

FEW PEOPLE TRY to mend broken reeds. When a reed bends, it usually
gets trampled on, so the instinctive thing to do is break it off. If a candle
is almost burned out on your dinner table, you snuff it out and get
another one. But God says his servant will not be like that. He will show
compassion.

Our world is full of bruised reeds. Perhaps you identify with that
description. You have been hit by something, and it has bruised and
broken you. You can hardly stand up under its crushing weight. Take
heart: God's servant will support you.

Perhaps you relate to the picture of a smoldering wick. There was a
time when you were burning with passion for the Lord, but now you're
running low. Your inner resources of faith, hope, and love seem to be
flickering. Having thrown yourself into ministry *for* God, you now stand
in desperate need of ministry *from* God.

Broken, bruised, and burned-out people will usually not be drawn to
the loudmouthed showman. People who feel that their lives are flickering will not be helped by high-impact promotions. The servant who
gets God's will done will have a quiet ministry that touches the lives of
wounded people with great compassion, right where they are.

This kind of ministry can seem slow and discouraging. Those who
are looking for quick results and glowing reports will not find ministry
like this easy or attractive. But God's servants will stick to their ministry
and "will bring justice to all who have been wronged"; they "will not
falter or lose heart" (Isaiah 42:3-4).

The servants God uses to get his will done in the world—any servant
that is useful to God—have hearts of compassion for the broken and the
bruised. They do not get discouraged but are sustained by the power of
the Spirit—not by seeing their own name in lights. If you want to be useful in God's ministry, cultivate humility, compassion, and faithfulness.

FOR FURTHER READING, SEE MATTHEW 12

THE SCALE OF THE CHALLENGE

*[He will] open the eyes of the blind . . . [and] free the captives from
prison, releasing those who sit in dark dungeons.* ISAIAH 42:7

THE PEOPLE TO whom God sends his servant are not only bruised and
broken, but blinded and bound. The servant faces an overwhelming
challenge. Sin *blinds* us to God's glory and *binds* us by its power. So if the
blessing of God is to flow to the nations, there must be healing from
sin's blindness and freedom from sin's power.

The scale of the challenge that God's servants face today points us to
the resources needed for ministry. If people had the capacity of spiritual sight, it would be enough simply to flood the world with the Good
News. People would immediately see their need of the gospel and come
to Christ.

But the problem God's servants face is that even when they have
described the glory of God and the Good News of the gospel, their
hearers lack the capacity to appreciate this truth and respond to it. They
are blind. Even if they had the capacity to see clearly, they are incapable of responding positively to God because they are bound. If sin
were simply a choice, it would be relatively easy to give people guidance
toward better choices. But sin is a power.

Effective ministry is never less than proclamation, but it is always
much more than that. God's servants are utterly dependent on him.
Unless he creates the capacity for spiritual sight and for spiritual life,
making it possible to see God's glory and respond to God's law when it
is proclaimed, the servants' hearers are like blind people in an art gallery
or bound prisoners with a map.

God's purposes do not depend on programs or personalities—even
those that declare God's glory and call people to repentance and faith.
His will is accomplished as his servants look to Jesus Christ, the Servant
of God, to create the capacity for spiritual sight and the ability to fulfill
his law.

FOR FURTHER READING, SEE 2 CORINTHIANS 4

WHO FITS THE PROFILE?

Israel my servant, Jacob my chosen one, descended from
Abraham my friend, I have called you back from the ends of
the earth, saying, "You are my servant." ISAIAH 41:8-9

AS GOD GAVE more information about his servant, his people would have become increasingly curious. Who might fulfill this role? Certainly Isaiah must have wondered who could possibly fit the profile.

When God first spoke about the servant, it must have seemed he was talking about Israel. God said to them, "I will be your God, and you will be my people" (Leviticus 26:12). God's people had been given the light of God's truth, and they had been given the Law and the sacrifices. They were to be the channel through which his name would be known and his blessing would flow to the nations.

But God's people could not live up to their calling. The servant was to bring sight to the blind and to release those who were bound, but God said, "Who is as blind as my own people, my servant? Who is as deaf as my messenger?" (Isaiah 42:19). And he added, "You see and recognize what is right but refuse to act on it. You hear with your ears, but you don't really listen. . . . [The Lord's] people have been robbed and plundered, enslaved, imprisoned, and trapped . . . and have no one to protect them, no one to take them back home" (42:20, 22).

The servants who were supposed to bring sight and freedom to others were blind and bound themselves! The servants, who were called to *give* ministry, turned out to be the very people who needed to *receive* ministry!

The prospect of God's blessing coming to the nations must have seemed bleak at this point. Israel was chosen as God's servant, but its people were not in a position to fulfill their role. Before Israel could bring light to the nations, it needed someone to bring light to it.

When Jesus Christ came into the world, he announced, "I am the light of the world. If you follow me, you won't have to walk in darkness, because you will have the light that leads to life" (John 8:12). Finally, Jesus is the servant who is in a position to bring hope to the nations.

FOR FURTHER READING, SEE ISAIAH 41

WHAT DID HE LOOK LIKE?

He said to me, "You are my servant." ISAIAH 49:3

WHEN GOD SPEAKS about the servant again, he is talking about an individual. It sounds as if God might be calling Isaiah to be that person.

Listen to the scope of this ministry: "You will do more than restore the people of Israel to me. I will make you a light to the Gentiles, and you will bring my salvation to the ends of the earth" (Isaiah 49:6). Isaiah knew the job was beyond him: "My work seems so useless! I have spent my strength for nothing and to no purpose" (49:4). That was true. The people were remarkably unresponsive to Isaiah's ministry.

No prophet in the Bible had ever achieved the ministry scope that God attributes to his servant. Isaiah was so staggered, he hardly knew what to say: "Who has believed our message? To whom has the LORD revealed his powerful arm?" (Isaiah 53:1). Isaiah seems to say, "If I tell you what I saw, you won't believe it."

What did the servant look like? "That's what I can't get over," Isaiah reports. "I saw him despised, and I saw violence poured out on him. He was so disfigured, people were hiding their faces from him, while others were saying, 'He's getting what he deserves.' It just doesn't make sense."

And yet, "it was the LORD's good plan to crush him" (Isaiah 53:10). His suffering and death were God's plan! God's servant would bring the blessing of God to all nations *through* his suffering and death, and "the LORD's good plan will prosper in his hands" (53:10).

Christ fulfilled what Isaiah saw dimly and could not fully understand: "He was pierced for our rebellion, crushed for our sins. He was beaten so we could be whole. He was whipped so we could be healed" (Isaiah 53:5). The cross was necessary because "all of us, like sheep, have strayed away. We have left God's paths to follow our own. Yet the LORD laid on him the sins of us all" (53:6).

All of the sin, failure, pride, and selfishness that belong to those who wish to be God's servants are laid upon Jesus, who is God's Servant. What no nation or prophet could ever accomplish, Christ achieved.

FOR FURTHER READING, SEE ISAIAH 53

THE TRADER REVEALED

Is anyone thirsty? Come and drink—even if you have no money!
Come, take your choice of wine or milk—it's all free! ISAIAH 55:1

IN THE TOWN where my wife, Karen, and I used to live in north London, market day was every Thursday and Saturday. The crews would arrive at around six in the morning to set up the scaffolding and the canopies for the stalls.

There were stalls with fruit and vegetables, a luggage rack, clothing stalls, and a man who, strangely, seemed to do nothing but sell parts for vacuum cleaners. The place was always teeming with people who were milling around, looking for a bargain.

One of the enjoyable things about markets is the noise and banter of the traders. When the market gets going, the whole place is a cacophony of voices. The traders' stalls were probably no more than six feet apart, and as you wandered between them, the traders would try to attract your attention . . .

"New towels—feel the softness!"

"Handmade luggage—unbeatable prices!"

It was almost a relief to go past the man selling parts for vacuum cleaners. He just sat there lost in a book he was reading.

Imagine yourself walking in the marketplace among the stalls of traders, with many voices calling out to you. Back there in the third row on the left, you see a stall. The trader is quiet compared to most, but ready to make a special offer.

God uses the picture of a marketplace to explain his incredible offer to us: "Come and drink—even if you have no money! Come, take your choice of wine or milk—it's all free! . . . Listen to me, and you will eat what is good. You will enjoy the finest food. Come to me with your ears wide open. Listen, and you will find life" (Isaiah 55:1-3).

Centuries later, Jesus took up these words and applied them to himself: "Anyone who is thirsty may come to me!" (John 7:37). Christ is calling out to attract the attention of any who will listen. He is one voice among many, and he invites you to come over to his stall, where he offers to satisfy your deepest thirst.

FOR FURTHER READING, SEE ISAIAH 55

CALLING OUT IN THE MARKETPLACE

Why spend your money on food that does not give you strength?
Why pay for food that does you no good? ISAIAH 55:2

JESUS' INVITATION GOES out, but some people in the marketplace are preoccupied at other stalls. They are within earshot of the invitation, but it is drowned out by other voices and interests. The street trader is competing for an audience, calling out to people as they rummage through the products displayed in other stalls.

Some people are preoccupied at the stalls marked "Sports" or "Marriage." Others are rummaging around in stalls marked "Careers" or "Popularity" or "Family." Many of those stalls have good things, but Christ is saying to us, "Come over here; I have something to offer that you will not find anywhere else."

Other people don't hear the invitation. When dinner is ready in our home, either Karen or I will usually shout, "Dinner's ready!" so that our boys know it's time to come. Sometimes there is no response, and one of us goes downstairs to investigate. Often the problem is very simple—headphones!

In one sense, it's not the boys' fault that they don't hear. The blockage over their ears prevents them from hearing the call. Some people do not hear Christ's invitation because there is a spiritual blockage in their lives. If we knowingly hold on to something that God forbids, it can prevent us from hearing the voice of God.

Others are not listening to the call of Christ because of prejudice. I'm like this myself with phone services. We've had so many calls from them lately that I've lost interest in hearing. I'm prejudiced. Their offer may actually be better than the phone service we have, but I'm not listening. If they call with another deal, I want to say, "No thanks. I've already made up my mind. Thank you and good-bye."

That's how some people feel about Christ—"I made up my mind long ago; I don't need to hear about him again." But Christ is still calling out in the marketplace to all who will listen. He has something to offer that is not available in any other stall, and he wants us to have it.

FOR FURTHER READING, SEE LUKE 14

ONE-OF-A-KIND OFFER

Come, everyone who thirsts, come to the waters. ISAIAH 55:1, ESV

WHEN YOU GO into a store, it's frustrating if you find that the sales assistant knows less than you do about the product being sold! A good trader will tell you what a product will do and why it is of value. What exactly is Christ's offer? The Trader offers to meet the fundamental thirsts of the human soul, to satisfy the deep desires God has created within us.

When Adam and Eve were in the Garden, their every thirst was fully satisfied. But when sin entered the world, they found that things went strangely wrong. Their marriage, which had been so wonderful, seemed to change as they blamed each other for their problems. Their work, which had given them such joy, was now mixed with frustration. Their bodies, which had been so healthy, began to age, and they began to experience pain. They wondered what was wrong with them.

Have you ever wondered why there are deep thirsts in your soul? Adam and Eve knew the answer. In the Garden, they had walked with God, but that changed when they were thrown out. Now they were separated from God, and they were thirsty.

We experience the same thirsts and find ourselves in the marketplace of the world trying to find fulfillment, satisfaction, and life. That is why Jesus announced one day, "Anyone who is thirsty may come to me . . . and drink!" (John 7:37-38). Christ is calling out to us: "Come over here! I can satisfy the deep thirsts in your soul."

That is why Jesus came into the world, "that [we] may have life, and have it to the full" (John 10:10, NIV). Jesus came to restore what was lost in the Garden to all who will receive him. At the end of the Bible story, we can read John's description of heaven, where the Shepherd "will lead them to springs of life-giving water" (Revelation 7:17). One of the joys of life in heaven is that we will always be satisfied, and yet Christ will continually lead his people into new discoveries of delight.

FOR FURTHER READING, SEE REVELATION 7

THE PRICE IS RIGHT

Come, buy . . . without money and without cost. ISAIAH 55:1, NIV

SELLING IS USUALLY about the trader arguing the customer up to his price, but here we have Christ arguing the price down! He conducts an auction in reverse, because he has chosen to sell to the lowest bidder.

Imagine the auction, where Christ is standing in his stall. "I am pleased to offer total forgiveness and reconciliation with God," he says. "This offer includes everlasting life, and it's available today to the *lowest* bidder."

A man in a pin-striped suit steps forward with the first bid. "I've led a good life and run an honest business," he argues. "I've been faithful to my wife, and I've served on the boards of three charitable organizations. I'd like to offer these good works." A murmur rises from the crowd. "It's with the man in the pin-striped suit," says the Seller.

Then a lady in a red coat lifts her hand. "I haven't done nearly as much as he has," she says, "but I've attended church faithfully, and I've had wonderful experiences with God."

The auctioneer motions. "It's with the lady in the red coat."

A girl in blue jeans raises her hand. "I haven't attended church, but I've tried to live a life that's pleasing to God."

The auctioneer says, "That's not much. Do I hear any other bids?"

A boy in tattered clothes stands up. "I'm not sure I'm truly sorry—there are some things I said I was sorry for, but then I did them again! At least I can say, 'I believe.'"

This isn't a battle of pride; it's a battle of blushes. People are opting out, not because the cost is too high, but because the offers are embarrassingly low. Then someone steps forward: "My works aren't what they should be. My repentance isn't what it should be, and neither is my faith. I have nothing to offer." The auctioneer brings down his hammer. "It's yours!" he says.

God has made it so that every one of us can make the lowest offer. Only pride stands in your way. If all you've ever done is offer things to God, your hands are full. Lay aside your works and come to Christ empty-handed so you can receive what he offers.

FOR FURTHER READING, SEE 1 CORINTHIANS 1

MAKING THE PURCHASE

Come, buy . . . ISAIAH 55:1, NIV

WHY DOES CHRIST talk about "buying" when there is no actual payment? Because salvation comes at a price, even though that price is not paid by us. How did he obtain the blessing he offers? He bought it, at the price of his own blood.

"Buying" also indicates that a transaction has taken place. There is a definite transaction in which what was obtained by Christ actually becomes yours. Unless this takes place, what Christ offers remains in the stall. It is his and not yours.

Some people enjoy window-shopping, and there's nothing wrong with that. That's where some people are spiritually. They hear Christ's invitation and come over to his stall, asking questions about the Bible and salvation. But looking isn't buying. The greatest commitment of your life is worthy of the deepest investigation, so look into the claims of Christ carefully. But don't confuse looking with buying.

Trying isn't buying either. I'm thankful for that, because if we had bought every dress my wife has ever tried on, we'd be bankrupt! But trying isn't buying. You can hang out in a store from nine to five, Monday through Friday, and never buy. And you can come to church, read the Bible, join a study group, and still never close the deal with Christ. You can feel that you *should* buy and never actually buy.

And knowing isn't buying. We were looking at washing machines a few months ago. We did our research and found a brilliant sales assistant; he was like an encyclopedia of washing machines. But eventually he told us he didn't own a washing machine. He knew all about the products, but he had never purchased one himself! Maybe that is where you are spiritually. You have learned many things about Jesus, but what he offers has not yet become yours. Knowing isn't buying.

There's a time for doing research, but if you are going to buy, there must come a point when you make a decision and close the deal. When you buy, what Christ offers becomes yours. Christ says, "Come, buy . . ." Are you ready to buy?

FOR FURTHER READING, SEE ROMANS 4

A BIG DISAPPOINTMENT

Judah has never sincerely returned to me. JEREMIAH 3:10

GOD'S WORD FIRST came to Jeremiah the prophet during the reign of Josiah. It must have been a great relief when Josiah came to the throne, because Israel had suffered under the rule of Manasseh for fifty-five years. Manasseh had promoted the worship of other gods and sacrificed his own children in the fire. There was so little interest in God's truth during his reign that God's Law was lost in the Temple.

But when Josiah came to the throne, the book of God's Law was found. The king asked for the Scriptures to be read to him, and when he heard them for the first time, he tore his clothes. That was an ancient way of saying, "We're not doing this! The way we're living is nothing like the way God's people are supposed to live!" Josiah personally supervised the dismantling of all pagan worship sites, reinstated the Passover feast, and called on the people to return to God (see 2 Kings 22–23).

Jeremiah's ministry began during this moral reformation, and God told him, "Jeremiah, you've seen this great campaign led by the king. The pagan shrines are gone, and the Passover is being observed. There has been some change of behavior, but it has not touched the hearts of my people."

Jehoiakim succeeded his father, Josiah, but the new king went in the opposite direction. The king had his secretary read a few columns of God's Word from a scroll, then he took his penknife, cut them off, and threw them in the fire (see Jeremiah 36:21-25). Jehoiakim threw God's Word into the fire piece by piece until the whole scroll was burned. What a contrast! Josiah heard the Word of God and tore his clothes in repentance. Jehoiakim heard the Word of God and tore the Scriptures, tossing them into the fire.

Jeremiah prophesied through the reigns of both these kings. He saw some outward change during the time of Josiah, but when the next king came to the throne, things went back to the way they had been. Jeremiah must have wondered, *If Josiah's massive moral crusade can't change the people, what will?*

FOR FURTHER READING, SEE JEREMIAH 3

A PROMISE FOR THE DISCOURAGED

This is the new covenant I will make with the people of
Israel. . . . I will put my instructions deep within them, and
I will write them on their hearts. JEREMIAH 31:33

GOD GAVE A wonderful promise to the discouraged prophet: "Jeremiah,
let me tell you what I am going to do. You experienced the disappointment of Josiah's noble attempt to change the nation. You saw how little
is achieved by imposing the truth on people. It simply cannot be done.
So, here's what I am going to do . . ."

God told Jeremiah he would make a new covenant, and the heart
of the new covenant would be a change in the heart. In effect, God was
saying, "In the new covenant, it will not be necessary for a king to tell the
people, 'You must . . .' I will change the heart, by my Spirit, bringing
people to the place of saying, 'We will.'"

Perhaps you have been searching for this for a long time. I have
lost count of how many people have said to me, "Pastor, I was taken to
church as a child, and I hated it. I didn't understand what was being
said, and when I did, it made me feel bad. It was boring, and I could
not see how it was relevant to life. The whole thing was a matter of duty
imposed on me, so as soon as I had the opportunity, I broke free."

If that was your experience, you have probably rejected a system of
religious rules and duties. But perhaps there is something within you
that still wonders if you can know and love God from the heart. This is
exactly what God is talking about here.

The "Good News" of the gospel is that God does more than just forgive your sins. Although this would clear away the penalty of your past
sins, you would be left with the same inclination to sin in the future.
The promise of the gospel includes a new heart. And if God gives you
a new heart, what once felt like a duty imposed on you can become a
delight that arises from within you.

FOR FURTHER READING, SEE JEREMIAH 31

THE PROBLEM WITH THE HEART

*The human heart is the most deceitful of all things, and desperately
wicked. Who really knows how bad it is?* JEREMIAH 17:9

THIS IS THE fundamental problem of the human heart: the heart is
devious and quite baffling. You cannot predict the direction the heart
will lean.

God gave Jeremiah this picture: "The sin of Judah is inscribed with
an iron chisel—engraved with a diamond point on their stony hearts"
(Jeremiah 17:1). Suppose thieves break into your home and ransack
it, spraying graffiti on the walls. That's what it's like when you sin—
an enemy comes in and writes all the wrong things on your heart!

But sin gets written not only on the human heart, but also "on the
corners of [the] altars" (Jeremiah 17:1). That's the place where God's
presence is. If I sin, my sin brings guilt into the presence of God, and
I need to be forgiven.

When sin gets written on our hearts, it becomes engraved on our
character. It creates the power of habit within us and sets up all kinds of
battles once it has gained access to the private world of the heart.

For some people, the heart has become a place where ugly, foul, and
obscene things are deeply engraved. It's not easy to live with a heart like
that. For others, the defacing effects of sin have been less severe, but
the Bible is clear in telling us that, to some degree, sin is scrawled over
every human heart.

When King David sinned, he knew his sin was written in God's presence, so he prayed, "Purify me from my sins, and I will be clean; wash me,
and I will be whiter than snow" (Psalm 51:7). But David knew he needed
more than forgiveness. He said, "Create in me a clean heart, O God"
(51:10). He asked God to deal with his heart because he knew that, unless
there was a change, his heart would lead him on the same path.

Our actions are not random; they're the fruit of the prevailing dis-
positions of our hearts. Our actions are the fruit grown in the secret
garden of the heart.

FOR FURTHER READING, SEE JEREMIAH 17

MORE THAN BEHAVIOR MODIFICATION

*You shall love the LORD your God with all your heart and with all
your soul and with all your might. And these words that I command
you today shall be on your heart.* DEUTERONOMY 6:5-6, ESV

WHEN GOD SPEAKS about the heart, he is talking about the prevailing
disposition of the soul that governs your thinking, your feeling, and
your choices. We sometimes talk about "the way we're wired." That gets
at it. When we talk about the heart, we're talking about the absolute
foundation of a person's whole being.

God said that he would write his law on the hearts of the people.
This would be quite a transformation, considering that the graffiti of
sin was scrawled all over their hearts. It would be like decorating a room
that had been vandalized and violated.

This is the fundamental change that every one of us needs. If you're
going to live the life that God calls you to lead, then his law will need to
be worked into the very core of your being so that it's not a set of external
rules but a set of inward desires.

The Old Testament story shows us that we cannot live a righteous
life simply because God says, "You shall." If we're to become who God
wants us to be, there must be an inner transformation that brings us to
the point of saying freely, "I will."

God is looking for more than behavior modification. It is not
enough simply that we stop stealing, lying, and coveting. God wants to
clean up the graffiti in the heart.

Some people think that in the Old Testament God was interested in
rules, regulations, and duties, but in the New Testament he introduced
a new religion of the heart. But there is only one God and only one
story. Right from the beginning, God made it clear that the only way
we can become who he calls us to be is through a change in the heart.
This has always been the purpose of God. The question is, how can we
get the law of God into our hearts?

FOR FURTHER READING, SEE GALATIANS 3

HOW SPIRITUAL LIFE BEGINS

*I will put my instructions deep within them, and I will
write them on their hearts.* JEREMIAH 31:33

YOU CANNOT ALIGN your heart with God's law, so God says, "I'll do
what you cannot do. I'll write my law on your heart." The technical
word for this is *regeneration*. When God does this, you have a new hunger
and a new thirst for the Word of God. You feel drawn to Christ and
responsive to God.

The best illustration I know of this is the way human life begins. The
living seed is planted, and in a secret, mysterious, and wonderful way,
new life is conceived. Hidden within the woman's body, there's a new
life—she may not even be aware of it! Weeks pass, and she begins to feel
something has changed. "Could I be pregnant?"

That's a wonderful picture of how spiritual life begins. It's a direct
work of God's Spirit to implant the seed of life in you. This has either
happened or it has not; there's no in-between. It may have happened
and you don't even know it yet. But like every pregnancy, it will eventually
show. Repentance and faith in the Lord Jesus Christ are the first visible
evidences, but it all begins with God.

This change is something only God can bring. That's why David
prayed, "Create in me a clean heart" (Psalm 51:10). He realized the
only way to change would be for God to change him. That's what God
promises to do in the new covenant.

You can look back now and see how God has done this in your life.
There was a time when you came to church, and it didn't mean much;
but then things began to change. You had a new hunger for God and
a desire to be clean. You didn't know it then, but the life of God was
implanted in you by the Holy Spirit.

Has this happened to you? Is there, at the core of your being, a deep
hunger and thirst after God? That desire is something God has placed
within you. He is fulfilling his promise and changing your heart.

FOR FURTHER READING, SEE TITUS 3

A BOOK WRITTEN IN TEARS

Jerusalem, once so full of people, is now deserted. LAMENTATIONS 1:1

JEREMIAH'S MINISTRY BEGAN during the reign of Josiah, the young king who led a crusade to remove the idols and pagan altars in and around Jerusalem. But Jeremiah realized that unless there was also a change in the hearts of the people, the changes in the land would be short-lived, and so they were . . .

When Josiah's son Jehoiakim came to the throne, he cut up God's Word and threw it into the fire. During Jehoiakim's reign, King Nebuchadnezzar of Babylon laid siege to Jerusalem until the city ran out of food and water. Then he went in, rounded up the most talented people in the city, and deported them to Babylon.

When your best leaders are taken, people of lesser ability step in. Jehoiakim's eighteen-year-old son, Jehoiachin, became king. His reign lasted only three months. Jehoiachin wasn't old enough to have a son, so when he died, his uncle Zedekiah took over.

When Zedekiah considered whether to form an alliance against Nebuchadnezzar, Jeremiah told him Jerusalem would fall—it was time to surrender (see Jeremiah 38:17). But Zedekiah ignored Jeremiah's prophecy and rebelled. The armies of Babylon laid another siege, burning every important building, breaking down the city's walls, and leaving behind only the poorest people (see 52:12-16). This was the darkest hour recorded in the Old Testament.

As Jeremiah was walking through the rubble, he wrote the book of Lamentations. Walls that had once been a strong defense against the enemies of God's people lay in ruins, with smoke still rising from the ashes of the Temple where God's presence had been known. There was hardly one stone on top of another.

When Jeremiah saw this, it broke his heart. That is why the book is called Lamentations. It is a lament, a book written in tears. It is the cry of a heart that is broken by the torn-down state of the work of God in the world. Jesus Christ, over five centuries later, experienced a similar grief as he wept over Jerusalem in his day. What about you? Do you mourn over the torn-down state of the work of God in the world? Don't be discouraged. Jesus promised, "God blesses those who mourn, for they will be comforted" (Matthew 5:4).

FOR FURTHER READING, SEE MARK 13

WEEPING OVER JERUSALEM

All the majesty of beautiful Jerusalem has been stripped away.
LAMENTATIONS 1:6

JEREMIAH THOUGHT ABOUT the Temple, the royal palace, and the exquisite craftsmanship—all reduced to rubble. There was no place for the sacrifices, no place for worship, no meeting place between God and man.

Jeremiah's tears began to flow: "I have cried until the tears no longer come; my heart is broken. My spirit is poured out in agony as I see the desperate plight of my people" (Lamentations 2:11). Jeremiah's tears did not come from personal pain. This godly man had a broken heart over the state of God's work in the world. He was weeping over Jerusalem.

If you set out in ministry with the idea that faith plus hard work mixed with prayer will lead to unbroken success, you'll be in for a big disappointment. God's work often advances through tears. God gave us a whole book of the Bible to teach us this.

Some people are naturally more moist than others, and Jeremiah was known as the weeping prophet. However you express emotion, you cannot serve God long without experiencing a broken heart. If you've never experienced this, it may be that your heart is insensitive or that you've never given yourself fully to his work.

A heart that cares will break over squandered opportunities—sin in the church, souls that might have been saved, the suffering of the persecuted, the hardness of an unbelieving world. But these are good tears. They're the tears of a person who cares, as Paul did: "I wrote that letter in great anguish, with a troubled heart and many tears . . . to let you know how much love I have for you" (2 Corinthians 2:4).

Perhaps you've thrown yourself into some venture to advance the cause of Christ in the world, but your heart is broken over major setbacks. Like David, you can ask the Lord to collect your tears in a bottle (see Psalm 56:8). The tears of God's people are of great value to God because they're the tears of people who care. These tears are a precious offering in the sight of God.

FOR FURTHER READING, SEE LUKE 13

NO MISSING LINKS

Yet I still dare to hope when I remember this: The faithful love of the
LORD never ends! His mercies never cease. Great is his faithfulness;
his mercies begin afresh each morning. LAMENTATIONS 3:21-23

IF THE PEOPLE God had chosen to bless were scattered and the place God had chosen to put his name was destroyed, what hope could there possibly be of God fulfilling his promise and bringing blessing to the world? If the last king's sons were all killed, what future could there be for the royal line of David?

The answer is found in Jehoiachin, the eighteen-year-old king whose reign lasted only three months before he surrendered and was taken off into exile in Babylon. Jeremiah tells us that Jehoiachin was eventually released from prison: "Jehoiachin put aside his prison clothes and for the rest of his life ate regularly at the king's table" (Jeremiah 52:33, NIV).

Jehoiachin's life was preserved, and the royal line continued. When Matthew lists the royal line of David into which Jesus Christ was born, Jehoiachin (or Jeconiah, in some translations) has an honored place (see Matthew 1:11-12). The king who lasted three months and did nothing but surrender to the enemy became a link in the chain that leads to Christ!

Jeremiah did not know this when he was walking through the ruined city of Jerusalem, writing the book of Lamentations. If we had asked him, "How will God's promise of a Savior from the line of David happen, given that all King Zedekiah's sons are dead?" I don't suppose he would have had the faintest idea.

But Jeremiah believed that God is faithful to his promise, and he staked his trust and hope on the faithfulness of God. Look back over the centuries of God's dealings with his people and you will see that even in the darkest hour, he is faithful. Because of God's amazing power, he keeps every one of his promises. That means you too can put your hope and trust in the unchanging faithfulness of God.

FOR FURTHER READING, SEE MATTHEW 1

IMAGINE GOD DOING THAT FOR YOU

*O Jerusalem, Jerusalem, the city that kills the prophets and
stones God's messengers! How often I have wanted to gather
your children together as a hen protects her chicks beneath
her wings, but you wouldn't let me.* LUKE 13:34

SIX HUNDRED YEARS after Jeremiah's ministry, Jesus Christ came to
the city of Jerusalem, and like Jeremiah, he wept over it, saying, "How
I wish today that you of all people would understand the way to peace.
But now it is too late, and peace is hidden from your eyes" (Luke 19:42).

God came to his own city only to be herded out of it and nailed to a
cross. But in his death and resurrection, Christ accomplished the purpose of God, and he is the channel by which the blessing of God will
come to all the nations of the earth.

People with sensitive hearts still weep over Jerusalem. But God
revealed to the apostle John how the story will end by showing him "the
holy city, the new Jerusalem, coming down from God out of heaven like
a bride beautifully dressed for her husband" (Revelation 21:2). That's
Jerusalem as God intended it to be, the place where God has put his
name and where his purposes will be fulfilled.

A voice from God's throne will announce, "Look, God's home is now
among his people! He will live with them, and they will be his people. God
himself will be with them. He will wipe every tear from their eyes, and
there will be no more death or sorrow or crying or pain. All these things
are gone forever" (Revelation 21:3-4). And the one seated on the throne
will say, "Look, I am making everything new!" (21:5).

God's work may advance through many tears, but God's purpose
will finally prevail. A day is coming when "God will wipe away every
tear from their eyes" (Revelation 7:17). Can you imagine God doing
that for you? Whatever circumstances you face in ministry, "always work
enthusiastically for the Lord, for you know that nothing you do for the
Lord is ever useless" (1 Corinthians 15:58).

FOR FURTHER READING, SEE REVELATION 21

WHAT ON EARTH IS GOD DOING?

> *On July 31 of my thirtieth year, while I was with the Judean
> exiles beside the Kebar River in Babylon, the heavens were
> opened and I saw visions of God.* EZEKIEL 1:1

MANY ADULTS LOOK forward to their thirtieth birthday. They're beyond
the age of just starting out but not yet over the hill, and their career may
be taking off. But for the prophet Ezekiel, his thirtieth birthday may
have been the hardest day of his life.

Ezekiel had spent his whole life preparing for ministry in the Temple, but when he was twenty-five and in the middle of his training, war
broke out and he was carted off to the Kebar River—which must have
seemed like the other end of the earth. Now, five years later, all that he
could think of was what might have been.

A priest's thirtieth birthday was the day on which his ministry in the
Temple began, and if Ezekiel had been back home, it would have been
a day of celebration. But what can a priest do when he's seven hundred
miles away from the Temple?

Ezekiel was a man with crushed hopes and shattered dreams. If only
he'd lived at another time. If only he were back home! But now his path
to ministry was blocked, and he found himself with a group of confused
people in backwater Babylon.

Perhaps you can relate to Ezekiel. Maybe you had high hopes and big
dreams, but in your wildest imagination you never thought you'd be in
the situation you find yourself in now. And you wonder, *What on earth is
God doing in my life?*

That's where Ezekiel was, but then something wonderful happened:
God met this displaced and disappointed man, and Ezekiel discovered
something far greater than lighting candles or offering sacrifices in the
Temple. God showed him his glory! And when Ezekiel saw the glory of
God, he was able to find his way forward.

When you face times of confusion or circumstances that are hard
to understand, or when you find yourself in a place you never thought
you'd be, look for God to meet you there and give you a glimpse of his
glory. He will do this by bringing you to see something new in Jesus
Christ.

FOR FURTHER READING, SEE EZEKIEL 1

HIDDEN IN THE CLOUD

I saw a great storm coming from the north, driving before it a huge cloud that flashed with lightning and shone with brilliant light. EZEKIEL 1:4

IT MUST HAVE been like gazing through smoke into a blazing fire. As Ezekiel looked into this cloud, he saw an amazing scene, full of symbolic meaning.

First he saw four cherubim. Each had four faces and four wings (see Ezekiel 1:6). The face of the lion speaks of nobility, the ox speaks of strength, the eagle speaks of compassion, and the man represents the pinnacle of God's creation. The four angels were in a square with their wings connecting at the corners, and above them was a "surface like the sky, glittering like crystal" (1:22). Above this platform rested the throne of God (see 1:26).

Then Ezekiel saw sparkling wheels facing north and south intersecting with other wheels going east to west (see Ezekiel 1:15-17). The wheels moved in four directions, which could be useful to parallel park your car. You could pull in sideways! The wheels gave mobility to the giant platform the throne of God sat on. The glory of God's presence is not fixed to any one location; he's free to move in any direction.

Then Ezekiel saw that the cherubim who were supporting the platform could rise or fall (see Ezekiel 1:19)—they could take off like helicopters! We're also told that the wheels were "covered with eyes" (1:18). This is simply a way of saying that nothing is hidden from the throne of God. There is nothing God cannot see.

Ezekiel tilted back his head, like a boy at the foot of the Washington Monument. Above the throne was "a figure whose appearance resembled a man" (Ezekiel 1:26). The higher Ezekiel looked, the more difficult it was to express what he saw. Finding words to describe what he saw would be like using a hand puppet to convey Shakespeare to someone who's never been to the theater. How could anyone do that?

The glory of God appeared, and while God's glory defies all description, Ezekiel's vision teaches us several key things about God. There is no place God cannot go and nothing he cannot see. He is high and exalted on the throne of the universe.

FOR FURTHER READING, SEE PSALM 139

SCANDAL IN THE TEMPLE

While the leaders of Judah were in my home,
the Sovereign LORD took hold of me. EZEKIEL 8:1

THE LEADERS OF the exiled community by the Kebar River came to Ezekiel's house. While they were there, the Spirit of God came on the prophet, and he saw a vision of the Temple in Jerusalem. From inside the Temple, he looked toward the north gate and saw a massive idol. Then looking toward the center of the Temple area, he saw the glory of the Lord (see Ezekiel 8:2-4).

It was as if God were squaring off with the idol. God was getting ready to destroy the false worship that had taken over his Temple, while at the same time, false prophets were telling the people that Jerusalem could never fall because the Temple of God was there (see Jeremiah 7:4-8).

But God was showing Ezekiel not only that Jerusalem would fall, but that it would fall because the days of the Temple were numbered. Judgment was coming to the household of God. God himself was coming to destroy his own Temple.

Then the Lord brought Ezekiel to a hole in the wall of the Temple court, where he found a secret door. When he looked inside, he found images of detestable animals and idols scrawled on the walls of God's Temple (see Ezekiel 8:7-10). These may have been astrological signs, going back to the time of Manasseh (see 2 Kings 21:5).

God was making it clear that even in the Temple, obscene things were happening in secret, and people were saying, "The LORD doesn't see us." (Ezekiel 8:12). That's what happens when people lose their vision of God. If they had seen Ezekiel's vision of the wheels full of eyes, they would never have dreamed of saying, "The LORD doesn't see us." God sees everything!

Maybe like David when he sinned with Bathsheba, you've lost your vision of God and have been telling yourself, "The LORD doesn't see me." Ask the God who knows all things and from whom no secrets are hidden to cleanse the hidden and secret places of your heart so that there will be no areas of your life you would be ashamed of in his presence.

FOR FURTHER READING, SEE PSALM 51

GOD IS ON THE MOVE

The glory of the LORD rose up from above the cherubim and
went over to the door of the Temple. EZEKIEL 10:4

WHEN EZEKIEL SAW what happened next, he must have been horrified. The wheeled platform was moving from the center of the sanctuary to the door. God's presence was on the move! The great question was, where was God's platform heading?

The glory of the Lord departed from over the threshold of the Temple and stopped. The cherubim under the platform spread their wings and flew, and the glory of God went with them. It stopped over a mountain east of the city (see Ezekiel 10:1-19; 11:22-23).

This must have been an awful thing for Ezekiel to see. He probably thought back to the days of Solomon when the glory of God filled the Temple. Jerusalem was the place where God had placed his name. It could never fall, for God was within it. But Ezekiel saw in his vision the glory of the Lord moving from the Temple to the edge of the city, and then to a mountain in the east.

God had already given Ezekiel a vision of this same flying platform by the Kebar River! That means that although God was abandoning Jerusalem, he had not abandoned his people or his promises. The focus of his redeeming work was moving away from Jerusalem and to a new place. Ten thousand of God's people would be preserved in that new place and eventually brought back to Jerusalem.

That's why God said, "Although I have scattered you in the countries of the world, I will be a sanctuary to you during your time in exile. I, the Sovereign LORD, will gather you back from the nations where you have been scattered" (Ezekiel 11:16-17). God promised that when they were brought back, they would have changed hearts and a new spirit (see 11:19-20).

This was wonderful news for Ezekiel, the man who thought his door of ministry was closed because he was seven hundred miles from the Temple. Yes, God's presence was leaving the Temple, but his glory would now be made known among an obscure group of people beside the Kebar River. Ezekiel was at the center of God's will after all!

FOR FURTHER READING, SEE EZEKIEL 11

IT'S BETTER TO BE IN BABYLON

*The glory of the LORD came into the Temple through the east gateway . . .
and the glory of the LORD filled the Temple.* EZEKIEL 43:4-5

EZEKIEL'S VISION OF the glory of the Lord reentering the Temple from the east was a reversal of his earlier vision. East was the direction the glory of God had headed twenty years earlier. In those days the Lord focused his redeeming work by the Kebar River. But there would come a time when God's presence would return to the great city, and his glory would fill a new Temple. This massive Temple would become the center of worship for people from every tribe and nation who turn from their idols to seek the true God.

There must have been times when Ezekiel sat down by the Kebar River, hundreds of miles from home, and said, "This isn't how it's supposed to be!" Maybe you've felt like that. Something happened that shattered your dream, and you found yourself saying, "I never imagined I'd be in this situation." Or maybe God has taken you from a place where you were happy and put you somewhere else.

Ezekiel's flying platform reminds us that God's glory and his blessing are not limited to one place. If God moves you to another place, his presence will go with you. He will never leave you nor forsake you (see Hebrews 13:5). Ezekiel discovered that it's better to be in Babylon with the presence of God than in Jerusalem without it!

Christ also spoke to the church in Ephesus about removing his presence from them if they did not repent (see Revelation 2:5). It's not difficult to find places that were once thriving churches but now show very little evidence of spiritual life.

A church without Christ's presence is like the Temple without God's glory—it is an empty shell. The church needs the presence of God like the human body needs blood, and without the Spirit of God, the church becomes like a corpse.

A local church may have many assets, but without the presence of God it won't amount to much. God's presence empowers the local church, so we must be careful not to grieve the Spirit. God's Spirit is a sensitive guest among his people.

FOR FURTHER READING, SEE EPHESIANS 4

GOD CAME OFF THE PLATFORM!

He was full of unfailing love and faithfulness. And we have seen his glory, the glory of the Father's one and only Son. JOHN 1:14

SIX HUNDRED YEARS after Ezekiel's visions, the glory of God came down among us.

God came off the platform! The Lord of glory came down from the throne, took human flesh, and was born in a small town outside Jerusalem. The one who sat on a throne held up by angels now lay in a manger as angels looked down on him.

Jesus Christ, who is the glory of God, also came to the Temple. And as he taught the things of God there day after day, he saw that the Temple had become a den of thieves and robbers. The people did not want him there, so he left the Temple, not on a flying platform, but in the custody of armed guards. The glory of God left Jerusalem, bearing a cross to the place outside the city wall where he was crucified.

On the third day, he rose from the dead. It was impossible for death to keep hold of him. And for forty days, he appeared to his disciples, proving "to them in many ways that he was actually alive" (Acts 1:3).

Then Christ went to a mountain east of the city—the Mount of Olives. He stood on the very spot where Ezekiel had seen the glory of God hovering as the platform left the Temple. As the disciples watched, Christ ascended to his throne in the presence of the Father. An angel appeared to them and said, "Why are you standing here staring into heaven? Jesus has been taken from you into heaven, but someday he will return from heaven in the same way you saw him go!" (Acts 1:11).

The glory of God appeared, and the glory departed from the city as Christ was rejected and crucified outside Jerusalem. The glory has returned to the throne in heaven, and the glory of God will come again. That is where all history is headed. On that day, we will be caught up to meet him in the air (see 1 Thessalonians 4:17), and so we will be forever with the Lord.

FOR FURTHER READING, SEE ACTS 1

PROPHETIC IMAGINATION

Prophesy against the false prophets of Israel who are inventing
their own prophecies. Say to them, "Listen to the word of the
LORD. This is what the Sovereign LORD says: What sorrow awaits
the false prophets who are following their own imaginations
and have seen nothing at all!" EZEKIEL 13:2-3

GOD SPOKE THROUGH Ezekiel to those who claimed to be prophets but replaced the Word of God with their own opinions. The prophet's role was to stand in the presence of God and hear the Word of God in order to speak that Word to the people. But these leaders looked at the market, discovered what people wanted to hear, and shaped their message to fit the need of the hour.

In Ezekiel's time, the prophets knew that the people wanted to hear a message of peace, so they gave them what they wanted. They led God's people astray by saying "peace" when God had said there would be no peace (see Ezekiel 13:10). What God said didn't concern them. Their ministry was driven by demand, not truth.

The health of the church today depends on the prophetic teaching of God's Word. This isn't a matter of revealing new truths received directly from God, because God's revelation has been completed in Jesus Christ. Every church needs a strong ministry of the Word so that God's truth may be known among God's people.

The leadership of the prophet is also important within the family. It is God's plan that in every home there should be a prophetic ministry of teaching God's truth to our children. Which father or mother feels adequate to do this?

But on the Day of Pentecost, Peter spoke about all of God's people prophesying (see Acts 2:17). That doesn't mean all of us are preachers, but it does mean God can use any of his people at any time to say something he will use to penetrate another person's life. A friend of mine used to say, "Every Christian is like a pilot light—always lit and carrying within him or her the potential to light a larger flame."

FOR FURTHER READING, SEE EZEKIEL 13

PRIESTLY COUNSEL

> *Your priests have violated my instructions and defiled my holy things.*
> *They make no distinction between what is holy and what is not.*
> *And they do not teach my people the difference between what is*
> *ceremonially clean and unclean. They disregard my Sabbath days*
> *so that I am dishonored among them.* EZEKIEL 22:26

THE ROLE OF the priest was the mirror image of the role of the prophet. The prophet spoke to the people on behalf of God; the priest spoke to God on behalf of the people.

The priests who operated in the Temple were to offer the prayers and sacrifices. Their ministry related to worship; it was all about bringing people into the presence of God. You could go to a priest in the Temple, and he would pray with you. The priests offered a kind of pastoral counsel to people in relation to their spiritual lives.

But instead of bringing people to God, the priests became like secular counselors who focused on helping people to be at peace with themselves. They were not exercising a ministry of prayer or showing people how to be reconciled with God. If you had gone to one of these priests, you could have gone through a whole session without any prayer or any reference to Scripture. They said very little about God.

The priests focused entirely on the horizontal ministry—human to human. But the church needs a ministry that is vertical, in which the needs of people are brought before God. This is the heart of pastoral ministry. When the needs of those who struggle with guilt and fear are brought before God privately and publicly, then the wounded are healed and the weak are strengthened. Parents are also called to the priestly ministry of praying for our children and encouraging them in their knowledge of God.

The apostle Peter wrote to Christians calling them "royal priests" (1 Peter 2:9). That means we can all pray for and minister to one another in the body of Christ. And every one of God's people can offer worship, not just the choir or a few worship leaders on the platform.

FOR FURTHER READING, SEE 1 PETER 2

KINGLY ACHIEVEMENT

> *You have not taken care of the weak. You have not tended the*
> *sick or bound up the injured. You have not gone looking for*
> *those who have wandered away and are lost. Instead, you have*
> *ruled them with harshness and cruelty.* EZEKIEL 34:4

IT IS AS if God were saying, "You kings have been given power; now what have you done with it?" The king's role was to lead the people into battle and protect them from their enemies. He was also responsible for leading the people in right paths so that they would continue to enjoy the blessing of God.

The exile to Babylon did not happen because of the sins of one generation but because of the repeated pattern of sin over many generations. God was pointing out a consistent pattern of abuse through the entire history of the nation.

Before the first king was appointed, God warned the people that a king would conscript their sons into the army, take their daughters into the service of the palace, and raise their taxes until the people "beg[ged] for relief" (1 Samuel 8:18).

That is exactly what happened. Many kings were wicked, but even the best kings placed great burdens on the people. Solomon is remembered for all his achievements, but his abuses of power were considerable. He built the Temple, but much of it was done under forced labor, and the taxes he levied were almost intolerable.

The church is called to fulfill a purpose, and we need leadership to help us move in that direction. There must be administration, organization, and order in the church of God. Church leaders must protect the flock from false teaching and keep them from sin that could hinder God's blessing on his people. And parents must protect their children from an evil world and lead them in paths of righteousness.

All God's people are kings. God has "raised us from the dead along with Christ and seated us with him in the heavenly realms" (Ephesians 2:6). In Christ you are positioned for victory over your enemies of sin, death, and hell, and you're given the Spirit of God so that you have the ability to move in right paths.

FOR FURTHER READING, SEE 1 SAMUEL 8

WHAT GOD FINDS INTOLERABLE

I myself will tend my sheep . . . says the Sovereign LORD. EZEKIEL 34:15

GOD FOUND THE situation among his people intolerable, so he determined to do something about it. In effect, God said, "I will be prophet, priest, and king to my people. I will personally bring the truth to them, care for them, protect them, and lead them in right paths. I'll be the shepherd to the sheep." It must have been hard for Ezekiel to understand how God could do that.

When Jesus Christ came into the world, he saw that instead of bringing people into the joy of knowing God, the religious shepherds were imposing unnecessary burdens on them. So Jesus "had compassion on [the people] because they were confused and helpless, like sheep without a shepherd" (Matthew 9:36).

Christ gave an uncompromising assessment of the "shepherds" of God's people: "All who came before me were thieves and robbers" (John 10:8). In other words, the shepherds were using the flock of God for their own advantage. Then Jesus identified himself as the shepherd of Ezekiel 34: "I am the good shepherd. The good shepherd sacrifices his life for the sheep" (John 10:11).

The Good Shepherd gives the sheep everything they need. He feeds the sheep with God's truth. Perhaps you've wondered how to grow in the Christian life or how you can be sustained in the difficulties you're facing. Christ will sustain you, and as you walk with him, you'll grow more than you ever thought you could.

The Good Shepherd came to seek and save lost sheep (see Luke 19:10). He is the kind of shepherd who will leave his sheep in the pen in order to find one who is lost, "and when he has found it, he will joyfully carry it home on his shoulders" (15:5). He doesn't wait for them to come to him; Christ goes out, finds people who are lost, and brings them back to God. Christ leads the sheep, protecting them from enemies: "My sheep . . . will never perish. No one can snatch them away from me" (John 10:27-28). He will guard you by all means, and when death comes, he'll bring you into everlasting life.

FOR FURTHER READING, SEE JOHN 10

CREDIBILITY GAP

On January 8, during the twelfth year of our captivity, a survivor from Jerusalem came to me and said, "The city has fallen!" EZEKIEL 33:21

THE BEDRAGGLED STRANGER was exhausted after his seven-hundred-mile journey. He walked into town, asked for directions to the house of the prophet, and said that he had bad news. Ezekiel never forgot that day.

It had been twelve years since the ten thousand exiles were deported to the Kebar River. In that time, they'd had endless discussion about what would happen next in Jerusalem. False prophets insisted the exile would be only for a short time and that soon God's people would be back in God's city—but that's not what God said.

When the news of Jerusalem's fall came, it's hard to imagine the impact it had. Jerusalem was the city of God, and these people grew up in Sabbath school singing, "A river brings joy to the city of our God, the sacred home of the Most High. God dwells in that city; it cannot be destroyed" (Psalm 46:4-5).

How could God allow this? Had he given up on his people? God promised, "I will give you a new heart, and I will put a new spirit in you. I will take out your stony, stubborn heart and give you a tender, responsive heart" (Ezekiel 36:26), but the people just said, "We have become old, dry bones—all hope is gone. Our nation is finished" (37:11).

They felt there was a credibility gap between their circumstances and God's promises. They were finding it difficult to connect the Word of God with the broken reality around them. Perhaps you've felt that way. The preacher talks about how the life of God, poured into the church, transforms the community. He reads the Bible's wonderful promises, but you see the godlessness of our time and say, "We're finished!"

There are times when the broken circumstances of life make us feel that we're beyond the range of God's promises, and that while they may be for other people at other times in other places, they are somehow not for us. If you have felt that, then the vision God gave to Ezekiel is for you. God did not abandon his people, and he will not abandon you.

FOR FURTHER READING, SEE PSALM 46

NO SIGNS OF LIFE

*The LORD took hold of me, and I was carried away by the
Spirit of the LORD to a valley filled with bones.* EZEKIEL 37:1

GOD TOOK EZEKIEL to a grim valley, a graveyard filled with human remains—perhaps the result of a great slaughter hundreds of years ago. He told Ezekiel the bones in the vision represented the house of Israel (see Ezekiel 37:11). The people had complained, "We have become old, dry bones," so God used a valley of dry bones to speak to them.

The first thing God did to show Ezekiel the scale of the problem was to give him a guided tour: "He led me all around among the bones that covered the valley floor. They were scattered everywhere across the ground and were completely dried out" (Ezekiel 37:2).

I don't suppose Ezekiel enjoyed the whole experience. The longer the tour continued, the more deeply the hopelessness of the situation was impressed upon him. There were no signs of life. God was saying, "You need to see how hopeless things have become." The only hope would be through God's direct intervention.

You have to begin in ministry with an honest assessment, and God essentially told Ezekiel, "I want you to minister in a place where there are no signs of life." Ezekiel had remarkable abilities, including an unusual flair for creative communication, but that would be of little use in a valley of dry bones. The first thing to understand in ministry is that what God calls us to do is impossible. If you don't grasp this, you won't survive long in ministry.

Perhaps God is showing you a valley of dry bones. You've been looking for signs of hope in the spiritual condition of someone you love, but there's not the slightest sign of life. When you talk with them about spiritual things, their eyes glaze over. They're about as unresponsive to the things of God as Ezekiel's dry bones.

God took Ezekiel over the valley of dry bones again and again until Ezekiel was convinced that the only hope would be a direct intervention of God. Do you see that? God can bring the dead back to life. Pray for God's intervention.

FOR FURTHER READING, SEE EZEKIEL 37

I DON'T KNOW, BUT GOD DOES

Son of man, can these bones become living people again? EZEKIEL 37:3

HOW WOULD YOU have answered that question? Ezekiel could have said yes. And there are some people who would agree with that answer today. I recently heard a well-known Bible teacher announce that America unquestionably is on the brink of the greatest outpouring of the Holy Spirit the world has ever seen. He was absolutely certain about it. I hope he's right, but I don't know how he knows that. There is a great danger in confusing naive optimism with faith.

Ezekiel could also have said no. There are people who would say that today too. It's very easy, in a culture where Christianity is becoming the minority position, to feel that the church will fade into insignificance. I've heard this predicted, and I hope it's wrong, but how can we know the future?

Ezekiel's response is a model of faith: "O Sovereign LORD, . . . you alone know the answer to that" (Ezekiel 37:3). The prophet was saying, "Lord, there's no way I can know what you're going to do with these bones." There's great humility in his response.

We need an attitude that says, "Lord, keep me from the arrogance that says yes. Keep me from the spirit that says, 'I know how it works; I can make it happen.' Keep me from the presumption that says, 'We can reclaim this country for Christ.'"

We also need an attitude that says, "Lord, keep me from the unbelief that says no. Keep me from the spirit that says, 'These are dark days, and the difficulties are so great that I cannot see any possibility of change.'" Ezekiel would neither despair nor presume; he found his rest in the sovereignty of God.

Similarly, we should say, "Lord, I don't know if the future of this country holds revival or decline, but you do. I don't know whether those I pray for will come to Christ or will remain hardened, but you know. I don't know whether we'll see a great missionary advance or we'll find the doors closing, but you know. The future of those I pray for is known only to you, and I'll rest in your sovereignty."

FOR FURTHER READING, SEE HABAKKUK 3

WHILE YOU'RE TRUSTING GOD

Speak a prophetic message to these bones. EZEKIEL 37:4

BELIEF IN THE sovereignty of God is never an excuse to sit back and do nothing. Ezekiel had trusted God with the future, but now God had something for him to do: preach to the bones.

This is one of the strangest commands in the Bible. Imagine what was going on in Ezekiel's mind: *You want me to talk to bones? Do I have to speak out loud? I'd feel stupid. Can't I just* think *my sermon?*

Why would God want the prophet to preach in a situation where hearing, understanding, and responding are impossible? The point of the exercise is simple—every time someone presents the Word of God to an unbelieving person, it's like appealing to dry bones. The Bible says that until God makes us alive through Jesus Christ, we're spiritually dead (see Ephesians 2:1-5).

There's something inherently absurd about sharing the gospel. Maybe you've felt the pain of this. You speak to a friend about Christ, and there's no response! Ezekiel might have objected that God was calling him to do something that had no chance of success. But God called him to preach anyway. So he did.

As he spoke, an amazing thing happened: there was movement in the graveyard. Nothing had moved in that valley for years, but now as Ezekiel preached, he saw bones coming together to form skeletons, he saw tendons connecting the bones, and then flesh and skin (see Ezekiel 37:7-8). It was incredible!

Bones speak of structure, tendons of unity (holding the bones together), flesh (which includes muscle) of strength, and skin of appearance—but there was still no breath. The church can have marvelous structures, united people, the great strength of resources, and an attractive outward appearance yet still have no life.

God does amazing things when his truth is proclaimed. Parents can teach their children God's truth; churches can run magnificent programs. We can pass out tracts and go on marches. All such activities are good. Yet none of these things, in themselves, will raise the spiritually dead. Our only hope is the Spirit of God breathing life into the dry bones.

FOR FURTHER READING, SEE EPHESIANS 2

THE BREATH OF LIFE

Speak a prophetic message to the winds. EZEKIEL 37:9

IN THE VERY beginning, when God made Adam from the dust of the ground, he formed a corpse made of bones, tendons, flesh, and skin. Then God "breathed the breath of life into the man's nostrils, and the man became a living person" (Genesis 2:7). God was about to do the same thing again in the valley of dry bones.

The prophet saw human structure and form in the bones strewn before him, but there was no life there. So God told Ezekiel to call on the wind of God's Spirit: "This is what the Sovereign LORD says: Come, O breath, from the four winds! Breathe into these dead bodies so they may live again" (Ezekiel 37:9).

Ezekiel began to preach, and as he did this, the breath of God entered the corpses. Ezekiel saw them coming to life, and then standing up, until right there, in what had been a valley of dry bones, there stood a vast army, ready for action (see Ezekiel 37:10).

Never, never, never underestimate what God can do when his Word is preached and his people pray. If the breath of the Spirit of God blows into a situation that is completely dead, a remarkable transformation will take place.

As Ezekiel looked at the vast army in the valley, he knew this was the work of God. But he also knew that God had done this miracle as Ezekiel preached and as he prayed. He must have wondered, *What if I had not spoken? What if I had not prayed?*

Where the wind of the Spirit blows is up to the sovereignty of God; it's not under our control. But God commands us to speak the truth and call on the Spirit of God in prayer.

What if our children's eyes glaze over as we present the truth, or if a colleague seems unresponsive as we share our testimony? We can try to introduce them to (or keep them in) an environment where they'll hear God's truth, and we can surround them with a ministry of prayer. God is telling us that amazing things can happen in the most unpromising places when his Word is preached and his people pray.

FOR FURTHER READING, SEE EPHESIANS 3

HIGH SCHOOL STUDENTS ABDUCTED!

The king ordered Ashpenaz, his chief of staff, to bring to the palace some of the young men of Judah's royal family and other noble families. DANIEL 1:3

DANIEL WAS TAKEN from his home and remained in Babylon for a period of about seventy years. Given a normal life expectancy, Daniel was, in all probability, of high school age when he came to Babylon.

Try to get a picture of this high school student in your mind. Daniel was one of the brightest and the best. He came from a good home and was a straight-A student. He was "well versed in every branch of learning" (Daniel 1:4). He was also fit and very good-looking. The world was at his feet.

Then one day during his junior year, Daniel was sitting at his desk when there was a knock on the door. Three Babylonian soldiers burst in, and Daniel was dragged off and, along with some of his friends, marched seven hundred miles to Babylon. These prize pupils were abducted, and the parents could do nothing to stop it!

Daniel's parents must have been distraught, and who knows what was going through Daniel's mind? *Maybe they'll torture us until we die.* He needn't have worried, though, because when he arrived in Babylon, far from being abused and imprisoned, he was treated like royalty and enrolled in a top-flight boarding school.

Daniel had grown up under the care of his parents, but now he was taken out of that environment and placed in a new situation where he had to stand on his own two feet. Daniel was completely anonymous in Babylon. Those who travel know all about this temptation. At home, many people know you, but when you get on a plane or check into a hotel, it occurs to you that you can be whoever you want to be.

This is a great test for those who leave home and head off to college. The watchful eyes of parents cannot extend to a new location, and that's when who you really are will be made known. When you can be whoever you want to be, then the person you really are will be revealed.

FOR FURTHER READING, SEE DANIEL 1

PRESSURE TO CONFORM

Train these young men in the language and literature of Babylon.
DANIEL 1:4

DANIEL HAD GROWN up under the care of his parents and the influence of godly people. Now suddenly he was taken out of that environment and placed in a new situation, where he had to stand on his own two feet and make his own decisions.

He and his friends were placed by the king under the care of a tutor named Ashpenaz to teach them a new language using a completely different set of textbooks than they were used to. Back in Jerusalem, they would have studied Hebrew and learned the Bible, but neither was on the curriculum in Babylon.

Daniel was exposed to a whole new spectrum of learning. Much of it would have been quite foreign to him, and a great deal of it would have been in direct conflict with what he had been taught from the Scripture as a child. Learning the literature of the Babylonians would have meant learning about their history and culture, as well as learning about the myths of their gods—Marduk, Bel, and Nebo.

There would have been all the usual discussions among the students over coffee. And there would have been challenges like these from their teacher and from the other students: "Do you seriously believe that your God is the only god?" "Don't you understand? Every culture has its own religious stories. They all point to the same spiritual reality." "Do you think you're the only ones who have the truth?" "These Bible stories are simply a way of describing the author's personal beliefs." It is not very different for many Christian young people in secular universities today.

Parents are sometimes distressed over the things their children are taught in secular schools. And students are often required to read books that are in direct contradiction to the truth. This is nothing new. It is exactly the situation Daniel faced.

God has given us a model of how one godly young person and a group of his friends stood against that pressure. Their secular education, far from overwhelming them, was actually the making of them. In the goodness of God, their Babylonian education became the anvil on which their faith was hammered out into maturity.

FOR FURTHER READING, SEE 1 PETER 1

TWO KINDS OF OPPRESSION

The chief of staff renamed them with these Babylonian names:
Daniel was called Belteshazzar . . . DANIEL 1:7

ASHPENAZ GAVE NEW names to his new students. He didn't want to use their Jewish names, so he gave them Babylonian names instead. *Daniel* means "God is my judge": *Belteshazzar* means "Bel [a Babylonian god] protects his life." Ashpenaz's plan was becoming clear. He was taking the brightest Jewish students and attempting to "Babylonize" them.

By moving Daniel and his friends to another location, filling their minds with another learning, and calling them by another name, Ashpenaz was attempting to erode their distinctive faith in God, so that at the end of three years in the royal college, they would emerge with a thoroughly Babylonian worldview. They would still be Jews, but they would think, act, behave, and respond like Babylonians.

There are two very different kinds of oppression. When Pharaoh persecuted God's people, he was ruthless and put them through hard labor—but all that happened was they multiplied and became stronger. Satan uses the same tactic today in many places where Christians are persecuted for their faith. The outcome is usually the same—God's people become stronger under persecution.

Nebuchadnezzar's plan was more subtle. He knew his history. What Pharaoh had attempted didn't work, so he decided to subdue these people not by persecuting them, but by blessing them. His strategy was to open doors of opportunity for them and place them on the fast track to success. They would find it so intoxicating, they would quickly forget all about their distinctive calling as the people of God. Before long, they would lose every trace of what made them different.

There are some places in the world where the enemy of our souls is using the crude tactics of Pharaoh. But he is increasingly using the tactics of Nebuchadnezzar, and they are proving very effective in his warfare against the church.

The strategy is simple: Intoxicate the people of God with the sheer splendor of this world. Gradually erode their distinctive practices and values, and it will not be long before they are assimilated into the culture. Some who would be heroes under the persecutions of Egypt are unable to resist the seductions of Babylon.

FOR FURTHER READING, SEE 1 TIMOTHY 6

A TASTE OF THE HIGH LIFE

The king assigned them a daily ration of food and wine from his own kitchens. They were to be trained for three years, and then they would enter the royal service. DANIEL 1:5

THIS WAS HEADY stuff for high schoolers, eating from the same menu as the king of Babylon. The message was getting through: "The king's palace is the place to be. This is where the doors of opportunity are." The king knew that once they got a taste for the high life, it would be hard to settle for anything else.

Daniel decided not to eat from the king's table. He resolved not to defile himself with the royal food (see Daniel 1:8). In addition to the potential scruples of conscience, I believe he abstained because he was realistic about the pressures of the culture. He would live, serve, and prosper there, but he would never allow Babylon to consume him. He would remember that he served a greater king.

Daniel needed some way of keeping that fixed in his mind, so he established a discipline for himself. He turned down the offer of a daily visit to the top restaurant in town and ate a brown-bag lunch instead. He didn't do this to keep an external law, but to sustain an internal desire. It was a voluntary discipline, designed to remind him of his distinctive calling and to increase his spiritual strength.

Daniel knew if he didn't exercise some restraint, he would eventually be consumed by the values of the culture. He determined not to get hooked on the things of this world, because then he would lose his freedom to be an effective servant of God.

Are you being realistic about the pressures that the world places on you? Every day you are bombarded by a view of life that is self-centered and has no room for God. "Nothing matters more than you do, so pursue your own pleasure," our culture seems to say. Once you identify the pressures you're facing, it's time to develop a strategy for resistance.

FOR FURTHER READING, SEE 2 TIMOTHY 3

CULTIVATING THE ABILITY TO SAY NO

But Daniel was determined not to defile himself by eating the
food and wine given to them by the king. DANIEL 1:8

THE GREAT SIGNIFICANCE of Daniel's decision to abstain from the king's table was that he was cultivating the ability to say no. This is critical to an effective Christian life: "The grace of God . . . teaches us to say 'No' to ungodliness" (Titus 2:11-12, NIV).

Daniel made a great decision. One day a future king would remove freedom of worship and call on everyone to pray in the name of the king or else face death in a den of lions. When that day came, Daniel would be able to stand firm.

If you do not develop the ability to say no on smaller issues, you won't be able to say no when larger tests and temptations come. That's why it's so important to develop the ability to withstand peer pressure and why there's great value in exercising voluntary restraint over some legitimate pleasures and opportunities.

Daniel was at liberty to eat from the king's table. But he perceived that the habit of eating at the king's table would exert a drawing power in his life that could subvert his loyalty to the Lord. So he used his freedom to exercise restraint. He wouldn't allow himself to get in a position where the good things of life consumed his heart.

This is full of practical significance for us today. Some Christians operate as if there were only one question to be answered in the practical decisions of life—is it right or wrong? And unless it's illegal, immoral, or it makes us fat, we eagerly affirm our liberty to enjoy. But there is another question to ask—is it wise?

What films should you watch? How large a mortgage should you take? What parties should you go to? What company should you keep? On what should you spend your money? Daniel's example reminds us that as we make these decisions, we need to consider the long-term potential for being sucked into the values and lifestyles of the world.

FOR FURTHER READING, SEE TITUS 2

FAITH AND SUCCESS

God gave these four young men an unusual aptitude for understanding every aspect of literature and wisdom. DANIEL 1:17

DANIEL COULD NOT change what they taught him at school. He could not change what Ashpenaz and the others chose to call him. But he could create a space in his life that was a daily reminder to him that he was a servant of God. He chose to exercise restraint, and his faithful fasting strengthened him for what lay ahead.

If we embrace every legitimate thing the world offers on the basis that there's nothing wrong with it, we may find we've been seduced into adopting the values of the world. God does not call us to a life of austerity, but a life of undisciplined indulgence will eventually erode away everything in our lives that distinguishes the people of God. Daniel determined that his success in Babylon would never do this.

God gave Daniel and his friends great success in their studies, so when they came to their finals, which would have been in the form of an oral exam before the king, they passed with flying colors. Daniel was appointed to a premier position of influence within the most powerful government of his day. Faithfulness and success need not be alternatives; they are natural partners.

Daniel had proved faithful in small things, and so God trusted him with greater things. That's always the pattern. Never imagine that faithfulness to Christ means being second rate or settling for small things. Daniel proved that he could be trusted, so God increased Daniel's gifts and abilities and opened the door of opportunity. Daniel would have influence beyond what he had ever dreamed, becoming second-in-command to the king.

Maybe you've been following Christ and you're seeing great opportunities on the horizon. The attractions of wealth, power, and pleasure are strong. Ask God to give you a love for him that is stronger. Ask him to show you how you can be different, not only in what you believe but in how you live. Ask him to show you where you can practice voluntary restraint so you can avoid drifting with the crowd. The rewards of faithful living far outweigh the temporary pleasures of indulgence.

FOR FURTHER READING, SEE MATTHEW 25

THE WEDDING

When the LORD began to speak through Hosea, the LORD said to him,
"Go, marry a promiscuous woman . . . for like an adulterous wife
this land is guilty of unfaithfulness to the LORD." HOSEA 1:2

IT'S UNLIKELY THAT Hosea phoned a dating agency to find the worst woman in town. The context seems to suggest that Hosea already knew Gomer. He'd fallen in love with her and was planning to marry her. But before the wedding actually took place, God told Hosea what the future would hold.

Imagine what this must have been like. One night, in a dream, Hosea sees Gomer with another man—and then another. He wakes up in a cold sweat, and somehow he knows God is revealing that Gomer will become an adulterous wife. Hosea is horrified, but he knows God is telling him to go ahead with the wedding. So he marries Gomer in the full knowledge of what lies ahead.

Picture the wedding. The minister welcomes everyone: "We're gathered here today to join Hosea and Gomer in marriage. If anyone knows of any reason why these two should not be joined together, speak now or keep silent forever."

Then he turns to Diblaim, the bride's father. "Who gives this woman to be married to this man?" If Gomer was as difficult at home as she would be after she got married, Diblaim must have been relieved to get her to the altar!

The minister continues: "Hosea, will you take Gomer to be your wife, to have and to hold from this day forward, for better, for worse?"

Hosea knows there will be a lot of "worse" in the days ahead, but without hesitation he says, "I will."

The minister turns to Gomer, "Will you have Hosea to be your husband? Will you love, honor, and obey him, forsaking all others, keeping only to him as long as you both shall live?"

"I will," she says. Hosea knows she won't, but he chooses to marry her anyway.

Throughout Hosea's life, God's people were two-timing. They had a covenant with God, but they also had other gods on the side. That was as offensive and painful to God as an unfaithful wife would be to her husband. Hosea's painful marriage became a mirror in which God's love for his people is wonderfully revealed.

FOR FURTHER READING, SEE HOSEA 1

LOVE'S CHOICE

So Hosea married Gomer. HOSEA 1:3

OVER THE YEARS a number of folks have told me, with great sadness, that if they had known the pain that the future would hold, they would never have gone through with their weddings. Of course, none of us who have made a marriage vow knew when we said "for better or worse" what the future would hold.

But Hosea did know, and his extraordinary decision to marry a woman he knew would repeatedly break his heart gives us a great insight into the love of God. God is telling us, "This is what I've done. I've made a covenant with my people in the full knowledge that they'll be unfaithful and bring me indescribable pain."

God knew before the beginning of time that men and women would choose the knowledge of evil, and that delivering us from it would involve God himself taking human flesh, entering our world, and being rejected by it. This would lead to unspeakable suffering and pain in the heart of God, but he did it anyway.

God knew from the beginning that Israel would turn to idols, and yet he set his love on these people. He had said to them, "I will be your God, and you will be my people" (Leviticus 26:12). He invited them into an exclusive covenant relationship with him, knowing that they would be hard-hearted, stubborn, and faithless.

God has shown the same love to us. Doesn't it strike you as amazing that God pledged his love to us in Christ in the full knowledge of what we would be like? He knew how slow, selfish, and stubborn we would be, and he loved us still.

That is why there is a profound sense in which you can never disappoint God. He loves you, even in the full knowledge of the deepest and most consistent failure of your life. God does not wait for us to sort out our lives before he takes us on. "While we were still sinners, Christ died for us" (Romans 5:8, NIV).

FOR FURTHER READING, SEE ROMANS 5

LOVE'S PAIN

> *"O Israel and Judah, what should I do with you?" asks the*
> LORD. *"For your love vanishes like the morning mist and*
> *disappears like dew in the sunlight."* HOSEA 6:4

APPARENTLY HOSEA AND Gomer enjoyed some good years after the wedding. They had three children, but the disturbing names given to them are a clue that trouble may have already been going on. The children were called Jezreel, which was the place of a massacre (see 2 Kings 10:1-11); Lo-ruhamah, which means "not loved"; and Lo-ammi, which means "not my people" (see Hosea 1:4-9).

Try to picture Hosea at home with the children. It's late at night, and Gomer has been gone for hours. She's evasive about where she's going and what she's doing, but Hosea is not naive. He knows what's going on. He has confronted his wife, but nothing has changed. So Hosea is pacing the floor in his own home, a man distraught with the pain of wounded love.

Over the years, Gomer's absences become longer and more frequent. She walks in one day and walks out the next. The whole situation is absolutely intolerable. Hosea is in an agony of soul. God told him that he would experience this pain, but now he is thrust into the heart of it.

Hosea's pain is a window into the heart of God. God's own people were as faithless to him as Gomer was to Hosea. Their love of other gods brought the same kind of pain to the heart of God as Hosea experienced when his wife went off with another man: "One minute you say you love me, but the next minute your love fades away! What am I to do with you?" Anyone who has experienced the pain of a broken home will know exactly what is pouring from the heart of God.

Gomer's behavior helps us to understand that sin is a deeply painful and personal offense against God. Every time we lie, cheat, steal, swear, lust, or blaspheme; every time we pursue self-interest over God's interest, we are inflicting a wound in the heart of God. If sin were merely breaking some principle or regulation, it would be much less serious. But sin is wounding the heart of God.

FOR FURTHER READING, SEE HOSEA 6

LOVE'S INITIATIVE

*How can I give you up, Israel? . . . My heart is torn within
me, and my compassion overflows.* HOSEA 11:8

OLD TESTAMENT LAW commanded the death penalty for both parties
involved in adultery (see Leviticus 20:10). Perhaps that's why Christ
allows the possibility of divorce following adultery (see Matthew 19:9).
If the full penalty were exacted, the unfaithful partner would be executed by stoning. So, by definition, the innocent party would be free to
remarry. Divorce was a legitimate option for Hosea.

God made an exclusive covenant with his people, but they violated
that covenant by turning to other gods. It seems clear that under these
circumstances, the appropriate course of action was for God to termi-
nate the covenant he'd made with these people. Something had to be
done. It was too late for the people to say they were sorry. Actions have
consequences, and this was the end of the road: "Though they call out
to the Most High, he shall not raise them up at all" (Hosea 11:7, ESV).

But it seems God cannot live with this conclusion. God's justice says,
"I have to bring this to a close," but his love says, "I cannot give up the
people I care about." Can you sense God's heart tearing? All the way
through the Old Testament story you have God in his awesome holiness and God in his incomparable love. It seems as if they're pulling in
opposite directions.

It's like Hosea saying, "I can't stand what Gomer is doing, but I can't
stop loving her." He goes back and forth. At night he says, "I have to
see a lawyer," but when morning comes, he can't bring himself to go. If
this dilemma is painfully close to home for you, then you have a unique
insight into the heart of God.

God told Hosea what to do. It's a wonderful picture of how he deals
with us: "Go and love your wife again, even though she commits adultery with another lover. This will illustrate that the LORD still loves
Israel" (Hosea 3:1). Hosea looked for Gomer, and when he eventually
found her, he "bought her back" (3:2). Imagine what this must have
been like for Hosea. It is a stunning picture of God's love for you and
me in the death of Jesus Christ!

FOR FURTHER READING, SEE HOSEA 3

WHERE JUSTICE AND LOVE COLLIDE

*I will win her back once again. I will lead her into the desert
and speak tenderly to her there.* HOSEA 2:14

THE DESERT, OF course, is the place where the couple can be alone. God is going to win back his bride. He is talking about a new honeymoon—together. Later, speaking of the whole nation, God says, "I will heal you of your faithlessness; my love will know no bounds, for my anger will be gone forever" (Hosea 14:4). God is telling us how the story of his relationship with his people will end.

God has taken love's initiative in Jesus Christ, and for all eternity God will share love's joy with his people. We do not deserve such love. Justice demanded something else. But the cross brings God's love and justice together.

Picture a mound of explosives. Two long fuses extend from the mound, one going to the right, the other to the left. At the end of one fuse, a sign points toward the explosives with the word *justice* written on it. At the end of the other fuse, a sign points toward the explosives, bearing the word *love*.

The two fuses are lit simultaneously. On one side, someone says, "This is terrifying; when that fuse gets to the explosive of justice, there'll be hell to pay!" But on the other side, they're saying, "This is wonderful; when the fuse gets to the explosive of love, heaven will be opened!" The fuses eventually burn into each other and the explosion shakes the whole earth. Justice and love collide at the cross.

That's the story of the Bible. On the day Adam sinned, God told him he would die—*and* he promised victory over the Curse. Someone born of the woman would crush the head of the serpent and deliver man from death.

God lit two long fuses called justice and love, and these two themes burn their way through the Old Testament story until they meet and reach their fullest expression at the cross. God's love and God's requirement for justice met as a perfect sacrifice was offered for our sins. What could ever make you turn away from love like this?

FOR FURTHER READING, SEE ROMANS 3

WHY DO YOU ALLOW IT?

How long, O LORD, must I call for help? But you do not listen!
"Violence is everywhere!" I cry, but you do not come to save.
Must I forever see these evil deeds? HABAKKUK 1:2-3

IMAGINE HABAKKUK AT home in Jerusalem, his head in his hands. He cannot pick up a *Jerusalem Journal* newspaper without reading about a shooting, a killing, or some other kind of violence. When he looks around the city, he says, "Wherever I look, I see destruction and violence. I am surrounded by people who love to argue and fight" (Habakkuk 1:3).

Everywhere he looks—businesses, government, neighbors, even in the Temple—there are disputes and arguments. You might expect a general civility among the people of God, and it had once been so, but now it's every man for himself. Habakkuk finds himself in a litigious society.

So "the law has become paralyzed" (Habakkuk 1:4). The courts are jammed with litigation, but when all is said and done, justice doesn't prevail because "the wicked far outnumber the righteous, so that justice has become perverted" (1:4). More cases are decided on the basis of money and power than truth and justice, and as a result, the whole legal system is coming apart at the seams. Does this sound strangely familiar?

The thing that made this so painful for Habakkuk was that all this was happening among God's people! God had called these people to be a light to other nations. Jerusalem was supposed to be the city where God's name was honored and where people lived according to his law. Habakkuk's heart was heavy because of the rampant injustice in the city of God. He wondered how long God would allow this to go on, and he longed for God to do something about the sins of his own people.

Why does God tolerate wrong? How are we to understand what is happening in our day? Habakkuk raises the great questions that believers in a fallen world face in every generation. Why is the world as it is? Why does God allow the evils that stalk the world today?

FOR FURTHER READING, SEE HABAKKUK 1

YOU WON'T BELIEVE THIS!

*Look around at the nations; look and be amazed! For I am
doing something in your own day, something you wouldn't
believe even if someone told you about it.* HABAKKUK 1:5

HABAKKUK HAD BEEN waiting for God to act, and now God was ready. Perhaps the prophet thought, *Great! What are you going to do, Lord? Are you going to bring a national revival? Will it impact us or the next generation?*

What God said next must have left Habakkuk speechless: "I am raising up the Babylonians" (Habakkuk 1:6). I imagine Habakkuk doing a double take at this point: *The Babylonians!*

If you want to know how Habakkuk must have felt about this, put in a more contemporary name. This would be like God saying, "Yes, I know that there are terrible things going on among my people, so I am going to raise up Saddam Hussein."

Habakkuk seemed to say, "But you can't do that, God! I know things are in a pretty desperate state among your people, but nothing like what's going on with the Babylonians! They deny everything you stand for." The cure seemed worse than the condition. But God's answer was clear: he would use the Babylonians to deal with the sins of his people. He would use their evil to accomplish his own purpose.

It is not surprising that Habakkuk asked a second question: "O LORD, our Rock, you have sent these Babylonians to correct us, to punish us for our many sins. But you are pure and cannot stand the sight of evil. Will you wink at their treachery? Should you be silent while the wicked swallow up people more righteous than they?" (Habakkuk 1:12-13).

Habakkuk's first question (Habakkuk 1:4) was about the sins of God's people. His second question was about the wider evil in the world. Habakkuk seemed to have accepted that God could use an evil power like Babylon to bring judgment to his own people, but that raised another question: what would God ultimately do with evil powers?

Sometimes the methods God uses to bring about his purposes seem counterintuitive—using a godless nation to punish God's people, using an instrument of death (the cross) to bring new life—but we can always trust God. His "ways are far beyond anything [we] could imagine" (Isaiah 55:8).

FOR FURTHER READING, SEE JONAH 4

WHERE HISTORY IS HEADING

*Write my answer plainly on tablets, so that a runner can carry
the correct message to others. This vision is for a future time.
It describes the end, and it will be fulfilled.* HABAKKUK 2:2-3

GOD WAS SAYING, "Habakkuk, write down what I am about to say, because this is something that everybody needs to know. It needs to have a permanent record, because what I'm about to tell you will not happen until the appointed time. I am going to unveil what will happen in the end."

Habakkuk pulled out a pen and a tablet and recorded God's five statements. Each one began with the word *woe*, which indicated that something would be stopped:

- "Woe to him who piles up stolen goods and makes himself wealthy by extortion!" (Habakkuk 2:6, NIV). This person has accumulated wealth without integrity.
- "Woe to him who builds his house by unjust gain!" (Habakkuk 2:9, NIV). This person has lost sight of truth and justice and will do anything to build power and achieve his own ends.
- "Woe to him who builds a city with bloodshed!" (Habakkuk 2:12, NIV). This person has placed a low value on human life.
- "Woe to him who gives drink to his neighbors, pouring it from the wineskin till they are drunk, so that he can gaze on their naked bodies!" (Habakkuk 2:15, NIV). Here is the abuser of drugs and the abuser of women.
- "Woe to him who says to wood, 'Come to life!' Or to lifeless stone, 'Wake up!'" (Habakkuk 2:19, NIV). This person is an idolater. What he has made he puts in the place of God. The greatest thing in this person's life is achievement.

God is promising that all the dimensions of evil in the world will finally be stopped. Their destruction is assured. God will completely overthrow all evil, and "as the waters fill the sea, the earth will be filled with an awareness of the glory of the LORD" (Habakkuk 2:14). That is where human history is headed: to the day when God's glorious presence will scatter all evil, and his glory will shine like the sun all over the world.

FOR FURTHER READING, SEE HABAKKUK 2

FAITH IS BETTER THAN SIGHT

The righteous shall live by his faith. HABAKKUK 2:4, ESV

WHEN HABAKKUK TALKS about "the righteous," he does not mean some people are in the right in every way. The Bible says, "No one is righteous— not even one" (Romans 3:10). But there are some people who desire it: "Blessed are those who hunger and thirst for righteousness, for they will be filled" (Matthew 5:6, NIV).

How are these people who, like Habakkuk, hunger and thirst after righteousness to make sense of this confusing world? And how are we to navigate our way through uncertain and unpredictable events? How are we to hold our course in the face of the great evils that arise throughout history? The answer is faith.

Sight is a wonderful gift, but it has a very limited capacity. It cannot look around corners. It can only look in one direction at a time, and when it turns to look in another direction, it loses the capacity to view what it saw before!

As long as we're living in this fallen world, faith is much better than sight. Sight looks at evidence, forms opinions, and draws conclusions, but the problem with sight is that it's only capable of looking at observable realities; it doesn't have the capacity to see any further than the objects in front of it.

Sight cannot reckon the invisible power of God. That's why sight is hopelessly inadequate when it comes to making sense of this world. By definition, sight leaves the invisible God out of the picture. So if you try to make sense of your life or the events of this world purely on the basis of sight, you'll be very discouraged.

This does not mean that people who exercise faith go through life with their eyes closed. Our eyes should be wide open to the problems, but faith goes further. Faith sees beyond the difficulties and counts on God.

Now we see the abuse of power in high places, the weakness and worldliness of the church, appalling acts of violence and terrible abuse, but when we're in the presence of Christ, sight will be altogether different. Then we will see him. Sight does not have that capacity now. So until then, we must walk by faith.

FOR FURTHER READING, SEE ROMANS 1

HOW FAITH OPERATES

This vision is for a future time.... If it seems slow in coming, wait patiently, for it will surely take place. It will not be delayed. HABAKKUK 2:3

GOD WAS INVITING Habakkuk to live by faith. God would prosper Babylon, and Jerusalem would be crushed. The apparent triumph of evil would make it seem like God's purpose was overturned, but God was saying, "My purpose will be achieved in the end. You have my Word. Trust me."

Faith trusts in the Word of God. That's what Abraham did. God promised to make Abraham's descendants like the stars in the heavens (see Genesis 15:5). The only problem was that Abraham was one hundred years old, and his wife was nearly ninety! The statistical probability of Isaac's birth was nearly zero!

Sight said, "There's no hope," but faith went beyond sight and found rest in God's Word. Paul said that Abraham "figured his body was as good as dead" (Romans 4:19), yet he gave glory to God, being "fully convinced that God is able to do whatever he promises" (4:21).

Six hundred years after Habakkuk received this assurance, the Babylonian empire was replaced by the Roman empire, but notice the same evil at work: a couple of false witnesses tell lies to a prejudiced jury. Why would God allow that? Soldiers stand around a man whose hands are tied and strike him, spit on him, and mock him. Why would God allow that? An innocent man is nailed to a cross, and as he dies, he cries out, "My God, my God, why?" (Matthew 27:46).

God allows evil to have its day, but he uses that evil to accomplish his purposes. Of course, sight will never tell you that. But when faith looks at the cross, it sees God at work and believes his promise. Faith sees that Christ came into the world and, through his death, accomplished the salvation God promised.

This is how faith operates. It looks beyond the observable realities and counts on God's promise. You may be looking at a pretty discouraging situation in your own life right now. Perhaps there's no basis for hope in what you see. God calls you to live by faith. Faith recognizes the realities but rests in the promises of God.

FOR FURTHER READING, SEE ROMANS 4

WHEN EVIL IS ADVANCING

Even though the fig trees have no blossoms, and there are no grapes on the
vines; even though the olive crop fails, and the fields lie empty and barren;
even though the flocks die in the fields, and the cattle barns are empty,
yet . . . I will be joyful in the God of my salvation! HABAKKUK 3:17-18

HABAKKUK DISCOVERED A joy that didn't depend on what was happening around him. He described the worst of all imaginable circumstances, and then he told God, "Even if everything goes wrong and all hell breaks loose—I won't live by sight, but by faith. I'll rest in your promise and find my joy in knowing that you are my Savior."

Habakkuk's joy was based on the assurance that even when the Babylonians came and overwhelmed the city of God, the Lord was in control. He'd grasped that history moves under the plan of God and is heading for the day when all evil will be brought to nothing.

This kind of joy doesn't depend on what's happening in the stock market or on who's in the White House. We should pray for fig trees to bud and for cattle in the barns, but our joy doesn't depend on these things.

Faith is better than sight. If I analyze my life in light of God's law, sight says that I've sinned and fallen short of the glory of God. Everyone, including me, can see that—so can my wife! It's the truth about all of us. "No one is righteous—not even one" (Romans 3:10).

But faith goes deeper than sight and rests on the promises of God. Faith says, "Christ died for my sins," and believes God's promise that "there is no condemnation for those who belong to Christ Jesus" (Romans 8:1) because Jesus carried our sin on the cross so we could be forgiven and reconciled to God. This faith in Christ brings lasting joy. I can say with Habakkuk, "I will be joyful in the God of my salvation!"

Habakkuk's joy was rooted in God, in the certainty that his purpose would be fulfilled. That gave Habakkuk stability, and he was able to worship God with joy at a time when evil was advancing in the world! What do you know about this kind of faith?

FOR FURTHER READING, SEE HABAKKUK 3

THE ULTIMATE OUTREACH

"I have always loved you," says the LORD. MALACHI 1:2

AS WE COME to the end of the Old Testament story, it's worth asking, where do things stand in the relationship between God and his people after all these years of alienation? Malachi does not give us an encouraging answer.

There is a pattern running through the book of Malachi: God makes a statement, but his people will not accept what he says. It is as if an argument develops between God and his people, rather like a counseling session in which one rather petulant person is unwilling to accept the truth of anything the other person says.

The book of Malachi opens with God affirming his love for his people. This seems reasonable when you think that God brought them out of Egypt, gave them promises, and restored them from exile, but God's people will not accept that. They fold their arms in defiance and say, "How have you loved us?" (Malachi 1:2).

God is seeking to restore the relationship with his people, so he raises the issues that have caused the relationship to break down. That is the only way in which a relationship can be restored—the issues that have caused offense must be brought to light and dealt with honestly. But God's people are in denial about the problem.

Have you ever seen an argument in which one person digs in and will not admit any responsibility for what's wrong? Those who have attempted to restore a broken relationship know what this is like. If you have one party who is reaching out to make peace and the other party is unresponsive and in denial about the problem, then you face an uphill struggle. That's what is happening here.

But while we were still dead in our sins, Jesus Christ came into the world, reaching out to us from the cross with open arms and giving his life as a sacrifice for sin. By his death, he bridged the gap of alienation between man and God, and he opens the way for the forgiveness of sins and reconciliation with God.

FOR FURTHER READING, SEE MALACHI 1

IN DENIAL

How have we ever shown contempt for your name? MALACHI 1:6

THE PRIESTS WERE supposed to order the worship of God and supervise the sacrifices. God said they were showing contempt for his name, but the priests wouldn't accept this. God elaborated: "You have shown contempt by offering defiled sacrifices on my altar," but the priests would not accept this charge either, so they asked, "How have we defiled the sacrifices?" (Malachi 1:7).

This pattern runs right through the book—denial, denial, denial. God raised the issue of repentance with the people because he wanted to restore the relationship—"Ever since the days of your ancestors, you have scorned my decrees and failed to obey them. Now return to me, and I will return to you"—but the people responded, "How can we return when we have never gone away?" (Malachi 3:7).

Then God raised the issue of tithes, "Should people cheat God? Yet you have cheated me!" The response was predictable: "When did we ever cheat you?" (Malachi 3:8). Then God pointed out that the people spoke about him harshly, to which they replied, "What do you mean? What have we said against you?" (3:13).

God was reaching out to his people. He told them that he loved them. He wanted to restore the relationship with his people, and he raised the issues so they could be resolved. But time after time, his people took the posture of denial and folded their arms in defiance toward God. And that's where the Old Testament ends!

This story, which began with a man and a woman in fellowship with God, ends with men and women alienated from God, in denial of the problem, unwilling to take any responsibility, and unable to do anything about it.

That's why Christ had to come into the world. He came to do what no religion could ever do. You can go to church, say your prayers, and try to live a moral life, but without Christ, you cannot be reconciled to God. But Jesus Christ can change your heart so that you are willing and able to be reconciled to him. The Old Testament is an unfinished story. It shows us our need for Christ.

FOR FURTHER READING, SEE MALACHI 3

THE HEART OF THE FATHER

The LORD witnessed the vows you and your wife made when you
were young. But you have been unfaithful to her, though she
remained your faithful partner, the wife of your marriage vows. . . .
"I hate divorce!" says the LORD, the God of Israel. MALACHI 2:14, 16

APPARENTLY, THE STORY of the people's relationship with God mir-
rored their relationships with each other. In the Garden, Adam and
Eve enjoyed perfect happiness, but at the end of the Old Testament era,
marriage among God's people was in shambles.

I've never met a couple who on their wedding day thought or hoped
they would one day stand in a divorce court. It must be one of the most
painful experiences in all the world. But as God spoke to the culture
of Malachi's time, it was clear that marriages were breaking and tearing
apart. The joy of shared hopes and dreams for the future was ending in
the tears of broken promises.

That is the story of the Old Testament. It began with a man and a
woman sharing the joy of a perfect life together in the Garden, and
it ends with men and women in the divorce court, unable to sustain
relationships of faithfulness and love. That is the tragedy of living in
our world.

The breakup of marriages has always had devastating effects on children. That's why God speaks about a day when he will "turn the hearts
of fathers to their children, and the hearts of children to their fathers"
(Malachi 4:6). The whole family unit was falling apart! Dads had lost
heart for their children, and sons and daughters didn't care about their
parents. Families lived without love, and long stories of accumulated
wrongs developed without forgiveness and, no doubt, with many tears.

Although the Old Testament ends in tears, the story of humankind
does not end here. It will end in a great city that is thronging with those
who have been redeemed by Christ—the one who is Faithful and True
(see Revelation 19:11). It will end with the heart of our heavenly Father
turned to his children, wiping away every tear from their eyes (see 21:4),
and his steadfast love will never fail.

FOR FURTHER READING, SEE MALACHI 2

THE UNFULFILLED PROMISE

Otherwise I will come and strike the land with a curse. MALACHI 4:6

THE PROBLEMS THAT began in the Garden continued throughout history, right up to the very last word of the Old Testament. But the Bible story is about more than sin's curse; it is also about a promise. On the day evil entered the world, God promised that someone born of a woman would destroy the evil one and all his works.

In the course of time, God appeared to Abraham and said, "All the families on earth will be blessed through you" (Genesis 12:3). Isaac and Jacob were born, and from them God raised up a great nation. That nation was oppressed in Egypt, but God brought them out and renewed his covenant with them: "I will claim you as my own people, and I will be your God" (Exodus 6:7).

Moses led them out of Egypt. Joshua led them into Canaan. But no deliverer had appeared to save them from sin. Then God gave a special promise to David: a king would be born into his line whose kingdom would last forever (see 2 Samuel 7:13). But after David, most of the kings were a disappointment. One king after another led God's people to imitate the worship and lifestyles of other nations, so that evil became rampant even among God's people.

God let the best and brightest of his people go into exile in Babylon. Jerusalem, along with its Temple, was utterly destroyed. But God never goes back on a promise, and after seventy years, a small group returned to rebuild the city. God sent Malachi to remind them of the problem and the promise.

"The Sun of Righteousness will rise with healing in his wings. And you will go free" (Malachi 4:2). There would be healing for the problem that had run all through human history. Evil had gained a grip on the world, and even God's people were imprisoned by it, but the day would come when God's people would experience freedom.

Despite this promise, the Old Testament ends on a dark note. It leaves us asking, when the Messiah comes, will the people be ready for him? Four hundred years passed before Jesus Christ came. Some were ready, but many were not. How about you? Are you ready for Jesus Christ today?

FOR FURTHER READING, SEE MALACHI 4

GOD'S "TO-DO" LIST

*There were fourteen generations in all from Abraham to David,
fourteen from David to the exile to Babylon, and fourteen
from the exile to the Messiah.* MATTHEW 1:17, NIV

THE NEW TESTAMENT opens by reminding us of the people to whom God made his greatest promises. Matthew arranged the genealogy of Jesus into three groups of fourteen generations—beginning, respectively, with David, Abraham, and the Exile.

Jesus is called "the son of Abraham" (Matthew 1:1, NIV). Two thousand years before Jesus was born, God promised that his blessing would flow through Abraham to every nation: "I will bless you. . . . All the families on earth will be blessed through you" (Genesis 12:2-3).

Abraham wondered how this could be since he had no children, but God stepped in and gave Abraham and Sarah a child in their old age. Isaac's birth was a miracle, but God's blessing to the world did not come through him. So the promise to Abraham remained on God's to-do list.

Jesus is also called "the son of David" (Matthew 1:1, NIV). God told David about a son who would build a house for his name, and he promised to establish that son's throne and kingdom forever: "I will be his father, and he will be my son" (2 Samuel 7:14).

David's son, Solomon, built a magnificent Temple for the glory of God, but Solomon did not fulfill God's promise. His Temple was eventually destroyed, and his kingdom certainly did not last forever. So this whole business of building a permanent house and establishing a throne was added to God's to-do list.

When God's people faced their darkest hour in exile, God promised to make a new covenant with them and write his instructions on their hearts (see Jeremiah 31:33) so they would live according to his law—not out of obligation, but out of an inner desire to follow God. These promises were made six hundred years before Jesus' incarnation, but they remained on God's to-do list.

Despite all that God had done for his people throughout the Old Testament story, God's greatest promises were still unfulfilled at the beginning of the New Testament. God wants us to know that the fulfillment of all he has promised to do was initiated in the coming of Jesus Christ.

FOR FURTHER READING, SEE HEBREWS 1

GETTING IT DONE!

This is how Jesus the Messiah was born. MATTHEW 1:18

MATTHEW TELLS US the story: Mary was found to be with child before she and Joseph were married. Joseph did not know what to make of this, but then one night God spoke to him in a dream—an angel told him not to be afraid: Mary was still a virgin; the child was conceived by the Holy Spirit.

Then Matthew writes, "All of this occurred to fulfill the Lord's message through his prophet: 'Look! The virgin will conceive a child!'" (Matthew 1:22-23). In other words, when Jesus Christ came into the world, the things God said he would do were done. As you read through the Gospels, you find this same point repeated again and again.

We're told how Joseph took Mary and Jesus to Egypt because Herod was trying to kill the child. Matthew explains that this too "fulfilled what the Lord had spoken through the prophet: 'I called my Son out of Egypt'" (Matthew 2:15). An event on God's to-do list was done.

Then the young family moved to the town of Nazareth. This "fulfilled what the prophets had said: 'He will be called a Nazarene'" (Matthew 2:23). Done! When Jesus began his ministry, he went to Capernaum, beside the Sea of Galilee. This "fulfilled what God said through the prophet Isaiah: . . . Beside the sea, . . . a light has shined" (4:14-16). Done!

Jesus stood up in the synagogue and read these words from the Old Testament prophet Isaiah: "The Spirit of the LORD is upon me, for he has anointed me to bring Good News to the poor. He has sent me to proclaim that captives will be released, that the blind will see, that the oppressed will be set free, and that the time of the LORD's favor has come." Then he announced, "The Scripture you've just heard has been fulfilled this very day!" (Luke 4:18-19, 21). In other words, "What God has promised is now being accomplished—by me!"

The detail is staggering! When Christ came into the world, it was as if God held up a massive to-do list of all he had promised since the beginning of time, and checked promise after promise off the list—it's done!

FOR FURTHER READING, SEE EPHESIANS 1

NOT JUST ANOTHER PROPHET

I did not come to abolish the law of Moses or the writings of the
prophets. No, I came to accomplish their purpose. MATTHEW 5:17

PEOPLE HAVE ALWAYS thought of Jesus as one of the prophets (see Matthew 16:14), but he made it clear that we must not understand him that way. "I came to accomplish [the prophets'] purpose," he said. Every time the prophets spoke, they announced God's promises, and God's to-do list got longer!

If Jesus were just another prophet, he would have announced more things God would one day do, but Jesus' coming would not have contributed much to actually getting those things done. Jesus did not come to make God's to-do list longer. He came so that God's to-do list would be done!

Jesus cannot be placed alongside the prophets or other religious teachers. If you want to know who Jesus is, you need to understand that he's altogether different from the Old Testament prophets or any other religious leader who has ever lived.

A friend of mine attended a religious seminar and was told that Judaism stops with Moses, Christianity stops with Jesus, and Islam stops with Muhammad. Many people see Jesus as just another figure in the long line of religious history. They see Abraham, Moses, David, Jesus, Paul, and others, continuing into contemporary times, as great religious teachers whose portraits all hang on the same wall.

Some opponents of Christianity suggest that Christianity is a new religion invented by Jesus, who lived a mere two thousand years ago. But the Bible story goes back to the beginning of time. It tells us what God said he would do, and it tells us that he has fulfilled his promises through Jesus Christ.

The prophets announced God's promise of blessing for all nations, a Kingdom that will never end, and a new heart for God's people, but the uniqueness of Jesus Christ is that all of these promises find their fulfillment in him. Have you begun to see why Jesus' portrait belongs on a wall all by itself?

FOR FURTHER READING, SEE MATTHEW 16

BRINGING THE LAW TO LIFE

I came to accomplish [the law's] purpose.   MATTHEW 5:17

ONCE YOU UNDERSTAND the uniqueness of Jesus, you will be better able to grasp what he has done. When Jesus announced what he would accomplish through his ministry, he made it clear that he came to fulfill not only the writings of the prophets, but also the law.

If the writings of the prophets represented God's to-do list, then the law, including the Ten Commandments and all the other commands given to Moses, represents *our* to-do list. In it God tells us what he requires us to do. This law will stand until heaven and earth disappear (see Matthew 5:18), and that hasn't happened yet!

So it would be a great mistake to think that God was concerned about the law and righteousness in the Old Testament but that somehow he changed his focus and switched to grace and forgiveness in the New Testament. The whole Bible is one story. God has always been gracious and forgiving, and his law stands forever.

The law of God is still our to-do list. But Jesus says that he came to fulfill the law. In other words, he came to move the law from the to-do list to the *done* list. The law is not an arbitrary set of moral rules but a description of God's character and glory. The reason we should not lie is that God is truth. The reason we should not commit adultery is that God is faithful.

The law tells us what God is like and describes his calling for our lives—how we're to live in this world. But consider the long list of names at the beginning of Matthew's Gospel. Not one of them fulfilled the law of God—and neither have you or I. Jesus came to live the life that God has put on your to-do list. He lifted the words of God's law off of the page and expressed them fully in his perfect life. That is why Jesus could say, "Anyone who has seen me has seen the Father" (John 14:9).

When Jesus came, he gave full expression to God's law—it was done.

FOR FURTHER READING, SEE MATTHEW 5

NO PAYMENTS UNTIL NEXT YEAR

I tell you the truth, until heaven and earth disappear,
not even the smallest detail of God's law will disappear
until its purpose is achieved. MATTHEW 5:18

THE LAW TELLS us what God requires of us and announces the consequences of sin. That's why the Bible talks about the curse of the law.
But throughout the Old Testament, God repeatedly postponed this
condemnation.

When Adam disobeyed in the Garden, he was excluded from
Paradise, but his life continued. Abraham lied about his wife, but he
remained a friend of God. David committed adultery, yet he remained
on Israel's throne. Isaiah confessed he was a man of unclean lips, yet he
was used as a prophet. None of them came under the full condemnation of God. Why? The reason cannot be that their sins didn't matter.

The whole point of the law is that sin *does* matter. But throughout the
Old Testament, God held back the condemnation of the law. He put off
the Day of Judgment. He didn't cancel it; he postponed it. He put dealing
with the consequences of human sin on his to-do list.

Advertisers often say, "No payments until next year!" It sounds
wonderful, and it's virtually free . . . until the letter arrives in January
telling you to pay up! The payment was not canceled; it was only postponed. At some point, the bill has to be paid.

Throughout the Old Testament, the sacrifices reminded God's people
that there would come a time when something had to be done. But the
consequences of sin remained, like an accumulating debt that one day
would have to be paid. Then Jesus arrived and said, "I have come to fulfill the law." That meant not only that he would fulfill everything the law
required in his life, but also that he would bear the condemnation of the
law in his death. That's why Jesus had to go to the cross.

God's time for dealing with the consequences of sin had come. The
judgment and condemnation described in God's law were poured out
on Christ, and when he'd absorbed it fully, he cried out, "It is finished!" (John 19:30). At that moment, dealing with sin was crossed off
God's to-do list, because for all his people, it was done.

FOR FURTHER READING, SEE HEBREWS 10

AT THE BOTTOM OF YOUR LIST

*[God] condemned sin in the flesh, in order that the righteous requirement
of the law might be fully met in us, who do not live according to
the flesh but according to the Spirit.* ROMANS 8:3-4, NIV

JESUS CAME TO bring you into a new life so you can begin to fulfill the
law of God. He died to bring you out of condemnation; he lives to lead
you into a righteous life.

Some things get pushed to the bottom of my to-do list—things I don't
like and things I feel I can't do. That's our problem when it comes to the
law of God: we don't like it, and we can't do it, so our instinct is to push
it to the bottom of our list.

Jesus came to save you from that and to make you the person God
always intended you to be. He does this by giving you a hunger and
thirst for righteousness and the power of the Holy Spirit, so your life
may move in the direction of God's law.

I recall vacationing as a teen in Torquay, England. The accommodations were poor, and the beaches were crowded. At one point in the
car ride home, I said, "Dad, I don't ever want to go to that town again!"
My mother pointed out this was the sort of thing a person might regret
saying. Six years later, I met a girl from that town, fell in love with her,
and married her. I've enjoyed going there ever since.

When God's Spirit begins working in you, you may be a long way off
from the law, but you'll have a new hunger. Jesus said, "Blessed are those
who hunger and thirst for righteousness" (Matthew 5:6, NIV). In other
words, you've come to want what God wants for you.

Christ accepts us just as we are, but he never leaves us as we are. It
is the purpose of God to make us righteous, so that we will reflect his
glory in a life that fulfills the law of God. What do you know about this
kind of life?

FOR FURTHER READING, SEE ROMANS 8

DEALING WITH DISASTER

*You are to name him Jesus, for he will save his
people from their sins.* MATTHEW 1:21

WHEN THE ANGEL announced the birth of Christ, he did not say, "You
are to give him the name Jesus, because he will *forgive* his people for their
sins." Forgiveness is only a part of what Jesus came to do.

Jesus will *save* his people from their sins. To *save* people from their
sins means to bring them out of their sins. Saving people from their sins
means delivering them from every dimension of this disaster.

On March 16, 1978, a supertanker called the *Amoco Cadiz* ran aground
off the coast of Brittany, France, and lost nearly a quarter of a million
tons of crude oil into the Atlantic Ocean. Oil swept onto more than a
hundred beaches—in some places up to a foot deep.

Now when a disaster like this happens, there's more than one problem.

The problem in the *courts* was an issue of justice—there was a price to
pay. In this case, a judge in Chicago awarded damages of $85.2 million.

The problem on the *beaches* was an issue of pollution—there was a
cleanup that needed to be done. Think of the crystal clear water and
the fish and plants and birds. Now imagine crude oil pouring from a
stricken vessel. That's what sin does—it pollutes.

The problem in the *hull* was an issue of repair—there was a hole that
needed to be fixed. If we don't deal with the source of the spill, the
problem will only get worse.

If Christ delivered us from the condemnation of sin without delivering us from its power in our lives, it would be like paying the fine for
the *Amoco Cadiz* but doing nothing to clean up the beaches or fix the hull.

The salvation that Jesus came to bring is much more than forgiveness and a free ticket to heaven. It has always been God's purpose to
deliver his people from sin *and* lead them into a holy life. Jesus came to
save you—to deal with your guilt and the pollution caused by your sin,
and to free you from the power of sin in your life.

FOR FURTHER READING, SEE TITUS 3

A GOLDEN OPPORTUNITY

*Repent of your sins and turn to God, for the Kingdom
of Heaven is near.* MATTHEW 3:2

JOHN THE BAPTIST'S message was essentially, "The long-awaited promise is about to be fulfilled. This is a golden opportunity. If you want to
take it, you're going to have to change." Notice heaven is a "kingdom,"
a place that's under the rule of a king. If you want to be in the Kingdom
of Heaven, you have to submit to the rule of the King of heaven.

For thirty-eight years, I was not subject to the laws of the United States
of America, because I was living in Great Britain. Then in 1996, I was
invited to serve as a pastor in the States, and when I came, I was immediately released from an old set of laws I'd been subject to in Britain, and
I became subject to a new set of laws in America.

Some of the new laws were difficult for me—like driving at low
speeds on open roads. But I've found—from experience—that if I'm
stopped by a police officer, it simply will not do to say, "I'm operating
under the laws of Her Majesty, the queen!" The officer would point out
that if I want to operate by another set of laws, I'd better go back to the
place where those laws hold sway.

Throughout human history, men and women have been kept at a
distance from heaven. The cherubim and the flaming sword barred the
way back into the Garden of Eden (see Genesis 3:24), where Adam and
Eve had known the blessing and the presence of God.

Abraham, Isaac, Jacob, David, and the prophets all looked forward
to the Kingdom of Heaven. God was gracious to them, but when they
died, they joined a long line of people waiting for God's promise to be
fulfilled (see Hebrews 11:13).

At last, through Jesus Christ, the borders of heaven have been thrown
open. But if you want to be in the Kingdom where Christ reigns, you
must place yourself under his authority, and that means you're going to
have to change. Repent, for the Kingdom of Heaven is near. You cannot have the benefits of the Kingdom if you will not bow to the King.

FOR FURTHER READING, SEE JAMES 2

DO WHAT YOU HAVE TO DO

Produce fruit in keeping with repentance. MATTHEW 3:8, NIV

FRUIT IS ALWAYS visible, and repentance will show up as a visible change in what you say and do. As the crowd listened to John's message, they were moved by what they heard and wanted to know what they should do (see Luke 3:10).

They probably thought John would tell them things they could do when they got home. But John called them to immediate action. Here was a crowd of people out in a desert—some would be cold and hungry—and John said, "If you have two shirts, give one to the poor. If you have food, share it with those who are hungry" (Luke 3:11). Repentance is not an intention to lead a new life in the future; it begins now, as you step out in obedience in your immediate situation.

Repentance is also specific. Tax collectors asked John what they should do, and he said, "Collect no more taxes than the government requires" (Luke 3:13). Soldiers asked what they should do, and he said, "Don't extort money or make false accusations" (3:14). Do what you have to do to bring your life into line with the commandments of God. That's repentance.

The Pharisees came to see what was happening, but they didn't feel the need to be forgiven. They never discovered repentance, so they went home unchanged. This must have caused John great sadness. He warned them about their smugness: "Don't just say to each other, 'We're safe, for we are descendants of Abraham'" (Matthew 3:9). Relying on heritage while refusing to repent is a sure formula for spiritual disaster.

Many Christians see repentance as an initial act that is completed at the beginning of the Christian life—a gateway we pass through. God's call to repent is immediate and specific, but it's also ongoing. God is gracious; he shows us our sins slowly. If he showed them to us all at once, we would be devastated.

As we come to know God more, we will discover more about ourselves, and our repentance will become deeper, touching areas that were hidden from us before. As God shows you sin in your life, remember that he is calling you to walk with him, and that always involves a life of repentance and faith.

FOR FURTHER READING, SEE LUKE 3

MATCHMAKERS

> *Someone is coming soon who is greater than I am—so much greater that*
> *I'm not worthy even to be his slave and carry his sandals.* MATTHEW 3:11

JOHN'S MESSAGE LED people to the point where they saw their need for change, but he could not give them the power they needed to follow through. John told them that they should go to Christ.

John was a great leader—he knew the limitations of his ministry. "I can baptize you and help you express your desire to live a new life. But I cannot give you the power to change. Someone greater is coming, and he will give you that power."

When Jesus began to preach, John identified him as "the Lamb of God who takes away the sin of the world" (John 1:29). Then those who had been following John left and began following Jesus. That's what John wanted them to do. He ended up with little personal following, but his ministry was the means of many coming to Christ.

My wife, Karen, and I have some friends in England who have been happily married for twenty years. They represent our one successful attempt at matchmaking.

I was speaking at a youth conference, and we persuaded them both to join us. She had her eye on him, but he found that hard to believe. She said, "I like him, but I don't think he's interested." He said, "I like her, but I don't have a chance."

"Ask her for a date," I said. "I can tell you on good authority that if you do, you'll get a positive response." Finally it happened. I have no idea what he said to her, but it obviously met with an enthusiastic reply. After that, Karen and I faded out of the picture.

I can tell you on good authority today that Christ will welcome you. He said, "Those the Father has given me will come to me, and I will never reject them" (John 6:37). Talking to a pastor, counselor, or Christian friend can be helpful, but it can never be a substitute for having a relationship with Jesus. They may encourage you or answer your questions, but at the end of the day, you have to make that move; nobody else can do it for you.

FOR FURTHER READING, SEE MATTHEW 3

DRENCHED IN THE LIFE OF GOD

I baptize with water those who repent of their sins and turn to God. . . .
He will baptize you with the Holy Spirit. MATTHEW 3:11

THE WORD *BAPTIZE* means "to dip, plunge, or immerse." The Holy Spirit is the Spirit of God, so when John says, "He will baptize you with the Holy Spirit," he is saying that Jesus will drench you in the life of God.

If you go to Christ, you will experience a divine invasion. The Holy Spirit will take up residence within you—completely. As water saturates what it is poured on, so the Holy Spirit gets into every portion of our lives. As fire purifies and destroys, the Spirit burns up the rubbish in our lives—"our God is a devouring fire" (Hebrews 12:29).

Picture John and Jesus standing with their followers around them. John baptizes with water; Jesus baptizes with the Holy Spirit. John helps people express their desire for a new life; Jesus gives them the power to live it. John cannot give the Spirit; only Jesus can do that.

Here's a testimony written by a person who wants to be baptized:

> I was brought up in a Christian family and attended church since I was very young. When I was sixteen years old, my friends were going to a Christian camp, and I went along. As I listened to the speaker, I began to realize that there was a lot wrong with my life. I really wanted to change, so I prayed a prayer of commitment to God. Since then, things have been different. It hasn't been easy, but I'm being baptized to show I want to live a life that's pleasing to God and to be with him in heaven.

This person wants John's baptism, not Christ's. He's in the same position as those who gathered around John: "brought up in a Christian family" (religious background), "listened to the speaker" (like hearing John in the desert), "wanted to change" and "live a life that's pleasing to God" (like those baptized by John).

There are many people like this in the church today, who have made a commitment but haven't come to Christ and haven't experienced the life of God invading their souls. John would say, "Go to Christ. He'll baptize you with the Holy Spirit."

FOR FURTHER READING, SEE ACTS 10

WHERE MANY STUMBLE

Are you the Messiah we've been expecting, or should we
keep looking for someone else? MATTHEW 11:3

IT'S TIME TO pause and ask some honest questions. That's what John the Baptist did when things didn't make sense. Remember, John announced that the Kingdom of Heaven was at hand, and when Jesus began his ministry, John identified him as "the Lamb of God who takes away the sin of the world" (John 1:29).

But then something happened that must have shaken John to the core: he was arrested and thrown in prison. When that happened, the man who had preached with such great faith found himself surrounded with doubts and questions. *If Jesus really is the Christ, then why is this happening to me?*

So, John sent messengers to Jesus with the question "Are you the Messiah we've been expecting, or should we keep looking for someone else?" (Matthew 11:3). You can see his point: if God was fulfilling his promise through Jesus, he was doing it in a strange way.

We have similar questions. If God's promises are true, what are we to make of the war, violence, and greed in the world? As we look at the church, what are we to make of the compromise, confusion, and complacency that are so prevalent? When I look at my own life, how am I to make sense of my ongoing battle with sin?

Jesus sent messengers to John: "Go back to John and tell him what you have heard and seen—the blind see, the lame walk, the lepers are cured, the deaf hear, the dead are raised to life, and the Good News is being preached to the poor" (Matthew 11:4-5). He was saying, "Yes, John, God is at work." It's not easy to live in the tension of what God has done and what he will do when Christ returns. This is where many stumble.

When Christ returns in glory, sin will be no more; sickness will be gone, and the church will be everything God has called her to be. God's Kingdom has come, and it is advancing. You will face many difficult circumstances and live with many unanswered questions, but what you have in Christ is more valuable than you can fully grasp now; it's only a foretaste of what is to come.

FOR FURTHER READING, SEE MATTHEW 11

July 14 | DAY 195

THE PARABLE OF THE BOMBER

He told many stories in the form of parables, such as this one: "Listen!
A farmer went out to plant some seeds . . ." MATTHEW 13:3

JESUS TOLD A story about a farmer who tossed seed on different kinds of ground. The story is so familiar that we may be in danger of missing the point. So here's an alternative parable that may help us see the power of Jesus' story more clearly: "The Parable of the Bomber":

A certain bomber went out to drop his bombs. He flew over an evil city with many kinds of buildings. Some of the buildings were nothing more than wooden constructions, so when the bombs hit them, the buildings were immediately flattened. Other buildings were made of concrete, reinforced by steel. They looked as if nothing would move them, but when the bombs hit them, they crumbled like powder. In fact, everywhere the bombs were scattered, the buildings were completely destroyed.

After the bomber had finished his work, he flew over the city to take photographs. No matter where the bombs fell, the effect was exactly the same. Bomb craters covered the ground like Bubble Wrap. Rubble was strewn everywhere. Enemy activity was reduced to zero. The bomber's mission was accomplished.

If Jesus had told this parable instead and the disciples asked him, "What does it mean?" imagine what Jesus might have said: "The bombs are the ministry of the Word of God. The buildings are the evils of the world, the flesh, and the devil. Some evils are deeply entrenched and strongly reinforced. But wherever the Word of God comes, evil is reduced to nothing!"

Sometimes I wish Jesus had given "The Parable of the Bomber," but he gave "The Parable of the Sower" instead. God works by sowing seeds, not by dropping bombs. Christ is telling us that the will of God gets done in people's lives not by earth-shattering explosions, but by the quiet teaching of the Word of God.

Where God's work gets done it will be like a farmer sowing seed. The seed will not grow everywhere, but where it is received, it will produce an abundant harvest. What is your approach to ministry? In what ways are you more like the bomber? Where are you more like the farmer?

FOR FURTHER READING, SEE MATTHEW 13

THE POWER OF PATIENCE

The seed that fell on the footpath represents those who hear the message about the Kingdom and don't understand it. Then the evil one comes and snatches away the seed that was planted in their hearts. MATTHEW 13:19

THERE ARE TIMES when I find this parable frustrating. I wish we could send a team of missionaries to an unreached people group and know for sure that when the Word is preached, the culture will be transformed, the darkness dispelled, the corruption ended, and faith in Christ born—that the whole community will become worshipers of Jesus. But God works by sowing seeds, not by dropping bombs.

I wish we could see our culture in America transformed. I wish abortion were unneeded and unwanted. I wish divorce would end and families would be happy and secure. I wish we would be delivered from the delusion that truth is whatever an individual happens to think. I wish we would all know the living and true God and fall before him in worship. But God works by sowing seeds, not by dropping bombs.

The problem with sowing seeds is that it takes patience. It's not very spectacular work, and things don't look very different when you're finished sowing than they did when you started. It's just the same old plowed field. The bomber can look at the immediate effects of his work, but the farmer can't.

If you teach Sunday school for an hour or pray with your children at home or share an encouragement with a neighbor, you will sometimes wonder if your work makes any difference. Remember that you are sowing seed.

God has chosen to grow his Kingdom slowly by planting the living seed of his Word in the lives of people. He calls us to sow that seed patiently and persistently. Jesus made it clear that a great deal of the seed is unproductive. Some falls on the path or among thorns or in rocky places, and nothing of lasting value comes from it. But the Word of God is living seed. It has life in it! And where the Word takes root, there will be a harvest. So keep sowing the seeds of God's truth.

FOR FURTHER READING, SEE MATTHEW 9

THE HARVEST IS COMING

He is ready to separate the chaff from the wheat with his winnowing fork.
Then he will clean up the threshing area, gathering the wheat into his
barn but burning the chaff with never-ending fire. MATTHEW 3:12

AS JOHN LANGUISHED in prison, he must have wondered why God wasn't bringing in the harvest. No doubt John was hoping that Christ would wield the winnowing fork and separate him from Herod!

That day of justice will come, but before God harvests his field, it has to be sown. Jesus makes it clear to the disciples that this is their ministry. When the seed is grown, God will announce the harvest, and then Christ will separate the wheat from the chaff, gathering the one into his barns and casting the other into the fire.

So be encouraged! Keep receiving the Word with faith and obedience. Keep believing God's Word and hiding it in your heart. Keep asking him to give you strength to do what he says. You will change and grow.

There may be times when you feel discouraged in ministry and feel like giving up. You dreamed of making an impact, but the work has been tougher and the progress slower than you thought it would be. Keep sowing the Word. Keep watering it with your prayers. Keep putting it out there, and God will bring a harvest.

I have a friend in England who has been praying for her rebellious son for fifteen years. I've prayed for the lad many times, so when I talked to her last, I asked, "How is it with your son?"

She told me that he recently said to her, "Just give me more time." Time? After fifteen years? I could feel my own frustration and disappointment rising. Then his mother said, "I'm just continuing to trust in God and to look for what he will do."

I have found this truth liberating. I cannot change the world; only God can do that. God has called us to plant seeds, not to drop bombs. Sowing takes humility and faithfulness, but it is something that, with his help, you can do.

FOR FURTHER READING, SEE COLOSSIANS 4

SABOTAGE IN THE FIELD

*The Kingdom of Heaven is like a farmer who planted good seed in his
field. But that night as the workers slept, his enemy came and planted
weeds among the wheat, then slipped away.* MATTHEW 13:24-25

JESUS TOLD A second story to help us understand the mystery of the
Kingdom. In this second story, the seed that is sown represents people,
and the field is the world (see Matthew 13:38). Jesus is telling us that
God plants his people in the world. Then he speaks about another
sower who comes to the field at night—an enemy who wants to sabotage
the farmer's work, so he sows weeds in the farmer's field.

The following morning, nobody knows what has happened. In fact,
for a long time it is difficult to distinguish the wheat from the weeds.
But when the wheat sprouts and the heads form, it becomes obvious that
an enemy has been at work in the field.

At this point, the farmer's servants want to pull out the weeds. But
the farmer refuses: "Let both grow together until the harvest" (Matthew
13:30). Then the whole field will be cut down, and the wheat will be
separated from the weeds.

If you are going to grasp the mystery of the Kingdom, you need to
know that there are two sowers, and they are sowing different kinds of
seed. God is sowing his people in the world and bringing a great harvest,
but the enemy is also at work, sowing his weeds. Jesus is telling us, "Let
both grow together until the harvest."

We live in the tension of a divided world. Christ has come and is
doing what God promised, but the enemy is still at work and his weeds
are also growing. God has determined that this is how it will be until
the harvest.

Why doesn't God pull up the weeds now? He is able to stop the work
of the enemy and bring his weed-sowing to nothing. Christ tolerates the
world, the flesh, and the devil because they're useful to him. They're
the anvils on which Kingdom character is painfully hammered out.
They're the hurdles we must jump and the pressure we must endure to
demonstrate that we truly love Christ.

FOR FURTHER READING, SEE JAMES 1

BURIED TREASURE

The Kingdom of Heaven is like a treasure that a man
discovered hidden in a field.   MATTHEW 13:44

JESUS USED A third picture to help us understand the Kingdom of God. What God is doing is like treasure buried in a field. That's different from treasure on display.

God's Kingdom is not like the crown jewels on display in London for everyone to admire. God's Kingdom is like treasure hidden in a field. That means many pass by it without ever knowing that they're missing something of great value.

Jesus spoke about the man who finds this kind of treasure. Perhaps he's hired to plow the field and suddenly he hits something, so he gets down and digs around in the dirt. Then he realizes he's just stumbled on buried treasure! What should he do? Jesus says he'll cover it up and sell everything he has to buy the field.

And he'll do it with joy! People who sell all they have usually do so because they're bankrupt and miserable. Folks in the marketplace must have wondered why this man, who was selling everything, wore a grin from ear to ear! He couldn't stop smiling because he knew he'd stumbled on the opportunity of a lifetime.

The marvelous thing is that even after he signed the papers to buy the field, he still didn't know the full value of what he had found. But he knew it was worth more than anything and everything else in his life.

The priceless treasure of Christ's Kingdom is ours. We are truly rich in Christ, but the day is still to come when the treasure will be dug up, each piece laid down, and its true value fully known. What we have in Christ right now is only a foretaste of what is to come; the full glory of what we have in him is hidden from view. But when he comes again, the treasure chest will be opened, and we will gasp as we see for the first time the full value of what he has done for us.

FOR FURTHER READING, SEE 2 CORINTHIANS 4

LIKE INTERNS FOLLOWING A DOCTOR

Not everyone who calls out to me, "Lord! Lord!" will enter
the Kingdom of Heaven. Only those who actually do the will
of my Father in heaven will enter. MATTHEW 7:21

THE GOSPEL IS often reduced to something like a "get out of jail free" card in the game of Monopoly: players receive a "get out of hell free" card—if they land on the "church" square and follow the directions. The result is "Christians" who are little different from the world, show no obvious signs of submission to the King, and are *dangerously* sure about everlasting life.

Jesus undermines such complacency. His first public sermon begins with the word *repent* (see Matthew 4:17), and he didn't mean "say you're sorry." He meant "turn around and move in a different direction." Then Jesus spoke about seed that springs up quickly, but when pressure comes, it withers away; and about seed that falls among thorns and is choked by worry or wealth (see 13:20-22).

True faith is like a tree filled with the fruit of obedience. That's why Paul talks about the obedience that comes from faith (see Romans 1:5). Faith joins us to Christ so his life can begin to flow into us and through us in order that we may bear fruit. Where there is no fruit of obedience, there is no spiritual life.

In the Gospels, Jesus calls people to a different kind of life. The first call of the Gospel is not to *believe* in Jesus, but to *follow* him. If we settle for something less, we miss authentic Christianity. We must discover what it means to be a disciple.

The word *disciple* was in common use at the time of Jesus. It was a term used for students and literally means "one who goes somewhere with someone." In Jesus' day, students learned by going where their teacher went, listening to what their teacher said, and watching what the teacher did. Disciples were like interns following a doctor on his rounds. An intern learns by observing and participating in what the doctor is doing.

Jesus' call to his disciples was "Come, follow me" (Matthew 4:19). A disciple of Jesus is a person whose life is bound up with his and is marked by a distinct loyalty to Christ. Could this be said of you?

FOR FURTHER READING, SEE MATTHEW 7

WALKING AROUND LIKE HE OWNS THE PLACE

Jesus called out to them, "Come, follow me, and I will show you how to fish for people!" MATTHEW 4:19

WHY DID THE first disciples follow Jesus? What did they find attractive in his offer? And why should we consider the same offer that he makes to us today?

Imagine that you are a secretary working on the second floor of a large multinational corporation. You have a pile of work on your desk, and you're rushing to meet several deadlines. As you pound away on your keyboard, a stranger walks into the office. You've never seen him before. He walks around like he owns the place, and people start getting annoyed. Then he arrives at your desk. He stops and waits for you to look up from your screen, and when you do, he says, "Follow me."

There's no way you're going to get up, leave your computer, and follow him! In fact, your first thought is probably to pick up the phone and call security. The next thing you'd be tempted to do is say, "Excuse me, but who do you think you are?"

Now, let's rerun that scene with one additional piece of information— as the stranger walks into the office, the receptionist scribbles a note on a piece of paper, and it's quickly passed from one secretary to the next, until it eventually comes to you.

The note says, "It's the CEO!" He's never visited the second floor before; this is the first time he's even been in the building. It is, after all, a multinational company. But the receptionist is sure it's him, and no one doubts that she's right.

It doesn't bother you now that he walks around like he owns the place. And when he stops at your desk and says, "Follow me," you get up and leave your computer, because you know that whatever he wants you to do is a higher priority than anything you were doing before.

You will never follow Jesus Christ until you are convinced that he's more than just a historical figure. But once you know who he is—the Son of God—you will jump at the great privilege of his offer to "come, follow me."

FOR FURTHER READING, SEE MATTHEW 4

WHO DO YOU SAY I AM?

You are blessed . . . because my Father in heaven has revealed this to you. You did not learn this from any human being. MATTHEW 16:17

ONE DAY JESUS asked his disciples, "Who do you say I am?" Peter answered, "You are the Messiah, the Son of the living God" (Matthew 16:15-16). What Jesus explained next is very significant: this was not something Peter had worked out on his own.

Peter had thought about the claims of Jesus and the miracles he'd seen. But Jesus made it clear: there was something beyond observation, reason, and deduction going on. God had opened Peter's eyes and given him the ability to see Jesus' glory. Spiritual sight is the gift of God.

On another occasion, Jesus invited a young man to follow him, but the young man chose not to (see Matthew 19:16-22). The immediate problem was that he didn't want to leave his wealth behind. But the deeper problem was that he never saw the glory of Christ. The Son of God called the man to walk with him, but the man's life went on exactly as it had before.

The same thing happens in churches today. Crowds of people gather, but only some of them see the glory of Jesus Christ. Others hear the same music, read the same Scripture, and listen to the same sermon, but they return home with nothing more than a religious duty fulfilled.

The Bible tells us why this happens: "Satan . . . has blinded the minds of those who don't believe. They are unable to see the glorious light of the Good News. They don't understand this message about the glory of Christ" (2 Corinthians 4:4). Satan has his work cut out for him to obscure such a radiant light.

But once you see the glory of God in the face of Christ, your mind and heart will be gripped by the wonder of his incarnation, the beauty of his perfect life, the power of his amazing words, the glory of his miracles, the love of his atoning sacrifice, and the glory of his life-giving resurrection and day of his coming. We see glory in Jesus. That's why we're not just believers, we're worshipers! Don't rest until God opens your eyes to see the glory of his Son.

FOR FURTHER READING, SEE EXODUS 33

A NEW KIND OF FISHING

I will show you how to fish for people! MATTHEW 4:19

WHEN JESUS CALLED the first disciples, he told them, essentially, "Place your life in my hands, and I will make something of it." I'm glad that's the order. Some people have the idea that they have to make something of their lives *before* they offer themselves to Jesus. But it is Christ who promises to make something of us.

I love the way Jesus uses an analogy from the disciples' world of fishing and gives it a whole new dimension—they will be fishing for people. He'll take what you can do and use it in a whole new way in his Kingdom.

Jesus trained his disciples the way a kindergarten teacher shows a child how to write. The teacher draws beautiful vowels that sit like plump fruit on the line. The child watches the way these letters are formed and copies them on the lines below.

That's what Jesus does for his disciples. He shows compassion to people who are like sheep without a shepherd, and he calls us to follow his example. As his Spirit flows into you, you'll break free from the insularity of the world around you and begin to feel God's heart for lost people.

Jesus met a woman whom others were ready to condemn, and he reached out to her in love and showed her a whole new way of life. But when Jesus spoke with a young man who wanted to add eternal security to his self-centered lifestyle, Jesus refused to compromise his message. When his Spirit flows into us, we'll learn to show the same kind of grace and truth.

Some disciples of Jesus have noticed that he healed the sick or fed the hungry or that when children came to him, he did not turn them away. And when these disciples heard him say, "Follow me," they established hospitals, started famine relief programs, or founded orphanages or schools in his name.

We're to show Christ to the world. Many will fail to see the Good News in our message, and all they will see is the bread given or the medicine dispensed. But some eyes will be opened to see the glory of Jesus.

FOR FURTHER READING, SEE MATTHEW 10

ON A COLLISION COURSE
WITH THE WORLD

You are seeing things merely from a human point of view,
not from God's. MATTHEW 16:23

FOLLOWING JESUS WILL be costly. When Jesus announced that he was going to Jerusalem to suffer, he called his disciples to follow him. They were reluctant. Peter even tried to persuade Jesus to pursue a less costly plan. That's when Jesus told Peter, rather bluntly, the problem with his mind-set.

Jesus refused to hide the cost of following him in the small print of his invitation. He said, "If any of you wants to be my follower, you must turn from your selfish ways, take up your cross, and follow me" (Matthew 16:24). He told his disciples plainly that he was sending them out "as sheep among wolves" (10:16) and "if the world hates you, remember that it hated me first" (John 15:18).

The world will not tolerate the exclusive claims of Jesus Christ. It has a definite opinion about him, and it is not favorable. Christ claimed that we cannot know God without him (see Matthew 11:27), and that insults our pride. He claimed that we're incapable of coming to God unless he brings us (see John 14:6), and that renders useless our strength. He claimed the authority to tell us what is right and what is wrong (see John 5:27), and that restricts our freedom.

That's why they crucified our Lord, and that's why our culture would crucify him again today. We probably wouldn't do it with wood and nails; we would likely crucify him on talk shows. Can you imagine what our media would make of Jesus' saying, "I am the way, the truth, and the life"? The world hates Christ. It has no room for his claims, and it will not look kindly on his disciples either.

If you follow Christ, you will have to take up a cross. He is on a collision course with the world, the flesh, and the devil. And if you follow him, you will find yourself in conflict with all three, and you will find yourself out of step with our culture. Only those who have seen his glory will be ready to pay the price.

FOR FURTHER READING, SEE JOHN 15

JUNKYARD DOGS

Everyone who calls on the name of the LORD will be saved. ROMANS 10:13

CHRIST IS ABLE to save us from our enemies precisely because he is able to subdue them. The fact that he is Lord qualifies him to act as Savior. That's why Scripture says, "Everyone who calls on the name of the LORD will be saved."

When I was five years old, my father would take me to a junkyard outside Edinburgh to get spare parts for our car. It was a marvelous place for a child with a vivid imagination to play.

The system was simple: you could strip pieces that you needed off the cars and then pay for them at the gate as you left. But some people were in the habit of taking parts off the cars, throwing them over the perimeter fence, walking past the gate without paying, and then picking up the stuff in the wasteland outside.

So the owners cleared a no-go area around the inside of the fence and barricaded it with a three-foot-high rail. They brought in German shepherd guard dogs, which were leashed to the railing so they could patrol the entire perimeter. As long as you did not go within a few feet of the fence, you were perfectly safe.

One day while my father was getting parts for our car, I found a truck and climbed into the cab. I was lost in an imaginary world of truck driving, when suddenly one of the dogs broke free from its chain and came bounding toward me.

I don't think I've ever been so terrified in my life. I screamed, as any small child would, and my father rushed over. After a struggle, he subdued the dog. The fact that he was able to subdue the dog was the reason he was able to deliver me from its power. If you can't subdue the dog, you can't save the boy.

Christ is able to save us from our enemies because he has authority over them. He is able to deliver us from sin because his power is greater than the power of temptation. He's able to bring us safely through death because he triumphed over the grave. He's able to open the doors of heaven because all authority in heaven belongs to him.

FOR FURTHER READING, SEE ROMANS 10

LORD OVER NATURE

Who is this man? . . . Even the wind and waves obey him! MARK 4:41

THE GOSPEL OF Mark records four stories that illustrate Jesus' author-ity over different dimensions of human darkness. Mark shows us that Jesus is Lord, and this is why we can trust him as Savior. The disciples learned this in stages. Every time they discovered a new dimension of his authority, they discovered a new sphere of his salvation.

It all began one evening when Jesus told the disciples to row over to the other side of the lake. They did what he asked, and halfway across the lake, they found themselves caught in a sudden storm.

Storms of this sort were not unusual, and the disciples had made their living on the lake, so they would have seen a few in their time. They knew how to handle a boat, but on this occasion, they were absolutely terrified. "Teacher, don't you care that we're going to drown?" (Mark 4:38). They pictured their obituaries in the following day's newspaper:

> Thirteen people died last night when a freak storm hit Lake Galilee. Meteorologists had failed to predict the weather system. Those who died included several local fishermen along with a former tax consultant, a religious teacher, and other unidentified friends. Eyewitnesses said the weather changed without warning. Rescue crafts were launched, but they were unable to identify any survivors.

There they were, in the middle of a life-threatening natural disaster, and the disciples must have been astonished at what happened next. Jesus stood up, "rebuked the wind and said to the waves, 'Silence! Be still!' Suddenly the wind stopped, and there was a great calm. Then he asked [his disciples], 'Why are you afraid? Do you still have no faith?' The disciples were absolutely terrified. 'Who is this man?' they asked each other. 'Even the wind and waves obey him!'" (Mark 4:39-41).

Think of the possibilities! If Jesus can subdue a storm, what about a volcano, a mudslide, a tornado, or a hurricane? If he is Lord over nature, then he can save us from its destructive power.

FOR FURTHER READING, SEE MARK 4

LORD OVER DEMONS

They saw the man who had been possessed by the legion of demons.
He was sitting there fully clothed and perfectly sane. MARK 5:15

WHEN THE DISCIPLES crossed the lake, they were immediately confronted by a man who was out of his mind. He lived among the tombs, and night after night he would cry out and cut himself with stones (see Mark 5:5).

No doubt everyone locked their doors at night because of him. Most likely nobody let their children play alone in the park in case he came around. This man cared little for his own life and nothing for the lives of others. He was extremely dangerous.

The local authorities tried chaining him hand and foot and throwing him in jail, but "he snapped the chains from his wrists and smashed the shackles. No one was strong enough to subdue him" (Mark 5:4).

After every breakout, people would say, "We need stronger chains at the jailhouse," or, "We need tighter gun laws or longer prison sentences." The community tried everything, but nothing worked. At night the locals heard this man crying out in the hills—it couldn't have been easy to sleep.

This man had a family (see Mark 5:19), and his wife and children must have gone through a thousand agonies as his outbursts worsened. Eventually, when it was no longer safe to have him at home, their hearts must have broken.

The Bible is clear—there were evil spirits (or demons) behind these outbursts. This is not the case with every violent or self-destructive person, but it was with this man. The devil is a thief who comes "to steal and kill and destroy" (John 10:10), and where this activity is most rampant, his activity can most directly be discerned.

Jesus commanded the spirits to enter a herd of pigs, and when the town came out to see what had happened, the man was "sitting there fully clothed and perfectly sane" (Mark 5:15). If Christ can do this, what about the deranged gunman or the suicide bomber? Imagine if each of them were restored to a right mind.

If Jesus is Lord over demons, then he can deliver us from their destructive power.

FOR FURTHER READING, SEE LUKE 8

LORD OVER DISEASE AND DEATH

*Immediately the bleeding stopped, and she could feel in her body
that she had been healed of her terrible condition.* MARK 5:29

WHEN JESUS RETURNED to the other side of the lake, a large crowd was
waiting. In the crowd was a woman who had suffered from a chronic
and disabling illness. She had spent all she had consulting numerous
doctors, but in spite of their efforts, her condition was no better; it was
even worse. She was suffering from an incurable disease.

This woman had heard about Jesus and joined the crowd that was
following him. In her condition, she would not have been able to move
quickly, but crowds move slowly, so she managed to push her way forward until she was just behind Jesus.

She thought if she could just reach him, she'd be healed. Then she
touched him, and immediately she was aware of a physiological change:
"The bleeding stopped, and she could feel in her body that she had
been healed of her terrible condition" (Mark 5:29). If Jesus can cure
diseases that are beyond the frontiers of medical science, what about
cancer or AIDS? If he is Lord over disease, he can deliver us from its
destructive power.

A man named Jairus asked Jesus to heal his sick daughter. But before
Jesus could get to her, "messengers arrived from the home of Jairus, the
leader of the synagogue. They told him, 'Your daughter is dead. There's
no use troubling the Teacher now.' But Jesus overheard them and said
to Jairus, 'Don't be afraid. Just have faith.'" (Mark 5:35-36). The time
Jesus had spent healing the woman had delayed his arrival, so that by the
time Jesus came to the house, the wake had already begun.

Jesus sent the mourners away, and while the parents of the dead girl
watched, he took her hands and said, "'*Talitha koum,*' which means 'Little
girl, get up!' And the girl, who was twelve years old, immediately stood
up and walked around!" (Mark 5:41-42).

If Jesus can deliver her from death, then what about you and me? If
Jesus is Lord over death, he can deliver us from its deadly power.

FOR FURTHER READING, SEE MARK 5

WHY DOESN'T HE DO IT?

The crowd began pleading with Jesus to go away
and leave them alone. MARK 5:17

JESUS DOESN'T FORCE himself on a community that does not want him. You would think after Christ delivered a town from the nightmare of a demon-possessed man (see Mark 5:1-15), the people would have asked him to stay. Imagine what he could do about their other problems! But they begged him to go, and that's why he left the area of the Gerasenes.

It is important to grasp this. They were pleading with Jesus to leave—pleading! "Please leave this area! We saw what you did, Jesus of Nazareth, and we don't want you here. This is not where you belong. Please go—now!"

Jesus gave the explanation for this on another occasion: "Judgment is based on this fact: God's light came into the world, but people loved the darkness more than the light, for their actions were evil" (John 3:19). Things haven't changed much.

Our culture has increasingly taken the position that we don't want Jesus around here, either. Of course, many people have no problem with the idea of religious people exercising their freedom to worship as they choose, but as far as the country at large is concerned, the prevailing consensus is that we do not want Jesus here.

His name is not welcome in public, unless it is placed alongside a list of alternatives. The suggestion that he is Lord is unacceptable because that would imply that he had authority over everyone, and we couldn't possibly entertain that idea—not here!

Some people ask, "If Jesus has the power to deliver us from the devastation of a hurricane, the ravages of cancer, and the peril of death, then why doesn't he do it?" We send Jesus away, but then we ask why he wasn't there in the middle of our calamity.

Sometimes it's impossible to make sense of the disasters, disease, and death that we read about in the newspaper. But we should read it alongside these words: "He came to his own people, and even they rejected him" (John 1:11). Before we criticize Jesus, we should examine ourselves: Are we in the crowd of people who have sent him away?

FOR FURTHER READING, SEE JOHN 3

WHAT ARE YOU WAITING FOR?

Christ must reign until he humbles all his enemies beneath his feet.
And the last enemy to be destroyed is death. 1 CORINTHIANS 15:25-26

JESUS DEMONSTRATED HIS power, but he was rejected again and again, until rejection eventually led to the cross—the ultimate expression of a community's saying, "Go away."

When Christ was crucified, nature convulsed as "the earth shook, [and] rocks split apart" (Matthew 27:51). The demonic powers of hell were set loose; as Jesus said, "This is . . . the time when the power of darkness reigns" (Luke 22:53). Jesus endured unspeakable suffering, and then he entered death itself. But that's not the end of the Bible's story.

Christ rose from the dead and ascended into heaven. Right now he is on the throne, where he will reign until he has put all his enemies under his feet. That time has not yet come, so we continue to live in a world that suffers under the curse of disasters, demons, disease, and death, and we wait for the day when Christ will put every one of them under his feet.

God gave the apostle John a glimpse of that day. One day all of nature's storms will be subdued—the sea will be "a shiny sea of glass" (Revelation 4:6). One day all demonic activity will cease—"the devil . . . [will be] thrown into the fiery lake of burning sulfur" (20:10). One day death will be no more—"death and the grave [will be] thrown into the lake of fire" (20:14).

The message is clear: You will face many storms in this world. You will see the enemy at work, and you will shed many tears over disease and death. But Jesus is Lord over all these things, and the day is coming when he will subdue them completely.

Until that day, Jesus has work for us to do. Jesus told the man who was delivered from the evil spirits, "Go home to your family, and tell them everything the Lord has done for you" (Mark 5:19). Jesus sent the man back to be a light in a culture that didn't want Jesus, and the man shared in the surrounding cities what Christ had done for him. That's our calling. He sends us back as light in a dark place.

FOR FURTHER READING, SEE REVELATION 20

UNDER A STORM CLOUD

*Anyone who doesn't obey the Son will never experience eternal
life but remains under God's angry judgment.* JOHN 3:36

JOHN THE BAPTIST didn't say that on the last day God's "angry judgment" (or wrath) would suddenly *come*, but rather that it would *remain*. The wrath of God toward sin is like a great storm cloud that hangs over us. It stays there unless and until sin is taken away.

Jesus came into the world to take this judgment away from us. He will do this for all who come to him in faith. But where Christ is rejected, the storm cloud of God's wrath remains.

The rest of the Bible story bears witness to God's relentless hostility toward all evil. God is determined to destroy evil, and on the day Adam sinned in the Garden, God pronounced a curse on the serpent. Evil will not stand forever.

The Old Testament records that sin kept growing, and God kept cutting it back. But at the end of the story, God will destroy sin altogether. When the apostle John was given a glimpse of this future judgment of God, he saw that the enemies of God will "drink the wine of God's anger. It has been poured full strength into God's cup of wrath" (Revelation 14:10).

Many people miss God's warning, not by denying what he said about judgment, but by ignoring it. When that happens, the message of Christianity will undergo a subtle change. The emphasis will be on coming to Christ to find a more fulfilling or satisfying life.

But that is not the heart of the gospel. Jesus came into the world to bring us from death to life. He died to deliver us from hell and bring us into everlasting life in his presence. God's salvation is about more than your experience of life; it's about where you will spend eternity.

Nobody ever spoke more clearly or powerfully about God's love or about God's implacable hostility toward evil than Jesus did. He never manipulated people's emotions, nor did he embellish the joys of heaven or exaggerate the pains of hell. Jesus is the Son of God, so I have to take seriously every word he spoke. If you claim to be a Christian, so do you. It's part of following him.

FOR FURTHER READING, SEE REVELATION 14

WHERE GOD'S JUSTICE IS FULLY KNOWN

His soul went to the place of the dead. There, in torment,
he saw Abraham in the far distance. LUKE 16:23

HELL IS THE place where God's justice is fully known, a place of punishment. When Jesus described a man who went to hell, he said that he was in *torment*. And the Bible speaks about God's enemies being "tormented with fire and burning sulfur in the presence of the holy angels and the Lamb" (Revelation 14:10).

As awful as this is, it is something for which we should be thankful. It is for this reason that God urges us to leave vengeance in his hands: "Dear friends, never take revenge. Leave that to the righteous anger of God. For the Scriptures say, 'I will take revenge; I will pay them back,' says the LORD" (Romans 12:19). God will execute perfect justice with total knowledge. God will bring all evil to light.

This world is riddled with injustice at every level. People who have been responsible for unspeakable evils have never been brought to face the evil for which they are responsible. Adolf Hitler would be one example, but there are many others who have slipped, through death, beyond the reach of justice in this world. And even with those who are living, the international community continues to struggle over how to bring justice to war criminals who have committed unspeakable atrocities.

But God has set a day of judgment from which no one can escape. All secrets will be revealed, and there will be no evasions. The dead will be raised, and the wicked will be brought to face their own sins as they stand before the judgment of God.

God will repay, so leave room for God's wrath. You don't need to take revenge into *your* hands when you know it is in *his*. God will deal with it. You can leave it to him.

On this foundation, God says, "If your enemies are hungry, feed them. If they are thirsty, give them something to drink. In doing this, you will heap burning coals of shame on their heads" (Romans 12:20).

FOR FURTHER READING, SEE LUKE 16

DEGREES OF PUNISHMENT

*Because you are stubborn and refuse to turn from your sin, you
are storing up terrible punishment for yourself.* ROMANS 2:5

THE PUNISHMENT EXPERIENCED in hell by a person who rejects the
Son of God will be a direct reflection of the particular sins committed
by that individual. God's justice is perfect, so nobody will be punished
for a sin he or she didn't commit.

Just as there are degrees of reward in heaven, so there will be degrees
of punishment in hell. Jesus referred to this on a number of occasions.
He spoke about a city that refused to receive the Good News: "It will be
more bearable for Sodom and Gomorrah on the day of judgment than
for that town" (Matthew 10:15, NIV). Receiving the Good News brought
a new level of responsibility and accountability.

Jesus also distinguished between a servant who knew what his master
wanted and a servant who did not: "A servant who knows what the master wants, but isn't prepared and doesn't carry out those instructions,
will be severely punished. But someone who does not know, and then
does something wrong, will be punished only lightly" (Luke 12:47-48).

Jesus makes it clear that the greater the light we have from God, the
greater our responsibility is to respond in obedience. The Bible also
points to degrees of punishment when it says, "Just think how much
worse the punishment will be for those who have trampled on the Son
of God" (Hebrews 10:29).

Some imagine that, having chosen the wrong path, they might as
well cut loose and live wildly. That's a terrible mistake. God will punish
sins with perfect justice. A person in hell would give anything to have
committed even one less sin.

If you see today that you've chosen the wrong path, that's God's
grace reaching out to you. It's not too late for you to turn around and
run to him. He has provided a way out of the punishment you deserve,
through the sacrifice of his Son. Through faith in him, you can live
under God's grace rather than his wrath.

FOR FURTHER READING, SEE LUKE 12

THE WORM

*It is better for you to enter the kingdom of God with
one eye than with two eyes to be thrown into hell,
"where their worm does not die."* MARK 9:47-48, ESV

JESUS SPOKE ABOUT a worm that never dies in hell. Notice this worm belongs to the person in hell. Jesus doesn't say *"the* worm," he says, *"their* worm." He is speaking of something personal and internal to every person in hell.

Several years ago, a storm destroyed a tree in our yard. It had become diseased, and when it fell, the extent of the damage was revealed: worms had been eating away the inside. That's what worms do—eat away at the inside of things.

Jesus is talking about something that eats away the inside of an individual in hell. He is talking about conscience. There is nothing more crippling than a bad conscience that never rests. Jesus says that in hell the sinner's worm will never die.

My father was on the police force for thirty years, and what surprised him most was that people who had committed the most dreadful acts seemed to have so little understanding of what they had done, even after long periods in prison.

Those who commit the greatest evils are sometimes least sensitive to the wrong they've done. But it won't always be so. Consciences will be fully activated in hell; denial will be futile. Every sinner in hell will be unable to block out the knowledge or responsibility for his or her own sins. Unbelievers' sin will always be before them. Those who loved sin in this world will see it for what it is and share God's abhorrence of it. This is part of the justice of God.

David had been living in denial about his sin, but God brought him to the point of facing what he'd done: "I recognize my rebellion; it haunts me day and night" (Psalm 51:3). God will bring every person to that point, either by bringing us to repentance in this life or by showing us the full horror of sin in hell. Pray that God would soften your conscience to respond to him today.

FOR FURTHER READING, SEE PSALM 51

THE FIRE

> Hell, *"where their worm does not die and the fire*
> *is not quenched."* MARK 9:47-48, ESV

A PERSON IN hell lives under the judgment of God, who is a "devouring fire" (Hebrews 12:29), forever.

The psalmist faced the awesome truth that no one can evade the presence of God when he said, "I can never escape from your Spirit! I can never get away from your presence! If I go up to heaven, you are there; if I go down to the grave, you are there" (Psalm 139:7-8).

When Paul said that the wicked will be "forever separated from the Lord" (2 Thessalonians 1:9), he meant they will be excluded from enjoying God's presence in the new Jerusalem. Every eye will see him—the righteous will see God in his beauty; the wicked will see God in his fury.

God revealed his presence to Moses and Elijah through fire. Malachi spoke of God as being like a refiner's fire, and the writer of Hebrews described God as a devouring fire. That is why it is a fearful thing to fall into his hands.

One of the most famous sermons on the subject of hell is a sermon by Jonathan Edwards called "Sinners in the Hands of an Angry God." It's a frightening sermon about the terrors of hell. Some have suggested that this is a good example of religious leaders trying to control people through fear.

Others have said that anyone who talks like this has a sick mind, but if that's your conclusion, you'd need to say the same thing about Jesus. The clearest teaching about hell is not from medieval theologians or Jonathan Edwards, but from Jesus Christ himself. He did not have a sick mind. Jesus is the Son of God, and he said these things because he wants us to know that hell is real—and he doesn't want you to end up there.

As troubling as the imagery of the fire of hell is, perhaps the greatest pain of hell is knowing that there is a God of love, and yet the opportunity of enjoying him is gone forever.

FOR FURTHER READING, SEE PSALM 139

TWENTY-FIRST-CENTURY SADDUCEES

The Sadducees . . . say there is no resurrection. MARK 12:18, NIV

THERE WAS ONE fundamental conviction buried deep in the mind of every Sadducee: there is no resurrection. This put them in dispute with the Pharisees, who believed wholeheartedly in a future resurrection. The Pharisees also believed in heaven and hell, but "the Sadducees say there is no resurrection or angels or spirits" (Acts 23:8).

A worldview is a set of beliefs through which we filter information. It's like a software program running in the mind, and it helps us sort out what we receive as true and what we reject as false. And it's not easy to change your worldview.

Once we've grasped a set of convictions, it's difficult for us to hear anything to the contrary. At one time, people believed the earth was flat and the sun revolved around the earth, but when it was discovered that the earth is round and it rotates around the sun, it was difficult for people to unlearn old assumptions.

Notice the pattern in the Sadducees' belief system—no resurrection, no angels, and no spirits. The Sadducees didn't like anything that smacked of the supernatural. They didn't buy any of it. As far as they were concerned, the only power available is the power inside of you. "You only live once," they seem to say, "and don't go looking to angels or spirits for help. That's an emotional crutch for weak people to lean on. Life is what you make it."

That was the Sadducees' worldview, and if you were to take off a Sadducee's robes, take away his scrolls, and take him out of the Temple; if you were to give him a job in the city, an Armani suit, and a cell phone, you'd have a picture of the twenty-first-century mind-set.

The twenty-first-century Sadducee worldview is clear: "Don't look beyond the grave because that cannot be known, and don't look to heaven because it's all up to you." Many of these modern Sadducees are in church, just as their first-century counterparts were in the Temple. They are good, upright, and successful people with sharp minds but blind spiritual eyes.

FOR FURTHER READING, SEE ACTS 23

THE *STAR TREK* RESURRECTION

Whose wife will she be in the resurrection?   MARK 12:23

ONE DAY A group of Sadducees came to Jesus with a question. They began by reminding Jesus of the Old Testament law that says that if a man dies without children, his brother must assume the care of his wife and raise children in his brother's name. The point of this law was to ensure the continuation of the line of Israel, which was central to the purpose of God.

Then the Sadducees told a story about seven brothers: the first brother dies with no children, so the second brother takes responsibility for his brother's wife. Then the second brother dies, and the third one steps up, and so on. By the time we get to the seventh brother, he too accepts his fate and dies, and eventually the wife dies too.

Now the Sadducees come to their question: at the resurrection, whose wife will she be?" This is the *Star Trek* view of the resurrection. Captain Kirk says, "Beam me up, Scotty!" Then Kirk disappears from view, only to rematerialize looking exactly the same but in a different place. That's how the Sadducees thought about the resurrection, and that's why they rejected it.

If heaven were simply a continuation of this life in another place, it would be terribly complicated. There are so many anomalies in life that it would be impossible for it to go on in the same way after death. Jesus makes this point clear when he says, "When the dead rise, they will neither marry nor be given in marriage" (Mark 12:25).

In heaven there will be no death and, therefore, no need for procreation. For those who are happily married, this sounds like bad news, because a happy marriage and the gift of children are among the greatest joys in this life.

It's hard for many to imagine life without their family, but that's why the Bible says we cannot imagine "what God has prepared for those who love him" (1 Corinthians 2:9). Marriage and family are among God's greatest gifts in this fallen world, but it's as if God is saying, "You ain't seen nothing yet!"

FOR FURTHER READING, SEE MARK 12

THE MORNING COMMUTE

Your mistake is that you don't know the Scriptures, and
you don't know the power of God. MARK 12:24

THE SADDUCEES REJECTED the Resurrection because they didn't know the Scriptures or the power of God. Many people today would say they believe in God, but they would never expect the god they believe in to do anything—you might say that their gods are along for the ride.

There is more than one way to commute into Chicago. You can drive a car, or you can take the train. Thousands of people travel by both means every day, and it's the same boring routine. You can ride the train down the tracks, stopping at all the same stations, or you can drive the car down the expressway, passing all the familiar landmarks. The whole thing is predictable.

This is how God has ordered the world—he holds the planets on regular courses, causes the sun to rise at predictable times, and makes things grow in consistent patterns. Science observes these patterns, which are just like the morning commute.

But there's one important difference between the train and the car: if you're a passenger on the train and one morning you decide to follow a different route, you can't because you're only a passenger. But if you're in the car and decide you want to take another route, you're free to do so because you're the driver.

Here's the question: Is God like a passenger on the train, or is he like the driver of a car? Is God imprisoned in a closed system in the universe in which he has no alternative but to follow the tracks of natural law? Or is God, despite the regularity of his actions, free to do something entirely different if he so chooses?

The Sadducees said, "God rides the train." Jesus said, "God drives the car." We can be thankful that God chooses to drive predictably, but if he should choose to do something completely different, he is absolutely free to do so. Once you know the God of the Bible, miracles don't seem so strange.

FOR FURTHER READING, SEE ISAIAH 43

GOD TAKES THE INITIATIVE

God sent the angel Gabriel to Nazareth. LUKE 1:26

THE BIRTH OF Jesus was entirely at the initiative of God. He chose Mary as the one who would bring Christ into the world, and he sent the angel Gabriel to announce to her, "Don't be afraid, Mary, . . . for you have found favor with God! You will conceive and give birth to a son, and you will name him Jesus" (Luke 1:30-31).

Mary did not see how she could have a child, given that she was a virgin. The angel's answer takes us to one of the great and wonderful mysteries in the Bible: "The Holy Spirit will come upon you, and the power of the Most High will overshadow you. So the baby to be born will be holy, and he will be called the Son of God" (Luke 1:35).

Joseph would have no role in the conception of Mary's child. If God had not told him what was happening, he would not have had the faintest idea. God completely bypassed him; Joseph made no contribution whatsoever.

The Bible contains other stories of miraculous births. Isaac, Samuel, and John the Baptist were all born as the result of special interventions of God. In each case, God worked through the union of a father and a mother, but Mary was a virgin. Not only did Joseph have no union with her before the child was conceived, but he had no union with her until the child was born (see Matthew 1:25).

The angel did not tell Mary to do anything. All she was told was that *God* would do something. It is God who acts. It is God who takes the initiative. Mary's privilege was that one of God's greatest miracles would take place in her body.

Human history has seen many remarkable leaders, but God did not wait for a deliverer to arise *from* the human race. He sent his Son *to* the human race. We can be thankful that God did not wait for us to save ourselves. He took the initiative.

FOR FURTHER READING, SEE LUKE 1

GOD'S INCREDIBLE JOURNEY

The virgin will conceive a child! She will give birth to a son, and they will call him Immanuel, which means "God is with us." MATTHEW 1:23

YOUR LIFE BEGAN when you were conceived in your mother's womb. Before that moment, you did not exist. God used the union of your father and mother to bring you into being. Before that you were not, and without that you would not have been.

With Christ it is different. His life did not begin in the womb. Speaking of Jesus' birth, the apostle Paul said, "He was rich, yet for your sakes he became poor" (2 Corinthians 8:9). Before he was born in the stable, God the Son already enjoyed the most marvelous life. That's something you cannot say about any other person.

The Son of God was always there: "In the beginning the Word already existed. The Word was with God, and the Word was God" (John 1:1). This "Word" is the Son of God who took human flesh and was born of the Virgin Mary. The one who has always shared the Father's glory came *to* us as a gift to the human race. He did not arise *from* us by the union of a father and a mother.

This is important because only God can reconcile people to God. The Old Testament was full of prophets, priests, and kings who were men and women just like us. They themselves shared in the problem of human sin, so they were in no position to rescue us from sin. The only way we could be delivered from sin was if someone came to us from outside the human race.

Imagine an air–sea rescue. You are in a dinghy out on the open sea, and you need to be rescued. There's a rope in the dinghy, but you cannot use it to climb up to the helicopter. Salvation has to come from the top down. The rescuer is lowered down with a winch. By embracing him, you are lifted up to the position from which he came.

Salvation has to come from above. Only God can save. Christ has come to us on an incredible journey from heaven to earth, and in him, God is reaching out to every person on this planet, including you.

FOR FURTHER READING, SEE PHILIPPIANS 2

IT MAKES SENSE OF EVERYTHING ELSE

The Word became human and made his home among us. JOHN 1:14

ONCE WE'VE GRASPED that Jesus is God, it's just as important for us to grasp that he is a human. He took human flesh and was born as one of us, sharing our life. This is the mystery that makes sense of everything else.

The fact that Jesus is a human is as important to our salvation as the fact that he is God. God the Son came from heaven because only God can reconcile people to God. But he became human because only a human can bear the punishment for human sin.

God appeared in visible form on many occasions in the Old Testament. These appearances are called *theophanies*. God was reaching out so that men and women could know him. God made himself visible to Adam and Eve in the Garden and to Abraham in the desert, but these appearances were only temporary.

A theophany is like an actor putting on a costume. When the show is over, the actor changes his clothes and leaves. But the birth of Jesus is entirely different. The Son of God took on human flesh. He became human, but he did not cease to be God.

You will never be able to fathom how God could become human, but when you believe that he did, you will not find it difficult to understand his claims, his miracles, or his resurrection. Everything else in the New Testament revolves around this one miracle. If God became human in Jesus, it all begins to fit.

If Jesus is "God with us," no one should be surprised that he claims to be the way to God or that he tells us there is no other way. If he has come from heaven, we may be astonished that he would allow his enemies to nail him to a cross, but it will not surprise us that he should rise from the dead.

If Jesus is the help that God has promised since the beginning of time, you can be confident that he is able to do in your life what no other person and no other teaching could ever do.

FOR FURTHER READING, SEE GENESIS 18

A NEW KIND OF HUMANITY

The baby to be born will be holy, and he will be
called the Son of God. LUKE 1:35

JESUS CHRIST IS like us in every respect except one—he is holy. He did not commit a single sin, but being holy means more than that. It means his thoughts, his intentions, and his character are holy too. He was not drawn to sin; he had no inner propensity to sin. This could not be said about anyone else in all of human history.

When Adam sinned, it changed his nature. He became a different kind of man, and he passed that on to his children. Parents pass on many good things to their children, but holiness is not one of them. We do not have that in us.

The apostle Paul was a good man who desperately wanted to live a holy life. He was born into a privileged family and educated in the finest schools. His parents may have given him everything he ever wanted—except for one thing: they could not give him holiness. When Paul tried to pursue a holy life, he found that there was a battle going on inside of him that he didn't know how to get free from.

When Jesus Christ came into the world, he broke the chain of sinful human nature, and for the first time since Adam, there was a holy human being in the world. It's difficult for us to imagine a human being who isn't subject to sin, but Jesus is the pioneer of a new kind of humanity.

Christ blazes the trail of a new humanity that will be holy, free from sin, and therefore no longer subject to death. This has always been the purpose of God. Christ began where his people will end. He entered at birth what his people will enter at death, and this is the life that he offers to you.

When Paul confessed his struggle with sin, he asked, "Who will free me from this life that is dominated by sin and death?" (Romans 7:24). Thank God there's an answer to that question: Jesus Christ our Lord! When you come to Jesus, he'll begin making you holy by the power of his Spirit. And when you're in his presence, what he has begun in you will be complete.

FOR FURTHER READING, SEE ROMANS 7

THERE IS NO FIREWALL

Because one person disobeyed God, many became sinners. But because one other person obeyed God, many will be made righteous. ROMANS 5:19

IF THE STORY of Adam and Eve were just an ancient story, it wouldn't be worth our time, but what happened in the Garden has direct consequences for your life and mine. Human beings are not like pebbles on a beach; we're like leaves on a tree.

If the root of a tree is diseased, then the disease will spread to every part of the tree. Adam's sin affected all who came from him. The disease flows from the root, and the blight of sin appears on every leaf of the human tree.

When sin entered the world, God announced that there would be an ongoing battle (see Genesis 3:15). In every generation, men and women would try to rise above the power of evil, but they would never be wholly free from its power. That's why the apostle Paul said, "Everyone dies because we all belong to Adam" (1 Corinthians 15:22). Through Adam's sin, a virus has entered into the human network, and there is no firewall.

But the New Testament makes it clear that just as we are all descended from Adam and in that way networked to him, so it is possible, by faith, for men and women to be networked to Christ—or as the Bible puts it, "joined with Christ" (Romans 6:3).

Just as the consequences of Adam's failure in the face of temptation flow to us through our union with him, so the consequences of Christ's triumph over temptation will flow to us through our union with him.

Paul called Christ "the second man" (1 Corinthians 15:47). The first man sinned in the Garden, and the result was the condemnation of the whole human race. Years of human history, recorded in the Old Testament, demonstrated conclusively that none of Adam's descendants were able to overcome the power of sin.

But God did not leave us in that place. The Son of God took on our human flesh and became another Adam. This "second man" confronted our enemy, and just as the first Adam's failure spelled death for everyone in his family, so the last Adam's triumph spells life for everyone in his family.

FOR FURTHER READING, SEE ROMANS 5

STALKING THE ENEMY

*Jesus was led by the Spirit into the wilderness to be
tempted there by the devil.* MATTHEW 4:1

IT WAS THE Spirit of God that led Christ into the desert. Christ was stalking the enemy. His first move was to confront Satan and triumph where Adam had failed, so he went looking for him.

Contrast the circumstances in which Adam failed and Christ triumphed: Adam and Eve were tempted in a garden where their hungers were fully satisfied. Christ was tempted in the desert, and he had been fasting for forty days—his hunger was raging. Adam had the company of his wife; Christ was completely alone.

When Jesus found his enemy, Satan's *first* strategy was to create confusion in Christ's mind about his identity. "Are you really sure you're the Son of God?" Satan was asking. "If God is your Father, he doesn't really care for you. Take matters into your own hands. Tell this stone to become bread" (see Matthew 4:3).

Then Satan moved on to his *second* strategy. Instead of questioning Christ's identity, Satan affirmed it: "Given, then, that God is your Father, you can be sure he'll take care of you. You can do anything you want! Throw yourself down from here, and God's angels will float you to the ground. Go ahead . . . do it!" (see Matthew 4:5-6).

Obedience to the will of God would be incredibly costly for Jesus, and Satan used this in his *third* strategy: "Think of what this will cost you—your own life! There must be an easier way. Just worship me, and it will all be yours!" (see Matthew 4:8-9).

Satan was doing what any general would do when faced with overwhelming odds—offering a truce. Satan would have settled for anything—except Christ proceeding in full obedience to the Father's plan. That plan would end in Satan being crushed and the people he'd enslaved for so long being set free by the ultimate sacrifice.

But Jesus was not negotiating. The strategy that worked so well in the Garden failed completely in the wilderness. Where Adam collapsed in defeat, Christ rose in triumph over the power of our enemy.

FOR FURTHER READING, SEE MATTHEW 4

THE INTERROGATION ROOM

*When the devil had finished tempting Jesus, he left him
until the next opportunity came.* LUKE 4:13

THE ENEMY LAUNCHED everything he had against our Lord Jesus Christ, but he could not break him. After he'd exhausted every strategy he knew, he was left with no alternative but retreat. Christ faced the full power of temptation. Even though he had a sinless nature, the temptation he faced was greater than we'll ever know.

Imagine three airmen flying jets over enemy territory during wartime. They're shot down, captured, and then taken by the enemy for interrogation. One by one they're brought into a darkened room . . .

The first airman gives his name, rank, and serial number. They ask him for the positions of his forces. He knows he must not give this information, but he also knows that the enemy is cruel, and eventually they will break him. So why go through all that? He tells them what he knows.

The second airman is brought in, and he gives his name, rank, and serial number. They pump him for information, but he's determined not to give in, so the cruelty begins. Eventually, they break him, and he tells them what he knows.

Then the third airman comes in and gives his name, rank, and serial number. "You will not break me," he says.

"Oh, yes we will," his captors reply. "We have broken every man who has ever come into this room. It is only a matter of time—you'll see."

The cruelty begins, but he doesn't break. It's intensified, and still he does not break. So it's intensified again, until it becomes unbearable, but still he doesn't break. There comes a point at which they've tried everything. "It's no use," they say. "He's unlike any other person we've ever had. We can't break him." So, they conclude, "If we can't break him, it looks like we'll have to kill him."

Which airman faced the full force of the enemy? The one who did not break. Don't ever think that Christ's temptations were less than yours. He is the only one who knows the full power of temptation, because he is the only one who has stood up under the enemy's assaults.

FOR FURTHER READING, SEE HEBREWS 4

GOD'S NETWORK PRINCIPLE

*Just as everyone dies because we all belong to Adam, everyone who
belongs to Christ will be given new life.* 1 CORINTHIANS 15:22

THE WHOLE OF human history revolves around two men—Adam and
Christ. Just as the consequences of Adam's sin run through his network,
bringing corruption and death to all his descendants, the consequences
of Jesus' righteousness run through his network, changing the eternal
destiny of all who are joined to him.

In other words, God has decided to plant another tree, and by faith,
you can be grafted onto it. When this happens, the life of Jesus will flow
into you, just like the life of a vine flows into its branches.

God's network principle is terrible when we consider Adam's sin,
but it's wonderful when we consider Jesus' righteousness. One man's
triumph can open the door of everlasting life for many. But there is this
one condition: that they are joined to him by faith. You and I are both
in Adam by nature. Are you in Christ by faith?

When we come to Jesus in repentance and faith, the Holy Spirit
joins us to him. We are still in Adam because we have sinful natures and
we live in this fallen world. One day we will die. But when you come to
Jesus, the most important thing is that you are in Christ, and that means
you will share in his triumph.

There is still a great deal of repair work that needs to be done, but
when you are in Christ, God begins his work of restoring you. One day
that work will be complete. Then all that was corrupted will fall away.
Even your body will be transformed and equipped for everlasting life.

So don't go through life telling yourself what a miserable failure you
are. If you are in Christ, hold your head high. You are a child of God,
a member of his family. The Holy Spirit is in you. His righteousness
makes you righteous before God, and when you see Christ, you will be
like him (see 1 John 3:1-2).

FOR FURTHER READING, SEE 1 CORINTHIANS 15

MORAL TEACHER, WONDER-WORKER, OR PROPHET?

But who do you say I am? LUKE 9:20

JESUS ASKED HIS disciples, "Who do people say I am?" (Luke 9:18). He wasn't doing market research. The point of the question was to see if the disciples understood their own culture.

The disciples explained three popular views of Jesus: "Some say John the Baptist, some say Elijah, and others say you are one of the other ancient prophets risen from the dead" (Luke 9:19). John was a great moral teacher, Elijah was a worker of miracles, and the prophets stood in the presence of God to bring his Word to his people.

Many people today put Jesus in one of these three categories. The world's view of Jesus hasn't changed much, and disciples today still confess their faith against the background of a culture that sees Jesus as a great moral teacher, a man endued with supernatural power, or a prophet through whom God speaks.

Then Jesus asked a second question: "Who do you say I am?" Having established the prevailing view of the culture, Jesus wanted to know if the disciples thought he fit into any of these three categories.

Peter stepped forward and said the one thing his culture was not prepared to hear: "You are the Messiah sent from God!" (Luke 9:20). Peter was convinced that Jesus was the one the whole Old Testament had been pointing to.

As Peter watched Jesus and listened to him, he became persuaded that Jesus could not be slotted into the neat categories of moral teacher, wonder-worker, or prophet. The prophets all pointed to someone who was to come, but Jesus did not point to anybody else; he was the one the prophets had pointed to.

This was a great breakthrough in Peter's understanding. Jesus said, "You are blessed, Simon son of John, because my Father in heaven has revealed this to you. You did not learn this from any human being" (Matthew 16:17). If you see Jesus not as just another great teacher or prophet or miracle-worker but as the unique Son of God, you're blessed, because God has revealed this to you.

FOR FURTHER READING, SEE LUKE 9

ARGUING WITH JESUS

The Son of Man must suffer many terrible things. . . . He will be killed,
but on the third day he will be raised from the dead. LUKE 9:22

HAVING GRASPED WHO Jesus was, Peter found the idea of his suffering and dying unthinkable. Peter was outraged. He took Jesus aside and began to rebuke him: "Heaven forbid, Lord. . . . This will never happen to you!" (Matthew 16:22). The other disciples must have stood frozen in their tracks, wondering what would happen next.

Then Jesus turned to Peter and said, "Get away from me, Satan! You are a dangerous trap to me. You are seeing things merely from a human point of view, not from God's" (Matthew 16:23). Peter's great confession of faith was immediately followed by an argument in which Peter acted not as Jesus' disciple, but as his adversary (that's the meaning of the name *Satan*).

Jesus went on to tell the disciples plainly that if they were serious about following him, they would also have their share of suffering: "If any of you wants to be my follower, you must turn from your selfish ways, take up your cross, and follow me" (Matthew 16:24). But Peter remained utterly opposed to the idea of Jesus' suffering and dying.

None of us find it easy to take up our cross and follow Jesus. Like Peter, we sometimes resist when Christ's way seems costly. There is no indication that this tense exchange was resolved. Luke skips over several days in the life of Jesus, and the other Gospel writers do the same. The text resumes with, "About eight days later . . ." (Luke 9:28).

These were probably among the saddest days in the life of Jesus. Jesus moved forward in a direction the disciples did not want to go. He was determined to go to the cross; they were equally determined that it should not be so.

Like those disciples, we experience times in the Christian life when we follow Christ without a glad heart because we don't like the direction he is taking us. But there is no greater encouragement when you feel the cost of following Christ than to look ahead and see where your painful path will end.

FOR FURTHER READING, SEE MATTHEW 16

A GLIMPSE OF THE FUTURE

The appearance of his face was transformed,
and his clothes became dazzling white. LUKE 9:29

EIGHT DAYS AFTER describing the suffering he would endure, Jesus
took Peter, James, and John and went on a prayer retreat. They climbed
a mountain together, and when they arrived at the top, Jesus gave these
discouraged men a glimpse of the future.

As Jesus prayed, his appearance changed so that the disciples saw
him as he would appear in the future. His face shone and his clothing
dazzled. Jesus was showing his disciples the glory he would enter after
his death and resurrection.

An awesome brilliance radiated from him, and it is clear that the
disciples were at the limits of language to describe how he looked, saying that Jesus' clothes appeared "far whiter than any earthly bleach could
ever make them" (Mark 9:3).

This is remarkably similar to the description John gave when he
saw the glory of the risen Christ, whose face was "like the sun in all its
brilliance" (Revelation 1:16). In his vision, John saw the same glory that
Jesus revealed on the top of the mountain.

The Transfiguration revealed the glory that lay beyond the cross.
There would be pain and suffering in Jerusalem, but Jesus wanted the
disciples to see where the story would end. They would see Jesus die,
but that would not be the end of the story.

When Christ leads you on a painful path, you need to know where
the story will end. You do not serve a weak or ailing Christ who is unable
to stop the tide of secularism and pluralism in our world. You serve the
risen Lord, who sovereignly moves history forward toward its climax,
when his own glory will be revealed.

So when you hear the world say, "We will not have this man to rule
over us" or you find that his work seems to be set back, remember that
history is moving toward the day when Jesus Christ will appear in glory.
Through all the suffering and darkness of this world, God is moving
toward the moment when his Son will be revealed and every person who
has ever lived will see his glory.

FOR FURTHER READING, SEE REVELATION 1

SOMETHING IMPORTANT ABOUT YOUR FUTURE

> *Suddenly, two men, Moses and Elijah, appeared and began talking with Jesus. They were glorious to see.* LUKE 9:30-31

HERE IS SOMETHING really amazing—two men appeared in glorious splendor and they *shared* in the glory that was radiating from Jesus. This is full of significance for us. When Jesus gave the disciples a glimpse of the future, they saw that Jesus would be exalted in glory *and* that other human beings would share in that glory too.

This must have been absolutely staggering to the disciples. They had seen something of the glory of Jesus in his miracles, but who would have imagined that ordinary human beings could be transfigured into glory?

Moses and Elijah were great men, but they both had their failures. Moses had a murder on his record and was unable to enter the Promised Land because of another failure. Elijah had been part of a great miracle (calling down fire on Mount Carmel), but at one point he regarded his ministry as a failure and lost faith in the ultimate victory of God.

Yet here were these two men, centuries after their earthly lives had ended, sharing in the glory of Jesus. This is telling us something important about our future. God created you for eternity. You will never cease to exist, and you will never become somebody else. The Bible emphasizes the continuity between this life and the next. Moses is still Moses, Elijah is still Elijah, and you will still be you.

The disciples immediately recognized Moses and Elijah—we're not told how. They certainly hadn't seen photographs of them! But somehow God caused them to know the identity of these men from earlier centuries whom they'd never met.

Sometimes people ask if we will know one another in heaven. Of course! We will know others because identity continues in heaven, and because God's purpose is to gather a great community of his people to share the joy of his presence. One of the greatest joys of heaven will be to see God's reflected glory in one another.

FOR FURTHER READING, SEE DEUTERONOMY 34

THE OVERWHELMING CLOUD

Then a voice from the cloud said, "This is my Son,
my Chosen One. Listen to him." LUKE 9:35

PETER, JAMES, AND John followed Jesus up to the top of a mountain, where they saw his glory. Imagine standing on the mountaintop as a thunderous and terrifying cloud moves toward you and then envelops you. It is hardly surprising that the disciples were terrified.

When God came down to meet with Moses at Mount Sinai, he spoke in an audible voice. At the Transfiguration, the audible voice of God was heard again.

This invisible God, whose presence was hidden in the cloud, cannot be known directly. But he does want us to know him, and he tells us that we may know him by listening to his Son, whom he has chosen.

This takes us to the heart of the Bible story. The Father has made himself known through the Son: "No one has ever seen God. But the unique One, who is himself God, is near to the Father's heart. He has revealed God to us" (John 1:18).

If we try to understand God directly, he will always be a mystery to us. I've met people who say they cannot understand God, and of course, they're right! You can't understand God, but you can come to know him if you will listen to what he says to you through his Son, Jesus Christ. This is how he makes himself known.

The disciples heard Jesus' words about the cross and refused to listen. For eight days Peter resisted what God was showing him through Jesus, and now he was enveloped in the presence of the Almighty, who said, "This is my Son; listen to him."

Peter tried to stand in the way of the cross, but now his resistance was overwhelmed as Moses and Elijah affirmed Jesus' plan to go to Jerusalem. And then God himself told Peter to start listening to what the Son of God was saying.

There may be times in your own life when you find yourself resisting God's purpose. In all your questions, doubts, and fears, God will point you to Jesus and say to you, "This is my Son; listen to him."

FOR FURTHER READING, SEE JOHN 1

IF JESUS IS WITH YOU

The disciples were terrified and fell face down on the ground.
MATTHEW 17:6

I'VE HEARD PEOPLE with grievances against God say that they will have a few things to say to God when they see him. It won't be like that. The disciples reacted like any human beings would when confronted with the presence of God. Peter fell face down, and you would have done the same.

But as the disciples lay terrified on the ground, something wonderful happened: "Jesus came over and touched them. 'Get up,' he said. 'Don't be afraid'" (Matthew 17:7). This is the same thing that happened when John later saw the glory of the risen Christ. He fell at the Lord's feet as if he were dead, and again Christ placed his hand on him and said, "Don't be afraid!" (Revelation 1:17).

The disciples must have been profoundly grateful that Jesus was with them when they entered the cloud. One day you will enter the presence of God, and if Jesus is with you, you will be able to stand in his presence with nothing to fear.

This takes us to the heart of the message of the Bible. This awesome, hidden, and sometimes frightening God points you to his Son so that through him you may be able to stand in God's presence.

The cloud then vanished. Moses and Elijah disappeared from view, and the disciples saw Jesus just as he had been before. Peter, James, and John had to return to the rest of the disciples and live by faith, not by sight.

But as they went down the mountain, they must have had a different attitude toward the difficulties that lay ahead. After seeing what they saw and hearing what they heard, being a disciple of Jesus must have seemed like the greatest privilege in the world, whatever the cost. The way ahead might be hard, but they had seen a glimpse of the glory that lay beyond the cross. And that glimpse gave them the hope and courage they needed to continue—even after Jesus ascended into heaven.

FOR FURTHER READING, SEE MATTHEW 17

FORGIVENESS RELEASED

Father, forgive them, for they don't know what they are doing. LUKE 23:34

HUMAN SIN REACHED its full horror and most awful expression on the cross when we crucified the Son of God. If there was ever a moment in human history when God's judgment had to fall, this was it. But at that moment, Jesus cried out, "Father, forgive them, for they don't know what they are doing."

Christ knew judgment would come, so he cried out to the Father, "Don't let it fall on them; let it fall on me." He was isolating himself under the judgment of God. "Let me be the lightning rod for your judgment on their sin. Allow me to be the sacrifice consumed on this altar of the cross; don't let your judgment fall on them."

When God pronounced his curse on the first sin, Adam must have thought that the judgment of God was going to fall on him, but God diverted it onto the ground (see Genesis 3:17). Sin always leads to God's judgment. But in his great mercy, God allows the judgment to be diverted away from the sinner so that room is created for reconciliation. This is at the very heart of the Good News.

Jesus stood under the judgment of God for sins that have been committed against him. Christ asked the Father to divert the punishment away from his enemies, and he absorbed it in himself. That is how forgiveness was released.

God's judgment for human sin was poured out on the cross, where Jesus bore it. That is how he built the bridge across which we can come and receive the forgiveness of God, even today. I love the broad way in which Jesus said, "Father, forgive them." Who is "them"?

Jesus' prayer included the crowds who mocked him, the soldiers who crucified him, and the disciples who deserted him, but it extends even further. It includes the Old Testament believers who had waited for him and all those in every generation who come to him. When Jesus says, "Father, forgive them," the word *them* is big enough for you to crawl inside.

FOR FURTHER READING, SEE LUKE 23

PARADISE OPENED

I assure you, today you will be with me in paradise. LUKE 23:43

ON THE CROSS, Jesus found himself in the company of two men who had pursued a life of crime, but the long arm of the law finally caught up with them. One of them joined the crowd in heaping abuse on Jesus: "So you're the Messiah, are you? Prove it by saving yourself—and us, too, while you're at it!" (Luke 23:39). But then something happened in the soul of the other one.

Perhaps for the first time in his life, he thought about his position. Earth was receding, and eternity was looming large—right on the horizon. He hadn't planned on this, nor had he prepared for it. As these thoughts ran through his mind, he heard the voice of his friend cursing, and he said to him, "Don't you fear God?" (Luke 23:40).

Then he said, "Jesus, remember me when you come into your Kingdom" (Luke 23:42). Jesus replied, "I assure you, today you will be with me in paradise" (23:43). This is extraordinary—a man who was destined for hell, right on the brink of eternal destruction, was given full access to eternal life with Jesus Christ.

Think about what happened to this man. He completely missed out on the Christian life! He had no battles with temptation and no struggles with prayer. He was not baptized, and he never became a member of a church. But the fact that he entered paradise shows with great clarity where our salvation lies. Salvation is by grace alone, through faith alone, in Christ alone.

This is the Good News: that your acceptance with God does not depend on your performance in the Christian life. "God saved you by his grace when you believed. And you can't take credit for this; it is a gift from God" (Ephesians 2:8). If our works were involved in any way in our gaining entrance to heaven, assurance would be impossible. We could never know if we had done enough.

Salvation depends not on your works for Christ but on Christ's work for you. When the judgment poured out on Christ was finally exhausted, Jesus cried out, "It is finished!" (John 19:30). Christ's sacrificial work is finished, so you can rest your life, death, and eternity on him with complete confidence.

FOR FURTHER READING, SEE EPHESIANS 2

NO ONE EVER DIED LIKE THAT

Then Jesus shouted, "Father, I entrust my spirit into your hands!"

LUKE 23:46

ON THE CROSS, Jesus became the sacrifice for our sins. The punishment that brought us peace was upon him. He endured all the dimensions of hell, and the love of the Father was beyond his reach. That's why he cried out in the darkness, "My God, my God, why have you abandoned me?" (Matthew 27:46). But the story doesn't end there.

The last words of Jesus were not uttered with an exhausted sigh, but with a shout. He came through it, and he said in triumph, "It is finished! . . . Father, I entrust my spirit into your hands!" (John 19:30; Luke 23:46). Do you see the significance of this? The hell is over. The price is paid. The infinite agonies endured by the Son have passed. The light of the Father now shines on him again.

Notice that Jesus was not overwhelmed by death. It did not overcome him. He did not run out of strength. He had said, "No one can take my life from me. I sacrifice it voluntarily" (John 10:18). Christ's life was not taken; it was given. He gave himself in death.

Mark adds, "When the Roman officer who stood facing him saw how he had died, he exclaimed, 'This man truly was the Son of God!'" (Mark 15:39). Do you see the glory of that? No one else ever died like that!

Then, on the third day, Jesus rose from the dead! Several weeks later, on the day of Pentecost, Peter began to preach the message that "God has made this Jesus, whom you crucified, to be both Lord and Messiah" (Acts 2:36).

Jesus is the one who brings salvation to you. He has cleared the enemies from the valley of death. He has opened paradise. He has borne the sentence of death for our sins, and he offers forgiveness to all who will come to him in repentance and faith. Don't push him away. Come to him and receive what he has purchased for you. Receive the gift of God by faith and make it your own.

FOR FURTHER READING, SEE JOHN 10

GOD GIVES THE EXPLANATION

Why are you looking among the dead for someone who is alive?
He isn't here! He is risen from the dead! LUKE 24:5-6

MARY MAGDALENE, JOANNA, and Mary the mother of James went to the tomb three days after Jesus died on the cross. They found that the rock in front of the tomb had been moved and the tomb was empty, but they had no idea what to make of it. They were lost for an explanation; the empty tomb left them wondering.

The women didn't immediately jump to the conclusion that Jesus had risen. Mary didn't say, "I have the feeling he must have risen from the dead." Joanna didn't say, "I have that feeling too. I think you're right." The thought didn't even occur to them. The first visitors had no idea what to make of the empty tomb.

So how did they know what had happened? God told them: "Two men suddenly appeared to them, clothed in dazzling robes. The women were terrified and bowed with their faces to the ground. Then the men asked, 'Why are you looking among the dead for someone who is alive? He isn't here! He is risen from the dead!'" (Luke 24:4-6).

God must have called two angels and said, "Go tell them what I have done. There's no way they're ever going to work out what happened." Christian faith rests entirely on grasping and believing what God tells us he has done.

We have seen this pattern throughout the Bible story. Adam had no way of knowing who he was until God told him. The Virgin Mary had no way of knowing what was happening to her until God sent an angel to explain it. The shepherds and wise men would never have known that the child in the manger was God in human flesh without God's explanation through the angels.

Christian faith does not rest on feelings, impulses, or personal insights. It is believing God's explanation of his actions given to us in his Word: "He is risen from the dead!"

FOR FURTHER READING, SEE HEBREWS 11

DEATH IS DEFEATED

Death reigned from the time of Adam to the time of Moses.

ROMANS 5:14, NIV

EVER SINCE THE first sin in the Garden of Eden, death has been relentless. It is like a tyrant exercising a reign of terror over the human race. Nobody can escape it.

In the Old Testament story, many great men of faith—Abraham, Isaac, Jacob, Moses, and David—believed God's promise, but death got every one of them. They did not enter condemnation, because by faith they were looking for a Savior who was still to come and for a sacrifice that was yet to be made.

But all of them died before the Savior came. Death brought them to a place where there was a way in, but no way out.

My kindergarten class had a pet mouse, and eventually my turn came to take the mouse home. One sunny Saturday afternoon, I took the mouse and several toys outside with me, including my one-foot-long, six-inch-high, bright red double-decker London bus. The mouse found my bus fascinating.

Before I knew it, the mouse climbed inside the bus, ran up the stairs, and was working its way along the top deck. It scampered over the little plastic seats, poking its nose out the windows, until it reached the front of the bus. Then we had a problem. The mouse couldn't move forward, and it couldn't move back. It was stuck!

I tried everything, including cheese at the back of the bus, but the poor mouse had no room to turn. There was no way out. I remember my father saying, "There's only one thing to do, Son. We'll have to destroy the bus!" So he took a knife, cut the roof open, and the mouse was free. But my bus was never the same.

People went into death before the time of Christ; no one came out. But death could not keep its hold on Christ. He cut a hole in death itself. He changed its nature, so that when we come to the moment of death, it will not be like entering a prison; it will be like going through a passage, which leads right into the presence of God.

FOR FURTHER READING, SEE LUKE 4

WHY BOTHER WITH IT?

Look at my hands. Look at my feet. You can see that it's really me.
Touch me and make sure that I am not a ghost, because ghosts
don't have bodies, as you see that I do. LUKE 24:39

JESUS WANTED THE disciples to know that what they were seeing was more than his spirit in visible form. The body that had lain in the tomb had been raised. The message of Easter is not, "Jesus is alive!" That's true, but Easter tells us much more: "Jesus is risen!" It's worth thinking about the difference.

The Son of God was alive in heaven before he ever took human flesh: "In the beginning the Word already existed. The Word was with God, and the Word was God" (John 1:1). He was actively engaged in the work of the Godhead, creating and sustaining the world, *before* he took on human flesh.

Why didn't he leave the crucified body in the tomb and return to the Father? It was only flesh and bone—why bother? The angels could have said on Easter morning, "His body is here in the tomb, but don't worry: his spirit is with the Father in heaven."

When a Christian dies, is this not precisely what we say at the funeral service? We visit the graveside, and we know exactly where the body is, but then we say, "Even though the body is here, the person's soul is with the Father in heaven."

God created men and women as unique integrations of body and soul. That's why death is such a terrible enemy: it separates the soul and the body that God has joined together. It's the undoing of our very nature. If only the soul were saved, that would not be victory over death. The only way death can be defeated is for the body and soul to be reunited in the power of a new life.

When Christ returns in glory and gathers his people together, it is not just some spiritual capacity within you that will enter heaven. All of you—body and soul—will be rejoicing in the presence of God. He will redeem every part of you, including your body.

FOR FURTHER READING, SEE LUKE 24

TAKING A VIRTUAL VACATION

*I am the resurrection and the life. Anyone who believes
in me will live, even after dying.* JOHN 11:25

THE RESURRECTION TELLS us that heaven is not merely a spiritual experience or virtual tour. It is not that some spiritual capacity within you survives death in a shadow of the life you now know. All of you will be redeemed!

Imagine that you're planning to take the vacation of a lifetime in Hawaii. But just before you leave, you fall down the stairs and break just about every bone in your body. In cartoon style, you wind up in the hospital, bandaged head to toe.

You cannot go to Hawaii—your body's just not up to it. But you have a friend who is a wizard with computers, and he says, "Don't worry; I'll take you there anyway. You'll have the time of your life. I'm going to take you on a virtual tour of Hawaii!"

So he brings in his laptop and sets it up on your bed. Sure enough, you can see Honolulu from different angles. He gives you a pair of headphones, and you can hear the sounds of the ocean. Then he places a little pad on your collar, and you can smell the flowers as you see them on the screen.

Your friend is excited, and you're grateful that he's gone to all the effort, so you thank him. "It's beautiful," you say. "I just wish that I had been able to go."

"What do you mean?" he asks. "You have gone! You saw Hawaii, heard its sounds, and smelled its scents. What more could you want?"

Your friend is a computer geek, so you humor him. But your body is stuck in the hospital, and whatever he says, you ain't been there! You may go there in your mind or in your imagination, but if your body doesn't go, you haven't really gone.

When Christ returns in glory and gathers his people, every believer will be there, not only in mind but also in body. Not just some spiritual capacity within you will enter heaven—*you* will be there, rejoicing in the presence of God. Grasp the resurrection of the body more clearly, and you'll have a greater anticipation of life in heaven.

FOR FURTHER READING, SEE JOHN 11

ADAPTED FOR ETERNITY

We will not all die, but we will all be transformed!
It will happen in a moment, in the blink of an eye, when the
last trumpet is blown. 1 CORINTHIANS 15:51-52

WHEN THE BODY of Jesus was raised, it was also changed. His flesh was adapted for everlasting life. This was something that had never happened before.

Lazarus was brought back to life in a wonderful miracle, but Lazarus came out of the tomb exactly as he'd gone into it. He might have been a few pounds lighter, but he was essentially the same. Then Lazarus carried on the process of aging at the point where he had left off, and eventually he had to go through the whole miserable process of dying all over again. Death was delayed; it was not defeated.

But when Christ was raised, his body was no longer subject to aging, sickness, or death. Nor was his resurrection body subject to pain or disability. It was Jesus' flesh, but it was transformed and adapted for eternity. This is the glorious future that awaits every Christian believer.

God has not prepared some kind of compensation package, like a reduced pension plan, for those who are unable to continue life on earth. He has sent Jesus Christ to redeem the whole of you, body and soul, and in the Resurrection, he will adapt your body, even as he is preparing your soul for eternal life in his presence.

The gift of the resurrection body is so wonderful that God holds it in reserve until the day when he will gather all of his children. That's what it was like on Christmas morning when I was a child—stockings were hung by the fire, and we were all eager to go in and open the gifts, but we weren't allowed to until everyone was standing at the door. Then, when everyone was ready, we all went in together.

We will experience the same transformation that Jesus did, in which our bodies are adapted for everlasting life. This gift will be given to the whole family together. Then all the faces of God's children will light up, as together we enter all that he has prepared for us.

FOR FURTHER READING, SEE 1 CORINTHIANS 15

LEARNING TO WALK BY FAITH

During the forty days after his crucifixion, he appeared
to the apostles from time to time, and . . . he talked to
them about the Kingdom of God. ACTS 1:3

AFTER HIS RESURRECTION, Jesus appeared to the disciples during a forty-day period. One of the reasons for these appearances was to prove "to them in many ways that he was actually alive" (Acts 1:3). It was important that Jesus' resurrection be established beyond a reasonable doubt, so Christ appeared to them, not once or twice, but repeatedly.

If you put the accounts of Jesus' appearances from the four Gospels and 1 Corinthians together, Christ appeared to the disciples on at least nine different occasions. Once Christ appeared to a group of more than five hundred people, and most of them were still living at the time Paul wrote about it. That means they were able to bear witness to the truthfulness of his account (see 1 Corinthians 15:6).

The resurrection appearances not only provided evidence that Jesus was alive, but they also prepared the disciples for the Kingdom work that lay ahead. Over these forty days, Jesus taught the disciples and brought them to a whole new level of understanding. Previously, they had thought of the cross as an unmitigated disaster, but now they saw that everything had happened exactly as God had planned it.

Christ was not with them constantly. He appeared to them, taught them, and then disappeared. In this way, Christ began to wean them away from dependence on his physical presence. For three years they had gotten used to talking with Jesus directly, face-to-face. They had witnessed his miracles, heard him speak, and asked him their questions. Their faith was built on sight. Now things would be different. The disciples would have to learn to walk by faith without sight (see 2 Corinthians 5:7). Over time, they gradually got used to trusting Jesus without seeing him.

What is true of the disciples is also true of you today, if you're a follower of Christ. You've been given the disciples' testimony in the Bible, which contains many convincing proofs of the resurrection of Jesus Christ. Your job, as you carry out the work that God has given you to do, is to learn to walk by faith, not by sight.

FOR FURTHER READING, SEE 2 CORINTHIANS 5

IN HEAVEN FOR YOU

He was taken up into a cloud while they were watching,
and they could no longer see him. ACTS 1:9

AS JESUS WAS taken from the disciples, they looked up and saw a cloud. The same Christ who had come from the Father was now returning to him. Having finished his work, Jesus was received by the Father. This was what filled the disciples with joy. Jesus had not simply disappeared into the sky; he was taken up into the cloud.

The significance of the cloud is clear in the Old Testament. When God's people were in the desert, he gave them a pillar of fire and a cloud as visible symbols of his presence. When the people saw the cloud, they knew God was with them. And in the New Testament when Christ was transfigured, a cloud came down on the mountain and the disciples fell on their faces, because they knew they were in the immediate presence of almighty God.

Think about the significance of Jesus' entering heaven. Adam was expelled from the Garden; now *a human was* in the presence of God. The Lord Jesus Christ not only assumed our humanity on earth, he has also taken our humanity into heaven. No wonder the disciples were filled with joy!

Can you imagine the celebration of Christ's entrance into heaven? Angels had seen Adam driven out from the presence of God. Now heaven erupted as *a human* walked right into the presence of God!

When Adam was expelled from God's presence, all his children were alienated from God. Christ has been welcomed into the Father's presence, and as a result, all God's children will be welcomed by the Father. The first Adam led us all out. The last Adam leads us all in.

Just as Jesus has been taken up into heaven, the day will come when all God's people will be caught up to meet him in the air. Jesus Christ lives in the presence of God, and once you grasp that he is there for you, you'll be filled with heaven's joy.

FOR FURTHER READING, SEE ACTS 1

GET A GOOD ATTORNEY

We have an advocate who pleads our case before the Father.
He is Jesus Christ, the one who is truly righteous. 1 JOHN 2:1

WHEN CHRIST ASCENDED into heaven, the disciples knew he was exactly where they needed him to be. It is far more important that Christ should represent us in heaven than that he should be physically present with us on earth.

Imagine you're in prison on a charge that carries the death penalty if convicted. You need a good attorney—the very best you can get. But as you get to know your attorney, you find that he is not only a skilled lawyer, he's also a man of great compassion. When he visits your cell, his presence is comforting, and you find that you can talk to him about how difficult life is on the inside.

All that is valuable, but what you need most from your attorney is not comfort in jail, but an effective performance in court. My greatest need as a sinner is not comfort on earth, but defense in heaven. I need a representative who will speak to the Father on my behalf, an advocate who will plead my case in heaven.

There are many ways of getting through this life successfully, but what use will that be if on the last day you find that almighty God has a case against you, and you have no effective defense?

The apostles were filled with joy because they understood that the ascended Christ, having entered heaven, was able to speak to the Father on their behalf. The apostle Paul says, "Who then will condemn us? No one—for Christ Jesus died for us and was raised to life for us, and he is sitting in the place of honor at God's right hand, pleading for us" (Romans 8:34).

If you are in Jesus Christ today, your Savior sits at the right hand of the Father as your advocate. He will defend you from every accusation, and you can be confident that on the last day, he will represent you before almighty God.

FOR FURTHER READING, SEE 1 JOHN 2

IN THE COURTROOM

I am writing this to you so that you will not sin. But if anyone does sin,
we have an advocate who pleads our case before the Father. 1 JOHN 2:1

JESUS CHRIST IS ready to defend sinners like you and me before God the Father. Aren't you glad that when we fail, we're no longer faced with the daily question of what we have to do to get right with God?

Imagine yourself standing in the courtroom of heaven. Satan, your accuser, has a case to present against you. The courtroom is filled with angels who rise as God the Father takes his place as the judge. Then the diabolical prosecutor begins to stride around the courtroom as he presents his case against you. The gist of it is that you are guilty of sin and deserve to be condemned.

He states that you were born in sin; your nature is corrupt. Then he brings allegations about sins you committed when you were young. He follows your life story, identifying moments of weakness, cowardice, complacency, pride, pettiness, and greed. You cringe as you listen. Other things he may use in his case against you come to mind, and you're afraid of what may happen if he brings them to light.

Finally, he clinches his argument by appealing to the weakness of your faith. He points out that even though you may have professed to be a believer in Christ, your faith was often weak and you had many doubts. His case is so compelling that you find yourself shaking and wondering how there could be any hope.

Jesus steps forward and begins to argue in your defense: "My client admits that every word spoken by the prosecution is true. We do not contest any of the charges, nor do we claim any mitigating circumstances. My client is guilty as charged."

"But," he continues, "I have here a full pardon, signed by God's own hand and purchased by my blood." Then, stripping off his robes, he shows his hands and side. The accuser has no answer. His whole case against you will be thrown out of court.

Our defense is not that we're without sin, but that Christ died for our sins, and they were judged at the cross. They cannot be brought to court a second time.

FOR FURTHER READING, SEE HEBREWS 10

THE BLESSING THAT NEVER ENDS

Lifting his hands to heaven, he blessed them. While he was blessing them, he left them and was taken up to heaven. LUKE 24:50-51

THE LAST TIME the disciples saw Jesus, his hands were raised, not in anger, but to bless them. Imagine what that must have been like. Try to imagine yourself kneeling down as Christ lifts his hands and speaks words of God's blessing into your life.

In the Old Testament, we saw that the blessing was more than just kind words expressing best wishes for the future. Jacob was prepared to deceive in order to get his father's blessing, because the blessing was a prophetic statement of what God would do through a person's life. When Isaac's blessing was given to Jacob, it was irreversible. God's hand would be on Jacob and on his children, and this man would be used to fulfill the purposes of God. That's what Jacob wanted.

Now Christ raises his hands over the disciples and imparts his blessing to them. God's anointing would be on them, and they would be used to fulfill his purposes.

The Ascension speaks to both the *completed work* and the *continuing work* of Christ. His completed work is the work of offering a sacrifice for sin. Jesus ascended to the Father, and the Bible says that "when he had cleansed us from our sins, he sat down in the place of honor at the right hand of the majestic God in heaven" (Hebrews 1:3).

The priests in the Old Testament never sat down. There was a table and a lamp in the Tabernacle, but there was no chair. This was a visual reminder that the priest's work was never done. But Christ's sacrificial work is finished. There is nothing more that needs to be done to satisfy the wrath of God and release his forgiveness. That work is complete, and that is why Christ sat down.

But there is also work that continues: Christ will go on blessing his people until he returns. "He lives forever to intercede" for us (Hebrews 7:25). If you belong to him today, you can be sure that Christ is sitting at the right hand of the Father with his hands raised, not in anger, but to bless you.

FOR FURTHER READING, SEE HEBREWS 1

IT'S THE REAL THING

Do not leave Jerusalem until the Father sends you the gift he promised. . . .
In just a few days you will be baptized with the Holy Spirit. ACTS 1:4-5

AFTER CHRIST ASCENDED into heaven, he would no longer be visible to the disciples, but through the Holy Spirit, his presence would be just as real as when they could see him. Jesus' presence would now be with all of them, in every place at one time.

This was not possible while Christ was on earth—human flesh can only be in one place at a time. Even after the Resurrection, when Christ was able to appear and disappear, there's no indication that he was in more than one place at a time.

Now Jesus told the disciples they were to be his "witnesses . . . in Jerusalem, throughout Judea, in Samaria, and to the ends of the earth" (Acts 1:8). They'd be scattered across the earth, but Christ would be with them in every place (see Matthew 28:19-20).

This is what Jesus was referring to when he said, "But in fact, it is best for you that I go away, because if I don't, the Advocate won't come. If I do go away, then I will send him to you" (John 16:7). After the Ascension, the disciples did not have the visible presence of Jesus *with* them, but they had the Spirit of Jesus *in* them.

The Lord Jesus Christ is at the right hand of the Father, and at the same time, the Spirit of Jesus is present in the believer. This is Christ's promise to every one of his children. Jesus is with you by his Spirit, and he will never fail you or abandon you (see Hebrews 13:5).

After Jesus was taken up, angels appeared and said, "Men of Galilee, . . . why are you standing here staring into heaven? Jesus has been taken from you into heaven, but someday he will return from heaven in the same way you saw him go!" (Acts 1:11).

God's promise is that just as Jesus was snatched up into the cloud, so when he returns, we will be caught up to meet him in the air. What happened to Jesus will happen to us when he comes in glory.

FOR FURTHER READING, SEE MATTHEW 28

THE DINNER PARTY THAT WENT SOUTH

Don't let your hearts be troubled. JOHN 14:1

IT WAS THE Passover, and Jesus had been looking forward to this last meal with his disciples before going to the cross. Early on in the evening, Jesus shocked his friends by saying that someone at the table would betray him. How do you carry on a dinner party after that?

There was more bad news: "I will be with you only a little longer" (John 13:33). Can you picture the faces around the table when Jesus said this? These men had left everything to follow Christ. They had built their whole lives around him, and now after just three years, he told them he would be with them only a little longer.

Peter could not imagine being separated from Christ, so he said he was willing to lay down his life for him. Jesus replied, "Die for me? I tell you the truth, Peter—before the rooster crows tomorrow morning, you will deny three times that you even know me" (John 13:38).

In a matter of minutes, the disciples discovered that one of them would betray the Savior, Jesus himself would be taken from them, and his leading disciple would make a total denial of his faith before the night ended.

Jesus' next words must have been staggering, "Don't let your hearts be troubled" (John 14:1). How could Jesus say this in light of all he had just said? I can imagine the disciples saying, "You tell us one of us is a traitor, you're about to leave, and Peter's testimony will collapse. Then you say we shouldn't be troubled?"

I imagine Jesus looking around at his disciples at this point in the evening saying, "Here's what I need you to do right now—trust God! Trust in me!" Jesus was not asking them to believe blindly. They'd seen his miracles, heard his words, and walked with him for three years. In this moment of great darkness, Christ called them to trust what he had taught them in the light.

FOR FURTHER READING, SEE JOHN 13

ONE HOUSE, MANY ROOMS

There is more than enough room in my Father's home.
If this were not so, would I have told you that I am
going to prepare a place for you? JOHN 14:2

WHEN JESUS BEGAN to speak about his Father's house, the disciples must have wondered what that had to do with Judas's defection, Christ's departure, and Peter's denial, but he had asked them to trust him, so they listened carefully.

If you're familiar with the King James Version of the Bible, you would have learned the phrase, "In my Father's house are many mansions." This has led many people to picture heaven as an upscale housing project with very large estates. Others, who think they've lived less worthy lives, have the idea that they'll find themselves in second-class accommodations—heaven's equivalent of a garden shed!

But there is really no basis for this in the Bible. Jesus spoke about one house with many rooms. The picture is of a great extended family being brought into the Father's home. The idea is not that everyone will be given a building plot, but that all of God's family will be together in the Father's house.

The irony is that when Jesus was born, there was no room for him in Bethlehem. There must have been a smile on his face as Jesus said, "Don't worry; when you come to my home, it won't be as it was when I came to yours—in my Father's house are many rooms!"

Later that evening, Jesus said, "All who love me will do what I say. My Father will love them, and we will come and make our home with each of them" (John 14:23). Literally, "We will room with him." Jesus was telling the disciples that God would move in with them by the Holy Spirit, until one day they move in with him!

Jesus emphasized the absolute certainty of the disciples' future: "If it were not so, I have told you" (John 14:2, KJV). If the future of the disciples was in doubt, he would have told them. But a magnificent destiny lies ahead, not only for them, but for all who love Jesus. That's why you don't need to be troubled, even when the bottom seems to be falling out of your world. Put your trust in Christ.

FOR FURTHER READING, SEE 1 THESSALONIANS 4

THE SUPER BOWL

I go to prepare a place for you. JOHN 14:2, KJV

WHEN JESUS SAID this to the disciples, he didn't mean he was going to heaven to get it ready for them! If God can create the cosmos out of nothing and hold the moon and the stars on course, he can get heaven organized with a single command.

When Jesus said this, he was telling the disciples that the place would be prepared *by his going*. Jesus was about to go to the cross. He was going to die, be buried, rise, and finally ascend to heaven. It is through Christ's death, resurrection, and ascension that the place for all his followers is prepared. His death and resurrection have made heaven ready, reserving a place for all who believe.

That's why the disciples didn't need to be troubled by the fact that Jesus was being taken from them. It was through his going to the cross that the way would be opened up for them to enter into the home Christ had described.

Imagine you are playing in the Super Bowl. The ball comes to you, and for a moment you see the goal line—thirty yards ahead of you. The crowd is cheering, and your heart pounds as you begin to run.

But there in front of you are the defensive linemen—huge guys looking right at you. Their names are "Law," "Sin," and "Death." There's another one—bigger, meaner, and uglier than the others—standing behind the linemen, and his name is "Satan."

There is no way past these guys. They stand between you and the goal line, and you know they'll flatten you before you get there. But now an offensive lineman comes at great speed toward them. They're looking to take you out, but he comes and knocks them down, opening your way to the goal line.

This is what Jesus Christ has done for you on the cross. "I go to prepare a place for you," he says. By his death and resurrection, Christ has opened the way into everlasting life for you.

FOR FURTHER READING, SEE JOHN 14

HE'LL BE BACK

*If I go and prepare a place for you, I will come back and take you to
be with me that you also may be where I am.* JOHN 14:3, NIV

JESUS WAS ABOUT to endure indescribable suffering on the cross, and
it was in this way that reservations would be made in the Father's house
for all his people. Since he would pay such a price for the reservations,
the disciples could be absolutely certain that Jesus would return to bring
them to the Father's home.

The logic of Jesus' words is powerfully persuasive: "If I go, . . . I will
come back and take you to be with me" (John 14:3, NIV). Jesus was saying, "If I go through the agony of death and rise on the third day and
ascend into heaven, all for the purpose of preparing a place for you,
then is it conceivable that I would not bring you there?"

This is why Jesus told the disciples that they were not to be troubled,
but rather to trust in him. They had seen Judas leave, they had heard
that Peter would fail, and they had been told that Jesus would be taken
from them. They felt that their world was falling apart, but it wasn't.
Jesus was going to prepare a place for them, and they could be absolutely
confident that he would bring them home.

Suppose you're buying a new car, and you want a particular model
in black. You go to the dealership and tell the dealer what you're looking for. He types a few things into his computer and then shakes his
head. "Well, we do have that model in stock, but unfortunately, we
don't carry it in black. I can locate one for you, but you'll need to pay
for it up front."

You really want the car *and* you really want it in black, so you agree
to his terms. If you've paid the full cost of the car, you'll come back to
that dealership to receive what you already purchased so you can take it
home. Christ laid down his life to purchase you. You can be certain that
he'll come back to take you home.

FOR FURTHER READING, SEE ROMANS 8

GOD IN THREE PERSONS

God said, "Let us make human beings in our image." GENESIS 1:26

WHY WOULD GOD refer to himself using the plurals *us* and *our* when he tells us so clearly and distinctively that he is one (see Deuteronomy 6:4)? The Old Testament raises some questions about the nature of God that don't get resolved until the New Testament.

The Bible tells us that "God is love" (1 John 4:8), but love needs an object. Whom did God love before Creation? God has always been love, and before anything else existed, that love was shared among the Father, the Son, and the Holy Spirit.

In the Old Testament, God said, "I AM," but in the New Testament, God was saying, "I am the Father, I am the Son, and I am the Holy Spirit." If we're going to know God, we must come to know him as Father, Son, and Spirit. If we do not know him in this way, we do not know him as he is.

This is more than a matter of knowledge; it's a matter of experience. Jesus told his disciples that they were to "go and make disciples of all the nations, baptizing them in the name of the Father and the Son and the Holy Spirit" (Matthew 28:19).

The word *baptize* means "to dip, plunge, or immerse." In the early church, believers were baptized in rivers. Either they were plunged under the water or water was poured over their heads. Either way, they got drenched! Jesus said baptism was to be given "in the name of the Father and the Son and the Holy Spirit." The Christian life is all about being drenched in the Father, plunged into the Son, and soaked in the Spirit. This is part of what baptism symbolizes.

The Father, the Son, and the Spirit permeate every part of a believer's life. You cannot separate one from the other—the Spirit draws you to the Son, the Son brings you to the Father, and the Son pours the Spirit into your heart. You cannot know the Father apart from the Son, or the Son apart from the Spirit. While you cannot fully understand the nature of God, you must grasp what is revealed about the Father, Son, and Holy Spirit if you're to know God as he is.

FOR FURTHER READING, SEE GENESIS 1

FIXING THE ANCHOR POINTS

*Go and make disciples of all the nations, baptizing them in the name
of the Father and the Son and the Holy Spirit.* MATTHEW 28:19

THE FATHER, SON, and Spirit permeate every part of a believer's life. To
try and grasp what this means, let's summarize what God has revealed
about his nature:

- *There is one God.* This is clear in both the Old and New Testaments.
  God says, "Hear, O Israel: The LORD our God, the LORD is
  one" (Deuteronomy 6:4, NIV). There is "one Lord, one faith,
  one baptism, and one God and Father" (Ephesians 4:5-6).
  Christians do not believe in three gods. There is one God.
- *God is three persons.* There's no place in the Bible where we read,
  "God is three persons." But within the limitations of human
  language, *person* is the best word we can use to describe the
  identities of the Father, the Son, and the Spirit.
- The distinct identities of Father, Son, and Spirit are written
  all through the New Testament. The Father sends the Son (see
  Galatians 4:4), the Son prays to the Father (see John 17:1), the
  Spirit glorifies the Son (see John 16:14), and the Son sends the
  Spirit (Acts 2:33). But don't confuse the three persons of the
  Godhead—the Father did not die on the cross; the Son did not
  send himself into the world; the Spirit did not rise from the
  dead. There is one God *and* God is three persons.
- *Each person is fully God.* The Father is God, the Son is God, and
  the Spirit is God. Christ said, "The Father and I are one"
  (John 10:30), and he talked about the glory he shared with the
  Father before the world began (see 17:5). When Christ spoke about
  sending the Holy Spirit, he was not talking about an alternative
  to his own presence; he was promising that his presence would
  be with the disciples, even though he was returning to the Father
  (see 14:16-18). If the Spirit was with them, Christ was with them;
  and if Christ was with them, the Father was with them (see 14:23).

The Father, Son, and Spirit are God, but there are not three gods.
There is one eternal God, who is Father, Son, and Holy Spirit. The
more you think about this, the more staggering it gets.

FOR FURTHER READING, SEE JOHN 17

HOW TO RESPOND TO A MYSTERY

*Can you solve the mysteries of God? Can you discover
everything about the Almighty?* JOB 11:7

THE NATURE OF God is a mystery, but it is not a contradiction. If Christians believed that there is one God *and* that there are three gods, that would be a contradiction. If we believed that there are three persons *and* that there is one person, that would be a contradiction. But to say that there is one God who exists in three persons is not a contradiction; it is a mystery.

There are a number of places in the Bible where we're presented with mysteries, and it's important to know how to respond to them.

Don't turn away from a mystery. Some people instinctively throw their hands in the air and turn away from anything they cannot understand, as if something that cannot be understood cannot possibly be true. If you do that, you will miss the unfathomable splendor of the glory of God.

Don't try to explain a mystery. You can't put "understanding the nature of God" on your to-do list and expect that one day some publisher will put out a book that explains it all, so you can cross it off your list and say, "It all makes sense to me now; I don't know why I didn't see it before." God will never let you get there; if you did, you would probably cease to worship.

The other day my wife said to me, "I knew you were going to say that. I've been married to you over twenty years, and I've figured you out." That's a rather intimidating phrase, "I've figured you out." And she has—I can't deny it. After twenty years, there isn't much mystery left. It's getting harder to surprise her.

God has revealed himself in such a way that we may truly know him, but we will never come to the point where we've "figured him out." Even in heaven, when you see God as he is, you will be lost in wonder and praise. You will look into the face of God and find yourself filled with more wonder than ever before. The way to respond to a mystery is to let it lead you into worship.

FOR FURTHER READING, SEE JOB 42

ACCESS TO THE PRESIDENT

If you had really known me, you would know who my Father is. JOHN 14:7

IT IS VERY significant that when Jesus spoke about the Father, he regularly said "*my* Father": "There is more than enough room in my Father's home" (John 14:2). "When I am raised to life again, you will know that I am in my Father, and you are in me, and I am in you" (14:20).

Jesus distinguished clearly between his relationship with the Father and the disciples' relationship with the Father: "I am ascending to my Father and your Father" (John 20:17). Why didn't he just say "our Father"?

There's only one occasion when Christ used the phrase "our Father," and that was when he was teaching his disciples how *they* should pray (see Matthew 6:9-13). Christ never referred to his relationship with the Father and the disciples' relationship with the Father in the same way—the distinction is always preserved.

If you wanted to see the president of the United States, it would be hard because he's not easily accessible. But there are options. If you knew his wife, she could help you. If you knew his father or mother or one of his brothers, they might be able to arrange a meeting. If you knew the secretary of state or the chief of staff, he or she might grant you access. The reason there are many ways to the president is that there are many people who are close to him and who know him.

But who knows God the Father? Jesus makes it clear—no one is close to the Father except the Son. He's the only one who has ever seen the Father, and he knows the Father: "No one has ever seen God. But the unique One, who is himself God, is near to the Father's heart. He has revealed God to us" (John 1:18).

The good news is not that God is everyone's Father. The good news is that Christ knows God as his Father, and for that reason, he is able to bring us to know God as our Father too. "But when the right time came, God sent his Son . . . to buy freedom for us who were slaves to the law, so that he could adopt us as his very own children" (Galatians 4:4-5).

FOR FURTHER READING, SEE GALATIANS 4

WHERE THE CHRISTIAN LIFE BEGINS

My nourishment comes from doing the will of God,
who sent me, and from finishing his work. JOHN 4:34

YOU CAN'T MISS this in the life of Jesus: He placed himself under the authority of the Father. The whole of his life was aligned with the Father's purpose.

This was never seen more clearly than in the garden of Gethsemane, where Christ said, "My Father! If it is possible, let this cup of suffering be taken away from me. Yet I want your will to be done, not mine" (Matthew 26:39). If it were possible to fulfill the Father's purpose without the awful pain of the cross, that would have been Jesus' choice. But if the Father's purpose required him to go through this agony, then he was ready.

If we want to come to the Father, the first question is whether we are ready to be subject to his authority. That was the big decision the Prodigal Son had to face (see Luke 15:11-24). He had resisted his father's authority for a long time. Then there came a point when his father's house seemed very attractive. But before he could return, he had to decide if he was willing to be under his father's authority.

Some people know so little of the Father's love because they're continually resisting his authority. No one can enter the relationship Jesus offers and at the same time resist him. When you pray, "Our Father . . . ," it won't be long before you're saying, "Your will be done." Christ brought these two together in Gethsemane when he submitted himself to the Father's will, even though it was indescribably painful. Are you ready for that kind of submission?

It is significant that the first time the most intimate title for God, *Abba*, is used in the New Testament, it is not from the mouth of an ecstatic worshipper, but from the agonized voice of Christ in Gethsemane (see Mark 14:36).

To know God as Father is to be subject to his authority. The Christian life does not begin with my deciding I would like to go to heaven; it begins when I come to the place of saying, "I want your will to be done, not mine."

FOR FURTHER READING, SEE LUKE 15

SECURE IN THE FATHER'S LOVE

I have loved you even as the Father has loved me. JOHN 15:9

JESUS OFFERS TO bring us into the love of the Father, the love he has experienced since before the world began (see John 17:24).

It's the special work of the Holy Spirit to let us know that we're loved by the Father by pouring out the love of God into our hearts (see Romans 5:5). Love is not something we believe; it's something we experience. It's a wonderful gift to be enjoyed!

This is a sensitive issue for some people. I was privileged to be raised in a happy family, and I thank God for a loving father. The security and love I knew makes me sensitive to the pain of those who did not know that privilege.

Folks whose experience of family life has been painful sometimes say that talking about God as *Father* is unhelpful and misleading. If that's how you feel, I have a question for you: How do you know your relationship with your father was bad?

You know because God has placed within your heart a sense of what a father should be. The very fact that you can identify your disappointment is an indication that you have a sense of what ought to be. God put that there.

Christ has come to bring you into a relationship in which you know the unfathomable love of God the Father for his children. Christ will bring you into the family of God as a wanted, loved, and welcomed child. The Holy Spirit will bond you to the Father so that you know you are secure in his love.

This kind of assurance does not always come immediately in the Christian life. Paul regularly prayed that Christians would experience more of God's love (see Ephesians 3:18-19). Sometimes our pain numbs us to the warmth of God's love for a time. But don't settle for anything less. Believe God's promises. Ask the Holy Spirit to pour out the Father's love in your heart. Go on asking; you will receive.

FOR FURTHER READING, SEE EPHESIANS 3

WHEN DID CHRIST BECOME THE SON?

*[Jesus] called God his Father, thereby making
himself equal with God.* JOHN 5:18

WHEN DID CHRIST become the Son? He has always been the Son. He's the eternal Son; his nature never changes. I became a father when my son Andrew was born in 1986. Before I had a son, I was not a father. When did God become Father? God has always been Father. He's the everlasting Father; his nature never changes.

The Father was never without the Son, and the Son was never without the Father. God did not gain a Son when Jesus was born. God sent his Son, who was already at the Father's side, into the world to be born of a virgin. Christ did not begin his existence in Mary's womb. Before he took on flesh, God the Son shared the Father's glory, the Father's life, the Father's activity, and the Father's love.

The Bible makes it clear that the Son has always been equal with the Father. There is no ranking of Father, Son, and Spirit in order of importance. To accomplish our salvation, the Son, "though he was God" (Philippians 2:6), chose to subordinate himself to the Father.

On one occasion, Jesus said to his disciples, "If you really loved me, you would be happy that I am going to the Father, who is greater than I am" (John 14:28). This is like me saying, "The president is greater than I am." I don't mean the president is more human than I am; I mean he has a more exalted position than I do.

When Jesus said, "The Father . . . is greater than I am," he didn't mean the Father is more divine; he meant that the Father had a more exalted position—which would become obvious as Jesus went to the cross. Christ was saying to his disciples, "If you loved me, you would be glad that I am going to the Father, because that means I am returning to share his exalted position."

Jesus is no longer on the cross. He died, was buried, and then was raised from the dead. Jesus ascended into heaven, and that's where he is now, exalted at the right hand of the Father—all glory and power and praise belong to him!

FOR FURTHER READING, SEE PHILIPPIANS 2

LIKE FATHER, LIKE SON

I have seen and have borne witness that this is the Son of God.

JOHN 1:34, ESV

WHEN JOHN THE Baptist says that Jesus is the Son of God, the word *Son* does not mean he's a dependent relative of the Father. The Father and the Son's relationship has no beginning and no end.

In the ancient world, if you were a boy, you did what your father did, and if you were a girl, you followed in the footsteps of your mother. By watching them, you'd learn how things were done. If it were still like this today and you were the son of a plumber, you'd be a plumber. If he was a good plumber, you'd likely be a good one too, but if he wasn't, your work would likely suffer. The father's work is normally reflected in the work of the son.

Names were given, in the ancient world, to describe character. For example, we're told that "the sons of Eli were sons of Belial" (1 Samuel 2:12, KJV). Notice that the word *sons* is used in two completely different ways in this one verse. These men were Eli's dependent children, but the character they reflected was not Eli's, but the devil's (or Belial's). This is not a very complimentary description.

On a more positive note, God referred to Israel as his "son." He said to Pharaoh, "Let my son go, so he can worship me" (Exodus 4:23). The Hebrew people were descended from Abraham, but God called them to reflect his holiness and to express his character in the world, so God called the nation his son.

In the New Testament we read about a man named Joseph, whom "the apostles nicknamed Barnabas (which means 'Son of Encouragement')" (Acts 4:36). "Barnabas" was a nickname given to Joseph because he was a great encourager—he was encouragement personified, encouragement in human flesh.

Jesus is called "the Son of God" not because he is a dependent relative of the Father, but because he reflects the nature of the Father perfectly. He is everything that God is, in the flesh. He shares the Father's nature and glory; he is "the visible image of the invisible God" (Colossians 1:15).

FOR FURTHER READING, SEE COLOSSIANS 1

WOMB, TOMB, AND DOOM

I tell you the truth, the Son can do nothing by himself.
He does only what he sees the Father doing.
Whatever the Father does, the Son also does. JOHN 5:19

JESUS IS SAYING that his activity is limited to what he sees the Father doing. He never does anything that's outside the range of what the Father would do. I wish I could say, "Everything I do is a reflection of the activity of my heavenly Father," but I can't. If that were true, I'd be perfect. But that is exactly what Jesus is saying.

Then Jesus says something even more astonishing—not only does he do *only* what the Father does; he also does *everything* that the Father does. All of his activity a reflection of the Father's activity, and all of the Father's activity also finds its reflection in Jesus.

We may do *some* things that reflect what God the Father does. We may love or forgive or make peace, and in that limited sense, we may reflect the nature of the Father, but there are some things the Father does that we can never do—like make a universe! Only God gives life; only God is in a position to pronounce final judgment; only God raises the dead.

And Jesus tells us that *he* does them: "Just as the Father gives life to those he raises from the dead, so the Son gives life to anyone he wants. . . . The Father judges no one. Instead, he has given the Son absolute authority to judge. . . . The time is coming, indeed it's here now, when the dead will hear my voice—the voice of the Son of God. And those who listen will live" (John 5:21-22, 25).

Our church recently completed a building expansion, and when the work was completed, keys were distributed. Keys reflect authority— if you have the keys to a place, you have the right to access it.

Some keys belong to God alone—the keys of womb, tomb, and doom. And Jesus holds all the Father's keys in his hand. They belong as much to the Son as they do to the Father.

FOR FURTHER READING, SEE JOHN 5

KNOWING GOD

*The Father has life in himself, and he has granted that
same life-giving power to his Son.* JOHN 5:26

GOD HAS GIVEN us the wonderful gift of life, but we don't have life *in
ourselves*. Our lives are the gift of God, through our parents. Without
them, we would not be. Only God has life *in himself*. He is the only being
whose existence does not depend on anyone else. Jesus' words help us
gaze into the mystery of the Trinity.

Notice Jesus did not say, "The Father has life in himself, and the Son
has life in himself." That would mean there are two gods, both with life
in themselves. Nor did Jesus say, "The Father has life in himself, and
he has granted the Son to have life." That would mean that the Son was
a created and dependent being like you and me.

The Father has always had life in himself and so has the Son—but
there's one life. The Father and the Son share in the one eternal life of
God. That's why Jesus could say, "Anyone who has seen me has seen the
Father" (John 14:9).

I have a brother in England. He is like me in some ways, but very different in others. I could not say to you, "If you have seen me, you have
seen my brother," because even though we come from the same parents,
we're entirely different. To know me is not to know my brother.

If the Son is close to the Father but is not God, then we are left guess-
ing about what the Father is like. We could assume that Jesus is like the
Father in some respects, but how could we know which ones? And if the
Son is not God, then by definition he must in some ways be different
from the Father. In what ways would he be different?

If the Son were not God, we would not know the Father. In that case,
the best we could say is that someone who was with the Father and is in
some ways like the Father has come to tell us about him. But Jesus isn't a
companion of the Father who has come to tell us about him. He is God
with us, and that means you can know the Father.

FOR FURTHER READING, SEE MATTHEW 1

AN ACT OF CRUELTY OR AN ACT OF LOVE?

God showed his great love for us by sending Christ to die
for us while we were still sinners. ROMANS 5:8

THE BIBLE TELLS us the Father laid the guilt and punishment for our sins on the Son. Think about it. If the Son were not God, the cross was an act of utter cruelty on the part of God. If the Son were not God, then God picked on some person in his creation and poured out on him what everyone else deserved. What kind of justice is that?

If the Son were not God, he was victimized by the Father—sentenced for crimes he did not commit. If the Son were not God, the cross was the greatest miscarriage of justice in history, not just by Pontius Pilate, but by God almighty. If the Son were not God, we would have to rewrite Romans 5:8 to read like this: "God showed his great injustice by sending Christ to die for us while we were still sinners."

Before God created the world, he knew the choice Adam and Eve would make and the disaster that would follow. But God had planned to redeem men and women out of this fallen world so that they would share his eternal glory forever. That plan involved a great cost. It would mean God giving himself, and that self-giving would be the ultimate display of his own nature and his own glory.

God's self-giving would involve all the persons of the Trinity. Before the world began, the Father said, "I will be the giver." The Son said, "I will be the gift," and the Spirit said, "I will bring the gift to all who will receive." The Father would send the Son; the Son would lay down his life; the Spirit would deliver this priceless gift and make it yours.

As the Father gave the Son and the Son laid down his life, God was reconciling the world to himself in Christ. The cross was not the act of a cruel and vindictive God. It was the outpouring of love by the God who chose to redeem his enemies at infinite personal cost, and the reason it is so is that the Son is God.

FOR FURTHER READING, SEE ROMANS 5

THE SUPREME COURT OF THE UNIVERSE

The Father . . . has given the Son absolute authority to judge.   JOHN 5:22

IF THE SON were not God, then we'd have an attorney acting for us, but at the end of the day everything would depend on whether he could persuade the judge.

That's why it is such good news that the Son *is* by very nature God and that the Father has entrusted all judgment to him. So when the Son says, "You are forgiven," you are forgiven! If the Son were not God, you could never be sure of your salvation.

I phoned my credit card company recently to exchange my card for a new one. "Can I do this over the phone?" I asked. The person on the line assured me that I could. After fifteen minutes on the phone, she told me that I would have a new card within the week. Well, a few days later, I received a letter:

> Thank you for your recent inquiry regarding your credit card account. Unfortunately, we are unable to change your account, as requested, at this time. If you have questions or we can help you in any other way, please don't hesitate to call us. Serving you is important to us, and we appreciate your business.

You know what happened—some poor telephone representative was overruled! From the information I gave her, she sincerely believed that my account could be changed over the phone, so she led me through the process. But later she was overruled by a higher authority who told her she had no right to make such promises and what she had told me was beyond her authority.

If the Son were not God, there would always be the possibility that however well-intentioned he may be, he could end up being overruled by a higher authority. If the Son were not God, we'd have to face the possibility that we might arrive at heaven's gate only to be issued a letter from a higher authority informing us that heaven is not currently available, but that there's another application process we may qualify for . . .

The Son is God, and he presides over the supreme court of the universe. If he settles your case, there is no other court of appeal. There is no higher authority.

FOR FURTHER READING, SEE MATTHEW 25

SIGNED, SEALED, AND DELIVERED

But in fact, it is best for you that I go away, because if I don't, the Advocate won't come. If I do go away, then I will send him to you. JOHN 16:7

THE BIBLE TELLS us that through his death, Christ made us the beneficiaries of a marvelous inheritance. He has opened the way for sinful people to be reconciled to God and enter everlasting life. The will of God has been signed by the Father and sealed by the blood of Christ, but it still must be delivered.

It's one thing for a gift to be offered; it's another thing for that gift to be received. All that Jesus Christ has done will be useless and of no value to us until we receive what he offers. So, how can the will of God, signed by the Father and sealed in the blood of Christ, be delivered to us? By the *Advocate*, or the Holy Spirit of God.

The Holy Spirit brings what Jesus has accomplished on the cross and applies it personally to us. He takes what Christ has made possible for all people and applies it to your particular case. If the Son of God had not come, you *could not* be saved. If the Spirit of God had not come, you *would not* be saved.

Imagine a Greek shipping magnate, Stavros, who's fabulously wealthy and over the years has amassed billions of dollars. One day Stavros dies and his lawyer opens the will. It's a lengthy document, running hundreds of pages, but the lawyer already knows the contents—he was there when it was written.

The beneficiaries of Stavros's will are all over the world. They have to be found, and according to the terms of the will, every one of them has to be brought to Stavros's home in order to receive what has been promised to them. The lawyer will have his work cut out for him for years to come.

Without the Spirit of God, salvation would remain a theoretical possibility, but it would never become a reality for any of us—no one would arrive in heaven. Without the Spirit, all that Jesus has done would be like a will that was never read, a gift that was never received, or an inheritance that was never made known.

FOR FURTHER READING, SEE JOHN 16

OPENING A CAN OF PAINT

And when [the Holy Spirit] comes, he will convict the world of its sin,
and of God's righteousness, and of the coming judgment. JOHN 16:8

CHRIST OFFERS US forgiveness of sin, righteousness from above, and deliverance from the judgment to come. But most people don't feel they need what Christ offers.

People in the business world know that you can't sell what people don't want to buy. You may have the most marvelous widget, but if people can't see a need for it, then you don't have much hope of success.

The Gospels tell us about a successful businessman who came to Jesus, wanting to know what he had to do to have eternal life. When Jesus spoke about the Ten Commandments, the man said, "I've obeyed all these commandments since I was young" (Mark 10:20). He was sincere: "I haven't trashed my life; you're talking to a highly successful achiever."

He wasn't suggesting he was perfect—no sane person thinks that. But he was not aware of any obvious sin in his life, and he felt he was walking on the right path. As he looked at his own life, his honest opinion was that he measured up to the law of God rather well. He expected to have eternal life; he just wanted to be sure.

Then Christ exposed the man's need: "There is still one thing you haven't done. . . . Go and sell all your possessions and give the money to the poor, and you will have treasure in heaven" (Mark 10:21). In a moment, the man saw himself for the self-centered person that he was.

Think about opening a can of paint. You use the rim of the can as a pivot for the screwdriver. If there were no rim, you wouldn't be able to pry the lid open. The gospel is like a lever that depends on a sense of sin as its pivot. If a person has no sense of sin, the gospel has no "pull" in that person's life. If it weren't for the Holy Spirit, we would never see our need for Jesus.

FOR FURTHER READING, SEE MARK 10

TIME TO WAKE UP

When [the Holy Spirit] comes, he will convict the world of its sin.

JOHN 16:8

THERE'S A HUGE gulf between what we are and what God calls us to be. When the Holy Spirit enables us to see ourselves clearly, we quickly realize that righteousness is far beyond our reach and that without Christ, we'd be liable to the judgment and condemnation of God.

The first work of the Holy Spirit is to show us what's wrong, so that we'll see our need and be ready to listen to the gospel. This is never comfortable. Nobody likes to be wakened when they're sleeping, but if there's a fire in your house, you'll be deeply grateful to the person who wakes you up. You may be angry at first, but as soon as you realize the danger you're in, you'll thank the person who warned you.

After the Second World War, the Allies set up a legal process for trying war criminals, and the hearings were held in the town of Nuremberg, Germany. The highest-ranking defendant was Hermann Göring. He sat in the courtroom as survivors of the most appalling violence were brought forward, and actual footage of the concentration camps in all their horror was shown.

After weeks of this, Göring still could not see how the cause he'd supported had been wrong. He felt there was reasonable justification for what he'd done, and that there was no good reason for judgment to be passed on him.

We hear a great deal today about "false guilt." False guilt is an inappropriate feeling of guilt over something we did not do and for which we were not responsible. There is nothing useful about false guilt. It's a snare of the enemy, and we need to expose it so we can be free from it.

But there is such a thing as *true* guilt, and it needs to be embraced. True guilt relates to sins we've committed, righteousness we haven't fulfilled, and the judgment that's due us on account of these things. True guilt is about facing reality and taking responsibility. A person who never discovers his or her true guilt will continue down the path of sin and never find reconciliation with God.

FOR FURTHER READING, SEE 2 CORINTHIANS 7

GOD'S THREE ALARM CLOCKS

When [the Holy Spirit] comes, he will convict the world of its sin.

JOHN 16:8

GOD HAS THREE ways to intercept sin in a person's life. You could think of them as three alarm clocks. As you consider each of them, think about which one you would most like God to use in your case.

The first is the quiet and gentle work of God's Spirit, opening up the conscience and revealing what's wrong so that you can change it.

If you sleep through that, the Holy Spirit speaks more loudly and directly, as he did with David. The king wasn't listening to the Spirit's prompting in his conscience, so God revealed David's secret sin of adultery to the prophet Nathan and sent him to speak to David. David's sin was exposed, and it became public knowledge. At that point, David turned to God in repentance. If that's what it takes, that is what God will do.

The situation of a person who ignores God's second alarm becomes perilous. That's what happened with Pharaoh. God sent Moses to him, but Pharaoh refused to listen to God's command, even when he was confronted directly. He continued to harden his heart, and eventually Pharaoh came under the judgment of God.

Karen and I have three alarm clocks in our bedroom. The first alarm wakes us gently with music. The second alarm is set a few minutes later, and it's more disturbing. We have it set in case we sleep through the first one. The third alarm is set later still, and it's our last resort. It makes a horrendous sound, and the day begins much better if we're up before it sounds its deafening blast.

Consider God's three alarms: the quiet work of his Spirit in opening the conscience, confrontation by another person, and the direct judgment of God Almighty. Which of these ways would you like God to use to stop you from sinning?

We should be deeply thankful to God for the work of his Holy Spirit, which is a wonderful expression of his grace, and determine to be sensitive to his voice. God is reaching out to you in the gentlest of ways.

FOR FURTHER READING, SEE 2 SAMUEL 12

TURNING ON THE FLOODLIGHT

He will bring me glory by telling you whatever
he receives from me. JOHN 16:14

ANOTHER WORK OF the Holy Spirit is to shine a floodlight on Jesus Christ. He illuminates the truth that was once obscure to us; he opens our understanding so that we can see the glory of Jesus. Like a floodlight, the Holy Spirit does not draw attention to himself; he directs our focus to Jesus Christ.

Have you ever been to our nation's capital, Washington, DC? If you were to go there, one of the things you would definitely want to see is the White House. Imagine going there at night, when the White House is floodlit. The building looks magnificent, but if it weren't for the floodlights, its beauty would be hidden in the darkness. I'm sure that millions of people have driven past the White House at night, but they don't comment on the floodlights; they talk about the building!

The Father, the Son, and the Holy Spirit are equally God. There is no order or rank or precedence among them. But for the purposes of our salvation, the Father, the Son, and the Spirit have different roles. The Father chose to be the giver, the Son chose to be the gift, and the Spirit chose to deliver the gift. The Son placed himself in the service of the Father, and the Spirit placed himself in the service of the Son.

The Holy Spirit disturbs us so that we see our sin and grasp our need of the Savior, and as he disturbs, he also illuminates so we can see that Jesus is precisely the Savior we need. Then he brings the two together.

The Holy Spirit is heaven's matchmaker. He brings us to Christ and forms a bond between the believer and Christ as faith and repentance are formed in our hearts so that everything Jesus accomplished on the cross becomes ours. The promises that are signed by God the Father and sealed by the death and resurrection of God the Son are delivered and made effective in our lives by God the Holy Spirit.

FOR FURTHER READING, SEE EPHESIANS 5

ANOTHER COUNSELOR

I will ask the Father, and he will give you another
Advocate, who will never leave you. JOHN 14:16

"OVER THE LAST three years," Jesus was saying, "I've been your advocate, but when the Holy Spirit comes, he'll be everything to you that I've been." This tells us two important things about the Holy Spirit. If he is to be everything to us that Christ was to the disciples, the Holy Spirit is a person and the Holy Spirit is God.

Jesus never referred to the Holy Spirit as "it," and neither should we. When talking about the Spirit, Jesus said, "The world cannot receive *him*, because it isn't looking for *him* and doesn't recognize *him*. But you know *him*, because *he* lives with you now and later will be in you" (John 14:17, emphasis added).

The Holy Spirit is a person, so we shouldn't think of him as a power or a force. The Bible talks about lying to the Holy Spirit (see Acts 5:3) and bringing sorrow to the Holy Spirit (see Ephesians 4:30). You cannot lie to a force or bring sorrow to a power. A burst of energy could never be to the disciples everything that Jesus was. The Holy Spirit is as much God with you as Jesus was God with the disciples.

Notice Jesus called the Spirit "*another* Advocate" (John 14:16, emphasis added). In other words, the Spirit and the Son have distinct identities. But then Jesus added, "I will not abandon you as orphans—I will come to you" (14:18). In other words, where the Spirit is, Christ is. He went another step: "All who love me will do what I say. My Father will love them, and we will come and make our home with each of them" (14:23). We learn that where the Spirit is, both the Father and the Son will make their home.

You cannot know one person of the Trinity without the others. There's no such thing as knowing the Father apart from the Son—it's through the Son that the Father has made himself known. Nobody knows the Son apart from the Spirit—it's through the Spirit that we come to faith and repentance in Jesus Christ.

FOR FURTHER READING, SEE EPHESIANS 4

MORE THAN ADVICE

You know [the Holy Spirit], because he lives with you
now and later will be in you. JOHN 14:17

NOTICE THE TWO words Jesus used to describe our relationship with the Holy Spirit. First, he said that the Spirit is *with* us—that reminds us that there's "the Holy Spirit" and there's "us," and we must never get the two confused!

Have you ever met people who have confused the two? They assume everything they say is from God. They cannot distinguish between their words and the Spirit's. It's almost impossible to reason with them. We must never confuse what we think with the mind of the Spirit. If we're wise, we'll humbly allow others to test what we say. The Spirit is with us, and we often need him to correct us.

That means the Holy Spirit is not some spiritual capacity within us. If that were the case, we would have no help outside of ourselves. When Jesus says that the Spirit is "with" the disciples, he is reminding us that God himself comes to us. He is our help and our shield. God is with you in the hardest situations of your life.

Jesus also said the Spirit would be *in* his disciples. The Holy Spirit is more than a mentor who shows us what to do. We need more than advice; we need the power to change. The ministry of the Spirit goes beyond the work of a counselor, pastor, or friend who may be able to shed light on problems and suggest possible solutions.

The Spirit is able to touch the deep places of our souls—renewing our minds, redirecting affections of the heart, molding and reshaping our wills, cleansing our imaginations, and healing our memories. He can create new desires within us to follow Christ not out of duty but with a heart that hungers and thirsts for righteousness. He can give us power to live a new life for the glory of God.

Don't ever say you can't change. Don't allow your enemy to talk defeat. The fullness of God is with you in Christ and by the Spirit. Think about the Spirit who dwells in you! The third person of the Trinity is at work *in* you and he is *with* you in everything you face from here to eternity.

FOR FURTHER READING, SEE GALATIANS 5

GET IN!

*If Christ has not been raised, then your faith is useless and
you are still guilty of your sins.* 1 CORINTHIANS 15:17

THE HEART OF Christianity lies not in a set of instructions, but in the ability of Jesus to take us to heaven. The Bible's teaching will not save you; Jesus Christ himself will save you. Christianity stands or falls on Jesus' ability to do what he has promised.

Suppose you're in a large city and you don't know how to get to a particular destination. Assuming you can't access the Internet, here are two options:

- *You could ask for directions.* Someone might tell you to catch bus #29, get off at the second stop, go over the bridge, and it's on your immediate right.
- *Or you could take a taxi.* You would ask the driver if he knew how to get to your destination, and if he did, you would get in.

Now suppose just after you get on bus #29, the man who gave you directions has a heart attack and dies. This unfortunate event will make no difference to your journey, because you already have the instructions. All that matters, as far as your journey is concerned, is that he gave you the information before he died.

But suppose you're in the taxi, and just as you're going past the second stop, the taxi driver has a heart attack and dies. If this happens, you're stuck! You don't know the way to your destination, and your driver is unable to take you there.

Other religious leaders present a program of spiritual disciplines and say, "This is the way," but Jesus said, "I am the way." Others present their teaching and say, "This is the truth," but Jesus said, "I am the truth." Others say, "Do this and live." Jesus said, "I am the life" (John 14:6). Jesus' claims all depend on his being raised from the dead. Apart from the resurrection, our faith is futile—he's unable to deliver us to our destination.

Jesus tells us that he can bring us to the Father. Like the taxi driver, he invites us to "get in." We face a decision that involves an act of trust, and since the issue at stake is your eternal destiny, it is not a decision you will want to make lightly.

FOR FURTHER READING, SEE 1 CORINTHIANS 15

YOU ARE THE JURY

These are written so that you may believe. JOHN 20:31, ESV

IMAGINE THAT YOU are in a court of law. You are part of the jury, and the apostle John wants to present you with evidence that shows Jesus is the Christ. When he is finished presenting his case, he will be looking for you to give a verdict.

He is not like a bully attorney, trying to intimidate you. Nor is he a tear jerker, trying to gain your sympathy. He is presenting key evidence of the things that he has seen and heard as a direct witness over the three years that he has spent with Jesus. All he asks is that you hear the evidence without prejudice.

Of course, that is precisely the problem. When a jury is sworn in, the key question is whether there are any ways they may be prejudiced with regard to the particular case that is going to be tried. You may be a very good member of the jury in one trial, but you may be highly prejudiced when it comes to another.

Many people have issues that cause them to prejudge their hearing of the evidence about Jesus. For example, our culture is highly preju- diced against the possibility that any one person could be the Savior of the world, so many dismiss this possibility before they've even heard the evidence.

There is also prejudice in our hearts. We know that if we come to the verdict that Jesus is the Christ, it will have a major impact on the direction of our lives. Many people are tempted to come to a conclu- sion before they've heard the evidence. They're not open to hearing the actual evidence, so they ask to be excused from the jury. "I'm sorry, but I cannot try this case."

If you are not in heaven on the last day, it will not be because God has failed to provide you with the evidence or with the opportunity. Don't excuse yourself from the jury, and don't allow the opinions of others to determine your verdict. He has given you firsthand evidence, so take the time to examine it carefully.

FOR FURTHER READING, SEE JOHN 20

WHY WE CALL JESUS "THE CHRIST"

These are written so that you may believe that Jesus is the Christ.
JOHN 20:31, ESV

IF YOU WERE asked to summarize the Christian faith, what would you say? John boils the essence of the faith down to just four words: "Jesus is the Christ." We know our Lord was given the name "Jesus," so why do we call him "Jesus Christ"?

Our English word *Christ* comes from the Greek word *Christos*, which means "Messiah" or "anointed one." *Christ* is a title that refers to one who was promised in the Old Testament, who would be anointed by God.

Throughout the Bible story, God "anointed" certain people as a sign that he would use them—to *reveal* himself so that we may know him (the prophets); to *reconcile* us to himself so that we can come to him (the priests); and to *rule* so that his purposes may be fulfilled (the kings).

God spoke to the prophets directly so that they could speak his Word to the people. At the end of Elijah's life, he was told to "anoint Elisha" to be a prophet after him (1 Kings 19:16).

While the prophets spoke to the people on behalf of God, the priests spoke to God on behalf of the people, offering sacrifices for them. When Aaron was installed as high priest, he stood before the people in elaborate clothing, and Moses poured oil on his head to show that God had chosen and anointed him for ministry (see Psalm 133:2).

The kings were anointed for the work of ruling. Samuel anointed David as king of Israel by pouring oil over his head. When he did this, "the Spirit of the LORD came powerfully upon David" (1 Samuel 16:13).

The prophets, priests, and kings of the Old Testament all pointed forward to one who would fulfill what they could only illustrate. God promised that there would be an Anointed One *par excellence* who would speak the Word of God, offer the sacrifice acceptable to God, and rout the enemies of God. How well does the phrase "Jesus is the Christ" summarize your faith?

FOR FURTHER READING, SEE 1 SAMUEL 16

ONCE YOU KNOW WHO JESUS IS

Jesus is the Christ. JOHN 20:31, ESV

JESUS IS THE CHRIST—that means Jesus is the prophet who speaks the Word of God. He is the priest who offers the sacrifice acceptable to God. He is the king who routs the enemies of God.

John presents his case like a lawyer in a courtroom.

He demonstrates that Jesus is the prophet who knows the hidden truth about a Samaritan woman. And when the woman says to him, "I know the Messiah is coming. . . . When he comes, he will explain everything to us," Jesus replies, "I AM the Messiah!" (John 4:25-26).

John brings a witness to the stand who will testify that Jesus is the priest. John the Baptist identifies Jesus as "the Lamb of God who takes away the sin of the world" (John 1:29). But how would Christ take away the sins of the world? Jesus speaks of "laying down his life"—the language of sacrifice. And when Jesus dies, John records his triumphant words, "It is finished!" (John 19:30), indicating that the sacrifice is complete and reconciliation between God and humanity is accomplished.

Then John produces evidence that Jesus is the king who delivers us from our enemies. He tells us how Jesus comes to the tomb of a friend who has died four days earlier and says, "I am the resurrection and the life" (John 11:25). The dead man's sister says, "I have always believed you are the Messiah" (11:27). Then Jesus asks for the stone to be rolled back, demonstrating his authority over death as he calls the dead man to come out. This king has authority over greater enemies than the Romans—he can deliver us from the tyranny of death and hell!

Once you know who Jesus is, you'll understand what it means to have faith in him. Jesus Christ is prophet, priest, and king, so believing in him means we trust what he says as prophet, taking his Word as the standard of truth by which all else is measured. It means we trust him as priest to bring us into the presence of God. It means we submit ourselves to him as king, living under his authority and rule.

FOR FURTHER READING, SEE JOHN 11

THE OUTCOME OF YOUR FAITH

These are written so that you may believe that Jesus is the Christ . . .
and that by believing you may have life in his name. JOHN 20:31, ESV

LIFE IS ONE of the great themes of John's Gospel. Since you're reading this book you are, by definition, alive. But Jesus spoke to people
about another kind of life he could give them, "life . . . to the full"
(John 10:10, NIV). What did he mean by that?

Jesus was talking about the life Adam and Eve experienced in the
Garden. They enjoyed a life free from the frustrations of age and the
fear of death. They knew a wonderful partnership together, in which
they pursued meaningful work in beautiful surroundings. But most of
all, they enjoyed the presence and companionship of God, who came
down and made himself visible to them so they could know him.

That was life to the full, and they lost it. They were driven out of
the Garden, and afterward, Adam must have known he was living half
a life. His children never experienced what their father and mother
had known; all they knew was life in this fallen world—disease, danger,
disasters, and death. Adam must have told them about the life he'd
known, but it would have been difficult for them even to imagine.

In high school, I had two friends who were blind. One was blind
from birth, the other became blind through an accident. Their experiences were very different. One knew what he was missing—you could
describe things to him more easily. The other had no notion of color
except what he produced in his own imagination.

Adam knew what life was like without the knowledge of evil. He
knew what it was like to walk with God. And he knew he was living half
a life. But we've only ever known this life. We find it difficult to imagine
what it would be like to be free from evil and to enjoy the visible presence of God.

Christ came so you could enter into a life beyond imagination. God
has anointed him for the task of taking all who will believe into this life.
Have you come to a verdict? Jesus is the Christ, and "by believing you
may have life in his name."

FOR FURTHER READING, SEE JOHN 10

A SOUND LIKE THE WIND

Suddenly, there was a sound from heaven like the roaring of a mighty windstorm, and it filled the house where they were sitting. ACTS 2:2

IN MANY ANCIENT languages, there is one word that can mean "wind" or "breath" or "spirit." In Hebrew that word is *ruach*. It is one of those words that sounds like what it means. If you pronounce *ruach* correctly, it sounds like the rushing of the wind.

If you think about it, the sound of wind is pretty much the same as the sound of breath, only it's much louder and it lasts longer. In the ancient world, people thought the wind was like breath on a larger scale, so they used the same word for both.

If we ask, "Where have we come across this before?" there are two answers. The first is at the very beginning of the Bible story, where we read about God breathing life into Adam. God shaped a lifeless corpse from the dust of the ground. It just lay there until God breathed into it. God gave Adam the kiss of life, and the first man became a living being.

The second is after the Resurrection. Jesus "breathed on [the disciples] and said, 'Receive the Holy Spirit'" (John 20:22). Jesus was explaining what would happen on the Day of Pentecost. Then he took a deep breath and blew it out toward them. It sounded like the rushing of the wind.

When the disciples heard a sound like the rushing wind a few weeks later, they would have immediately associated it with the sound of Jesus breathing on them and recognized that this was the fulfillment of what Jesus had promised.

Think about an Olympic sprinter taking in great gulps of air that pulsate through his chest as oxygen fills his lungs and energizes his body. That's what happened at Pentecost. God breathed new life into the disciples, and they were never the same.

Jesus had sent the disciples out to do ministry before, and they would not have been able to do what they did without the power of the Spirit. But this was something entirely new—the Spirit of God was not only *with* them, but *in* them.

FOR FURTHER READING, SEE ACTS 2

GREAT BALLS OF FIRE

What looked like flames or tongues of fire appeared
and settled on each of them. ACTS 2:3

TRY TO IMAGINE yourself among the 120 people when this happened. What they saw at first must have looked absolutely terrifying. A great ball or pillar of fire was coming right toward them. The astonishing thing was that none of them was burned.

Where have we come across a fire that rested on something but did not burn it up? In the story of Moses and the burning bush: "The angel of the LORD appeared to him in a blazing fire from the middle of a bush. Moses stared in amazement. Though the bush was engulfed in flames, it didn't burn up" (Exodus 3:2). Then God told Moses, "I AM WHO I AM," and Moses realized he was in the immediate presence of God.

When God appeared to Moses, Moses was a believing man whose life was going nowhere. He had settled into semiretirement in the desert. God came to him in the fire to give him a new commission—to deliver God's people from the land of Egypt. God called this man out of an aimless retirement and gave him a ministry that was for the glory of God.

At Pentecost, the church was like Moses in the desert: nothing was happening through them to advance God's purpose in the world. Then God's fire came down. Imagine the fireball coming nearer and then dividing into individual flames, or "tongues of fire." You remember that when the fire came to Moses, he was commissioned to advance God's purpose, so you wonder who the fire will rest on now. Will it be Peter, or perhaps James and John? Maybe it will be all three of them?

You look up with awe as you see one of the flames coming toward you. Then you look around at the others in the room, and a flame of fire rests on every one of them. God is commissioning *every* believer to advance his purposes in the world. The presence and power of almighty God rests on you.

Everyone, including you, has a part to play in advancing God's purposes for the world. God's Spirit rests on all those who love Jesus and follow him.

FOR FURTHER READING, SEE EXODUS 3

THIS PROMISE IS FOR YOU

When they heard the loud noise, everyone came running,
and they were bewildered to hear their own languages
being spoken by the believers. ACTS 2:6

ON THE DAY of Pentecost, suddenly and spontaneously 120 believers were "filled with the Holy Spirit and began speaking in other languages" (Acts 2:4). They found they were able to speak in languages they had never learned!

Where else have we seen a group of people suddenly begin to speak in languages they had never learned? Answer: the tower of Babel (see Genesis 11:1-9). As humanity's rebellion against God was growing, God broke their momentum by introducing the confusion of multiple languages.

At Babel, God used the curse of languages to slow down human self-promotion. At Pentecost, God used the gift of language to speed up the advance of Christ's Kingdom. God had gathered a vast crowd from every nation under heaven to Jerusalem for Pentecost, and when they heard the sound of the wind, they hurried to see what it was (see Acts 2:5-6).

Some who were there on that day thought the believers were drunk, so Peter stepped forward to give an explanation: Jesus was crucified seven weeks ago, but God raised him from the dead, and now he is at the right hand of the Father, pouring out the Holy Spirit on his people.

The people believed Peter, and they cried out, "What should we do?" (Acts 2:37). Peter said, "Repent of your sins and turn to God, and be baptized in the name of Jesus Christ for the forgiveness of your sins. Then you will receive the gift of the Holy Spirit" (2:38).

But the promise didn't end with the three thousand people who responded to Peter's invitation that day: "The promise is for you and your children and for all who are far off—for all whom the Lord our God will call" (Acts 2:39, NIV).

The promise of forgiveness and new life is for *you*, if you believe in the Lord Jesus Christ and turn from your sins. It is for *your children*—it is not limited to one generation. And this promise is for *all who are far off*, people from every background, and especially for you if you feel far from God today.

FOR FURTHER READING, SEE GENESIS 11

CROSSING CULTURAL BARRIERS

*Saul is my chosen instrument to take my message to the Gentiles
and to kings, as well as to the people of Israel.* ACTS 9:15

AS THE NUMBER of disciples grew in Jerusalem, the Jews who had believed in Jesus faced growing opposition, including a rather sinister character who was determined to stamp out these Jewish communities of believers in Jesus. He sought authorization to arrest them in other cities and bring them back to Jerusalem.

The first city he targeted for his roundup was Damascus. But while he was on the way, the risen Lord Jesus Christ intercepted him: "A light from heaven suddenly shone down around him. He fell to the ground and heard a voice saying to him, 'Saul! Saul! Why are you persecuting me?' 'Who are you, lord?' Saul asked. And the voice replied, 'I am Jesus, the one you are persecuting! Now get up and go into the city, and you will be told what you must do'" (Acts 9:3-6).

This angry man was completely stopped in his tracks, and the whole direction of his life was turned around. The greatest enemy of the church became its greatest evangelist. We know him better as the apostle Paul. The intervention of God in his life represents a major turning point in the Bible story.

Christ commissioned this new convert and Jewish believer to bring his name to Jews *and* Gentiles. Paul later wrote about his commission, saying, "I am not ashamed of this Good News about Christ. It is the power of God at work, saving everyone who believes—the Jew first and also the Gentile" (Romans 1:16).

The gospel crosses cultural barriers. It belonged first to the Jews, and then it came through them to the Gentiles. It is the fulfillment of God's promise to bless Abraham and then to bless all the nations of the earth through him. As Jews and Gentiles came to faith in Jesus, they discovered that the old barriers between them were broken down and that they were truly one as they worshiped together.

The gospel is able to break down every wall that would separate you from God, and every wall that would divide us from one another, making it possible for people from every race and culture to come to God through faith in Jesus Christ.

FOR FURTHER READING, SEE ACTS 11

IS FAITH ENOUGH?

Some men from Judea arrived and began to teach the believers:
"Unless you are circumcised as required by the law of
Moses, you cannot be saved." ACTS 15:1

THERE WAS NO problem as long as only a few Gentiles professed faith in Jesus, but soon the trickle became a flood, and some of the leaders in Jerusalem became alarmed. The Gentiles who professed faith in Jesus were not being circumcised or embracing Judaism; they were simply professing faith in Jesus and being baptized.

Even in Old Testament times, God's people had opened their arms to outsiders. The question was whether a Gentile could be accepted as a follower of Jesus without embracing Judaism first. The men from Judea were telling young Christians at Antioch that faith in Christ was not enough for them to be saved. Something else had to be added. But as soon as people say that, they have undermined the gospel.

Had Jesus done everything that was needed to save those who would come to him, or were other "rites of passage" necessary? Was it necessary for Gentile believers to embrace the traditions of Judaism as they came to Christ, or was it possible for Gentiles to come from their varying traditions directly to faith in Jesus Christ?

It is not surprising that this led to "arguing vehemently" (Acts 15:2). Paul and Barnabas were appointed by the believers in Antioch to go to Jerusalem and meet with the apostles and elders there. The issue was discussed openly, and the result was clear and decisive: Jesus Christ had opened the way for people from every background to come to God, and they determined not to put anything extra in the way.

The apostles and elders also wrote a pastoral letter making two points: First, the new believers must make a decisive break with sin—patterns of sexual immorality that were notorious among the Gentiles must stop. Second, new Gentile believers were asked to show sensitivity toward the Jewish believers, refraining from food that their Jewish brothers and sisters would not eat—not as a condition of the gospel, but as an expression of love (see Acts 15:23-29). Whenever you restrain your liberty out of love for others, you are demonstrating the unity of the body of Christ.

FOR FURTHER READING, SEE ROMANS 14

PRIVILEGE AND DESPERATION

My heart is filled with bitter sorrow and unending grief for my people,
my Jewish brothers and sisters. I would be willing to be forever cursed—
cut off from Christ!—if that would save them. ROMANS 9:2-3

WHY DOES THE apostle Paul have great sorrow and unceasing anguish over his own people? Because it's possible to be in a position of great privilege and yet miss out on the greatest thing God wants to give you. "My heart would break," Paul was saying, "if my own people, with all their rich heritage of God's blessing, missed the greatest blessing of God, which is in Jesus."

The apostle Paul spoke from experience, having thrown everything he had into the pursuit of an exemplary life. He had a great education and would have held a distinguished teaching position and earned a high salary. But when Christ intercepted his life, all that he had going for him seemed to fade in importance compared with "the infinite value of knowing Christ Jesus" (Philippians 3:8).

Paul discovered that privilege doesn't save anybody, so he longed for his own people, who'd been richly blessed by God, to know Jesus. I'm not Jewish, but I feel the high privilege of having a stable home, a good education, and open doors of opportunity. Perhaps you feel the same. Remember, privileged people need Jesus too.

Paul also wrote about the desperate spiritual condition of the Gentiles: "You Gentiles used to be outsiders. . . . You were excluded from citizenship among the people of Israel, and you did not know the covenant promises God had made to them. You lived in this world without God and without hope" (Ephesians 2:11-12). That's about as far from God as you can get!

This desperate position was illustrated in the way the Temple was set up. There were distinct areas marked off for different classes of people. The most distant area from the Most Holy Place—where God's presence was made known—was on the outside perimeter and was called the court of the Gentiles.

The Good News is that Jesus has broken down every wall that separates you from God, so even if you are far from God today, even if you are in the most desperate situation, you can come to him.

FOR FURTHER READING, SEE ROMANS 9

GAME, SET, AND MATCH

Once you were far away from God, but now you have been brought near to him through the blood of Christ. EPHESIANS 2:13

IN THE TEMPLE, there were different levels of access, and Paul reminded the Gentile believers that they were about as far away from God as they could possibly get.

The structure of the Temple reminds me of the tennis championships at Wimbledon. When I lived in London, you could get into the grounds in late afternoon for about eight dollars, but that gave you access only to the outer courts. Usually that meant watching players few people had heard of.

I wanted to get to the center court, but for that you needed a different ticket, and they were very hard to find. I succeeded in getting on center court a few times, but I never once got into the locker rooms. They're restricted to a very select group of people.

When Jesus died on the cross, the curtain shielding the Most Holy Place was torn in two—from top to bottom—as if God reached down from heaven and ripped it apart. But if that were all that had happened, it would be like inviting those on center court to visit the locker rooms. That would be marvelous for a privileged few, but it would only heighten the frustrations of those who were outside.

Paul reminds us that Christ has done more than tear the curtain: "He himself is our peace, who has made the two groups one and has destroyed the barrier, the dividing wall of hostility" (Ephesians 2:14, NIV). Paul is talking about the walls that separated the Gentiles from the Jews. But the dividing walls farther out were also demolished so that those who were far off could also come all the way into the presence of God.

Imagine a series of concentric walls. When Christ died on the cross, it was as if God took a bulldozer and plowed through all of them, creating a path from the farthest horizon right into the Most Holy Place. *All* the walls came down. *All* the divisions of privilege and race and gender came down, and equal access to God was opened up to *all* through Jesus Christ. Even if you're far from God today, you may come. Christ has opened the way.

FOR FURTHER READING, SEE EPHESIANS 2

THE STREAM BURST ITS NARROW BANKS

There is no longer Jew or Gentile, slave or free, male and female.
For you are all one in Christ Jesus. GALATIANS 3:28

PAUL WAS COMMISSIONED to take the name of Christ to the most privileged people in the world and to tell them that they *must* come. The Jews need Jesus. But Paul was also commissioned to take the name of Christ to the most desperate people in the world and tell them that they *may* come.

Perhaps you feel about as far from God as anyone could be, and you wonder how God could ever be interested in you again. Picture a bulldozer demolishing one wall after another, creating a path between you and the presence of God. The rubble is piled high on either side of the pathway. That's what Jesus Christ has done for you. There is grace and forgiveness for the most desperate person in the world.

Paul described the backgrounds of some of the early Gentile believers in Corinth. Some were prostitutes, some thieves, others drunkards or sexually immoral. But when they came to Christ, they were washed and accepted into the fellowship of believers.

Paul was commissioned to take that Good News to Jews *and* Gentiles. And as he did, God raised up communities of believers where the privileged worshiped alongside those who had been desperate, and they discovered that they were one as they walked on the same path that had been opened up for them by Christ Jesus.

The stream of God's blessing had burst out of its narrow banks. God's blessing began to flow through Abraham's descendants to all nations. The most privileged and the most desperate found themselves worshiping together at the feet of Jesus.

Your life will intersect with thousands of other people's lives. Some of those people will be very privileged—they need Jesus. Others will be very desperate—they can come to Jesus. We must tell the privileged not to presume, and we must tell the desperate not to despair. Our mission, like Paul's, is to carry the name of Jesus to the privileged and to the desperate and invite them to come to him.

FOR FURTHER READING, SEE GALATIANS 3

LOVE'S OPPOSITE

Don't just pretend to love others. Really love them.
Hate what is wrong. ROMANS 12:9

LOVE AND HATE are often found together in the Bible because they're two sides of the same coin. If we do not hate what is evil, then there's no sincerity in our claim to love. The opposite of love is not hatred but indifference. True love hates all that destroys the one who is loved.

In our journey through the Bible's story, we have discovered that God is love—he is absolutely committed to seeking the good of all that he has made. The Bible also tells us God is holy—he is absolutely opposed to anything that would destroy the objects of his love. God's holiness is a dimension of his love. In the same way, we cannot love others without at the same time hating what would destroy them.

I will never forget being with a family whose son was dying of cancer. The boy's mother said to me, "I hate this cancer." She said it with some venom, and understandably so. She hated what was destroying the object of her love.

Another lady's husband is an alcoholic. Over the years, alcohol has destroyed his life and every area of their marriage. She has remained loyal to him at great personal cost. One day she said to me, "I love him, but I hate what he's become." Her hatred of what was destroying her husband and of what he has become is a component of her love. The day she stops hating what he has become is the day she stops loving him.

God loves the world, and he hates all that destroys it. He hates what sin has done to us, precisely because he loves us. That's why God cannot and will not leave the world as it is; to do so would be a denial of love. Because God loves the world, he relentlessly opposes evil. God hates evil; he cannot be indifferent to it.

It's helpful to regularly ask yourself, *According to the Bible, does God love this or hate it?* If you choose to love what God hates, then you're taking sides against him, and when you do that, you're heading down a path that leads to destruction.

FOR FURTHER READING, SEE PROVERBS 6

WHAT MAKES GOD ANGRY?

The wrath of God is being revealed from heaven against
all the godlessness and wickedness of people, who suppress
the truth by their wickedness. ROMANS 1:18, NIV

THE WRATH OF God is not some kind of flaring rage, and we should not think of God as losing control and lashing out in random acts of frustration. God's wrath is his strong and settled opposition to all that is evil.

God is love—that is in his nature, and there has never been and never will be a time when he is not love. But God's anger is different. The Bible never says "God is wrath"; in fact, God is "slow to get angry" (Psalm 103:8). The Bible story demonstrates his great patience and tolerance toward an evil world. But God's anger can be provoked by *godlessness* and *wickedness*.

A godless person doesn't want anything to do with God, and a wicked person refuses to obey God. But in order to sustain this response to God, a person must suppress what God has revealed about himself.

It takes energy to go on resisting God. Picture a man pressing down on a powerful spring. He has to put his whole weight on it to keep the spring compressed. If the man lets up for a moment, the spring will recoil. Those who want nothing to do with God have to work hard at avoiding him because God has revealed his divine power and his glory all around us in creation (see Romans 1:20).

The person who wants to keep God at a distance has to close his or her eyes to this revelation and keep up the pretense that all the beauty and order in the world are just products of chance. Many people choose to believe this because they find the alternative unacceptable. They're determined not to acknowledge the glory of their Creator because they've already decided they will not obey him.

When people say, "We'll pour our energy into beliefs and behaviors that keep God's truth as far away from us as possible," God reveals his wrath. God loves the world, and he cannot be indifferent and shrug his shoulders as his world destroys itself.

FOR FURTHER READING, SEE PSALM 103

FREE FALLING

God gave them over in the sinful desires of their hearts. ROMANS 1:24, NIV

WHEN PEOPLE THINK about the wrath of God, they sometimes envision God targeting bad people with lightning or causing volcanoes to erupt over rebellious communities, but that's not what we find in Romans 1. We may wish that God would directly strike the perpetrators of torture and mass murder, and one day he will. But that is rarely how God's wrath operates today.

Where an individual or a society says, "We don't want and won't obey God," God expresses his wrath by allowing their choice—he *gives them over*. God stands back from those who don't want him and won't obey him, and he allows them to live with the reality of their choice.

God surrounded our first parents with good gifts in the Garden, but they chose not to obey him—this was an expression of godlessness and wickedness. They suppressed the truth by choosing the knowledge of evil, and God gave them over to it.

I brought a crystal vase into the pulpit one Sunday, held it up high, and asked the congregation what would happen if I "gave it up." If I gave up the vase, it would become subject to the pull of gravity. The vase would have no way of overcoming the powers that surround it, and it would fall like a stone and shatter.

What happens when God "gives up" the godless and wicked? They find themselves at the mercy of powers greater than themselves. Paul identifies these powers as "sinful desires" (Romans 1:24, NIV), "shameful desires" (1:26) and "foolish thinking" (1:28). If the evidence that God's wrath is being revealed in a society is that those who don't want and won't obey God find themselves in the grip of these powers, I can't avoid the conclusion that the wrath of God is being revealed in our nation today.

Maybe you can see how sinful and shameful desires and foolish thinking are pulling you down. God has given you over to what you have chosen. Your only hope is that he may have mercy and save you. That opportunity is open to you today, but if you keep saying to God, "I don't want and won't obey you," the powers that now hold you will lead to your destruction.

FOR FURTHER READING, SEE ROMANS 1

WAS THE CROSS REALLY NECESSARY?

God put forward [Christ Jesus] as a propitiation by his blood,
to be received by faith. ROMANS 3:25, ESV

GOD CHOSE JESUS as the one on whom his wrath would fall, satisfying the requirements of God's justice. That's what *propitiation* means. God's relentless opposition to all that destroys us was poured out on the Lord Jesus Christ when he died on the cross.

Some would question whether this was really necessary. Jesus himself raised the question in Gethsemane: "If it is possible, let this cup of suffering be taken away from me" (Matthew 26:39). Jesus was saying, "If there is any other way for people to be saved besides your wrath being poured out on me, then let's not do this. But if it's the only way, let your will be done."

And so it was: "[God] did not spare even his own Son but gave him up for us all" (Romans 8:32). Notice the phrase "gave him up." God took his hand off his Son. He let Christ fall. He dropped him for you. That's why Jesus cried out, "My God, my God, why have you abandoned me?" (Matthew 27:46).

Jesus lived a perfect life. The reason God's wrath was poured out on him was that "God made Christ, who never sinned, to be the offering for our sin" (2 Corinthians 5:21). God found a way of separating the sins he hates from the people he loves by laying them on Jesus. Jesus endured our punishment.

If I were to drop a glass vase, it would fall as it was overwhelmed by the force of gravity. But the vase would not have to be destroyed, because having dropped it from my right hand, I could catch it a few feet from the ground with my left. Giving the crystal vase up to the power of gravity would lead to its destruction, but by catching it, I could deliver it from that same power.

That's what God does for us in Christ. He offers to save those who otherwise would fall to their destruction. Jesus Christ went to the lowest point so he could lift you up. You can call out to God, even as you're conscious of the power of sinful and shameful desires and foolish thinking. You can ask him to save you.

FOR FURTHER READING, SEE ROMANS 3

GOING UNDER

All people, whether Jews or Gentiles, are under the power of sin.

ROMANS 3:9

HAVE YOU EVER had one of those days when you worked hard, but at the end of the day, the work to be done was greater than when you started? The pressures were piling up, and you didn't feel you had the ability to rise above it. You began to feel overwhelmed, and eventually you might have even felt like you were going under.

That's the picture Paul uses when he says that all people are under sin. Ponder the word *all*. It crosses cultural barriers—Scots, Swedes, Poles, and Texans are all under sin. It includes people who are single, married, separated, divorced, and widowed. It embraces people at every point on the economic spectrum, from peasants in Mongolia to executives in Manhattan. It includes you and me.

Paul also speaks about people who are "under the law" (Romans 3:19, ESV). This is God's world. Our Creator writes the rules. Sin is breaking the rules that God has written.

In a recent survey on values and morality, only 17 percent of Americans defined sin as a violation of God's will. That means 83 percent of those interviewed do not really understand what sin is. They grasp that sin is doing something wrong, but they do not understand that it is doing something wrong *as defined by God*.

If each of us were free to make our own definitions of right and wrong, life would be a lot easier! I love the story of the man who tried archery for the first time, and then came back claiming that he'd hit the center of the target *every time*. When his friends asked him how he did it, he said, "It's easy—I just shoot all my arrows, and then I paint circles around each one!"

God paints the targets; we don't. "Shoot at this," he says. "You shall have no other gods before me. Do not covet. Be holy because I am holy." God is the lawgiver, defining right and wrong. Sin is breaking his commandments; it's a personal offense against God.

FOR FURTHER READING, SEE PSALM 51

LIKE A FISH OUT OF WATER

Obviously, the law applies to those to whom it was given,
for its purpose is to keep people from having excuses, and to show
that the entire world is guilty before God. ROMANS 3:19

THE LAW TELLS us we're sinners, but does it really matter? After all, nobody is perfect and everybody makes mistakes. "To err is human; to forgive, divine," the saying goes, but if it's natural for us to fail and for God to forgive, then why should Christians make such a big deal about this? Isn't it obvious God will forgive our sins?

The natural consequence of crime is not forgiveness but punishment, and the natural consequence of sin is not forgiveness but condemnation. God is holy. He abhors sin and has a settled disposition of unrelenting hostility toward it, wherever it is found. It is God's unflinching purpose to eradicate sin from his universe. He will destroy it forever. So the fact that we're "under sin" matters big time!

It is hard for us to understand the holiness of God because we're not holy. It's like asking a fish to comprehend life outside water. When a fish is taken out of the water, its mouth opens, its eyes glaze over, and before long it is dead. It cannot survive in the new environment. That's what it's like when even the best people are taken out of their normal environment and exposed to the holiness of God.

Isaiah was the finest preacher and moral leader of his day, but when he saw the holiness of God, he said, "I am doomed" (Isaiah 6:5). The apostle John was known as the disciple whom Jesus loved, and he had reclined next to him at the Last Supper, but he wrote that when he saw the unveiled holiness of the Lord, "I fell at his feet as if I were dead" (Revelation 1:17).

If Isaiah and John reacted that way, what would it be like for you and me? Sinners cannot live in the white heat of God's holiness. When we stand in the presence of holiness, we will be silent. All the excuses and justifications that come so easily now will dry up in our mouths. Nobody will have anything to say.

FOR FURTHER READING, SEE REVELATION 1

A TRULY REMARKABLE FRIEND

God has shown us a way to be made right with him without keeping
the requirements of the law, as was promised in the writings
of Moses and the prophets long ago.   ROMANS 3:21

GOD IS DOING something to make our wrong position right "without keeping the requirements of the law." In other words, it's not a matter of God saying, "Get your act together." That would be an unbearable burden, because we do not have the ability to obey God as we ought.

But this way of being right with God was anticipated by Moses and the prophets. Christ is not an alternative to the law; he is its fulfillment. The law was never intended to be a ladder to heaven. God gave it to us to show us that we *need* a ladder to heaven.

The only way sinners can come into a right relationship with God is by redemption. "All have sinned and fall short of the glory of God, and all are justified freely by his grace through the redemption that came by Christ Jesus" (Romans 3:23-24, NIV). *Redemption* is erasing a debt by paying a price. A person in the ancient world who went bankrupt could pay his debt by selling himself as a slave. He was *redeemed* when someone else paid his debt.

Suppose a woman loses her job and is no longer able to pay her mortgage. After a few months, she is so far behind that she has no hope of paying the debt. Now suppose a friend offers to pay the debt for her. He writes a check to pay the outstanding amount and agrees to assume payments for the life of the loan. This friend has acted as a redeemer.

The Bible tells us about a truly remarkable friend, Jesus Christ, who came to pay our debt to God. He offers not only to bring us up to date on our late payments of obedience but to service the lifetime of the loan. To secure this benefit, Christ assumed the price of our sin—that's why he died on the cross. "The wages of sin is death" (Romans 6:23). Are you still trying to work off the debt you owe God? You cannot pay it back, but by his death, Jesus offers to pay your debt in full.

FOR FURTHER READING, SEE HEBREWS 9

THE NIGHT OF THE PARTY

> *Redemption . . . is in Christ Jesus, whom God put forward as a propitiation*
> *by his blood, to be received by faith.* ROMANS 3:24-25, ESV

A *PROPITIATION* IS a payment that's offered to placate the anger of an offended person. The best way to explain it is by introducing you to Neil and Sally.

Neil was in his twenties when he began dating Sally, an attractive girl from the office. One night Neil took Sally to a party, and he had more than a few drinks. On the way home, the unthinkable happened: the car spun out of control, smashed into an embankment, and rolled over. Both Neil and Sally were unconscious.

Hours later, Neil came around in the hospital. "How is Sally?" he asked. The doctor told him Sally was paralyzed and would never walk again, but Neil's nightmare had only just begun. Sally refused to talk to him, and it wasn't long before he received a letter from Sally's lawyer.

Here are the factors in this case: 1) *There's an offense*—Neil acted recklessly when he decided to drink and drive. 2) *There's an offended person*—Sally is angry, and rightfully so. 3) *There's an offender*—Neil knows he's to blame, and he's sorry for what he's done, but that won't change that Sally is paralyzed.

Neil's lawyer talks with Sally's lawyer about what it would take to settle the case. It doesn't matter what Neil thinks. It's all about Sally, because she is the offended party. Neil must find a way to satisfy Sally, or he will stand before the judge.

If the lawyers agree on an acceptable sum of money, the payment would be a propitiation. A propitiation is offered to placate the anger of the injured party and satisfy the need for justice so that the case cannot be raised in a court of law again.

Our sin is an offense against God; *he* decides what the propitiation should be. We may be sorry, and we may have ideas about what's appropriate, but that's irrelevant—the question is, what will satisfy God? His staggering answer is, "I put forward Jesus' death on the cross as a propitiation." That's why the Bible says, "Now there is no condemnation for those who belong to Christ Jesus" (Romans 8:1).

FOR FURTHER READING, SEE ROMANS 8

A QUESTION FOR MEDIEVAL THEOLOGIANS

Since we have been justified by faith, we have peace with God.
ROMANS 5:1, ESV

EARLY ON IN the church's history, the New Testament was translated from Greek into Latin. This translation—the Vulgate—became the standard Bible used by the church for over a thousand years.

The word that the Vulgate used for the English word *justified* meant "made righteous." So when medieval theologians studied Romans 5:1, it read like this: "Since we have been *made righteous* by faith, we have peace with God."

This translation led to the conclusion that the only way to have peace with God was to become a righteous person, and if one ceased to be righteous, that person would lose peace with God. If you had asked a medieval theologian, "How can I have peace with God?" he would probably have said, "You have to be righteous."

If I could ask a medieval theologian one question, I would ask, "Are you righteous?" That would be difficult for our medieval friend to answer. It would be hard to say yes because Jesus warned about the dangers of being confident in our own righteousness, but if he said no, he had no way to peace with God.

For over a thousand years, the church's understanding was this: justification is the way God makes a bad person good. Christ gives you a spotless robe; it is your responsibility to keep that robe clean by living according to God's law. If you fail, confession and penance are God's appointed means of restoring the purity of the robe.

The big question was, have you preserved the righteousness given to you by Jesus Christ? That left honest people desperately scouring their memories to make sure all their sins were confessed and appropriate penance performed.

This is a crushing burden. If our salvation depends on preserving the righteousness Jesus gives us, the best of us could only be agnostic about our salvation. We might hope to enter heaven; we could never be sure.

But you can know that you're in a right relationship with God through faith in Christ. When faith unites you with Jesus, he assumes your debt and you are credited with his righteousness. Justification doesn't depend on your performance; it depends on God applying the benefits of Jesus' death and resurrection to your life.

FOR FURTHER READING, SEE ROMANS 5

THE COACH AND THE UMPIRE

We have been justified by faith. ROMANS 5:1, ESV

A YOUNG MONK named Martin Luther passionately desired to be right with God, so he poured his energy into fulfilling God's law. But he found the burden of trying to maintain a spotless righteousness to be more than he could bear. When he thought of how he had blotted the spotless robe of righteousness, he confessed and did penance. But even during the act of penance, he would think of other ways in which he had sinned.

Luther began to study the New Testament in the original Greek, and as he did, he made a fascinating discovery: the original Greek word that we translate "justified" did not mean "make righteous" as he had been taught. It meant "declare righteous." Justification has nothing to do with God *making* us righteous; it is about God *declaring* whether we're righteous or not. These two things are entirely different.

Picture yourself in the afternoon sun at Chicago's historic Wrigley Field. The crowd is enjoying the game, even though the Cubs pitcher is struggling. To the great frustration of the crowd, he has thrown ten balls in a row, and he has already walked two batters. He's looking defeated.

The umpire crouches behind the catcher, waiting for the pitch. The crowd groans as the umpire calls another ball. But then to everybody's surprise, the umpire walks toward the mound. He puts his arm around the pitcher's shoulder. "I know you're having a bad day," he says, "but I can help you with your pitching."

The story is absurd—it's not the umpire's job to improve the pitcher's performance. That job belongs to the coach. The umpire's job is to score the pitcher's performance. He calls balls and strikes, and he must do this with consistency, accuracy, and integrity. If he fails to do so, forty thousand fans will want to know why.

God acts as our coach *and* our umpire, but we must never confuse the two. The Holy Spirit leads us into an effective Christian life. The Bible calls this *sanctification*. But in *justification*, God acts as the umpire. He observes us and makes one of two calls: justified or condemned. Justification has nothing to do with making you a better person; it's about God declaring your standing before him.

FOR FURTHER READING, SEE LUKE 7

WHOSE PERFORMANCE?

All have sinned and fall short of the glory of God,
and all are justified freely by his grace through the redemption
that came by Christ Jesus. ROMANS 3:23-24, NIV

IF JUSTIFICATION IS about God observing my life and declaring whether I'm in the strike zone of righteousness or not, what hope is there of my ever being justified? The apostle Paul gives us the marvelous answer to that question: we "are justified freely by his grace through the redemption that came by Christ Jesus" (Romans 3:24, NIV).

In other words, the way God declares a person to be in the right is not on the basis of that person's performance, but on the basis of the redemption and propitiation that were offered by Christ on the cross. We're not justified by pitching a perfect game, but because God makes his declaration about us while he is looking at Jesus.

Jesus' perfect righteousness becomes ours when a living connection is formed between us and him. This bond is formed by faith. That's why Paul says God justifies sinners "when they believe in Jesus" (Romans 3:26).

When you come to faith in Jesus Christ, God credits you with Jesus' righteousness. He counts Jesus' righteousness as if it were yours. If God measured my life against his law, he could only make one call, and that would be "condemned." That remains true of my life, even though I came to faith in Christ decades ago. Our righteousness is "nothing but filthy rags" (Isaiah 64:6), and Paul makes it clear that nobody will be declared righteous in God's sight by observing the law (see Romans 3:20).

God justifies us freely by charging our sins to Jesus. This free gift is ours because two thousand years ago Jesus paid the cost in his death on the cross. God justifies us because the charges we have incurred have been paid by Jesus. He picked up the tab. Someone has to pay if God is to say, "No charge!" to sinners like you and me, and that is precisely what Jesus has done for us.

FOR FURTHER READING, SEE ISAIAH 64

FORMED BY FAITH

We are made right with God by placing our faith in Jesus Christ.
ROMANS 3:22

THE ONLY BASIS for justification is Jesus' death and resurrection. God will justify those who are connected to him—a connection formed by faith. The moment you put your faith in Christ, God will apply all the benefits of Christ's death and resurrection to you. If you believe in Christ now, you will be justified—God says so.

That's how God justified Abraham: "Abraham believed God, and God counted him as righteous because of his faith" (Romans 4:3)—two thousand years before Jesus was born. Abraham believed God's promise. He trusted God to send a Redeemer (see John 8:56).

God justified Abraham as he looked forward in faith to the coming of Jesus. In the same way, God justifies us when we look backward to Christ in faith. Faith seals a relationship between you and Christ in which the benefits of his death and resurrection flow into your life.

Faith begins by coming to know Jesus—who he is, where he has come from, and what he is about. It begins with discovering that he is the Son of God, that he came from heaven, and that he has come to redeem sinners.

But faith is more than knowledge—the devil knows *about* Christ. It is possible to learn about Jesus and be no better off than if you had never heard his name. Faith involves a two-way commitment in which Christ receives me and I receive him.

Think of what being joined to you meant for Jesus: the holy Son of God had to take your sin as if it were his own. But now think of what being joined to Jesus means for you: you possess the righteousness of Christ as if it were your own!

Christ has declared his readiness and desire to be your Savior. He is ready to take your sins, and he offers you his righteousness. But the transaction is not made until by faith you take him as your Savior. At that moment the redemption that is possible for everyone becomes an actual fact for you.

FOR FURTHER READING, SEE ROMANS 4

WHERE DO I STAND WITH GOD?

Since we have been justified by faith, we have peace with God through our
Lord Jesus Christ . . . and we rejoice in the hope of the glory of God.
ROMANS 5:1-2, ESV

IF YOU ARE unsure about your standing with God, it will be difficult for you to rejoice in him. The apostle Paul says that "we have peace with God through our Lord Jesus Christ" (Romans 5:1, ESV).

Having "peace with God" is not the same thing as feeling peaceful. There may be times in the Christian life when we are very troubled. "Peace with God" means that God holds nothing against us. The reason for this is that he has charged all your sin to Jesus, and Jesus dealt with it on the cross.

The case against you is closed; the hearing is over, and the court is dismissed. Through Jesus' death and resurrection there is peace with God, access to grace, and the certainty of glory for every person who trusts in the Lord Jesus Christ.

That is the transformation that takes place when you are justified. It is a miracle of God's grace, and it brings you into peace with God. That is your standing, and it is secure. It doesn't vary from day to day or swing with your moods, and it isn't canceled when you let God down.

Imagine a business partnership in which you had to call your partner every day to find out if he or she still wanted to work with you. Or imagine a marriage in which you didn't really know if your spouse loved you. Either of these relationships could be endured but not enjoyed.

Many Christians have the idea that the Christian life begins with forgiveness but is sustained by performance. That's completely false. When we're justified, we live in the world of God's grace.

You can look to the future with confidence because the Christ who died to save you lives to keep you. Your final salvation does not rest on your performance in the Christian life. It has been sealed by the blood of Christ, and knowing this, you can rejoice in God through the Lord Jesus Christ.

FOR FURTHER READING, SEE PHILIPPIANS 3

WHY IS THIS HAPPENING TO ME?

We can rejoice, too, when we run into problems and trials, for
we know that they help us develop endurance. And endurance
develops strength of character, and character strengthens
our confident hope of salvation. ROMANS 5:3-4

WHEN THINGS SEEM to be going wrong in your life, your enemy will try to use the situation to undermine your confidence in God. Satan loves to sow doubts, because he knows that if you lose your joy, you will struggle in every other area of your life.

One of the "joy killing" questions he will attempt to plant in your mind is this one: Why is this happening to me? Whether a health issue, a family problem, or some disappointment, the struggle makes you wonder why God would allow such a terrible thing to happen to you. And if you don't know how to answer this question, it will sap your faith, undermine your hope, and kill your joy.

But God wants you to know that your suffering is not meaningless. Your suffering will produce endurance, character, and hope. God uses the most difficult times in your life to achieve something of infinite value. He can take the greatest pain you've experienced and transform it into a remarkable resemblance of Jesus Christ in you.

If you have understood that the whole of this life is a preparation for eternity, you will say with the apostle Paul, "Our present sufferings are not worth comparing with the glory that will be revealed in us" (Romans 8:18, NIV). God's purpose is not just that you will be in glory, but that glory will be in you.

Your life is in God's hands. That means you can be confident that God is working out his purpose, even in the darkest days of your life. Your suffering is not accidental, meaningless, or out of control. It's the place where God will form the image of Christ in you.

If you can see that, then you will be able to rejoice in God even through the hardest days of your life. You may look up to God through your tears, but you will be able to say, "Thank you that this is not the end, but only a painful passage on the way to all that you are preparing for me."

FOR FURTHER READING, SEE JAMES 1

DOES GOD REALLY CARE?

*God showed his great love for us by sending Christ to die
for us while we were still sinners.* ROMANS 5:8

TO MANY PEOPLE, it is not immediately obvious how Jesus' death is a demonstration of God's love. After all, there are many things that God could give us that might seem to be a more relevant expression of his love.

If the Bible said, "God showed his love for us by giving us a cure for cancer," we would have no doubt about the relevance of the message. We can think of several ways God might show his love for us, but for many people, Jesus dying on the cross is not one of them.

Imagine a couple sitting in a car on a moonlit night near Niagara Falls. The man puts his arm around the woman's shoulder and whispers in her ear, "I love you."

She looks up at him doubtfully. "Do you really? Sometimes I wonder."

"Okay," he says. "I'll prove it." He gets out of the car, walks over to the edge of the falls, and with one huge leap, throws himself over the side. As he is falling, he screams, "I looooove youuuuu!"

This would surely be an unforgettable experience, but it would not be a demonstration of love at all—it is a demonstration of utter stupidity. The man's death is of no value to the woman.

In the same way, the death of Jesus is of no value to us unless it achieved something for us. That is exactly what the Bible teaches. Through Jesus' death, the debt of our sin was paid, and God's wrath was satisfied.

God showed his love for us on the cross. Jesus laid down his life at the point of our greatest need—"while we were still sinners." When you are tempted to wonder if God really cares for you, look at the cross and contemplate the wounds and sufferings of Jesus. Then reflect on the fact that all this was for you.

FOR FURTHER READING, SEE 1 JOHN 4

WHERE IS YOUR CONFIDENCE?

We have now been justified by his blood. ROMANS 5:9, NIV

"JUSTIFIED BY FAITH," a phrase we find so often in the Bible, is short-hand. We are actually justified by Christ, through his blood applied to us when we put our faith in him. But what does the justifying is Christ's blood. Faith is simply the means by which this justification comes to us. God does not invite us to have faith in our faith but to have faith in Christ.

I am a sinner in the process of being restored. God's work in me has truly begun, but it is not yet complete. So while it is wonderfully true that I love Christ, am committed to serve Christ, and have faith in Christ, not one of these things is what they might be or what, one day, they will be.

We are not yet what we will be, and that is why we can never find a basis for security or confidence before God through anything in ourselves. There is only one solid ground of assurance, and it has nothing to do with me. It is the blood of Christ. We are "justified by his blood."

If you want to cultivate assurance and joy in God, the question you should be asking is not, "How strong is my faith?" or "How warm is my heart?" or "How deep is my commitment?" Instead you should ask, "Is the blood of Jesus Christ rich enough and strong enough to wash away every sin and to cover every weakness, failure, and inadequacy in my life until the day I arrive in the presence of God?"

The answer to that question is absolutely, without question, yes! Since our standing before God is not based on anything in us but rather on the perfect sacrifice of Jesus Christ on the cross, we can be fully confident that all will be well on the last day, because our salvation will rest, then as now, not on us but on him.

No wonder Paul said, "We also rejoice in God through our Lord Jesus Christ" (Romans 5:11, ESV). We rejoice because our final salvation rests not on our performance in the Christian life but on the blood of Jesus Christ.

FOR FURTHER READING, SEE HEBREWS 10

SIN IS MORE THAN A CHOICE

Sin ruled . . . ROMANS 5:21

MOST CHRISTIANS EMBRACE the idea that sin is a choice. We make choices every day, and we like to think that most of them are reasonably good ones. We might also have the humility to admit that we occasionally make bad choices, and we may even be willing to call these bad choices *sin*.

But the Bible makes it clear that sin is a bigger problem than a few stupid mistakes. Sin is more than a choice; it's a power. That's why Paul talks about sin *ruling*.

Rule is a power word. Imagine that you and a large group of your friends are heading off for the vacation of a lifetime on one of the Pacific islands. You gather at the airport and board the plane. Many of your friends are traveling in economy class, some are traveling business class, and a few are in first-class seats.

The journey begins with a smooth takeoff. You enjoy the food and the in-flight entertainment, until suddenly an alarm sounds. Smoke fills the cabin, and then, to your absolute horror, three masked gunmen appear. You quickly realize that the unthinkable has happened: the plane has been hijacked, and you're all hostages.

Most of your friends are economy hostages, some are business-class hostages, and a few have the distinction of being first-class hostages, but you're all in the same position. The hijackers are in control, determining the destiny of the plane. That's what *ruling* means. When the Bible says that "sin ruled," it means sin invaded our world. Sin took charge of our ultimate destiny—it was in control.

The problem is that most of us see sin not as a dangerous hijacker, but as a harmless pest. In the book *Gulliver's Travels*, Gulliver comes to a town where the people are so tiny that he seems like a giant. During his visit, Gulliver becomes tired, and while he sleeps, the little people climb all over him, tying him with thousands of tiny threads. The individual threads have very little strength, but together they have great power, so that when Gulliver wakes up, he can't move.

Sin is not simply a choice; it's a power that has taken over your world. It may seem innocuous at times, but its many threads are too strong for you to break on your own.

FOR FURTHER READING, SEE ROMANS 7

UNDERSTANDING THE NEWSPAPER

Sin ruled over all people and brought them to death. ROMANS 5:21

THE FINAL OUTCOME of the tyranny of sin over the human race is death. The final destination to which the hijacker "sin" takes us is death. The outcome of sin's hostile invasion of our lives and the end result of being bound in sin is death.

When death comes, it doesn't make any difference whether you're traveling first-class, business, or economy. At the point of death, it makes no difference whether you were a pauper on the streets of Calcutta or Princess Diana in Paris. There is nothing any of us can do about it. It may seem like some of us are able to cheat death for a while, but death eventually takes us all. Its tyranny is cruel and relentless.

Paul's teaching about the rule of sin helps us to understand the newspaper. We read and hear about school shootings, military takeovers, drug cartels, broken homes, and financial fraud, and we say to ourselves, *This is not how things are supposed to be*. So, why is the world like this?

God's answer is, "You're right. This is not how the world should be, and the reason it's like this is that it has been invaded by an enemy. You are living under a tyranny. Sin reigns."

If sin were simply a choice, we could all choose to have happy homes, strong families, peaceful nations, and contented hearts. But sin is a power, and that's why our dreams are always beyond our reach.

This doesn't mean that we're all as bad as we could be or that the world is as bad as it could be. God is gracious in restraining some of the worst effects of sin. But it does mean that we cannot get free from this power. While we can all avoid some sin, none of us can avoid all sin.

The fact that sin is a power helps me to understand myself. I find these lines from DC Talk's "In the Light" very insightful: "What's going on inside of me? I despise my own behavior." Have you ever felt like that? We're often a mystery to ourselves, and the only explanation of that mystery is that sin is a power.

FOR FURTHER READING, SEE 1 JOHN 3

CUT THE CORD

Sin is no longer your master. ROMANS 6:14

WHEN CHRIST SAVES you, he sets you free from the tyranny of sin. Grace invades your life, and Christ flies his flag over you. You will still have many struggles with sin, but sin is no longer your master.

Grace puts you in an altogether different position. Sin is still a powerful enemy, but when Christ invades your life, sin does not rule over you. You belong to Christ. Grace reigns where sin once ruled, but two flags cannot be planted on the same ground. Sin and grace may both be present in the same place, but they cannot both rule. Where grace plants its flag, sin no longer reigns.

Sin will still be a menace to you, but you are no longer under its rule. There is all the difference in the world between a menacing neighbor and an occupying army.

Many Christians feel defeated. They understand that God loves them and that Christ died for them, but their problem lies in the habits of thought or patterns of behavior that have become ingrained over many years.

Some think of grace as God smiling down benignly, rather like a helpless parent who has no idea how to control an unruly child. They have tried to change but have lost heart. You've no doubt experienced what the power of sin does to you. You feel its pull and may even feel defeated by it, but the power of grace is greater than the power of sin. God's grace sets prisoners free.

Think about Gulliver in *Gulliver's Travels* tied down by thousands of tiny threads. Now picture someone cutting the cords that bind him. It may take a long time to cut all the threads, but every stroke of the knife brings greater freedom. That's a picture of how God's grace works in our lives.

The apostle Paul tells us he was once an angry, violent blasphemer, but when God's grace invaded his life, he was completely changed: "I persecuted God's church. But whatever I am now, it is all because God poured out his special favor on me—and not without results. . . . [God] was working through me by his grace" (1 Corinthians 15:9-10). God's grace in your life will not be without results either.

FOR FURTHER READING, SEE 1 CORINTHIANS 15

A LICENSE TO SIN?

Should we keep on sinning so that God can show us more
and more of his wonderful grace? ROMANS 6:1

IF GOD HAS made a promise to me in Jesus Christ, and by his grace my eternal destiny is secure, doesn't that mean I'm able to sin without consequence?

Some people feel it's dangerous to teach the security of our salvation in Christ because it may have the effect of making Christians lazy. After all, what is the point of praying, giving, or serving if I already know my eternal destiny is secure?

This important question arises out of the nature of the gospel itself. The teaching of Romans 5 leads directly to the question of Romans 6: "Should we keep on sinning so that God can show us more . . . grace?"

If this question has never occurred to you, it is probably a sign that you haven't understood, or you haven't reflected deeply on, the free gift of God's salvation in Jesus Christ. Once you understand the teaching of Romans 5, you will inevitably ask the question of Romans 6. And you need to know how to answer this question, because it goes to the heart of our motivation for living the Christian life.

What would you think of a man who, knowing that his wife was absolutely committed to him, said to himself, *My marriage is secure, so why would I bother with caring for my wife?* There is something despicable about that. It is a travesty of the high calling of marriage.

God invites us into a relationship that is both secure and intimate. It is secure because God makes a covenant with us, and he never goes back on his Word. But it is also intimate because it involves union with Christ.

Jesus spoke about this when he said, "I am the vine; you are the branches" (John 15:5). Just as sap rises from the vine and flows into the branches, so the life of Christ flows from him into his people. This is more than a legal transaction in which your sins are forgiven and your passport is stamped for heaven. This is the life of God entering into you. It's hard to imagine a more intimate picture.

FOR FURTHER READING, SEE JOHN 15

DISCOVER WHO YOU ARE

Have you forgotten that when we were joined with Christ Jesus in baptism,
we joined him in his death? . . . Since we have been united with him in
his death, we will also be raised to life as he was. ROMANS 6:3,5

THE WORD *BAPTISM* literally means to be "plunged," "immersed," or "saturated." The apostle Paul tells believers they are "joined with Christ Jesus in baptism." When you come to faith in Jesus, the Holy Spirit connects Jesus' death two thousand years ago with your life today. You are plunged into him, and the benefits of his death and resurrection flow into your life.

Many churches symbolize this by baptizing believers in water that completely covers them. This is a powerful picture of our immersion in Jesus Christ. The Holy Spirit brings the believer into a deep spiritual union with Christ, formed through the bond of faith. The believer is "in Christ."

Being baptized into Christ's death means that who you were before ceases to exist. I find it helpful to think of it like this: there was once a fellow by the name of Colin Smith . . .

Because he was descended from Adam, he was under the reign of sin, alienated from God, and powerless to do anything about it. If he had stayed in that condition, he would have ended up under condemnation. But that fellow no longer exists. He died. He went down with Jesus at the cross. That's what Paul means when he says we joined Christ in his death.

But Paul also writes about being raised to life as Christ was. When the Holy Spirit plunged me into Christ, he brought a whole new person into being. This new person, who also goes by Colin Smith, is under the rule of grace. He is a child of God, and his destiny is everlasting life. The Spirit of God lives in this person. He has been raised to live a new life to the glory of God (see Romans 6:4).

This is the consistent teaching of the New Testament: "Anyone who belongs to Christ has become a new person. The old life is gone; a new life has begun!" (2 Corinthians 5:17). This is so much more than turning over a new leaf or making a decision.

FOR FURTHER READING, SEE 2 CORINTHIANS 5

THE TROUSERS AND THE SOCKS

God . . . has blessed us with every spiritual blessing . . .
because we are united with Christ. EPHESIANS 1:3

ALL OF THE blessings of salvation come to us in Jesus Christ, and none of them come to us apart from him. Forgiveness is found in him, eternal life is found in him, holiness is found in him, and victory over sin is found in him. These gifts are all joined together inseparably in him. If you are in him, all of these blessings are yours. If you are not in him, none of them are yours.

Consider the difference between a pair of socks and a pair of trousers. When you put a pair of socks in the wash, one of them can get lost. The problem, of course, is that there is nothing that unites them together. But trousers are different. Over the years, I've put plenty of pants in the wash, but I've never once had a pair come out with one leg missing. They are joined together; they're intrinsically one!

Some people have the idea that the blessings of God are like socks. They think of God sending out isolated blessings, like forgiveness or everlasting life, from heaven. But God's blessings do not come to us like that. He has chosen to unite all the blessings of salvation together in one, and he offers us one blessing: Jesus Christ.

Paul was writing to Christian believers, and he said, "Don't you know? You've been baptized into Christ's death and resurrection. Don't you see? Being a Christian is much more than a decision to believe and a passport to heaven" (see Romans 6:3-5). All of the blessings of salvation come to us in Jesus Christ, and none of them come to us apart from him.

Forgiveness and everlasting life are wonderful gifts, but they come to you because you are "united with Christ," and that means the person you used to be has truly ceased to exist. God has brought a whole new person into being by the power of his Spirit, and the purpose of your new life is to live for the glory of God.

FOR FURTHER READING, SEE EPHESIANS 1

YOUR NEW POSITION

Do not let sin control the way you live; do not give in to sinful desires. . . . Give yourselves completely to God, for you were dead, but now you have new life. ROMANS 6:12-13

CHRISTIANS STILL FACE a lifelong battle with sin; it's a real struggle. But while the old person was destined for defeat in the battle, you are now positioned for victory.

Some Christians say, "That's just the way I am," as if there were nothing they could do about their sin. That was you *without* Christ, but that person has died! You are risen with Christ. You have power! Sin is no longer your master.

Imagine working under the same boss for thirty years. Every morning you check in with Fred, and he tells you what he wants you to do. You get along with him, but if you question his judgment, he gets angry. You've learned to do things Fred's way.

One day the chairman of the company comes to see you. He says he has big plans for you, including an immediate promotion to management. Next Monday you will have a new position in a new office upstairs.

You arrive on Monday, and it dawns on you. *Fred answers to me!* Over the next couple of weeks, Fred continues telling you what to do. He's done it for thirty years! He comes right into your new office and tells you what he thinks you should do. Fred will always think of himself as your boss, even though he no longer is. You have a tendency to listen to Fred and do what he says, even though you don't answer to him anymore.

Six weeks later, the chairman comes to see you: "If we wanted Fred in charge, we would've given him the job, but we gave it to you. We've given you authority; use it. From now on, he does what you tell him, not the other way around."

Discovering the authority of your new position in Christ is an important key to living the Christian life. Sin is no longer your master, so don't let sin rule over you. When temptation comes, deal with it as you would deal with someone who's subject to you. Half the battle is knowing you have the authority to do that.

FOR FURTHER READING, SEE ROMANS 6

HOSTILE: NO DESIRE AND NO ABILITY

The sinful nature is always hostile to God. It never did
obey God's laws, and it never will. ROMANS 8:7

THE APOSTLE PAUL speaks about a person whose nature is hostile to God, so we're going to call him *Hostile*. Hostile has neither the desire nor the ability to follow God's law. We have already met Hostile several times in the Bible's story.

The first time was in the story of Adam and Eve's two sons. Cain brought an offering to God, but God did not accept it, so Cain became angry. He was hostile toward God, and his hostility was deflected to his brother, Abel, who loved God. Cain's anger became so intense, he eventually killed his brother.

Pharaoh was hostile. God said, "Let my people go, so that they may worship me," but Pharaoh refused to recognize God's authority over his life. He was unwilling to submit to the Word of God, and he became Hostile.

But Hostile's greatest day, as he saw it, was the day we call Good Friday, when Jesus was brought before a crowd of people, and they cried out, "Crucify him!" There was real feeling there, and it was hostile!

In the early days of Christianity, Paul launched a mission to destroy the church, "uttering threats with every breath" (Acts 9:1). That's Hostile! He was on the road to Damascus when the risen Lord Jesus Christ appeared to him and said, "Why are you persecuting me?" (Acts 9:4). Paul's violent anger against Christians was a reflection of a deeper rage against Christ.

You may have noticed that many kind and respectable people are hostile when it comes to the things of God. A conversation can be quite civil until God comes up. Then, as if a switch were flipped, a deep hostility is opened up.

If you're hostile, know that God has loved you through all your struggling, resisting, and fighting against him. He offers you peace with him. He invites you to repent. Repentance is giving up your resistance to God. God invites you to surrender to him. Lay down your arms now. Jesus came into the world and went to the cross so that enemies like you and me could become his friends.

FOR FURTHER READING, SEE GENESIS 4

HELPLESS: DESIRE WITHOUT ABILITY

I don't really understand myself, for I want to do what is right,
but I don't do it. Instead, I do what I hate. ROMANS 7:15

THE PROBLEM FOR this character is that he isn't able to do what he wants, and that's why we're calling him *Helpless*. The big difference between Helpless and Hostile is that while Hostile hates God's law, Helpless loves it: "I agree that the law is good" (Romans 7:16). That is something Hostile would never say. Helpless loves God's law and wants to keep it: "I love God's law with all my heart" (7:22).

Though Helpless wants to fulfill the law of God, he finds it beyond his power. Helpless is a mystery to himself: "I don't really understand myself" (7:15). He ends up doing what he never intended.

We've met Helpless before in the Bible. When Moses announced the laws of God, the people said, "We will do everything the LORD has commanded" (Exodus 19:8), but they found it impossible to live up to their good intentions. When they got to Canaan, Joshua challenged them to choose whom they would serve. They said, "We . . . will serve the LORD" (Joshua 24:18). Desire is one thing; ability is another.

The law is "unable to save us because of the weakness of our sinful nature" (Romans 8:3). The law tells us what to do, but since we don't have the power to do it, it leaves us helpless. And Helpless cries out, "What a miserable person I am! Who will free me from this life that is dominated by sin and death?" (7:24). God's answer is Jesus Christ!

If you are helpless, God is saying, "Jesus Christ will deliver you. The Christian life is not about you keeping my law. It is about my power entering your soul, breaking the power that is ruling over you." Come to Christ in faith, and tell him you cannot live the Christian life on your own. Tell him you need his Holy Spirit's power so you will have the ability and the desire to live a new life.

FOR FURTHER READING, SEE JOSHUA 24

HOPEFUL: DESIRE WITH ABILITY

Those who are controlled by the Holy Spirit think about
things that please the Spirit. ROMANS 8:5

THE APOSTLE PAUL introduces us to another character, *Hopeful*. Like Helpless, Hopeful wants to live in a way that is pleasing to God. The difference between them lies in the area of ability.

Paul tells Hopeful to "put to death the deeds of your sinful nature" (Romans 8:13). That is precisely what Helpless could not do. He says, "I'm a prisoner!" He doesn't have the ability to overcome the enemy. But Hopeful is in an entirely different position. He has the desire to fight against sin in his life, but he also has the ability to prevail, and the reason for that is the Spirit of God living in him.

Hopeful and Helpless face the same struggles. They feel the power of the same temptations. The difference between them lies not in the battle but in the outcome. Helpless faces inevitable defeat; Hopeful faces ultimate victory.

You might think that the power of the Holy Spirit at work in a person's life must be a special experience known mainly by pastors, saints, and martyrs. But Paul makes it clear that this is the normal Christian life. Salvation in Christ and the gift of the Spirit are inseparable. You cannot have one without the other. "Those who do not have the Spirit of Christ living in them do not belong to him at all" (Romans 8:9). Period.

God says to Hopeful, "If through the power of the Spirit you put to death the deeds of your sinful nature, you will live" (Romans 8:13). He's saying, "Start an intentional battle against the sin that remains in you, Hopeful. Learn to fight, and don't say you are Helpless. You're not! The Spirit of God is within you. Christ has put you in a position to fight!"

Can you identify specific sins you're launching an assault on? Are you praying about them? Have you formed a strategy for change, knowing the power of the Spirit has been given to you for this purpose? Are you feeding on God's Word and building relationships with other Christians to strengthen your soul for battle?

FOR FURTHER READING, SEE GALATIANS 5

THE MARK OF A SON OR DAUGHTER

*If through the power of the Spirit you put to death the deeds
of your sinful nature, you will live. For all who are led by the
Spirit of God are children of God.* ROMANS 8:13-14

WHEN YOU ARE in Christ, you are able to destroy the deeds of your sinful nature by the power of the Holy Spirit. This is a long campaign with many setbacks, but it will end in victory for all of God's people.

Paul tells us why it's so important for us to fight this battle: "For all who are led by the Spirit of God are children of God" (Romans 8:14). Notice the word *for*. *For* shows that the second half of a statement is an explanation of the first.

The reason you must "put to death the deeds of your sinful nature" is that "all who are led by the Spirit of God are children of God." In other words, the distinctive mark of the sons and daughters of God is that they follow the Holy Spirit into battle against the deeds of their sinful natures.

When Barnabas is described as the "Son of Encouragement" (Acts 4:36), the word *son* is describing character. That's also how we're to understand the Bible's description of Adam as "the son of God" (Luke 3:38). Adam was created in the image and likeness of God; he reflected something of God's glory.

God called Israel his *son* because the nation was to reflect his character (see Exodus 4:22). That's why Israel was given the Ten Commandments, which reflect the character of God. As God's children lived by these laws, his glory would be seen among the nations. But throughout the Old Testament, God's people turned out to be unlike the Father.

They did not reflect the Father's glory, so the Father sent someone who did. God himself took human flesh in Christ—the Son of God par excellence. He is the image of the invisible God, the exact representation of his being (see Colossians 1:15; Hebrews 1:3). Jesus said, "Anyone who has seen me has seen the Father" (John 14:9). The apostle Paul takes up the same language and talks about our being "children of God" (Romans 8:14). Think about that! God wants his character and likeness to be reflected in your life.

FOR FURTHER READING, SEE JOHN 14

LET'S PLAY BLANKETY BLANK

All who [blankety blank] are children of God. ROMANS 8:14

FOR MANY YEARS, one of the popular game shows on British television was called *Blankety Blank*. In this game, contestants had to fill in missing words from a sentence. It's a good game to play with familiar phrases from the Bible, because it helps us see great truths we might otherwise miss.

If you'd never seen Romans 8:14, how would you fill in the blanks? You might say, "All who [receive Christ] are children of God." You have good biblical basis for that answer. The apostle John wrote that "to all who believed him and accepted him, he gave the right to become children of God" (John 1:12).

But Paul is not dealing with the question of how to enter God's family; he's talking about how to become a person who reflects the likeness of God. That's what being a child of God is all about. Will this happen by saying a prayer or making a decision? No. Being *led by the Spirit* is how you will reflect the image and likeness of God.

The Spirit will lead you into battle against the sins that have dug themselves into your life. He will lead you to fight them, and through his overwhelming power, you have the ability to put them to death.

Paul is talking about a marvelous possibility in your life. Those who are led by the Spirit of God into an intentional onslaught against the sins that hide within us will be marked by an increasing likeness to God himself; they will be children of God.

God created Adam in his own image and likeness. That likeness was defaced and the resemblance distorted when sin entered the world. But God has determined to restore that likeness in his people.

Imagine watching the restoration of a defaced painting. Gradually you see the original image appearing. Slowly the shades of original color become visible, and what was once an ugly mess begins to look like a masterpiece. This is the work of the Holy Spirit. That is where he is leading you.

FOR FURTHER READING, SEE JOHN 1

WAGING WAR

You should examine yourself. 1 CORINTHIANS 11:28

IMAGINE YOURSELF ON the field of battle in the desert. About a mile ahead of you, the enemy has dug in, and you've been charged to reclaim that ground. Obviously, the enemy is not going to stand on top of his bunker, wave his flag, and invite you to fire at him, so your first task is to identify the enemy's position.

This is precisely how we're to approach the campaign against sin in our lives. We have to get specific. We are to identify the positions sin may have taken up in our souls so that we may launch an assault against them in the power of the Spirit.

God has given us a checklist of what to look for when we examine ourselves. It's called the Ten Commandments. Here are some questions you may use to examine yourself in the light of God's commands:

- "You must not misuse the name of the LORD your God" (Exodus 20:7). Have I become flippant or casual about the things of God? Does God carry weight in my life?
- "Remember to observe the Sabbath day by keeping it holy" (Exodus 20:8). How does my use of time reflect the place I've given to God in my life? When in the last week have I given God my focused attention? Could someone sustain a quality relationship with a spouse on this basis?
- "You must not murder" (Exodus 20:13). What has made me angry this week? (Jesus related murder to issues of anger— see Matthew 5:21-24.) How did I respond? Have I forgiven the offender, or am I becoming bitter? Am I angry with anybody now? What can I do to promote reconciliation?

No matter how long you've been a Christian, the enemy will always attempt to establish new footholds in your life. The trouble is that many Christians are waiting for God to make them holy, not realizing that God is calling them into battle. But God's promise is that as you engage in this warfare, you'll prevail, and you'll increasingly reflect the likeness of God: "All who are led by the Spirit of God are children of God" (Romans 8:14).

FOR FURTHER READING, SEE EXODUS 20

GREAT EXPECTATIONS

The creation looks forward to the day when it will join God's children in glorious freedom from death and decay. ROMANS 8:21

GOD MADE HUMANS a little lower than the angels and placed everything under their authority (see Psalm 8:5-6), but humanity was not able to maintain its position. We do not see everything subject to humanity as God intended. Our governance of this world has left the creation groaning, longing for deliverance and waiting for a change.

The whole creation is looking forward to the day when the children of God will be revealed. The Curse will be removed, and the created order will be placed under the care of people who reflect the image and likeness of God.

That's why Jesus has come into the world. He is the image of God, and the whole creation finds its hope in him. He is bringing people to glory by sending his Spirit to lead his people into battle against sin. His purpose is that we become a people in whom God's likeness and image can be increasingly seen.

On the last day, the work will be complete, and Jesus will stand before the Father and say, "Here I am, and here are the children you've given me." He will be the first of many brothers who will all reflect God's image and likeness.

Creation is waiting because when the children of God are revealed, the creation itself will be liberated! When God's final purpose is fulfilled, there will be a new heaven and a new earth, the home of righteousness (see 2 Peter 3:13). All creation will rejoice when the Curse is removed, and even the trees "will clap their hands" (Isaiah 55:12).

Are you a child of God? I want you to notice that it is by faith in Christ that you become a child of God. It is Christ who will bring you into the family: "To all who believed him and accepted him, he gave the right to become children of God" (John 1:12).

If you're a child of God, are you living like one? Does your life have the marks of an intentional assault on the sins in your life? That's how God's glory is seen in you. All creation is waiting for the day when that will be brought to completion.

FOR FURTHER READING, SEE ISAIAH 55

A THORN IN THE FLESH

To keep me from becoming proud, I was given a thorn in my flesh,
a messenger from Satan to torment me. 2 CORINTHIANS 12:7

THERE HAS BEEN a lot of speculation about Paul's thorn in the flesh. Suggestions include malaria, depression, epilepsy, an unusual temptation, or blindness. The truth is that we don't know what it was.

Since Paul connects the thorn with the remarkable revelation he had received before writing this letter (see 2 Corinthians 12:2), we can assume he'd been suffering from this affliction for fourteen years. We can also be confident it was a serious affliction.

Paul was no stranger to suffering. Five times, he'd endured thirty-nine lashes; three times, he'd been beaten with rods, and he'd been stoned once (see 2 Corinthians 11:24-25). Receiving thirty-nine lashes would be enough to make some folks quit the ministry, but not Paul. He was a man of extraordinary courage, and he wouldn't have made a big deal of the thorn if it were only a minor irritation.

If you had a thorn in your flesh, you'd be aware of it every time you moved. You wouldn't be able to do anything without wincing as the thorn buried itself deeper into your flesh. Perhaps that's a picture of a painful issue in your life. You can't escape it. Whatever you do, you're aware of it, and it's been like that for years.

Paul faced this situation with prayer. When something is troubling us, prayer is always the right thing to do. No doubt Paul prayed with great intensity. "I begged the Lord," he wrote (2 Corinthians 12:8).

There was every reason to expect God would answer Paul's prayer request positively. Paul describes the thorn as "a messenger from Satan" (2 Corinthians 12:7). If Satan was involved, wouldn't God bind the enemy and deliver Paul? But apparently it's not as simple as that, because Paul also tells us the thorn was "given" to him, and clearly he means it was given by God!

Satan caused great suffering and loss in Job's life too, but behind the devil's activity was the sovereign hand of God, who used this suffering to lead Job into a new understanding of his Creator and Redeemer. It may be Satan's intention to harm you, but God can use it for good.

FOR FURTHER READING, SEE 2 CORINTHIANS 11

MY GRACE IS ALL YOU NEED

Three different times I begged the Lord to take it away.
Each time he said, "My grace is all you need. My power
works best in weakness." 2 CORINTHIANS 12:8-9

PAUL BEGGED GOD for relief from the thorn in his flesh (see 2 Corinthians 12:7), but God chose not to give him what he asked for. There may be times when God's Word to us is, "You are more useful to me with this thorn than without it."

Consider the cross. When wicked men nailed Jesus to a piece of wood, he said, "This is your moment, the time when the power of darkness reigns" (Luke 22:53). But then Peter tells us that "God knew what would happen, and his prearranged plan was carried out" (Acts 2:23). Nobody had the power to take Jesus' life from him. He chose to lay it down (see John 10:18). In fact, it was for this very reason that he came into the world.

Paul prayed three times that God would remove the thorn. When I read that, it reminds me of when Jesus prayed three times in Gethsemane, "My Father! If it is possible, let this cup of suffering be taken away from me" (Matthew 26:39). God didn't take the cup from him, and our salvation is possible because Jesus accepted the Father's answer.

God the Father didn't remove the suffering of the cross, but when Jesus prayed in the garden, an angel came and strengthened him (see Luke 22:43). And when Paul prayed, God gave him a particular promise: "My grace is all you need" (2 Corinthians 12:9). The person who walks with God will often know what it is like to draw strength from that promise and to discover that God has a purpose in the hardest things in life.

There will be times when God does not give you the answer you are looking for in your prayers, but you can be certain that when you seek him in prayer, he will always give you the strength you need. The mark of true spirituality is not that God gives you everything you ask, but that you walk with him when he does not.

FOR FURTHER READING, SEE LUKE 22

OUTSIDE YOUR COMFORT ZONE

I am glad to boast about my weaknesses, . . . for when I am weak,
then I am strong. 2 CORINTHIANS 12:9-10

I HAVE HEARD many testimonies over the years in which Christians have spoken about how they used to feel weak but now they are strong. But that's not what Paul says here. His experience of weakness is in the present tense. It's continuing, and he's not expecting it to change.

This seems surprising given the overwhelming power of the Holy Spirit. Why would Paul say he felt weak? Was he lacking faith? Had he forgotten God was with him? Paul was certainly not inadequate or unable to handle the challenges of life. He had extraordinary courage. By any standards, Paul was one of the most remarkable people who ever lived.

The reason Paul experienced weakness was that God had given him an overwhelming task: "I have the daily burden of my concern for all the churches. Who is weak without my feeling that weakness?" (2 Corinthians 11:28-29). God had put the apostle in situations that pushed him well beyond his comfort zone. He knew what it was to feel unbearably crushed. At one point he was "overwhelmed beyond [his] ability to endure" (1:8).

Perhaps you've known this in your own experience. If God gives you the weight of a demanding task, there will be times when, like Paul, you may feel crushed by it, and you will begin to experience what Paul calls "weakness."

Those who choose to live within cautiously safe limits cannot discover the strength in weakness that Paul is talking about. Nor can those who are sure and confident in their own abilities. Only when you let God take you outside your comfort zone will you begin to feel weakness.

This weakness is not something to be afraid or ashamed of. It is one of the most significant opportunities in your Christian journey. Paul says that he's "glad" about it, because this is where Christ's power has rested on him. It will be the same for you. Jesus did not live within cautiously safe limits. Jesus wept, and he was crucified in weakness. If you follow him, he will lead you outside your comfort zone. You will experience weakness, and Christ's power will rest on you.

FOR FURTHER READING, SEE 2 CORINTHIANS 12

WHAT MAKES THE ANGELS GASP

*God's purpose in all this was to use the church to display his
wisdom in its rich variety to all the unseen rulers and authorities
in the heavenly places. This was his eternal plan, which he carried
out through Christ Jesus our Lord.* EPHESIANS 3:10-11

GOD'S PURPOSE HAS always been to display his wisdom to a vast audience
in heaven, and the way he's doing this is through the church. The church
was not tacked on to God's plan; it has always been in God's heart.

When God created Eve and brought her to Adam, it was the beginning of human community. But sin separated us from God and from
each other. It has brought conflict and division at every level of society,
from the first relationship, through the first family, to the scattering at
Babel (see Genesis 11) and the hostility of nations. History is the story
of our alienation from God and from one another.

At the same time, God has been advancing a plan to reconcile people
to himself and to each other. He had told Abraham, "All the families on
earth will be blessed through you" (Genesis 12:3). The mystery of how
God would accomplish this was revealed when God sent his Son into
the world (see Ephesians 3:4-6).

After Jesus' death, resurrection, and ascension, the Holy Spirit was
poured out at Pentecost, and the church was established. God had now
gathered together the groups that had been scattered at Babel from all
over the known world (see Acts 2:5-12).

God was drawing people to faith in Christ, gathering them into a
community called *the church*. From the very first day, it crossed barriers
of race, language, and culture. Humanity is always trying to achieve this
kind of unity, and it will never succeed. But God is making people from
every culture and generation one in Christ.

The distinctions of culture, race, education, social standing, income,
gender, and generation exist only for a time; the unity of God's people is
for eternity. It makes the angels gasp, and that's what Paul is talking about
when he says God is putting his wisdom on display for a vast audience in
heaven through the church.

FOR FURTHER READING, SEE EPHESIANS 3

CINDERELLA WILL GO TO THE BALL

Christ loved the church. He gave up his life for her to make her
holy and clean, washed by the cleansing of God's word. He did this to present
her to himself as a glorious church without a spot or wrinkle or any other
blemish. Instead, she will be holy and without fault. EPHESIANS 5:25-27

THE CHURCH IS the bride of Christ, and Christ will present her to himself. And when he does, the church will not be in rags and tatters. She will be beautiful, radiant, "without a spot or wrinkle or any other blemish."

Once upon a time, there was a little girl who had a wicked stepmother and two ugly stepsisters. She was made to work in the kitchen, and she used to sit in her ragged clothes among the cinders, so they called her "Cinderella."

One day the king invited all the maidens in the land to a grand ball in the palace. He wanted his son, the prince, to fall in love and to marry. The ugly sisters were taken to the ball, but Cinderella had no dress to wear, and she was left at home.

Then the fairy godmother touched her with her wand, and Cinderella's rags were turned into a beautiful dress. Mice turned into horses, and a pumpkin turned into a carriage—but only until midnight.

When Cinderella arrived at the ball, she captivated the prince's heart, and they danced until midnight, when she had to leave. Cinderella ran from the ballroom, but as she did, one of her glass slippers fell off.

The prince was determined to find the woman he loved, so he ordered that the slipper be tried on the foot of every maiden in the land. Once the rightful owner was found, she was to be brought to the palace.

That's a wonderful picture of the church. It sometimes looks a bit ragged, and there are some rather ugly brothers and sisters who despise her and count her of little value. In some parts of the world, there are even wicked stepmothers who persecute the church and imprison her leaders. But Christ loves the church, and he will one day bring her to his palace.

FOR FURTHER READING, SEE EPHESIANS 5

WHAT MAKES THE WORLD SIT UP AND TAKE NOTICE

There is no longer Jew or Gentile, slave or free, male and female.
For you are all one in Christ Jesus. GALATIANS 3:28

THE HOLY SPIRIT baptizes into one body all who believe (see 1 Corinthians 12:13). God brings us together in Jesus Christ. He makes us one as he reconciles us to himself.

I'm a Scotsman and proud of it, but I have more in common with a Bedouin who loves Christ than with a Scotsman who doesn't. A Christian physics professor has more in common with an illiterate believer than with a fellow academic who doesn't know Christ. A multimillionaire who knows Christ has more in common with the poorest believer in India than with friends at the yacht club who know nothing of Jesus.

Christian high school students have much more in common with an old man who listens to Brahms and Mozart and knows Christ than with their friends who do not love Christ. And the old man has more in common with the Christian youngster whose jeans hang off his waist, who listens to rock music, and who loves Christ than with his friends at the symphony center who've never seen their need of a Savior!

If angels gasp at the way God gathers people together from diverse backgrounds, is it not also glorifying to God when people with different backgrounds gather for worship on a Sunday morning? I've always had difficulty with the idea of a church having a clearly defined "target audience." I know that every church has its own culture and that this both attracts and repels, but that's a reflection of our limitations rather than our success.

God is glorified by unity across diversity. There is nothing surprising to the world or to angels about a narrow band of people gathering together for worship because they like the same kind of music or a group who gathers together because they're at ease with each other socially. That looks to the world, and probably to the angels, suspiciously like a religious version of the golf club.

But when people come together across the great divides of generation, race, class, and education to worship and serve Christ, the angels gasp. Even the world has to sit up and take notice, because only God could do that.

FOR FURTHER READING, SEE GALATIANS 3

EVEN WITH HER WRINKLES

Christ loved the church. He gave up his life for her. EPHESIANS 5:25

BE CAREFUL HOW you speak about the church, because Jesus Christ loves the church and gave up his life for her. We should have appropriate humility whenever we speak about the church.

God sees the church's failures and so does the world, and it does us little good to pretend they don't exist. It will be difficult for unbelieving people to take us seriously if we can't see what is obvious to them. But those who are continually criticizing the church may find themselves embarrassed on the last day, when they stand in the presence of Christ and discover just how much he loves her.

A number of years ago I was invited to conduct a wedding in a beautiful church in the bride's hometown in England. The couple had asked me to preach a sermon during the service, and I was happy to do so, much to the chagrin of the photographer, who was used to ceremonies that were over in about fifteen minutes.

He was waiting outside during the message, pacing back and forth. I know this because my wife had taken our boys, who were very young at the time, into the foyer. Eventually, the photographer came up to Karen and said, with obvious irritation, "Who is that man going on and on and on in there?"

"Oh, that's my husband," she said with style.

The photographer's face quickly turned a bright shade of red . . . until Karen was kind enough to relieve his embarrassment. It is wise to be very careful about how you speak of someone who is loved!

When you know that Christ loves the church, you will begin to love the church too, even with her wrinkles and blemishes. And when you know that Christ gave himself for her, you will look for ways in which you can give yourself for the church too.

You can start by asking, How can I be most useful in building the church of Jesus Christ? How can I contribute to God's work of reconciling people from every background to himself and to each other through Jesus Christ?

FOR FURTHER READING, SEE 1 CORINTHIANS 12

HIDING UNDER THE BLANKETS

*God's light came into the world, but people loved the darkness more
than the light, for their actions were evil. All who do evil hate the light and
refuse to go near it for fear their sins will be exposed.* JOHN 3:19-20

THERE WAS A time when Adam and Eve were at home in God's light.
They were comfortable in God's immediate presence as they walked
with him in the Garden. But when they sinned, they ran for cover (see
Genesis 3:8). Having chosen darkness, they didn't want to come into
the light, so they stayed in hiding. Sin makes us reluctant to come near
God and incapable of standing in his presence.

Parents know how difficult it can be to get kids up in the morning.
When our children were young, I often woke them up with a hearty, "Rise
and shine!" When I turned on the light, they hid under the blankets.

The light that was quite comfortable for them the evening before
was now disturbing because they'd become used to the darkness. That's
how it was for Adam. The man who was once at ease in God's presence
would now do anything to avoid it. He ran for cover and hid in the
trees, hoping God would not find him.

The idea that all people are engaged in a sincere search after God is
a fallacy. When our first parents were expelled from the Garden, they
went out into a darker world, and people in the darkness are reluctant
to come into the light.

When God chose to reveal the brightness of his glory in Jesus Christ,
those who saw it were overwhelmed by the brilliance of light. Like children under the blankets, they found the radiance of God's glory more
than they could bear.

But if you put out the light, you will be in darkness. That's why there
was darkness for three hours when Jesus was hanging on the cross. God
put out the light. He would not allow natural light to shine while men
had chosen this darkness.

But darkness didn't reign forever. On the third day, Christ rose
from the dead and ascended to heaven. Through faith in him, people
who have become used to darkness may be made ready for entrance into
the light of God's presence.

FOR FURTHER READING, SEE JOHN 3

BLINDED BY THE LIGHT

The one who is the true light, who gives light to everyone,
was coming into the world. JOHN 1:9

THE GOD WHO lives in unapproachable light veiled his glory, took human flesh, and was born as a human baby. When the Gospel writers announced the coming of Jesus into the world, they repeatedly explained his coming in terms of light.

At the Temple Jesus said, "I am the light of the world. If you follow me, you won't have to walk in darkness, because you will have the light that leads to life" (John 8:12). Later on Jesus took Peter, James, and John to the top of a mountain, and he was transfigured. The veil was taken away, and they caught a glimpse of his glory.

Dazzling light radiated from Jesus. The Gospels record that his clothes were "far whiter than any earthly bleach could ever make them" (Mark 9:3). John must have recalled that experience when he said, "We have seen his glory, the glory of the Father's one and only Son" (John 1:14). John knew that he had seen the glory of God in the face of Jesus Christ.

Years later, a man named Saul saw the same glory and was blinded by the intense light of the immediate presence of the risen Lord Jesus Christ. He fell to the ground, and then he heard the voice of the Son of God (see Acts 9:3-5). Jesus' glory was no longer veiled. Saul was overwhelmed by the dazzling brightness of the risen Lord in the same way Moses, Isaiah, and Ezekiel had been overwhelmed by God's glory in the Old Testament.

The Son of God shares the Father's glory (see John 17:5). But he put a veil over this glory so that it would be possible for us to know him and come to him. The intense light of God's presence came among us in Jesus Christ. And when he came, he opened the way for people who walked in darkness to live in the light.

Jesus is the way by which a man or woman can live in the light of God's presence. You can come to God through Jesus' offering and sacrifice. You come in the power of the Holy Spirit, who is the gift of God to all who put their faith in Jesus.

FOR FURTHER READING, SEE MARK 9

Y'ALL ARE LIGHT

Once you were full of darkness, but now you have light from the Lord.
EPHESIANS 5:8

IN THE ENGLISH language we use the same word *you* when we're referring to individuals or groups, except in the South, where the distinction
is preserved by the delightful expression *y'all*. When Paul wrote to the
church in Ephesus, he addressed them as a group: "Y'all were full of
darkness, but now y'all have light from the Lord."

The problem was not just that these believers had been in darkness,
but that darkness had been in them. The problem is in our nature
as well as our environment. Sin darkens our minds, diminishes our
capacity for feeling, and disables our wills so that we cannot get free
from evil by the exercise of choice. Sin put out the light in us, and
our greatest problem is not the darkness around us, but the darkness
within us.

But now through the gospel, a remarkable change has taken place in
the lives of Christian believers. Paul says, "Now you have light from the
Lord." It is not just that God has brought us into the light; he brought
the light into us! What had happened to these believers was more than
a change of environment, it was a change of nature, and of course that
is our greatest need.

God puts his light within his people so that we may shine in a dark
world. So when Paul writes to the church at Ephesus, he says, "Y'all
have light from the Lord." Jesus taught the same truth to the disciples:
"Y'all are the light of the world" (see Matthew 5:14). It was not just that
the disciples had *seen* the light; Christ put his light within them.

Christ is the light of the world, and when we get connected to him
through faith, his life flows into us and we will shine. Jesus said, "Put
your trust in the light while there is still time; then you will become
children of the light" (John 12:36). If the life of Christ is in you, you
will shine.

FOR FURTHER READING, SEE MATTHEW 5

Y'ALL MUST SHINE

Live as children of light. EPHESIANS 5:8, NIV

LIVING AS CHILDREN of light means being different from the darkness that surrounds us. So, what does that look like?

In a world of hype, exaggeration, ludicrous claims, and downright lies, let your "Yes!" be yes and your "No!" mean no. "Stop telling lies. Let us tell our neighbors the truth, for we are all parts of the same body" (Ephesians 4:25). Then you will be light—people will discover they can trust what you say. That's why keeping your word is so important. It's part of being the light.

Some people approach life by asking, "What is the minimum I have to do?" That's part of the darkness, and God calls his people to be different: "If you are a thief, quit stealing. Instead, use your hands for good hard work, and then give generously to others in need" (Ephesians 4:28). Do something useful. Be industrious—see how you can make the greatest contribution to your company, your home, your family—and you will be light.

Words have great power either to build up or to tear down. We cannot avoid hearing dark words of criticism, pride, or fear, but God calls us to make sure we're not the source of them: "Don't use foul or abusive language. Let everything you say be good and helpful, so that your words will be an encouragement to those who hear them" (Ephesians 4:29). If our speech has the effect of building others up, then we will be light in a culture where so many words are aimed at tearing other people down.

Don't ever expect the world to shine for you. God calls you to shine for the world. The world is a dark place, and God has put us where we are able to be lights. That's the challenge for the whole church. If Paul could visit your church and speak with a southern accent, he would say, "Y'all are the light. Y'all are the people who claim to know that eternity itself is secure. Y'all have the Holy Spirit of God in you, and y'all live in a dark place. Now live as children of light."

FOR FURTHER READING, SEE EPHESIANS 4

A CANDLE IN THE DARK

Their minds are full of darkness; they wander far from
the life God gives because they have closed their minds and
hardened their hearts against him. EPHESIANS 4:18

PAUL GIVES US a powerful description of the human condition: sin darkens the mind, hardens the heart, renders the conscience insensitive, and distorts our desires. And the way God has chosen to break into this darkness is by placing his light there.

God may have put you in a dark place—perhaps you work with people who are like this. If you're the only Christian in your family or if your colleagues at work are unsympathetic to your faith, you might easily feel discouraged.

Listen: if you take a candle outside in the middle of a summer day, its light will not be impressive. But if you light a candle in a dungeon, its flame will change the whole environment. The greater the darkness, the more effective the light.

My parents were in Scotland during the Second World War, and my mother lived in the town of Leith, where there are still some shipping docks. That area was a natural target in the nighttime bombing raids.

It was essential that the city lights not be seen by incoming planes, and so each family was required to cover their windows with "blackouts." Wardens would patrol the streets, and if they saw a chink of light coming through one of the windows, they would shout, "Get those lights out!"

Never underestimate the importance of your light in a dark place. When everything else is dark, even the smallest light can be seen for miles. God may have placed you in the darkness so that he may use your light as the means of leading someone home who is lost in the darkness.

If you belong to Jesus Christ, the light is in you, and the day is coming when you will be in the light. In the book of Revelation, John wrote of a beautiful city that doesn't need the light of lamps or the sun—God is its light.

The radiance of God's immediate presence will be suffocating fire for those who have hidden from God in the darkness and cool light to those who have come into God's light through Christ. What will God's presence be for you?

FOR FURTHER READING, SEE REVELATION 21

THE ENEMY

*[We are fighting] against evil rulers and authorities of
the unseen world, against mighty powers in this dark world,
and against evil spirits in the heavenly places.* EPHESIANS 6:12

WHEN YOU BECAME a Christian, four things happened. First, you were brought into a new relationship with God in which your sins were forgiven and your condemnation removed. Second, you became a new creation. Third, you became part of God's family, the church. And fourth, you provoked the attention of an enemy whose purpose is to oppose and destroy the work of God.

We met this enemy at the beginning of the Bible's story, when he came to Eve in the form of a serpent. Having rebelled against the authority of God himself, his great objective is to destroy God's handiwork. That is why when God began a new work in your life, you took on new significance for the devil.

Satan used to be your master: "You were dead because of your disobedience and your many sins. You used to live in sin, . . . obeying the devil. . . . He is the spirit at work in the hearts of those who refuse to obey God" (Ephesians 2:1-2). He held you unresponsive to God and moving along with the flow of this world. But when God made you alive with Christ, your old master became your new enemy.

Having lost you, Satan's objective is damage control. He is determined that you should not pose any further threat to his kingdom. That means he'll do everything in his power to make you ineffective and unproductive in the Christian life. Becoming a Christian is not the end of your battles; it's the beginning of new warfare.

This means your primary problem is not with people—"we are not fighting against flesh-and-blood enemies" (Ephesians 6:12). Obviously, people do cause problems in our lives, so we tend to assume that if we can get free from them, our struggles will be over. But that is never the case.

When we fall into the error of identifying people as the problem, it's wise to remind ourselves that they're not the enemy; they're victims of the enemy. The real enemy has taken many hostages—blinding their eyes and keeping them bound. Our objective is not to fight the hostages, but to rescue them.

FOR FURTHER READING, SEE EPHESIANS 2

November 22 | DAY 326

THE FIELD OF BATTLE

*Put on all of God's armor so that you will be able to stand firm
against all strategies of the devil.* EPHESIANS 6:11

OUR ENEMY IS the devil, and he is a created being. That means he's not present everywhere, he doesn't know all things, and he doesn't have all power. These things belong to God alone. So, the enemy normally works through two infrastructures, which the Bible calls "the world" and "the flesh."

We may rightly say that we're engaged in a great battle against the devil, just as during the Second World War, a woman sewing army uniforms in the north of England would have said she was fighting Hitler, even though she never actually came within a hundred miles of him or saw him directly. Practically speaking, though, the reality is that we are normally contending with what Paul calls the devil's *strategies*. These are the primary ways in which Satan tries to make you fall.

The field of battle is a lot closer than many people think. The primary battles of your life will be fought in four areas: your mind (see Ephesians 4:22ff), your home (5:21ff), your work (6:5ff), and your church (4:1ff).

These are the areas where your enemy will launch his main attacks, so you must be careful to defend them. God's spiritual armor is the equipment we need for maintaining a pure mind, a strong family, a God-honoring career, and a healthy church. This is where the real battle is fought.

The first objective of your warfare is to *stand*. This is so important that Paul uses the word four times in Ephesians 6 to make his point clear. The enemy is going to come against you and try to push you back to a position in which your life will count for very little in the advance of Christ's Kingdom.

You will need more than willpower and good intentions if you are to stand against the devil's onslaught. You will need the help of someone who can defeat him, and that means you need to learn to find your strength in the Lord (see Ephesians 6:10).

FOR FURTHER READING, SEE EPHESIANS 6

DON'T TRIP ON YOUR TUNIC

Stand your ground, putting on the belt of truth. EPHESIANS 6:14

DECEPTION WAS SATAN'S first scheme in the Garden. He confused Eve into thinking she was doing good when in reality she was disobeying God (see Genesis 3:1-13).

A woman spends her morning at Bible study, but when her husband comes home, she is cold and distant. She thinks she is pleasing to God because she's studying the Bible, but she's blind to the falling temperature of her marriage. A man is involved in ministry, but at work he is arrogant and irritable. He thinks he is pleasing to God because of his ministry, but he's blind to the loss of his testimony.

Our enemy will be content for us to pray, study, and serve the Lord as long as we don't discover what he's up to. He hides his work in a fog of unreality, deceiving us into thinking ourselves spiritual, when actually we are living in defeat—at the very point where the enemy is waging the battle. That's deception!

The only way to stand against deception is to put on the belt of truth. Paul is not referring to the truth of the Bible here; that comes later (see Ephesians 6:17). The belt of truth is what David was talking about when he said, "You delight in truth in the inward being" (Psalm 51:6, ESV).

Putting on the belt of truth is an intentional action. You must build self-examination into your spiritual life. Ask God to search you and show you your heart. Use the Bible as a mirror, and don't lie to yourself. Learn to listen to close friends and counselors who will hold you accountable.

Regularly review your thought life: Have your thoughts become negative, critical, or self-centered? Do they reflect faith in God? Review your reputation: What would people say about your attitude? Your work ethic? Are you building others up?

In Paul's time, a belt was used to hold up the tunic. Without a belt, the rest of the armor would be useless, because you could easily trip on your own tunic and fall without even being attacked. The picture would be comical, if it weren't so tragic. Too many Christians are tripped up simply because they live an unexamined life.

FOR FURTHER READING, SEE PSALM 51

CLOSING THE DOOR ON COMPROMISE

Stand firm then . . . with the breastplate of righteousness in place.
EPHESIANS 6:14, NIV

ONE OF SATAN'S favorite ways of leading us into compromise is by suggesting that God's standards are only ideals.

God says, "Don't let the sun go down while you are still angry" (Ephesians 4:26). We respond, "Well, we all know that that's how it should be—in an ideal world." God says, "Obscene stories, foolish talk, and coarse jokes—these are not for you" (5:4). We respond, "That's something we can work toward." God says, "Get rid of all bitterness" (4:31). We say, "But I have good reason to be angry."

The enemy will be happy if we regard God's commands as ideals we should work toward rather than instructions we should obey. There's a big difference. One of my professors pointed out, "This college holds the standard that students don't beat up the faculty. The day people start talking about it as an 'ideal,' I'm out of here!"

A person who calls God's standards "ideals" has opened the door to a compromised life. That's one of the enemy's strategies, and the only defense against it is the breastplate of righteousness. This is not the righteousness of God that is counted as ours when we come to faith in Christ but the daily, personal choices we must make to do what is right. You need to be intentional about putting it on.

It's the choice to get rid of bitterness so that you can be light in a world that's full of bitterness. Or the choice to pay back money that's owed, even when that is costly. Or the choice to tell the truth, even when it is uncomfortable.

Without intentional choices of righteousness, your testimony will not be credible. This is where the battle is fought. It's not surprising that Paul says, "Be strong in the Lord" (Ephesians 6:10). The only way to prevail in the battle against compromise is to determine what is right before God and make the choice to do it, irrespective of the cost.

FOR FURTHER READING, SEE ACTS 5

GET YOUR BOOTS ON

*For shoes, put on the peace that comes from the Good News
so that you will be fully prepared.* EPHESIANS 6:15

ONE OF THE enemy's goals is very simple—to use our natural love of comfort to keep us from doing anything that might cause significant damage to his kingdom.

The only way to stand against this scheme is to put on the shoes of the gospel. Shoes are meant for movement, and Paul links that movement with the gospel. Putting on shoes means that I have to become intentional about asking, *How can I best contribute to the advance of the gospel in this world?*

If that question seems remote to you, it may be a sign that the enemy has already had considerable success with this strategy in your life. He is happy to see the whole church wearing slippers. Slippers are comfortable footwear for those who are planning to stay inside and who have no intention of going out. But God calls us to take off our warm slippers and put on work boots, because our calling is not to sing songs by the fireside but to take the gospel to every nation and people.

The advance of the gospel is always in tension with our comfort. We'll always be faced with choices between what's most comfortable for us and what's most useful to Christ. Every Christian and every church will move in one direction or the other. Do you see signs of the enemy using this strategy in your life? Have you ever felt that your own personal comfort was becoming more important than God's call?

The gospel advances as Christians move from a mind-set that says, "The church exists for me, and what matters is how I like it," to a mind-set that says, "The church exists for Christ, and what matters is how his work can best be accomplished." That means being ready to adapt, respond, and initiate in new ways.

Now here's the question: Are you walking with Christ in such a way that you can discern what he wants you to do? When was the last time you discerned the voice of God calling you to some new venture for him? Are you living with the expectancy that God will lead you forward?

FOR FURTHER READING, SEE ACTS 16

LEAN ON ME

*In addition to all of these, hold up the shield of faith to stop
the fiery arrows of the devil.* EPHESIANS 6:16

THE ROMAN SOLDIER would have protected himself using a round, handheld shield used in hand-to-hand combat, but it wouldn't have been much use against a volley of flaming arrows. The shield Paul is referring to was a larger, rectangular shield—four feet high and two feet wide—rather like a modern police riot shield, but covered with leather, for extinguishing the enemy's pitch-covered fiery arrows.

Soldiers would have used these larger shields in a *phalanx*—a Roman innovation in which a small group of soldiers would stand together and arrange their shields so that they formed a protective cover around the whole group, rather like the shell of a turtle.

Paul is telling the whole church, "Y'all are to take the shield of faith." When the day of evil comes, and you find yourself under special attack, you are to bind yourself together with other believers around you under the protective cover of faith.

The Gospels record a wonderful story about four men who brought their friend to Jesus. They climbed onto the roof of a house where Jesus was teaching, dug a hole in the roof, and lowered their friend to the feet of Jesus. You can't fault their initiative or their determination.

When Jesus saw their faith, he said to the man who was carried in, "Your sins are forgiven" (Luke 5:20). Never underestimate the degree to which God may bless you through the faith of other believers who care for you.

Maybe you're facing the day of evil right now, and you're trying to fend off a ferocious attack with your little shield. You're fighting a losing battle in your mind or in your home that no one else knows about. Satan wants you isolated in the battle, but God never intended for you to fight alone. Take up the shield of faith, and share the struggle with someone you trust who will stand with you. And when brothers or sisters share a burden with you, exercise faith and stand with them.

FOR FURTHER READING, SEE LUKE 5

GRADUATION DAY

Put on salvation as your helmet. EPHESIANS 6:17

IT'S ONE THING to start; it's another thing to finish. If you are to sustain a lifetime of useful service to Jesus Christ, you will need to overcome discouragement.

There will be times when the results of your work will be disappointing. Prayers won't seem to be answered as you had hoped. You will find yourself facing problems to which there are no obvious answers. Tiredness will cloud your judgment, and you may begin to despair. Paul knew all about this (see 2 Corinthians 1:8-9).

The apostle was writing to believers, so when he said, "Put on salvation as your helmet," he was not inviting them to come to Christ to be saved. They'd already done that. The Bible talks about salvation in the present and the future tense. When Paul writes about salvation as a helmet, it's the confident expectation of final victory that he's talking about (see also 1 Thessalonians 5:8). When the immediate outlook is bleak, take time to meditate on the final outcome.

Students struggling through their final exams do well to think about graduation day. That was Paul's regular practice. He placed his present sufferings alongside the glory that would ultimately be revealed and concluded it was well worth the cost of staying in the battle every time: "Our present troubles are small and won't last very long. Yet they produce for us a glory that vastly outweighs them and will last forever! So we don't look at the troubles we can see now; rather, we fix our gaze on things that cannot be seen. For the things we see now will soon be gone, but the things we cannot see will last forever" (2 Corinthians 4:17-18).

That's how you stand—with rigorous honesty, uncompromised personal integrity, total commitment to the advance of the gospel in all circumstances, unity with other believers, and confidence in the final outcome of the battle. When the armor is in place, you will stand. And if you are standing, you will be in a position to go on the offensive, using "the sword of the Spirit, which is the word of God" (Ephesians 6:17).

FOR FURTHER READING, SEE 2 CORINTHIANS 4

THREE STRIKES, AND YOU'RE OUT!

[Christ] disarmed the spiritual rulers and authorities. He shamed them
publicly by his victory over them on the cross. COLOSSIANS 2:15

OUR ENEMY'S DEFEAT comes in a series of three strikes. Strike one took place at the cross, where our Lord Jesus Christ disarmed the powers of evil. He blew open the kingdom of darkness to make a way out for all who believe. Satan's power to hold the captives was broken. This does not mean the enemy has given up or that his activity has ended. But Christ has inflicted a fatal wound on him.

Strike two comes through the ministry of the church. Jesus said, "I will build my church, and the gates of Hades will not overcome it" (Matthew 16:18, NIV). He didn't mean the gates of hell would be advancing against the church; the church will be advancing against the gates of hell. And as the light of the gospel spreads around the world, people are saved and hell itself is on the retreat.

That has been the story of the church over the last two thousand years. As the church takes the light of the gospel from generation to generation and from culture to culture, men and women are brought out of Satan's kingdom and into the Kingdom of our Lord Jesus Christ (see Colossians 1:13).

That is why we need to stand in the battle. It is only as believers stand against the devil's strategies that they will be in a position to advance on Satan's kingdom using the sword of the Spirit, which is the Word of God, and the ministry of prayer.

Strike one: the enemy's power has been broken. Strike two: his territory is being invaded. Strike three: when Jesus Christ returns in glory, he will overthrow the enemy "with the breath of his mouth" (2 Thessalonians 2:8).

The apostle John describes what will happen: "The devil, who had deceived them, [will be] thrown into the fiery lake of burning sulfur, joining the beast and the false prophet. There they will be tormented day and night forever and ever" (Revelation 20:10). That's strike three, and you don't need me to tell you, "Three strikes, and you're out!"

FOR FURTHER READING, SEE 2 THESSALONIANS 2

GET THE MAXIMUM RETURN

*Store your treasures in heaven, where moths and rust cannot destroy,
and thieves do not break in and steal.* MATTHEW 6:20

JESUS APPEALED OPENLY and unashamedly to our desire for gain. He is appealing here to people who want to gain a maximum return on the investment of their lives, and he's saying, "Let me tell you how to do it."

Jesus also spoke powerfully about guarding against unacceptable losses: "And what do you benefit if you gain the whole world but lose your own soul? Is anything worth more than your soul?" (Matthew 16:26). There are some losses you can't afford to take.

Remember the parable Jesus told about how we should invest our lives? Three servants were trusted with resources by their master. When their master returned, the servants who made wise investments and showed a profit were commended, and the servant who wasted his opportunity to invest was punished (see Matthew 25:14-30).

You may be wondering how this talk about gain fits with Jesus' words about the cost of following him. The Bible never hides the cost. Jesus said, "If any of you wants to be my follower, you must turn from your selfish ways, take up your cross, and follow me" (Matthew 16:24).

But that's only the first half of Jesus' statement. Immediately after this, he said, "If you try to hang on to your life, you will lose it. But if you give up your life for my sake, you will save it" (Matthew 16:25). Even the cost of taking up the cross is a sacrifice with a view to ultimate gain. Jesus wants to show you how you can invest your one journey through life in such a way as to gain the maximum return.

The whole Bible story is about making up for an incredible loss. God filled the world with good gifts for our first parents to enjoy; then an enemy came, and in one day, paradise was lost. The Bible tells us how it will be restored. Christ came into the world so that we may have life to the full (see John 10:10). An enemy has come to steal, kill, and destroy, but Christ has come to restore the priceless gifts of God. This desire for gain is deeply imbedded in you. God put it there.

FOR FURTHER READING, SEE MATTHEW 6

WHAT'S IN YOUR PORTFOLIO?

*Yes, everything else is worthless when compared with the infinite
value of knowing Christ Jesus my Lord.* PHILIPPIANS 3:8

THE APOSTLE PAUL was saying, "For the sake of Christ, I've lost everything in my portfolio, but I don't care about that now." Paul was born
with a silver spoon in his mouth. He had studied at the ancient equivalent of Harvard, and he prided himself on living a highly disciplined
moral life as a Pharisee. But none of that mattered now.

While he was on a journey to Damascus, the risen Lord Jesus Christ
appeared to him. A light from heaven flashed around him, and he fell
to the ground. He knew he was in the presence of overwhelming power:
"Who are you, Lord?" (Acts 9:5, NIV)

The voice answered, "I am Jesus, the one you are persecuting!" (Acts
9:5). God's presence left Paul in the sand, overwhelmed by his holiness.
After assembling an impressive portfolio, all Paul could do was fall
prostrate before the risen Lord, whose claims and cause he'd pledged
to destroy. He saw Jesus and thought, *If that's righteousness, I'll never make it.*

At that moment, his whole life changed completely. He caught a
glimpse of what it would be like to stand in the presence of God on
the last day and realized that his life portfolio was filled with the wrong
stock.

His position, achievement, and power were of no use to him on the
Damascus road, and they'd be of no use to him when he slipped through
death into the immediate presence of almighty God. He discovered that
what finally matters is not how we do against a system of rules, but how
we relate to the person of Jesus Christ.

Thirty years later, Paul looked back on that remarkable day and
reflected on his gains and losses, saying, "Let me tell you about my
portfolio now. I've been disowned by my people. I once had a brilliant
career, but I've spent the last three decades building tents. I once had
the authority to put other people in prison, but now I'm chained like a
criminal. All this happened, but I don't care!"

As you look back on your own life, reflect on your losses and gains.
What's in your portfolio that will matter on the last day?

FOR FURTHER READING, SEE ACTS 9

DON'T FEEL SORRY FOR ME

I have discarded everything else, counting it all as garbage,
so that I could gain Christ. PHILIPPIANS 3:8

PAUL WAS SAYING, "The great passion and investment of my life has been to get more of Jesus Christ. I want to gain Christ; I want to know him. That's what I've been investing in the last thirty years."

If we were to ask Paul why he invested his life in Christ, he'd say, "I've seen the value of his righteousness. I want to be found in him. 'I no longer count on my own righteousness through obeying the law; rather, I become righteous through faith in Christ'" (Philippians 3:9).

Then Paul would explain, "Ever since I caught a glimpse of the future on the Damascus road, I've been investing in the day of Resurrection. It won't be long before I stand in Christ's presence, so I'm trying to live every day in the light of that awesome reality. That's why I want to know him and the power of his resurrection. Whatever suffering is involved in following Christ, I will gladly embrace, so that, somehow, I may attain to the resurrection from the dead" (see Philippians 3:10-11).

When Paul used the word *somehow*, he was not expressing doubt over whether he would share in the Resurrection but only about how it would happen for him. He did not know whether he would pass through death into Christ's presence or whether he would be alive when Christ returned. Regardless, Paul had invested his life with a view to the final resurrection.

The apostle was saying, "Don't feel sorry for what I've lost. My position, achievement, and power would have been of no value on the last day. My portfolio is now loaded toward the Resurrection, and I wouldn't trade that for all the world."

Many people hold back from following Jesus because they're worried about the cost. They focus on the cost of following Christ and fail to see the value of following him. It will cost you to follow Christ, to have his righteousness, and to share in his resurrection. I don't know if it will cost you your career, your financial prosperity, or your freedom, like it cost Paul, but I know it will cost you your pride and your sins.

FOR FURTHER READING, SEE PHILIPPIANS 3

INSIDER INFORMATION

To me, living means living for Christ, and dying is even better.
PHILIPPIANS 1:21

PAUL DISCOVERED THAT knowing Christ, his righteousness, and his resurrection is of supreme value now, and at death, this portfolio goes through the roof!

Imagine you were given a glimpse of the stock market in five years' time, and you knew your information was accurate. What would you do? What if you knew that your pension fund would lose half its value in five years and that another stock would soar in that same time frame? You would move as much as possible out of the stock that's going down and into what you know is going up.

Paul had seen the future. The risen Lord appeared to him on the road to Damascus, and he caught a glimpse of what it will be like on the last day. He understood that what was in his portfolio would be of no use to him. He needed Christ, his righteousness, and his resurrection, whatever the cost, so Paul recalibrated his life.

We are surrounded by people who are afraid to die because they know that everything they have will be lost to them when death comes. Paul invested his life in such a way that the day he died would be an incredible gain.

One day the market will be closed. The opportunities of investing your life will be over. God will call, "Time's up!" and then we will cash in our investments. On that day, some people will open their portfolios, and they will be worthless. Jesus said that people who are outside will weep, saying, "If only I had Christ and his righteousness. I'd give anything to hold that stock now!"

The Bible tells us what God will reward: praying and fasting (see Matthew 6:6, 17-18), having compassion for the vulnerable (25:34-40), bearing insults and being excluded for following Jesus (Luke 6:22-23), loving your enemies (6:35), giving generously (6:38), hospitality that cannot be repaid (14:12-14), enduring ministry pressures (2 Corinthians 4:17-18), performing quality work for your employer (Colossians 3:23-24), keeping faith through trials (1 Peter 1:6-7), and being faithful to the truth (2 John 1:7-8).

These are the great investment opportunities. God tells you what will be rewarded; the choice of how to live is yours.

FOR FURTHER READING, SEE PHILIPPIANS 1

THE WAY THINGS OUGHT TO BE

God's peace . . . exceeds anything we can understand. PHILIPPIANS 4:7

THE HEBREW WORD for "peace" is *shalom. Shalom* is a common greeting that means "May things be the way they ought to be." Paul describes God as the "God of peace" (Philippians 4:9). That means everything in God is exactly as it ought to be. There is nothing disordered, out of place, out of control, or out of character in him.

Peace begins by coming into a right relationship with God. Without this foundation, it is impossible to have shalom in your life. That was Adam's problem when he went into hiding after he disobeyed God's command in the Garden.

Do you remember playing hide-and-seek as a child—how your heart thumped in your chest when the person who was "it" came near your hiding place? Can you imagine what that was like for Adam when the Lord came looking for him? It must have been his first experience of fear. Shalom was broken, and he was afraid that God would find him. Things were not as they ought to be.

It takes a lot of energy to hide from God. As long as we're hiding from God, we cannot be at peace with him. That is why God says, "Those who still reject me are like the restless sea, which is never still. . . . There is no peace for the wicked" (Isaiah 57:20-21).

The great invitation of the gospel is to come out of hiding and surrender into the loving arms of God. Christ came into the world to make things as they ought to be between God and you. You do not need to continue fighting an unwinnable war of disobedience against God. You can come out of hiding and be reconciled to him. You can have shalom with God through Jesus Christ.

The starting point of shalom is that things are the way they ought to be between you and God. That happens when you come out of hiding, give up your rebellion against his commands, put your trust in his Son Jesus Christ, and submit to his rule over your life.

FOR FURTHER READING, SEE ISAIAH 57

LIVING AT PEACE

Do all that you can to live in peace with everyone. ROMANS 12:18

IN A FALLEN world, it is simply not possible for things to be right in every relationship. Conflict will end when Jesus Christ returns, but that day has not yet come.

When Jesus said, "Love your enemies," he clearly implied we'd have some enemies to love. We may wish that everything was as it should be in all of our relationships, but there are some things we don't have the power to change. Conflict is a two-way street, and sometimes there are crazy drivers on the other side of the road.

The Bible recognizes this, and it never requires you to resolve every conflict in your life before you can experience the peace of God. But God does call you to be a peacemaker: "Do all that you can to live in peace with everyone" (Romans 12:18).

There is a wonderful insight in the Bible about how to pursue the path of peace in fraught relationships: "Let your gentleness be evident to all" (Philippians 4:5, NIV). Paul deals with pursuing peace in our relationships *before* he deals with finding inner peace: "Don't worry about anything" (4:6).

This is the opposite of the popular psychology and spirituality offered on many talk shows today. The secular approach always begins with *me*. The idea is that I need to be at peace with myself, and then, once I have found my own peace, I can deal with relationships, and lastly, maybe I can think about God.

That's upside down, and the Bible turns it the right way up. The Bible always begins with God. True peace begins by getting right with God through faith in Christ. There can be no peace for you when you are hiding from God. When you have that foundation, the next priority is the pursuit of peace in your relationships with others. How can you know peace in your heart if you are causing pain to others?

The peace of God is a gift enjoyed by those who have come into a right relationship with God through faith in Jesus Christ, who show grace toward others, and who learn to lift their anxieties to God in prayer. This peace passes understanding because it is the gift of God.

FOR FURTHER READING, SEE PHILIPPIANS 4

THE SHOCK ABSORBER OF THE SPIRIT

If you are presenting a sacrifice at the altar in the Temple and you
suddenly remember that someone has something against you, leave
your sacrifice there at the altar. Go and be reconciled to that person.
Then come and offer your sacrifice to God. MATTHEW 5:23-24

PUTTING THINGS RIGHT with others comes before worship and prayer.
Peter made this point about marriage: husbands should treat their wives
well so that nothing will hinder their prayers (see 1 Peter 3:7). A man
who is rude to his wife and then goes to a prayer meeting is wasting his
time. His prayers will be ineffective. Spirituality must never be used as
a cloak to cover up harsh attitudes toward others.

If you want to know peace in your heart, you have to approach it
indirectly. It rests on the pillars of getting right with God and pursuing
peace with others. That's why Paul dealt with this matter of our relationships and attitudes to others before he spoke about prayer and the peace
of God in our hearts (see Philippians 4:5-6).

One striking feature of American cars is the quality of the suspension. When I first drove our minivan, I remember thinking it was like
floating on air. But after sixty thousand miles and countless potholes,
the suspension is not quite so good.

My mechanic told me, "You might want to replace those shock
absorbers. It will give you a smoother ride." The shock absorbers provide some give between the road and the vehicle. They cushion the
harshness of travel, and they play an important role in softening what
otherwise would be an uncomfortable ride.

Gentleness is the shock absorber of the Spirit. We live in a harsh
world, where there is a great deal of conflict, and when we travel over
the potholes of life, we can easily become like the shock absorbers in
my van—rigid, rusted, and with no give, transmitting the harshness we
experience to other people.

One way to cultivate gentleness in a conflict is to think of every
reasonable defense you possibly can for the other person's behavior.
Imagine yourself defending their position. Bend over backwards to
identify something good in their actions or in their motives. You will
be amazed how much this softens your spirit.

FOR FURTHER READING, SEE MATTHEW 5

THREE WEAPONS AGAINST ANXIETY

Do not be anxious about anything, but in every situation,
by prayer and petition, with thanksgiving, present your
requests to God. PHILIPPIANS 4:6, NIV

PAUL USES THREE words to describe the way we're to fight anxiety—prayer, petition, and thanksgiving. That word *prayer* will cause some readers to lose interest, because they are already convinced that they've tried this and it doesn't work.

Ask yourself if you have really prayed about the things worrying you now. It is possible to think that we've prayed when in reality all we've done is worry on our knees, adding "Father" at the beginning and "Amen" at the end.

Prayer is entering the presence of God and filling your mind with who he is. Like a good marinade, a sense of his greatness and glory should permeate into the recesses of your mind—God is sovereign; God is good; God is for you; God is with you. True prayer begins as you allow these truths to soak into your mind.

Petitions are specific requests that we bring before God. You might find it helpful to think of anxiety as a large bag that you carry on your shoulders. We aren't always entirely sure what is worrying us, and we're often afraid to look inside the bag to find out what's there. The only way to fight back against worry is to open the bag.

Take that great burden off your back and open it up. Face your fears. Bring them out of the darkness where they thrive. Put them into words and bring them to God. That's petition. Spell out your "what ifs" to him, and keep in mind the greatness of God. That's why marinating your mind in truth comes first. You need to know that God is great enough to handle the darkest fear in the corner of the bag.

Thanksgiving expresses confidence in God: "I know you're with me. I know you're for me. So whatever happens, I trust you, and I'm grateful that my life is in your hands." God wants to hear our requests; he also invites us to count our blessings.

Cultivate the practice of bringing to mind the great things God has done for you. Thanksgiving refreshes your soul and brings joy to the heart of God.

FOR FURTHER READING, SEE EPHESIANS 1

WHAT HAPPENED WHEN JESUS DIED?

He suffered death for us. . . . By God's grace, Jesus
tasted death for everyone. HEBREWS 2:9

THE BIBLE SPEAKS about death in two dimensions: *Physical death* is the familiar event that happens to over six thousand people in America every day. But the Bible also speaks about the *second death* (see Revelation 2:11; 20:6, 14; 21:8). This is the judgment of God that will be poured out on the last day.

When Jesus died on the cross, he "tasted" both dimensions of death: Jesus suffered a slow, painful physical death *and* he bore the wrath of God. God laid our sins on Jesus and poured out the judgment that was due us on him.

On the night he was arrested, Jesus cried out, "My soul is crushed with grief to the point of death" (Matthew 26:38). Nothing else had crushed him, but as Jesus looked toward his death, he said, "My Father! If it is possible, let this cup of suffering be taken away from me" (26:39). Jesus was appalled at what he was about to experience.

Since then, a long line of martyrs have died for their faith in Christ. The extraordinary thing is that when you read their stories, you find a very different attitude toward death.

Come with me to Oxford, England. The year is 1555, and two men, Nicholas Ridley and Hugh Latimer, stand before a court on charges arising from their faith in Christ. They refuse to recant their faith, so they're sentenced to be burned at the stake.

As they are brought out, Latimer says to Ridley, "Be of good comfort, Master Ridley, and play the man. We shall this day light such a candle, by God's grace, in England, as I trust shall never be put out." Were Ridley and Latimer more courageous than Jesus? Or was Jesus' cup filled with suffering that Ridley and Latimer never knew?

Ridley and Latimer endured excruciating physical suffering in their deaths, but they never knew anything of the cup that was so overwhelming to Jesus. And as a Christian believer, neither will you. You will never see the second death. Christ "tasted" this death for you so that you should never know what it is like.

FOR FURTHER READING, SEE REVELATION 20

AT THE MOMENT OF DEATH

Don't be afraid. . . . Take courage! I am here. MARK 6:50

TRY TO IMAGINE yourself in a boat with the disciples in the middle of a storm. You look out into the darkness and see a figure walking toward you on the water. What would you be thinking? It's not surprising the disciples were terrified.

Mark tells us, "When they saw [Jesus] walking on the water, they cried out in terror, thinking he was a ghost. They were all terrified when they saw him. But Jesus spoke to them at once. 'Don't be afraid,' he said. 'Take courage! I am here'" (Mark 6:49-50). He climbed into the boat with them, and the wind died down. They were completely amazed.

That's a great picture of what happens for the believer at the moment of death. Jesus comes to take you home, and the experience itself may be frightening. Some Christians die peacefully, but others, like the disciples, experience great fear, even though Jesus is near.

If you've experienced the traumatic death of a Christian loved one, it may have made you wonder if all was well. Remember the disciples straining at the oars and their terror as they wondered what was happening? What's important is this: in their moment of fear, Jesus was coming to take them home.

Viewed from earth, death is Christ coming to take us home, but viewed from heaven, death is the moment of arrival. When you arrive in heaven, you will not stand alone in God's presence. Jesus Christ will stand beside you and present you to the Father. He has promised that if you acknowledge him before people, he will acknowledge you before his Father in heaven (see Matthew 10:32).

We can be certain that when we stand in the presence of God, Jesus will gladly identify with all his people. He will stand with us before the Father and say, "Here I am and the children [you have] given me" (Hebrews 2:13, NIV).

On that day, Jesus' word will be the one thing that matters. Entrance into everlasting life will not depend on your getting everything right in life. Christ will confess you before the Father, and he will usher you into the joy of everlasting life. That's his promise, so what is there for you to fear?

FOR FURTHER READING, SEE MARK 6

WHO'S THE NEW GUY?

*There were many priests under the old system, for death
prevented them from remaining in office.* HEBREWS 7:23

THERE WERE MANY high priests throughout the history of God's people, because death prevented them from carrying out their duties and continuing in office.

The Old Testament records the moving story of how the role passed from Aaron, the first high priest, to his son Eleazar (see Numbers 20:22-29). God spoke to Moses and Aaron, telling them that Aaron was about to die and that he would not enter the Promised Land. Then God gave them instructions about how Aaron's son Eleazar was to assume the role of the high priest.

An alien arriving from another planet who knew absolutely nothing about Israel would immediately understand the importance of the high priest simply from the clothes he wore. With jewels hanging all over his colorful robes and a turban on his head, the high priest looked like royalty on a state occasion.

Moses, Aaron, and Eleazar climbed Mount Hor in full view of the whole community of God's people. Aaron was wearing the high priest's robes and must have looked overdressed for climbing. But at the top of the mountain, hidden from the view of the people, Moses removed Aaron's robes and put them on Aaron's son Eleazar. Then Aaron died up on the mountain.

Imagine yourself in the crowd, waiting for their return. Someone shouts, "They're coming back!" You look, but you see only two men returning. You can clearly identify the high priest's robes, so you assume one of them is Aaron, but as they come closer, you realize that it's Eleazar. There is a new high priest.

When the time came for Aaron's robes to be passed on to his successor, no doubt some struggled with this younger, less experienced high priest. "Will he be too busy to help me?" "Will he be harsh with us or merciful?" "Does God hear his prayers?"

God has given us one High Priest, Jesus Christ, who has a permanent priesthood because he lives forever (see Hebrews 7:24). There will never be a time when the robes are taken from him. He has been through death and splintered its gates. He lives in the power of an endless life.

FOR FURTHER READING, SEE NUMBERS 20

HAVE A SEAT

*Unlike those other high priests, [Jesus] does not need
to offer sacrifices every day.* HEBREWS 7:27

THE OLD TESTAMENT high priest had a tough job. Sacrifices were
offered for specific sins, and since there were always new sins, there
was a constant need for sacrifices. Today we use the phrase, "A woman's
work is never done." You could definitely say that about the high priest.

Old Testament law required that people who sinned unintentionally must come to the priest with a goat as a sin offering (see Leviticus
4:27-31). The priest would then pour the blood of the animal around
the base of the altar, remove the fat from the animal, and burn the car-
cass on the altar. Some job—I'm truly thankful I was called to be a New
Testament pastor, not an Old Testament priest!

Some jobs involve a lot of repetition and can become boring, but
the work of the priest was about as repetitive as they come. Imagine the
priest at the end of a hard day's work offering prayers and sacrifices.
It's three minutes to five, and he's just about to go home when John
Doe turns up with his scrawny goat and announces that he has sinned
unintentionally. Not again!

The priest asks John what he has done this time. It's a familiar routine. The priest offers the sacrifice, and John goes back to his tent, but
the priest knows it won't be long before John is back with another goat.

The relentlessness of the high priest's work was illustrated by the
way the Tabernacle was designed. The main area was where the priests
operated—there was a lamp and a table with some bread, but no chair.
The priest could never sit down in the Tabernacle because his work was
never done.

Now God has given us a High Priest who made a sacrifice for the sins
of his people "once for all" (Hebrews 7:27). In Old Testament times,
the priests offered one sacrifice for one sin. But Jesus has offered one
sacrifice for every sin. And after his death, resurrection, and ascension,
"he sat down in the place of honor at the right hand of the majestic God
in heaven" (1:3). He sat down because his work was completed. No
other sacrifice for sin would ever be needed again.

FOR FURTHER READING, SEE LEVITICUS 4

HE TOOK IT AWAY

*He canceled the record of the charges against us and took it
away by nailing it to the cross.* COLOSSIANS 2:14

THINK OF YOUR sins as rocks that you carry in a large backpack over your shoulders. In Old Testament times, every time you felt the weight of a rock in the bag, you would go to the priest, who offered a sacrifice for that particular sin. Every time you committed another sin, you had to go back for another sacrifice.

The Old Testament priests were taking rocks out of the bag, but Jesus takes the bag off of your back! He deals with all our sin by separating it from us through his one act of self-sacrifice. He has dealt with the whole sin issue fully, finally, and completely by taking our sins—past, present, and future—and nailing them to the cross. That is why, when he died, he cried out, "It is finished!" (John 19:30).

The reason there's no condemnation for me in Christ is not that there are no rocks in my bag, but that the bag itself has been lifted from my back. Jesus took it from me. He carried it to the cross and dealt with it for me. But many people in church still live as if they were in the Old Testament era. When they sin, they feel as if they come under condemnation and that they need a new sacrifice.

The Bible makes it clear that if we claim to be without sin, we are deceiving ourselves (see 1 John 1:8). Our bags are never empty. We may not be aware of some of the rocks, but they are there. The Christian believer is never wholly free from sin in this life. No matter how deeply we reach into the bag, we can never empty it completely. There is always another rock.

Christ has set us free by removing the burden from us. This does not mean that we should become complacent about the rocks. God calls us to deal with the sin in our lives. But our salvation does not depend on emptying our own bags. It depends on Christ's removing the bags from our backs, and there's all the difference in the world between these two things!

FOR FURTHER READING, SEE COLOSSIANS 2

WHAT JESUS IS PRAYING FOR YOU

> *[Jesus] is able, once and forever, to save those who come to God through him. He lives forever to intercede with God on their behalf.* HEBREWS 7:25

JESUS *INTERCEDES* FOR you. That means he speaks to the Father on your behalf, bringing before God the specific needs and particular situations you're facing.

Here's a beautiful illustration of this: Jesus knew Peter would come under great pressure after he was arrested, so he told Peter, "Satan has asked to sift each of you like wheat. But I have pleaded in prayer for you, Simon, that your faith should not fail" (Luke 22:31-32).

Jesus did not pray that *Peter* wouldn't fail, but that Peter's *faith* wouldn't fail. God can use our failures as well as our triumphs. Jesus was saying, "The bad news is the enemy is going to attack you. But the good news is I've prayed that your faith won't fail."

Satan really worked Peter over, and Peter failed big time. That would have been the end of Peter's story, but Christ had prayed for him, and Jesus' prayers are always answered. That's why Peter's failure became an opportunity to discover God's mercy. When Peter came to the tomb and saw the risen Lord, his faith was renewed. A few days later, the Lord restored him and commissioned him for ministry.

What Jesus did for Peter is a wonderful picture of what he continues to do—pray for you. Be careful not to imagine Jesus on his knees in heaven, agonizing like he did before the cross. He's seated on the throne, and his word is the angels' command.

Jesus Christ, your great High Priest, is aware of every circumstance of your life. Nothing escapes his attention. He speaks with authority in the Father's presence, and his word releases the resources of heaven for every pressure you face today.

I wonder what Jesus is praying for you right now. That your faith may not fail? That you'll be sustained under a great burden? That you'll face up to an issue of sin and deal with it? It's marvelous to know that Christ intercedes for you. He will bring you through every circumstance of life. He lives for that very purpose.

FOR FURTHER READING, SEE LUKE 22

POTENT PRAYERS

*You will ask the Father directly, and he will grant your
request because you use my name.* JOHN 16:23

ONE OF MY greatest struggles in prayer is that my prayers often seem weak and ineffective. I sometimes find that I'm not sure what to ask. I feel I lack insight to understand what's best, and sometimes I wonder if my feeble prayers can make any difference. This is why Jesus told us to pray in his name. That means much more than tagging the formula "in Jesus' name" to the end of our prayers.

My home country of Scotland is known for several things, and unfortunately, one of them is whiskey. It's fascinating, even for a life-long teetotaler like me, to see how this venomous stuff is made. Whiskey is made by the process of distilling, in which liquids are separated as they boil and condense at different temperatures. What is distilled is so potent that a wise man would never touch it.

Now think of that picture in relation to your prayers. They may seem feeble, but Jesus distills them down so that they come to have a potency in heaven that is different from anything you could ever have imagined on earth. That's true even of the simplest prayer of a brand-new Christian.

The apostle John was given a vision of this. He saw what happened to the prayers of God's people when they ascended to heaven: the prayers were mixed with incense in heaven and then fire fell on the earth (see Revelation 8:3-5). That's a wonderful picture of what happens when you pray. Christ receives your weak prayers and distills them so that in his name they carry weight in heaven and have effect on earth.

The Holy Spirit is involved every time you pray, authoring prayer within the Christian. Your prayers may arise from a desire for God's glory and some insight into God's purposes; they may also include a great deal of confusion and selfishness.

But you should never hold back from praying because you don't know what to say or feel your prayers are inadequate. All that matters is you're coming to the Father through his Son, Jesus Christ. The Spirit of God will help you. Don't worry about getting it right. Your prayers will be heard because of Jesus.

FOR FURTHER READING, SEE REVELATION 8

SPIRITUAL SURGERY

God said, "Let us make human beings in our image, to be like us."

GENESIS 1:26

THE BIBLE TELLS us that we were made in God's image. Adam and Eve were not like God in every respect, but if you had seen the first man and woman, you'd have seen a reflection of what God is like in them.

A woman I know named Joy was on vacation in a trailer park in the south of Europe when a gas bottle exploded, trapping her inside the trailer. Remarkably, she managed to open the door and stumble clear of the inferno, but her burns were so severe that she almost died. She was taken to a local hospital, where it soon became clear they could not give her the help she needed, so arrangements were made to fly her back to Britain.

I'll never forget the first time I saw her. Her face was completely destroyed—she was unrecognizable. Her recovery took months, and it involved many operations. After her accident, Joy needed two things: first, she needed to get a surgeon who could help her, and second, she needed a long process of reconstructive surgery.

Joy's story has helped me to grasp the heart of the gospel. God made Adam and Eve in his image, and they reflected his character. There were no lies to confuse their minds, no hate to pollute their hearts, and no greed to bend their wills. Even the devil would admit that the image of God was reflected in them, though it was an image he hated and was determined to destroy.

What followed was a great disaster. Sin defaced the image of God so that it was scarcely recognizable. The Bible story is about how God's image can be restored. If this is to happen, like Joy after her disaster, we must be brought to the Physician who can restore not our faces, but our souls. We'll need to undergo a long process of spiritual surgery in which our minds, hearts, and wills are renewed.

The process will be painful at times, but the image of God will be restored in us. That is why Jesus Christ came into the world. He came to save his people from the devastating effects of sin. He came to restore what was lost and destroyed.

FOR FURTHER READING, SEE COLOSSIANS 3

SEVEN DEADLY SINS

Faith is dead without good works. JAMES 2:26

JAMES, THE BROTHER of our Lord Jesus Christ, wrote as a pastor who was deeply concerned about people who were confident of their spiritual health yet had shown little evidence of spiritual life. He deals with one of the most common misunderstandings of the Christian faith—that spiritual health is nothing more than a set of beliefs.

Some people believe in God, heaven, and even Jesus' death and resurrection, but apart from these beliefs, there's nothing that shows the image of God is being restored in them. James saw some of these "believers" as he traveled around the churches, and he noted seven disturbing patterns of behavior:

1. Some people gave preference to the rich. They sought out friendships with those who could benefit them, showing little interest in others (see James 2:1-13).
2. Other people couldn't control their tongues. He'd heard some cursing, and the way they spoke to other people was disturbing (see James 3:1-12).
3. Too many people wanted their own way, and they ended up butting heads as they pursued their own agendas (see James 4:1-3).
4. Some folks were arrogant. There was little evidence of the repentant spirit that comes to Christ with nothing to offer and everything to receive (see James 4:6-10).
5. Some "believers" spoke unkindly about their brothers and sisters in Christ. They seemed to enjoy talking about the deficiencies of the others (see James 4:11-12).
6. Some visionaries were so confident about their plans for the future that they showed little evidence of a daily dependence on God (see James 4:13-16).
7. A few people failed to make good on the debts they owed, withholding wages from their employees (see James 5:4).

Beliefs that do not change your life, making you merely a religious version of what you were before, are useless to you and dangerous to everyone else. There is no saving power in a faith that does not lead to a changed life.

FOR FURTHER READING, SEE JAMES 4

THE FLIGHT THAT SAVES

Having been justified by faith, we have peace with God
through our Lord Jesus Christ. ROMANS 5:1, NASB

IT IS NOT our faith that justifies. Faith is simply the way we come to Christ. It is the way you receive what Christ gives.

A notorious woman came to Jesus and poured perfume over his feet and wiped them with her hair. Jesus said to her, "Your faith has saved you" (Luke 7:50). But the reason her faith saved her was that it brought her to Christ! The men who brought their friend to Jesus lowered the lame man through the roof (see Mark 2:4). Their faith caused them to bring their friend to Jesus so he could heal him.

The world rightly objects to the idea that certain people will be saved just because they happen to believe the right things. After all, Muslims believe one thing, Hindus believe another, and Buddhists still another, not to mention us Christians. So we're often asked, "How can any sane person possibly think that one group will be saved just because they happen to have the 'right' beliefs?"

The next time somebody challenges you with that question, tell the person that he or she is absolutely right. We do *not* believe that faith has some magical or mystical power to save people. We do not believe that we are taken into heaven by certain beliefs. Now you may be thinking, *Wait a minute, doesn't the Bible say, "We are justified by faith"? And "Whoever believes in Jesus will not perish but have everlasting life"?* Yes. But it is not faith that saves us; it is Christ who saves us.

My friend Joy, who had been severely burned, was flown by medevac to a hospital that specializes in treating burn victims. When we say, "The flight saved her life," we understand that it brought her to the physician who treated her condition. The flight saved her only in the sense that it brought her to the doctor.

Faith is like the flight that brings us to Christ. The reason you will enter heaven on the last day is not your faith. It is Christ. Faith is simply the way you come to Christ, the one who saves you.

FOR FURTHER READING, SEE LUKE 7

ARE YOU IN GOOD HANDS?

You believe that there is one God. Good for you! Even the demons believe this, and they tremble in terror. JAMES 2:19

THERE IS ALL the difference in the world between saying that you believe in Jesus and signing yourself over to him for radical spiritual surgery. James's point is that simply holding certain beliefs about God is of no saving value whatsoever.

The demons are all too aware that God exists, that his Son, Jesus Christ, was born of a virgin, died on the cross, rose on the third day, sent the Holy Spirit, and is coming again to judge the living and the dead. They know all that, and they tremble when they think about it!

But one thing they'll never do is come to Christ and say, "Lord Jesus, do your surgery on me. Reconstruct my life in your image. Deal with my selfishness and pride, and reshape my life in your image." They refuse to put themselves in his hands.

The central claim of Christianity is not that we have a better set of beliefs. It is that Jesus Christ is able to do what nobody else who has ever lived can do. He can restore the image of God in you. He can reconstruct what sin has devastated in your life. He can rebuild your life. No one else can do that.

If your body needed radical surgery, you would do all kinds of research on the abilities of different physicians. Then you would place yourself in the hands of the one you trusted with your life. Faith is placing yourself in the hands of Christ to do whatever he has to do to restore the image and likeness of God in you.

Have you come to Christ in that way, or are you among those who have reduced Christianity to a set of beliefs but have never placed themselves in the hands of the Great Physician for major reconstructive surgery? A set of beliefs will never save you. True faith only brings you to Christ, who does the restorative work.

FOR FURTHER READING, SEE JAMES 2

GET A CHECKUP

Examine yourselves to see if your faith is genuine. Test yourselves.

2 CORINTHIANS 13:5

THE BIBLE WARNS against the dangers of presuming that we are spiritually healthy. Nothing is more tragic than the blind and empty self-confidence of a person who is sure of salvation while showing no evidence of spiritual life.

Most sensible people go to the doctor for a checkup on a regular basis. They make an appointment because they want to make sure that everything is well. If something is wrong, they want to be in a position to do something about it before the problem gets serious. If people do that with their bodies, why would they not do it with their souls?

Examine yourself in the light of the seven sins of the book of James (see December 15's devotion), and where you find disease in your soul, place yourself in the hands of Christ. Ask him to restore his beauty in you. Then look for ways to reflect the image of Christ in the brokenness of the world around you.

Discovering hidden sins you had not seen before can be alarming, but it is a normal feature of the Christian journey. You will never get beyond it in this life, so be patient, and don't become discouraged. God deals with us gently and reveals our sins gradually. A growing sensitivity to our sins is a sign of spiritual growth.

The process of restoring the image of Christ takes a lifetime. The day we're discharged from the hospital will be the day we enter the presence of Christ in heaven. But while progress is slow, it is also sure: "All of us who have had [the] veil removed can see and reflect the glory of the Lord. And the Lord—who is the Spirit—makes us more and more like him as we are changed into his glorious image" (2 Corinthians 3:18).

God's ultimate purpose is that his glory will be reflected in you. That process is already begun in Christ, and when he returns, it will be complete. One of the great joys of heaven will be seeing the glory of God reflected in one another. Are you placing yourself unconditionally in the hands of Jesus Christ to do whatever is necessary, however painful, to restore the image of God in you?

FOR FURTHER READING, SEE 2 CORINTHIANS 3

THE MOUNT EVEREST OF CHRISTIAN EXPERIENCE

Our fellowship is with the Father and with his Son, Jesus Christ. 1 JOHN 1:3

NEARING THE CONCLUSION of our journey through the Bible story is like trekking through the Himalayas. We're surrounded by breathtaking snow-covered mountain peaks, so the moment we look at one and think, *That's magnificent!* we see another that's even higher! We've seen many breathtaking peaks in the Bible story, but now we come to the highest of them all. Fellowship with God is the Mount Everest of Christian experience—our greatest privilege on earth; our highest joy in heaven!

At the beginning of the Bible story, God breathed life into Adam. So in his first moment of conscious existence, Adam stared into the face of God. God put Adam and Eve in the Garden of Eden and visited them there, taking on a visible form and walking with them. God was cultivating a relationship with them.

Fellowship is sharing a common life and a common purpose. It is "doing life together," and in the Garden, Adam and Eve "did life" with God. But our first parents chose the knowledge of evil, breaking fellowship with God. So they were alienated from God and placed outside the Garden. God did not come to them or talk with them. But that severed relationship was not the end of the story. From the day sin entered the world, God has been at work to bring men and women back into fellowship with himself.

God gave his people two wonderful gifts that make this possible. First is the sacrifices. God is holy, and if sinful men and women were to have fellowship with him, something would have to be done about sin. The sacrifices pointed us toward what God would do by sending his Son, Jesus Christ, to deliver us from sin's condemnation. We are saved *from* our sins *for* a life of fellowship with God.

Then God gave us the commandments. God saves us *from* sin in order to bring us *into* a life in which we love him. We reflect that love by obeying him as we honor our parents and remain faithful in marriage, truthful in speech, prompt in our payments, and content with what God has given us. We are saved for a life of fellowship with God.

FOR FURTHER READING, SEE 1 JOHN 1

THIS IS ETERNAL LIFE

If you don't personally go with us, don't make us leave this place.

EXODUS 33:15

WHILE GOD WAS giving the Ten Commandments to Moses at the top of Mount Sinai, his people were rebelling down below. This caused a breach in the relationship, and God told the people that they could go up to Canaan, but his presence would not go with them.

God was offering them a life of freedom and prosperity in a land of abundance, and the only thing that would be missing was the presence of God with them. But when God's people heard this, they mourned. They were cut to the heart because they had seen something of God's glory and could not face the thought of life without him (see Exodus 33:3-4).

They knew that even the freedom and abundance of life in Canaan could not satisfy the hunger in their souls if God was not with them. So Moses went up the mountain and said to God, "If you don't personally go with us, don't make us leave this place" (Exodus 33:15). If it came down to a choice, they would rather have God without Canaan than Canaan without God. Would you have made that choice?

Rediscovering a taste for fellowship with God is one of the greatest needs of our time. It is not unusual to hear testimonies of people who have professed faith in Christ that appear to amount to little more than a desire to avoid hell. The decision is announced with the smugness of a person who has just picked a winner at the races.

Jesus defined eternal life as a relationship with God. If we asked a hundred people to complete the sentence, "This is eternal life: _____" many would say, "to be in heaven" or "to never die." But Jesus said, "This is eternal life: that they know you, the only true God, and Jesus Christ, whom you have sent" (John 17:3, NIV).

The purpose of the gospel is to bring us out of condemnation and into this fellowship with God. This has always been central to the purpose of God. If you do not have fellowship with God, you have missed what the Bible is about.

FOR FURTHER READING, SEE JOHN 17

WHERE THE GARDENER IS AT WORK

*We are lying if we say we have fellowship with God but go on living in
spiritual darkness; we are not practicing the truth.* 1 JOHN 1:6

IT IS CLEAR that some folks in the early church had deceived themselves
(see 1 John 1:8). They claimed to have fellowship with God but were
walking in darkness. They lived a double life, and their claim was empty.
Others genuinely thought they had fellowship with God but did not.

When Mary and Joseph made their annual visit to the Temple, they
no doubt were part of a larger group with many children, uncles, aunts,
cousins, and friends. Returning home, they thought Jesus was with
them. Everybody assumed it, but along the road they realized he wasn't.
He had remained at the Temple. It would be a terrible thing to go
through life thinking Jesus is with you and to find on the last day that
he never was. John makes it clear: this is an area where some people are
deceived.

Jesus said, "On judgment day many will say to me, 'Lord! Lord!
We prophesied in your name and cast out demons in your name and
performed many miracles in your name.' But I will reply, 'I never knew
you'" (Matthew 7:22-23). Here are people who had no doubt impressed
many with their ministries but knew nothing of fellowship with God.
Jesus says he doesn't know them.

Some years ago my parents bought a home in the country. It was a
wasteland, with an impenetrable swamp in the front yard and an over
grown path in the back. The perimeter was unfenced, and the whole
place was a mess, but they saw its potential, so they bought it. Over the
past ten years, the swamp has been transformed into a pond, the lawn
is green, and a fence has been put around the perimeter. The evidence
of a gardener at work can be clearly seen.

Think of your life like a garden. There are flowers to cultivate and
weeds to pull. The flowers and plants are always growing, and the work
of pulling weeds is never done. The garden is always a work in process;
it is never complete. But where the Gardener is at work, the evidence
can be clearly seen.

FOR FURTHER READING, SEE MATTHEW 7

CULTIVATE THE FLOWERS

God is light, and there is no darkness in him at all. 1 JOHN 1:5

IF WE ARE to have fellowship with God, we must walk in the light. This means pursuing obedience, growing in love, and holding to the truth. These three flowers grow in the life of every person in fellowship with God. You may not see them everywhere, but they will be planted and growing.

The first sign of an authentic relationship with God is that we obey his commands (see 1 John 2:3). John brings further clarification when he puts it in the negative: "If someone claims, 'I know God,' but doesn't obey God's commandments, that person is a liar and is not living in the truth" (2:4).

If obedience grows, it is a sure sign of the work of the Gardener, because this is what he cultivates in the lives of those he owns. But if obedience is not growing, there is little reason to think that the garden belongs to God.

Loving others is the second evidence of walking in fellowship with God: "Anyone who loves another brother or sister is living in the light and does not cause others to stumble" (1 John 2:10). Again, John puts it in the negative: "If anyone claims, 'I am living in the light,' but hates a Christian brother or sister, that person is still living in darkness" (2:9).

Some people claim to have fellowship with God, but without love, their claim is empty. There may be a neon sign flashing, "This garden belongs to God," but if you don't see love growing there, you can be pretty sure God isn't the gardener.

The clearest test of fellowship with God is a person's response to Jesus Christ: "All who confess that Jesus is the Son of God have God living in them, and they live in God" (1 John 4:15). The one sure evidence of God's work in a life will be that person's clear confession that Jesus is the Son of God. But the person who denies this truth does not have fellowship with God (see 2:22-23).

Where God is at work in a person's life, the flowers of obedience, love, and truth will all be clearly seen. They're the seeds God plants in every garden he owns.

FOR FURTHER READING, SEE 1 JOHN 2

ONCE YOU SEE THE WEEDS

*If we claim we have no sin, we are only fooling ourselves
and not living in the truth.* 1 JOHN 1:8

NO CHRISTIAN IS ever totally free from sin in this life, and John makes it clear that the person who thinks his or her life is a weed-free garden is deceived.

John identifies some of the weeds that need to be pulled when he writes about physical cravings, cravings for things we see, and boasting (see 1 John 2:16). These weeds spread quickly, and their roots can go deep. If they're allowed to continue growing, they will destroy our lives. People who have come into the light are able to identify sins more clearly so that they can intentionally uproot them.

Even though you have worked your garden for years, you must continue to pull weeds. This work never ends. Some weeds grow because a root remains planted. Others grow because a seed has blown in from outside. Weeds are a constant challenge, and if they are left, they will quickly take over the garden and choke the flowers.

Walking in fellowship with God doesn't mean that everything in your life will be as it ought. It means you're intentional about identifying the sins in your life and weeding them out. When we walk in the light, we begin to see sins that were previously hidden, and when we see them, we're able to confess them to God.

Ray began to study the Bible for the first time. He didn't cheat on his wife or on the government, so Ray couldn't see how he was a sinner. Then one day Ray said to God, "Lord, if you say I'm a sinner, then I'm a sinner, and I want Jesus Christ as my Savior." When he came to that point, it was as if his mind was opened, and he began to see his anger, pride, and envy for what they were.

If you feel you have no sins to confess, it may be that you're walking in darkness and deceived about your spiritual condition. A person who can't identify weeds won't make much of a gardener. Once you see the weeds in your life, you will discover how much you need the Gardener.

FOR FURTHER READING, SEE ROMANS 3

THE THRONE

*Instantly I was in the Spirit, and I saw a throne in heaven
and someone sitting on it.* REVELATION 4:2

WHEN JOHN SAW heaven opened, he was confronted not by streets of gold, but by a throne. Everything else in heaven takes its point of reference from this throne.

John saw *someone* sitting on the throne. In the Bible, when men like John are given a vision of God, all they can do is describe his splendor: "The one sitting on the throne was as brilliant as gemstones—like jasper and carnelian" (Revelation 4:3). John saw a dazzling display of brilliant light as it would be reflected in sparkling jewels or a kaleidoscope. Think laser light show.

Surrounding the throne were twenty-four elders, "clothed in white [with] gold crowns on their heads" (Revelation 4:4). These angels guard the throne of God, just as the cherubim guarded the entrance to the Garden of Eden (see Genesis 3:24). Like an entourage, a host of attendants surround the throne of God (see Psalm 89:6-7).

Suddenly, this glorious scene became quite terrifying. The awesome light that radiated from God's throne was the source of a terrifying thunderstorm (see Revelation 4:5). When God came down on Mount Sinai, the mountain was burning with fire, and even Moses trembled with fear (see Hebrews 12:21). John witnessed something similar here.

Between John and the awesome throne in the distance was "a shiny sea of glass" (Revelation 4:6). John would have thought of God's people after the Exodus and the miracle of God's parting the Red Sea. Now John recognized that if men and women were to come into the presence of God, it would take another, even greater miracle.

Then John saw four living creatures. Like the seraphim that Isaiah saw (see Isaiah 6:1-3), they covered their eyes with their wings and never stopped saying, "Holy, holy, holy is the Lord God, the Almighty—the one who always was, who is, and who is still to come" (Revelation 4:8).

God's throne is too glorious, his presence too terrifying, and his holiness too great for us to ever draw near on our own. If you are ever to come into his presence, a way must be opened up for you.

FOR FURTHER READING, SEE EXODUS 19

THE SCROLL

I saw a scroll in the right hand of the one who was sitting on the throne. There was writing on the inside and the outside of the scroll, and it was sealed with seven seals. REVELATION 5:1

PAPYRUS STRIPS LAID horizontally on top of a layer of vertical strips formed a papyrus sheet. These sheets were then joined together into a scroll, a stick was attached to each end, and the scroll was rolled up and sealed with blobs of wax in the middle.

Normally you would write only on the inside of a scroll. But if it was important to have all the information relating to a legal transaction in one place, you could use both sides. The scroll written on both sides is a picture of everything God has planned for the world. God holds this scroll in his hand. There's nothing else to be written. The entire purpose of God is contained here.

Throughout the Bible's story, God had promised to destroy evil and restore men and women into his presence. This is the whole purpose of God. But notice the scroll was sealed. In the ancient world, a will was sealed until the one who wrote it died. Then the seals would be slit, and the person who opened the seal would execute the will. The will of God had been declared, but not yet executed.

Then a mighty angel issued a challenge: "Who is worthy to break the seals?" (Revelation 5:2). Who could withstand the thunder and lightning that radiated from God's throne? And after crossing the sea of glass and taking the scroll from God's hand, who would have the authority to put God's plan into effect?

"No one in heaven" could do it (Revelation 5:3); it was beyond the ability of the cherubim or the seraphim. "Or on earth" (5:3)—John knew it was way beyond his ability. "Or under the earth" (5:3)—Abraham couldn't do this, nor could Muhammad, Krishna, or Buddha, nor any other religious leader.

When John saw that no one could destroy evil and restore humanity to God's presence, he wept (see Revelation 5:4). Who was worthy to break the seals and open the scroll? Many have dreamed about a better world, and some have even promised it, but who can actually deliver a better world?

FOR FURTHER READING, SEE REVELATION 5

THE LION AND THE LAMB

One of the twenty-four elders said to me, "Stop weeping! Look, the Lion of the tribe of Judah . . . has won the victory. He is worthy to open the scroll and its seven seals." Then I saw a Lamb . . . REVELATION 5:5-6

THE ONE WHO is able to bring the purpose of God to pass is described as both a lion and a lamb. No single image can describe his glory.

This person now becomes the focus of the whole vision as he emerges from the dazzling light around the throne. His origin is not with us, on this side of the sea of glass. He comes from the inscrutable light of the throne.

Although the "Lion of the tribe of Judah" emerges from the throne of God, he is identified with one of the tribes of Israel. John is told, "He has won the victory," yet he is depicted as a lamb with its throat cut. A slaughtered lamb spoke of sacrifice, so John was seeing that the one who emerged from God's throne entered human history as a Jew and laid down his life as a sacrifice.

This Lamb bears the marks of death, but he is very much alive. Standing triumphant in the presence of God with seven horns, the symbol of perfect power, and seven eyes, a picture of complete knowledge, he does what no other person in heaven, on earth, or under the earth could do. He approaches the throne of God and takes the scroll from the hand of the Almighty (see Revelation 5:7).

Then all of heaven erupts in "a new song" about Jesus Christ, who is able to open the seals and execute the will of God because of his death and resurrection (see Revelation 5:9). That's why we read later in Revelation that there is no more sea (see 21:1). For those who are purchased by Christ's blood, there is no longer thunder and lightning coming from God's throne, and nothing can separate them from his presence.

Christ has not yet come in power and glory to destroy his enemies and take his rightful place as King on earth, but the scroll is in his hand; the future is secure. Every one of God's purposes will be accomplished through him.

FOR FURTHER READING, SEE REVELATION 4

A NEW HEAVEN AND A NEW EARTH

*I saw a new heaven and a new earth, for the old heaven and
the old earth had disappeared.* REVELATION 21:1

WE CAN UNDERSTAND why God would make a new earth, but why would he make a new heaven? Answer: before there was ever rebellion on earth, there was rebellion in heaven. Satan wanted to ascend God's throne, and he was cast out of heaven. The possibility of evil existed both on the earth and in heaven.

In his vision, John saw evil consigned to destruction forever, and he saw a new heaven and a new earth, free not only from the presence of evil but even from its possibility. The sea speaks of all that separates man from God, and John saw "the sea was also gone" (Revelation 21:1). The first heaven and the first earth had passed away. Human history as we know it had been brought to a close.

John saw a "new earth." These two words are significant—*new* means it will be wonderfully different; *earth* means it will be strangely familiar. The destiny of the Christian believer is not dreamlike existence in a spiritual never-never land. God will reshape, re-create, replenish, and renew the whole earth—"the creation looks forward to the day when it will join God's children in glorious freedom from death and decay" (Romans 8:21).

The Resurrection teaches us the same truth about ourselves. We will have new bodies. The resurrection body will be wonderfully different in that it will not be subject to aging, sickness, or death. But it will be a body, enabling us to live on the new earth, the home of righteousness.

The Bible begins with God creating the heavens and the earth. It ends with God creating a new heaven and a new earth. Everything Adam lost will be restored—and much more. If you are among the people of God, you will one day enjoy life here as you always dreamed it might be but never imagined that it could be.

FOR FURTHER READING, SEE ROMANS 8

THE CITY

*I saw the holy city, the new Jerusalem, coming down
from God out of heaven.* REVELATION 21:2

THE CITIES OF world history had been laid bare in the heat of God's judgment. London, Chicago, Jerusalem, Cairo, Beijing, Moscow, Baghdad, Bangkok, and Calcutta were gone! Then John saw a city coming from heaven, recognizing its outline, just as you would recognize the skyline of New York. It was Jerusalem!

Jerusalem is full of significance. God warned his people not to choose their own places of worship; he would choose the place and meet with them there (see Deuteronomy 12:5-7). David discerned that Jerusalem was the place. Solomon built the Temple there. Jerusalem was where God would meet with his people, but access to God's presence was limited to the high priest on only one day a year.

The new Jerusalem is vast, "1,400 miles" (Revelation 21:16). That's the distance from New York to Houston. The area of the city would cover about three-quarters of the United States! John had already seen that God's redeemed people numbered more than anyone could count. God has a place for every one of his people.

This city is as wide and long as it is high—a perfect cube. John would have seen the significance of this immediately. When Solomon built the Most Holy Place, where the cloud of God's immediate presence came down, it was constructed as a perfect cube—thirty feet on all sides (see I Kings 6:20). The old Jerusalem *had* a holy place where God's presence came down; the new Jerusalem *is* a holy place where God's presence will remain.

There is "no temple in the city" (Revelation 21:22). The whole place is one massive temple, where a vast crowd of people live in the light of God's presence. That's why a loud voice said, "God's home is now among his people!" (21:3). John saw the dazzling light of the invisible God on the throne, but the throne had come down into this city. All God's people have access to him; they live in the light of his glory, so there's no need for the sun and no night (see 21:23-25).

It's as if heaven and earth are joined together. Heaven is made suitable for the people of earth, and earth is made to reflect the glory of God.

FOR FURTHER READING, SEE REVELATION 21

THE BRIDE AND THE PROSTITUTE

I saw the holy city, the new Jerusalem, coming down from God out of heaven
like a bride beautifully dressed for her husband. REVELATION 21:2

THE CITY SPEAKS of a vast community of people in the presence of God.
But you can get lost in a city, so God gives us the more intimate picture
of a bride. You will never be lost in a crowd in the new Jerusalem. You
will know and walk with Christ.

The book of Revelation is the tale of two cities, each represented by a
woman. The first city is Babylon (see Revelation 18), another manifes-
tation of the tower of Babel, which reminds us that throughout human
history, right up to the end of time, humanity will continue in its defiance of God. That city is represented as a prostitute. The second city is
the new Jerusalem, and it is represented as a bride.

There is all the difference in the world between a prostitute and a
bride. The prostitute sells herself; the bride gives herself. The prostitute is motivated by greed; the bride is motivated by love. The world is
divided between those who trade their lives for the things of this world
and those who give themselves freely to the Lord.

Imagine the contrast of these two women, projected simultaneously
on a split screen. The prostitute sits on a garbage heap, destitute and
filthy. Unclean birds fly around her head, and her soul has become a
haunt for evil spirits (see Revelation 18:2). She can still remember her
glory days when she was the desire of rich and famous men, but nobody
wants her now.

The bride is about to begin her procession. She is dressed in white,
and her face is radiant. The one who waits for her loves her more than
words can tell. The bride of Christ steps forward to the sound of trumpets. She knows that this is the moment of her destiny.

The bride and the prostitute give us a picture of the eternal destiny
of every person who has ever lived. Your eternal destiny will either be
one of desolation or one of delight; one of everlasting loss or one of
everlasting love. There is nothing in between.

FOR FURTHER READING, SEE REVELATION 18

December 30 | DAY 364

THE GARDEN

> *On each side of the river grew a tree of life, bearing twelve crops of fruit, with a fresh crop each month.* REVELATION 22:2

IN HIS VISION, John had been looking at the new Jerusalem from the outside, but now he was invited in. And as he entered, John saw a garden. The Bible story began in a garden, and as John entered the city, he would have immediately seen it—Paradise restored!

This paradise is even more glorious than the one Adam lost. The great difference is the tree that's missing: the tree of the knowledge of good and evil. This garden is free not only from the presence of evil, but even from the possibility of evil.

There is free access to the tree of life, which bears twelve different crops of fruit—one each month. Winter never comes. The variety speaks of the richness of life continually replenished in God's presence. The pleasures of God's new garden-city will surpass anything Adam knew in Eden. You will taste fruits Adam never tasted and enjoy pleasures Adam never knew.

In the first garden, Adam served God by ruling over the animals. But when the serpent came, Adam became subject to his lies. That's been our story ever since. When John described us reigning "forever and ever" (Revelation 22:5), he was telling us that our lives will be ordered, our work fulfilled, and our relationships whole. Life itself will be brought under our control, freeing us to fulfill all the purposes of God.

John saw twelve entrances to the new garden-city—gates facing north, south, east, and west—letting people into the city from every direction. The old Eden was enjoyed by just one man and one woman, but now a great crowd that no one could number was streaming in through the gates to this new paradise of God.

God had come to Eden and cultivated a relationship with the man and the woman in the cool of the day. He came down as a visitor. But now God has gathered a vast community of people who have come to love him freely. He is no longer a visitor, and he announces this with a note of triumph: "God's home is now among his people!" (Revelation 21:3).

FOR FURTHER READING, SEE REVELATION 22

THE INVITATION

The Spirit and the bride say, "Come." Let anyone who hears
this say, "Come." Let anyone who is thirsty come. Let anyone who
desires drink freely from the water of life. REVELATION 22:17

THE QUESTION OF where you will spend eternity is more important than any other issue you will ever face. The whole Bible story is about how God has opened the way into everlasting life through Jesus Christ for all who will come to him in repentance and faith. The Bible story ends with the greatest invitation you will ever receive!

The marvelous thing about John's vision of the city is that all its gates are open. John saw an angel at each gate (see Revelation 21:12), reminding us of the beginning of the Bible story where the cherubim and a flaming sword guarded the entrance to the tree of life (see Genesis 3:24). But now Jesus Christ has come, and the sword of God's judgment has been broken on him. Now the angels stand by the gates not to forbid entrance, but to welcome all who will come.

The bride is the church, and she invites you to come. If you have not yet come to faith in Christ, it is quite likely there's a Christian somewhere who has been praying for you and longing that you will. It is my privilege to speak for the bride: the Lord Jesus Christ has come into the world for you. He has gone to the cross and opened the way to everlasting life. He offers all this to you, but you must come!

Enter by repentance and faith into what Jesus Christ has opened up for you. Come and receive the life he offers to you. Come to him, because one day every one of his people will enter into this marvelous city.

Alongside the invitation of the bride, the Holy Spirit also says, "Come!" God wants you to be part of this, and he invites you. Jesus Christ died to open these gates for you. God will not force eternity in his presence on you, but he wants you to enjoy his blessing and presence forever, so he invites you to come. Do not stand at a distance from the priceless gift that God offers to you. Come!

FOR FURTHER READING, SEE ISAIAH 55

Additional books available by Colin S. Smith

Unlocking the Bible Story
volumes 1-4